Penguin Health
The Fertility Handbook

Dr Joseph Bellina is the director of the Omega Institute of New Orleans, widely recognized as one of the most advanced research and treatment facilities for infertility.

Josleen Wilson is a science writer and author of *Surviving Family Life* and *Live Longer – Control Your Blood Pressure*.

The Fertility Handbook

A Positive and Practical Guide

Joseph Bellina and Josleen Wilson

This edition revised by Robert Newill, MD

Penguin Books

Penguin Books Ltd, Harmondsworth, Middlesex, England
Viking Penguin Inc., 40 West 23rd Street, New York, New York 10010, U.S.A.
Penguin Books Australia Ltd, Ringwood, Victoria, Australia
Penguin Books Canada Limited, 2801 John Street, Markham, Ontario, Canada L3R 1B4
Penguin Books (N.Z.) Ltd, 182–190 Wairau Road, Auckland 10, New Zealand

First published as *You Can Have A Baby* by Crown Publishers, Inc. 1985
Published in Penguin Books 1986
Copyright © Joseph H. Bellina, MD, and Josleen Wilson, 1985
Preface to the British edition and revision © Robert Newill, 1986
All rights reserved

Typeset by CCC in Great Britain by William Clowes Limited, Beccles and London

Typeset in Ehrhardt

Contents

The Female Check-up

The Male Check-Up

Causes and Treatment: Women

Causes and Treatment: Men

Special Considerations

Alternatives

Appendices

List of Illustrations

Consultants to
The Fertility Handbook

The Omega Institute of New Orleans, Louisiana, incorporates under one roof all medical specialists involved in the science of infertility: microsurgery and laser surgery, urology and andrology, gynaecology and endocrinology, laboratories devoted exclusively to infertility analyses, psychology, cardiology, and radiology. Some specialists in these fields work only with the institute; others are in private practice and/or affiliated with universities and offer their services to the Omega Institute on a consulting basis. Twelve specialists acted as consultants to this book, providing current research and expert technical advice in their respective fields. They answered innumerable questions, kept their sections in perspective, and gave the best of their personal experience and knowledge. Alphabetically by speciality, the consultants to *The Fertility Handbook* were:

CARDIOLOGY
Bruce Iteld, MD
Richard Mautner, MD

GYNAECOLOGY
Janos I. Voros, MD

HEALTH CARE
Jeanette Bellina, BA, RN
Bobette Dudley, RN

PSYCHOLOGY
Susan Avery, PhD
Craig McCaskill, MSW
Jay Seastrunk, MD

RADIOLOGY
V. Philip Bellina, MD

UROLOGY
Deborah Bell, BS
Donald Bell, MD
Ronald Lewis, MD

Acknowledgements

We are indebted to our colleagues, friends, and families for their contributions to this book. We all learned a great deal about the science of infertility during this project, and we learned even more about working together to bring a large-scale work to fruition. Several professional researchers worked closely with us: Peggy Eastman in Washington, DC, Jeanette Bellina, Jeff Jackson, and Deny Gregar in New Orleans; and Carolyn Fry and Jeanne Schuman in New York.

The Omega Institute is a large organization devoted solely to the treatment of infertility in both women and men. It has its own private consulting rooms, laboratories, and hospital unit, staffed by various medical specialists. There are thirty people working in the outpatient departments and another thirty in the hospital unit. As word filtered through the group that this book was under way, virtually everyone – nurses, physicians, researchers, technicians, administrators, accountants, and clerks – freely offered us help and expertise.

A trio of excellent computer typists – Ana Fick, Debbie Dorsey, and Damian Knight – devoted innumerable nights and weekends to help the manuscript through its many revisions. Their skill at word processing made at least one writer who cherishes a note pad and pencil learn to love the computer. Vivian Buu and Nancy Doan also pitched in at the keyboard; and Mary Haman and Beth Leonard, who managed the office and the accounting department, kept us all going by seeing that we always had what we needed, when we needed it.

The good humour and optimism of every member of the Omega team did much to lighten the stress that accompanies a project of this size, and we offer our warmest thanks to each of them. We are also indebted to Louise Voros and Bobette Dudley for their review and critique of parts of the final manuscript.

Certain people not only contributed their professional skills but helped in every way conceivable to make this book a success, from listening with critical ears to new ideas and concepts, to digging remote historical information out of the library, to sacrificing their personal needs to the needs of the book. Our special thanks to Delia Malone, the gifted illustrator of this book; Jeanette

Bellina, the director of nursing at the Omega Institute; and Neil Felshman, who contributed the basis of the complex final chapter, 'Brave New World'. We can say, with gratitude, that *The Fertility Handbook* would not have been possible without them.

Preface to
the British Edition
by Robert Newill, MD

Probably no human affliction causes more distress than the inability to have children, when all one's friends and relations seem to be able to start families without any difficulty. Today, infertility has reached epidemic proportions in America, Britain and Western Europe. One reason is that young couples are often putting off starting a family until their most fertile years have passed.

Until recently, the investigation and treatment of infertility, throughout the world, was very inadequate and rudimentary. This was partly because the majority of people had no difficulty in producing children and were unable to comprehend the distress which infertility causes. Also, in an already overpopulated world, it may be thought difficult to justify the diversion of scarce medical resources to the treatment of people who do not appear to be ill. None the less, these young couples do deserve full medical treatment because they have all their lives before them, and the inability to have children can be devastating in its effects.

In the past, and even today in most areas, the local gynaecologist has always been considered adequate to deal with the problems of the infertile couple. This is no longer the case: gynaecologists have no knowledge of male fertility problems and, in addition, the whole subject of human reproduction has become so vast that it is difficult for a single specialist to keep up to date with new research.

In recent years this has been recognized by many gynaecologists who have a particular interest in human fertility, and we are now seeing the establishment of comprehensive infertility clinics, almost all of them in teaching hospitals in the larger cities. The Omega Institute, from which this book hails, is one such clinic in the USA; in Britain, clinics have started up in London, Edinburgh, Birmingham and other large cities.

Our knowledge of the subject is increasing rapidly, thanks to recent advances. In the 1960s the fertility drugs were discovered; now we are seeing the introduction of laser surgery and microsurgery, which allow delicate operations to be carried out with minimal damage to tissue, and are particularly valuable in the repair of blocked or damaged tubes.

Unfortunately, because of lack of funds, our practice is not able to keep up with our knowledge. Microsurgery and laser surgery are far from being generally available in Britain, and advanced infertility treatment can only be given at a few centres; there are only two private clinics which do *in vitro* fertilization, and a very few NHS clinics. Other hospitals which would like to open such clinics are unable to do so because they do not have the resources. This means that you may find that some of the techniques described in the text are not in fact available in your area at present, but it is to be hoped that availability will improve in the future.

Sadly, there are still many cases of infertility which cannot be cured, even in the best and most up-to-date of clinics. This book will help you to know whether you have had a full investigation by your local hospital; if you are not satisfied, you should ask to be referred to an infertility clinic which has facilities for advanced investigation and treatment. This may mean that you have to travel some distance, but it will give you the benefit of the best treatment available, and if the treatment is still not successful, you will at least know that you have done everything you could.

Preface:
Breakthroughs in Fertility

Call it cosmic spark or spiritual fulfilment, biological need or human destiny –
the desire for family rises unbidden from our genetic souls. In centuries past, to
multiply was to prevail – the family was stronger, and better able to survive, than
the individual.

Emotionally, the concept still holds true. The yearning for family has never
subsided. Despite our individual powers and achievements in the world, most of
us long to have our own children to be close to, and to create within our lives a
family that offers retreat and affection as the world churns around us.

A single child can satisfy this wish. Yet millions of men and women are denied
their wish because, through circumstances beyond their control, they are infertile.
Their numbers are astonishing. One out of every six couples in Britain and
America is infertile, and this is a skyrocketing statistic – more than twice as high
as it was ten years ago. If any other disease had showed such an overwhelming
surge, an epidemic would have been proclaimed and medical research centres
would be working on the problem in a desperate attempt to stem the tide. Yet
this has not happened. Though widely discussed in the popular press, infertility
is pushed under the carpet when research funding is distributed. The scientific
investigation of infertility has an uneasy place in a world threatened with
overpopulation.

As a result, infertile couples are in a bind. Their parents, relatives, and friends
press them to have children. Everything seems to revolve around family life –
from television programmes and commercials to church meetings and suburban
cocktail parties. Children, and talk of children, seem to abound. On the other
hand, the efforts of infertile couples to have children are often condemned. A
recent television programme on fertility enhancement techniques posed this
question: 'Do you think people should have test-tube babies?' A member of the
audience replied: 'No, infertility is nature's way of controlling the population. If
you're infertile, that's just the breaks.'

XVI · PREFACE: BREAKTHROUGHS IN FERTILITY

This is not an uncommon observation. People seeking help for infertility problems are sometimes viewed as traitors to the rest of humankind, fighting nature's process of natural selection. But the rest of humankind already has children. War too can be viewed as a way of controlling population, but no one would put that rationale on a recruiting poster. Cancer and heart disease can control population, yet no one suggests that we stop spending large amounts on cures for these disastrous diseases.

Some people believe that infertile couples should not have children because there is something genetically wrong with them. If fertility specialists make it possible for the couple to conceive, won't the offspring be riddled with birth defects? For the vast majority, infertility has nothing to do with genetics.

Infertility is a problem shared equally by women and men: 35 per cent of the time the cause can be traced to the female partner, 35 per cent of the time it can be traced to the male partner, and 20 per cent of the time both partners have a fertility problem. For the remaining 10 per cent of infertile couples there is no traceable problem.

In women, infertility is most often caused by faulty hormonal signals or obstructions within or around the reproductive organs. In men, the most common cause of infertility is a swollen vein in the testicle. In only 2 per cent of all infertile couples can the disease be traced to a chromosomal defect, and these couples are unable to conceive under any circumstances. Genetic defects are passed along in the 'normal' fertile population just as frequently as they are in the 'abnormal' infertile population.

More important than society's viewpoint about infertility, however, are the couple's own thoughts about the predicament. The desire to have children is powerful, rooted in something deeper than discussions about population control. People who want children but cannot have them speak of their need in ambiguous terms, for there is little precise vocabulary for the feelings they want to express. Some have suggested that the terms used by psychology to deal with the process of dying might apply – anger, fear, rage, acceptance. But acceptance is a long time coming for most infertile couples.

Infertility is an intangible. There is little or no awareness of what it feels like until you have crossed the threshold and must face the problem for yourself. The desire for children becomes amplified as answers to the problem recede. Perhaps for the first time in their lives, infertile couples have lost control, and as they reach out for help only a handful of straws is offered.

Infertility is not a medical speciality; rather, it is a sub-speciality of at least six different sciences: gynaecology, urology, microsurgery, endocrinology, psychotherapy, and genetics. Infertile couples may have to consult many different specialists merely to discover *why* they are infertile. Each of these specialists may have a different approach and recommend different treatment. Some doctors approach infertility in a haphazard, hit-or-miss fashion that creates enormous anxiety for the couple. Many couples are guilt-stricken because they're convinced they've brought the problem on themselves. (Part of the reason for the soaring incidence of infertility is the rapid spread of sexually transmitted diseases such as gonorrhoea and chlamydial infection.)

These worries are compounded by a sense of frustration and helplessness. Being shunted from doctor to doctor, taking fertility drugs, undergoing surgery, and contributing an endless stream of semen samples is enough to drive any couple crazy.

The search for a solution begins to override every other purpose in life. The more confusing the proffered medical advice, the more obsessed the couple becomes. There must be an answer – somewhere – so the couple continues relentlessly, going from doctor to doctor, investigating every new avenue that might offer hope. If treatment is possible, what are the chances of success? How long will it take? How much will it cost? This vital information – information that can profoundly affect every aspect of a couple's life – is not always provided.

In some religions, hope is expressed by the symbol of an anchor. Infertile couples are looking for such an anchor and will go to any lengths to find it. Today, American couples will travel to all points of the globe in search of a successful outcome, particularly to England and Australia, where ground-breaking research is being done.

Chaotic as the picture seems, there is hope. Out of chaos, experts are beginning to fashion reason. In the last ten years scientists have been able to grasp significant facts about reproduction that had eluded them in the past. Even though institutional funding has been denied, researchers and fertility specialists in the private sector have made brilliant advances in the areas of drug therapy and microsurgery.

Thanks to prizewinning research in chemistry, we can now identify the unique brain chemical that triggers reproductive hormones in both men and women. Fertility drugs have been developed that offer hope to thousands of couples who only a few years ago would have remained infertile. Technology also has come to grips with infertility. The marriage of the microscope and the surgical laser has made it possible to rebuild delicate reproductive structures within the pelvic cavity. These two advances – high technology and applied science – have catapulted infertility science into the twenty-first century.

If the new supertechniques do not succeed, the couple still has a wide array of 'fertility enhancement techniques' from which to choose: artificial insemination, *in vitro* fertilization, embryo transfer, and others. The immediate future holds tremendous promise for infertile couples. Yet there remains the problem of getting the technology to the people who need it; in the United Kingdom, advanced infertility treatment is at present only available in a few centres around the country. After years of struggle, the average infertile couple knows as much about infertility as some doctors.

The objective of *The Fertility Handbook* is to give you a running start: to provide under one cover the latest and the best that infertility science has to offer. There is hope, and there are answers. Today, the odds of a successful pregnancy have been tipped solidly in your favour.

The Anatomy of Reproduction

1
The Egg and the Sperm

Only in the last hundred years have we really understood where babies come from. From the dawn of history, fertility has been a human obsession. Primitive tribes and advanced civilizations puzzled equally over the miracle of childbirth. The ancient Hindus thought the ibis brought children. The Teutons believed it was the stork. And the Japanese honoured the butterfly. The less poetic people of the East Indian islands thought pregnancy was caused by bathing in streams inhabited by eels. Most of these ancient tribes made no connection between sex and pregnancy. A few enterprising groups came close when they theorized that an accumulation of seminal fluid built the flesh and blood of a baby. It followed that pregnancy could occur only after repeated intercourse. Small surprise that this lively idea caught on quickly.

When the connection was finally made between intercourse and childbirth, men quickly took all the credit, and it was soon universally accepted that male semen was responsible for new life. The woman merely provided the soil for the child to grow in. The man was the farmer, the woman farmland.

The difference in anatomy was partly accountable for the unequal distribution of responsibility. The reproductive organs of a woman were completely hidden, while a man had a clearly visible organ that ejected a mysterious life-giving fluid.

Even the Greeks, the most advanced culture of ancient times, had meagre knowledge of conception. Aristotle strongly opposed any theory that women contributed seeds of any kind to the embryo. Only male semen could transmit the dynamic life force.

The physician Hippocrates held a more enlightened view. He believed that during pregnancy menstrual blood accumulated in the uterus and formed the flesh of a new child. He thought that ovaries, like testicles, produced semen, and was convinced that a child's resemblance to its parents was due to the semen from both. Hippocrates raised a voice in the wilderness, but he could not compete with the authority of Aristotle.

In the second century, another Greek physician tried to prove that women played some small role in conception. Galen knew that a woman could not conceive alone, but he stubbornly clung to the belief that she must have something to do with making babies. His theory was difficult to prove because the female reproductive organs had never been viewed. Scientific thinkers believed the uterus was some kind of freely moving animal.

In the middle of the sixteenth century Gabriel Fallopius, an Italian anatomist, examined the ovaries in search of semen. He found none and so agreed with the historical concept of woman's inferior role in conception. However, he did discover the tubes on either side of the ovaries, which were later named fallopian tubes.

All these rudimentary findings served to support the patriarchal society. The concept of male superiority in making babies persisted, even though no one had any firm understanding of how conception happened.

The Discovery of Sperm

A major breakthrough occurred in 1677. In these early days of microscopic viewing, everything from a hair on the head to a sliver of a toenail was put under the lens for a close-up. Little wonder that Ludwig Hamm, a student of the Dutch lens-maker Anton van Leeuwenhoek, decided to examine a sample of seminal fluid (most likely his own). And little wonder that what he saw there, swimming furiously through the fluid, caused him to call his teacher in excitement. The two scientists observed organisms that swam like the 'little animalcules' they had seen in pond water. They theorized that these little creatures were the seeds of life, and they named them spermatozoa, or seed animals.

As Hamm's mentor, van Leeuwenhoek had the privilege of presenting these revolutionary findings to the Royal Society of London. He assured the members that the semen sample was his own 'excess', taken during ordinary conjugal intercourse. (In the seventeenth century masturbation was considered the ultimate sin.)

Instead of clearing up the mystery of reproduction, the discovery of sperm led to even greater controversy. Most scientists were now convinced that sperm held all the components of a new life. They eagerly placed great quantities of semen samples under the microscope and let their imaginations run wild. Most were sure that they saw tiny men inside each microscopic sperm. In the sperm of stallions, they saw miniature horses, and in donkey sperm, long-eared animals. The concept of little men floating in semen persisted through the century, putting scientists no further ahead than their ancestors thousands of years earlier.

A hundred years later scientists were still entertaining themselves with their microscopes. In 1775 the brilliant Italian biologist Lazarro Spallanzani came up with a colourful experiment. Spallanzani dressed up a bevy of male frogs in little taffeta trousers. He then put the frogs together with female frogs. The male frogs clasped the females in amorous embrace and released their sperm. Instead of falling upon the female's deposit of eggs, the semen was caught and encased in the froggy pants. When eggs failed to produce tadpoles, the inventive Italian knew he was on to something.

He collected some of the frog semen from the trousers and mixed it with female eggs. The eggs became fertilized. Did Spallanzani make the connection? Unfortunately, despite his novel experiment, the scientist concluded that an embryonic tadpole was already coiled up inside each egg; some vague element in seminal fluid made it uncoil and grow. Spallanzani's firm espousal of this theory helped delay until the late nineteenth century the true discovery of conception.

In the 1870s it was still generally believed that conception occurred when one or more sperm entered an egg and dissolved. Finally, in 1877, the German anatomists Oskar Hertwig and Hermann Fol, studying the eggs of a sea urchin and a starfish, both described the actual penetration of a single sperm into the egg, and the merging of the two cells to form a new cell. The papers published by Hertwig and Fol generated considerable criticism, but the puzzle that had stymied humankind throughout history was finally solved.

The discovery surely ranks among the most important in the annals of science, yet today almost no one remembers either of these dedicated scientists. Their names do not appear in textbooks, nor do schoolchildren learn about them in science. It was just over a hundred years ago, and in that brief span of time scientists have learned to protect fetal life and have made great strides in curing infertility. The great discovery of conception lies forgotten in the rush of high technology and miracle drugs. But these were the two men who finally figured out how babies were made.

From that time forward, scientists have agreed that conception occurs when one ovum provided by a woman merges with one sperm provided by a man.

How Babies are Made

Biologically speaking, human life is created when two cells – an ovum and a sperm – meet and fuse within one fallopian tube in a woman's body. The match takes place unheralded and largely unnoticed. On impact the body feels no shudder, nor do the other cells tremble. Yet this simple union is the cataclysmic finale of two elaborate journeys. For these are no ordinary cells.

The ovum, no bigger than a grain of salt, is the largest cell in the female body. The sperm is one of the male body's smallest cells. They are an unlikely pair, one plump and round, the other a tiny projectile, yet their twenty-three chromosomes match and fuse perfectly.

The journey of these two miniscule cells to the one place in the body where fertilization usually takes place is an intricate maze, fraught with obstacles. In later chapters we will talk about the origin of sperm and ova from reproductive organs. Here we will examine how these two mature cells meet during sexual intercourse between a man and a woman.

When a man ejaculates, the small ducts from the testicles eject up to 300 million sperm cells; they continue to produce millions more daily over the man's lifetime. The ovaries, however, produce only one ovum each month. The life of this egg is so brief – only twenty-four to thirty-six hours – that the whole reproductive system of a woman's body is designed to protect it. Hundreds of thousands of sperm are squandered lavishly in the hope that one will seek out and fertilize the single egg.

The meeting of one particular egg and one particular sperm is mere chance. The odds are greater than the accidental meeting of any two people born at opposite ends of the earth.

The two small ovaries, attached to the uterus by short fibrous stalks, house a full complement of ova – roughly 400,000 eggs – that will last a woman's lifetime. Each month, at the beginning of the menstrual cycle, a single ovum matures inside an ovary and works its way towards the surface. About half-way into the cycle the ovum breaks through the surface of the ovary and the egg pops out, leaving its shell or follicle behind.

The egg falls through space. This is a critical point, for now a slender fallopian tube leading to the uterus must catch the egg with its open end and draw it inside. The tube is not a very good catcher. About 40 per cent of the time the egg falls off the ovary and disappears into the abdomen. To broaden the catching surface of the narrow fallopian tube, the fringed open end, called a fimbria, splays open like a flower. As the egg falls off the ovary, it seems suspended for a moment; then, if luck holds, it tumbles on to a single fringe of the fimbria and is pulled into the tube. The lining of the tube is like velvet. Millions of tall cells with soft hair-like tips called cilia brush the egg along in undulating waves toward the uterus. Cilia, mucus, and gentle muscular movements provide the sensitive ovum with a ride as smooth as a conveyor belt.

The middle of this tube is the one point in the body where the egg can usually be fertilized.

When a man reaches orgasm, sperm are ejected from the pocket of the testicles up through a series of ducts. Seminal fluid pouring into the ducts from adjacent storage areas flush the sperm through the system and out from the tip of the penis. The semen floods the woman's vaginal vault and bathes the cervical opening of the womb.

Most of the millions of sperm die instantly, destroyed by harsh acid fluids that continually cleanse the vagina. Only a few hundred, swimming furiously, make it to the cervix, and even these have no guarantee of entry, because most of the time the tiny portal is completely blocked by a thick plug of mucus. The mucus is essential to the health of a woman's body, for this blockade prevents bacteria from invading the abdominal cavity. Sperm rush up against the cervix, only to be turned back by a solid mucus wall. Obviously, were this protection sustained, procreation would come to a complete halt. Nature, fortunately, has designed a cunning loophole.

For a few brief hours each month, at the exact moment when an egg drops from an ovary, the composition of the cervical mucus changes from a dense plug into a thin, fluid stream that sperm can swim through. The mucus becomes so abundant that it literally pours out of the cervical opening. The sperm swim against the flow, gaining a strong sense of direction from the resistance.

Even at its most watery, the mucus is elastic and stretchable. The sperm first bounce against the slippery barrier; then one sperm finds a swimming channel and others quickly follow. A flotilla of sperm launches itself forward into the cervical canal. Those sperm that survive to this point now have about forty-eight hours remaining to reach and fertilize the ovum before they die of old age.

If the egg is already midway along the 4 in (10 cm) fallopian tube, fertilization may take place within minutes. But if the egg has just entered the tube or is in transit somewhere along the way, it may need several hours to reach the optimum point. Sperm and egg are not synchronized. Whether they arrive at the exact point of fertilization at the same time is largely a matter of coincidence. Nature again meets this new challenge imaginatively. And the solution helps explain why so many sperm are needed to effect a single pregnancy.

Sperm are working against time in two ways. They must move quickly or their lifespan will run out. If they move too quickly, however, they may overshoot the fertilization point before the egg gets there. If a sperm and egg meet before or after the optimum fertilization point, the result may be a misplaced pregnancy or a union too little developed to successfully implant in the uterus. Therefore, even though sperm have the power to swim up into the tubes within minutes, a series of obstacles in the female reproductive tract conspire to slow them down and keep some sperm near the fertilization point for as long as they remain alive.

Little crypts inside the walls of the cervix provide the first stopping places. Some sperm wait here while others swim straight through. (Once in the uterus, these sperm may be helped along by the natural contractions of the uterine wall, possibly caused by a chemical in the semen. There is some speculation, but no direct evidence, that the contractions of female orgasm also assist the movement of sperm.)

At the top of the uterus sperm enter the passageway of both fallopian tubes;

but since only one tube receives an egg each month, many sperm are lost by misdirection. Their numbers now vastly reduced, the remaining sperm enter the correct tube. Inside the tunnel, gauzy mucosal folds entrap and delay them. The fine hairs of cilia streaming towards the uterus also work against them. Once more, the sperm must swim against the tide to reach their destination, a course seen repeatedly in nature.

On their journey through the tube the adult sperm have undergone a final transformation. Every mature sperm has an invisible membrane protecting its head. Without this covering, the sperm would release its chemicals helter-skelter and try to merge with any cell in the body. As the sperm swims toward the fertilization point, the coating slowly wears away until the head is completely bare.

The sperm that make it this far face one final obstacle, the egg itself. The ovum is present in the tube for only a few hours during the whole month. Sperm that reach the tube at any other time during the cycle will find it empty. As the well-cushioned egg is slowly tumbled along the length of the fallopian tube, dozens of microscopic sperm rush out to meet it. The force of their attack actually makes the egg spin. All the sperm are fully capable of penetrating the egg. Which one succeeds is a matter of chance.

To succeed, a sperm must first dig through the thick, sticky outer coating of the egg. Spraying chemicals from its naked warhead, the sperm dissolves a hole in the outer layer and exposes another, tougher membrane underneath. This is the most formidable obstacle yet, the zona pellucida. If the sperm now sprays its chemicals wildly, the egg may be damaged. Instead, it concentrates the chemicals in a narrow jet that slits a small opening in the shield. At that moment, the sperm locks on to the egg and stiffens its tail; then, with all the strength in its body, it injects its blob of nuclear chromosones (DNA) into the egg. The sperm and the egg are one.

This is the moment of fertilization. The membrane surrounding the egg is transformed into a rigid barrier. No other sperm, despite the strength of its chemicals, can enter. If the mechanism fails and more than one sperm penetrates, the egg will die from a lethal excess of DNA. Twins are never formed by two sperm entering one egg. Two eggs may be fertilized by separate sperm, or the fused cells of a sperm and egg may divide into two separate embryos. But only one sperm can enter one egg in which a human develops.

In three days' time the fertilized egg divides into two cells; each cell divides to make four, and again to make eight. At this point the eight-cell embryo is ready for transfer into the womb, where it clings to the inside wall of the uterus. For the next forty to sixty days the pregnancy will be supported by progesterone manufactured by the empty egg sac (corpus luteum) that is left behind on the surface of the ovary. After that, the placenta will take over the hormonal workload of quieting the uterus.

Considering the complicated nature of human reproduction, the question is not why people have so many fertility problems, but how the human race manages to propagate as well as it does. Other animal species manage reproduction in a much more efficient manner, with sexual intercourse being closely tied to ovulation. Only in humans is pregnancy an occasional byproduct of continual sexual activity.

Under the best circumstances, human pregnancy is chancy. A couple has only a 20 per cent likelihood of conceiving in any given month. The fallopian tube has only one moment each month to catch an egg, and four times out of ten it misses. If the egg doesn't make it into the tube, fertilization cannot take place, no matter how many sperm are waiting. Besides egg-catching, there are dozens of other steps in the game. If a single move is missed, you lose.

Based on studies in primates and also on experiments in *in vitro* fertilization, we know that 15 per cent of the time the ovum is incapable of being fertilized; 25 per cent of the time it is fertilized, but silently aborts; and 40 per cent of the time the ovum never makes it into the fallopian tube. With only 20 per cent odds, it may take up to a year for the average couple to conceive.

Before we can begin to understand the multiplicity of factors that can go wrong in the system of reproduction, it is enlightening to view the sexual anatomy when it's working perfectly. In both men and women the system is beautifully elaborate and exquisitely complex.

2
The Female Anatomy

At the moment of fertilization all the properties of a new human life are determined, including its sex. Whether the fetus will be a boy or a girl is determined by which sperm enters the ovum. Although rare aberrations arise, the ovum itself almost always carries an X sex chromosome. If the sperm that penetrates its sticky surface also carries an X, the baby will be a girl. If it carries a Y, the baby will be a boy. The small blossom of human life begins with the fusion of these two 'half' cells: the sperm, perhaps the smallest cell in the body, and the ovum, one of the largest.

A whole human being is made from this new cell, which divides millions and millions of times. Newborn cells quickly become specialized. Some cells make blood; others grow hair. Some are sensitive to light, and others detect odours. Some distinguish between sweet and sour, and still others digest food.

Cell societies form to make up different organs and organ systems. The lungs control breathing. The kidneys and liver control excretion. The lymph system, heart, and blood vessels control circulation. And so on.

As different as these groups of cells are, they all have a common ingredient: every cell in the body has the same forty-six chromosomes (forty-four plus two sex chromosomes) that carry the genetic code. In all the cells except those few designated 'reproductive', the first forty-four chromosomes dominate the two sex chromosomes. The few reproductive cells are fundamentally different from the rest.

The reproductive cells begin to sort themselves out in the early weeks of embryonic life. The female and male gonads (ovaries and testicles) arise from similar tissue, and for the first eight weeks of fetal life it is impossible to distinguish a boy or a girl from the amorphous mass of cells. Then, slowly, a hazy imprint begins to show through.

By the tenth week external genitals take shape from a small groove near the fetal tail. The upper portion of the groove develops into the clitoris in a girl, and becomes the tip of the penis in a boy. Two cords of cells known as the Mullerian system move down toward the pelvic floor. In a girl, the lower portions of the cords fuse and hollow out into the vagina and uterus. The upper segments remain separate and later become the fallopian tubes. In a boy, the Mullerian cords almost completely disappear.

Another pair of cords, called mesonephric ducts, form the major ducts of the male gonads. In a boy, the upper portion of the mesonephric cords forms the ejaculatory ducts, and the lower portion becomes the vasa deferentia. In a girl, these cords disintegrate.

A baby girl should be born with an intact vagina, cervix, uterus, and fallopian tubes, and two ovaries. A newborn boy should be born with his penis and testicles fully formed and the two vas deferens in place. The major difference between these two sexual systems is that the reproductive organs of a man are external and easily seen, while the vital organs of reproduction in a woman are buried within the body cavity. To observe these elaborate organs inside the female body, we must approach them through the closely guarded vaginal opening.

The Vulva

The vulva is not a particular organ, but a series of outer folds that protect the vagina. These external genital formations include the mons pubis, the outer and inner lips (labia majora and minora), the clitoris, hymen, vestibule, and urethra, and two pairs of lubricating glands.

Except for the round, plump mons pubis, all these sexual structures are well hidden. The distribution of curly pubic hair over the mons can sometimes provide a clue to fertility problems. For example, the usual pattern of pubic hair is an inverted triangle, with the top forming a nearly straight line across a woman's stomach. (Only in Asian women, who typically have less pubic hair, is the line less defined.) If the pattern is more diamond shaped, with hair growth pointing towards the navel, as it does in men, it suggests an increase of male hormone production.

Every woman normally produces a certain amount of the male hormone testosterone, and possessing a little extra is probably the result of genetic chance. The excess doesn't affect a woman's femininity or her sexual preference, although she may have a stronger sex drive. But it can affect her fertility. Excess male hormone, as we will see later, may interfere with ovulation and cause infertility.

Labia Majora

Lying along either side of the vaginal entrance, and merging at the top into the mons pubis, are two large, round pads. These are the labia majora, or large lips, which are analogous to the scrotum of the male. If the labia majora could be pulled forward and two testicles placed inside, the result would be a scrotum.

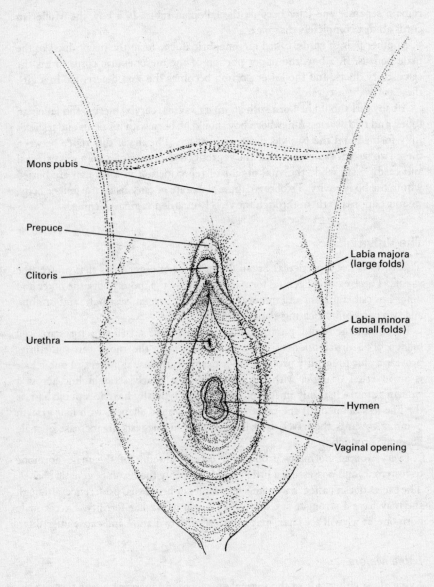

Mons pubis

Prepuce

Clitoris

Urethra

Labia majora
(large folds)

Labia minora
(small folds)

Hymen

Vaginal opening

The vulva

The labia majora are firm and covered with pubic hair. As a woman ages, the fat pads under the skin thin out and the lips become more flaccid.

The labia majora contain sebaceous glands that produce sweat and oil around the hair follicles. These firm lips cover the vaginal opening and protect against infection and disease.

Labia Minora

When the large lips are pulled back, the smaller inner folds of the labia minora are exposed. There is no pubic hair on these lips; they fold over the vagina, completely sealing the entrance from invasion by any bacteria lingering around the labia majora. At the top, the small lips form a small tent over the urethra, directing the stream of urine downward.

These small lips, whose upper portions surround the clitoris, are the equivalent of the uncircumcised foreskin in a man. They are highly erotic and sensitive, responding easily to sexual stimulation. During sexual arousal, the veins of the labia minora constrict, the blood rushing into them cannot flow out. The engorged lips grip the penis; this gripping action also helps prevent semen from spilling out of the vaginal vault after a man ejaculates.

Sebaceous glands in the labia minora release a white lubricant, just as the male foreskin does. Some of this soapy discharge, called smegma, is released every day and, unless washed away daily, can irritate and inflame the skin.

In childhood the small lips are completely hidden by the bigger labia majora. But as a girl enters womanhood, the inner lips begin to grow larger and eventually extend past the large lips. In the recent past male physicians had the notion that relatively large labia minora proved that a woman was a chronic masturbator. And, they suggested, such a woman was, if not emotionally disturbed, then certainly morally corrupt. Physicians today are usually more knowledgeable. Masturbation in both sexes is normal. If anything, masturbation increases sexual sensitivity and improves other sexual pleasures. As far as the female anatomy is concerned, masturbation has little effect on the size of the labia. To increase the size of the inner lips, a woman would have to masturbate strenuously and repeatedly for several decades.

There are, of course, normal variations in the size of the labia minora, mainly determined by genetic factors. Just as genes determine physical height and the size of the nose, so they determine the size of the sexual organs in both men and women. Strong manipulation and intense sexual activity stretch the small lips to some extent; childbirth may also enlarge them. (Only rarely are the minora so large that they interfere with sexual pleasure. In these instances the excess flap of skin can be removed surgically.)

The Clitoris

The clitoris lies just under the mons pubis, where the top of the large and small lips come together. This highly erotic tissue is comparable to the penis – in fact, both develop from identical buds of fetal tissue. For protection, a small fold of skin called the prepuce lies across the sensitive clitoris. The prepuce is very tight in a young girl but loosens as a woman matures.

The shape and size of the clitoris vary and, as with the male penis, size has no bearing on sexual pleasure. Blood vessels that lace the surface tissue engorge during sexual foreplay. The clitoris expands, increasing in size from about $\frac{3}{4}$ in (2 cm) to $1\frac{1}{2}$ in (4 cm).

For many women the clitoris is so sensitive that direct manipulation causes pain. However, the entire vulva and vaginal area is covered with residual nerve endings that come off this erotic centre; sexual stimulation anywhere in the area, even when the clitoris is not directly touched, can bring orgasm.

The small oval of skin around the clitoris is called the vestibular bulb. Sometimes this bit of tissue will fuse over the clitoris and reduce sensitivity. Removing the fused portion surgically, sometimes called a female circumcision, frees the clitoris and increases the responsiveness of the organ.

Female Orgasm

Not so long ago there was only one 'good' way for a woman to achieve orgasm. Sigmund Freud made famous the idea that vaginal orgasm – that is, orgasm achieved during penile intercourse – signified maturity and mental health in a woman. Any other kind of orgasm was considered childish. The trouble with Freud's idea, at least from a female point of view, was that many women never experienced orgasm during vaginal intercourse. They were thus labelled by Freud, and the generations of psychoanalysts who came after him, as an infantile lot.

Of course, it's easy to criticize Freud as we look down from the enlightened plateau achieved by climbing the great ramparts of his work. Freud admittedly was working on a dark continent. He lived in an age in which the mere mention of sex was loathsome to most people, while pornography flourished among a few. These polarized attitudes provided a spindly foundation for any serious scientific investigation of sexuality. Any attempt to conduct a sexual survey among thousands of women would have been impossible in Freud's time, even if he had thought of it. As it was, Freud believed that psychoanalysis was the only way to investigate sexuality. He confined his research to examining his own creative mind and analysing a relatively small group of patients, all of whom were very much products of their nineteenth-century upbringings.

Even though Freud admitted that his understanding of female sexuality was limited, only one of his disciples took exception to his theories. Dr Karen Horney first began to challenge Freud's assumptions in the 1920s. Among other things, Horney believed that a woman's sexuality was strongly influenced by the culture in which she lived. When the society at large denied the very existence of female sexuality, as the Victorians did, women responded to that denial. Horney also took issue with Freud's theory of penis envy, suggesting instead that men envied a woman's ability to bear children. However, she set the analytical world spinning when she also questioned Freud's distinction between vaginal and clitoral responses.

When Horney came to the United States from Berlin, she found support from a new wave of cultural anthropologists and psychologists, including Ruth Benedict, Margaret Mead, and Harry Stack Sullivan. These scientists concluded that women have an innate capacity for orgasm that can be developed with learned techniques. They were still a long way from discovering the extent of this capacity.

It was not until Alfred Kinsey conducted wide sexual surveys in the 1950s that women had the opportunity to speak out as a large group. When they did, they described a multitudinous array of orgasmic experiences – clitoral orgasm, anal orgasm, multiple orgasm, and even the old standby, vaginal orgasm. Kinsey theorized that all the various forms of orgasm radiated from the erotic centre of the clitoris. His surveys confirmed the idea that cultural background influenced a woman's capacity for orgasm. Kinsey found that devoutly religious upbringing, sexual restraint, and lack of higher education correlated with difficulty in reaching orgasm.

The later work of William Masters and Virginia Johnson, who observed the physiological changes of orgasm for the first time, continued to broaden the female sexual panoply. Researchers still do not agree on precisely where a woman's orgasmic centre lies, or even if she has an orgasmic centre. However, they have confirmed what women have been saying for years: different women experience orgasm in different parts of their sexual anatomy. And the orgasms they experience vary in character and intensity.

Arousal and orgasm are directly related to the surface area of the sexual organs. The pudendal nerve divides into three portions, carrying sensory fibres to the clitoris, around the vulva and vagina, and to the anal area. That means that all three of these areas are orgasmic. During sexual arousal, the rectal area, the clitoris, and the vagina swell as the veins constrict and the arteries pump blood into them. Via the spinal cord, the nerve fibres receive and transmit heat impulses from the skin to the sex centres of the brain.

Where a woman is most sensitive, and where she most often experiences orgasm, is directly related to the number of nerve fibres in a given area, the thickness of the tissue, and how much stimulation a particular area receives. The more nerves present in one area, the greater the erotic zone. A woman may be sensitive around the anus, but if this area receives no stimulation she will not climax there. Similarly, if the sensitive clitoris is located so high up in the vulva that the shaft of the penis cannot come in direct contact with it, the frictional surface is lost during intercourse. For some women, a simple change in position during intercourse improves clitoral orgasm. Certainly, oral or manual stimulation can also increase sexual arousal.

The controversial G-spot, named for German obstetrician and gynaecologist Ernst Grafenberg, is believed to be another orgasmic centre. Grafenburg and his American collaborator, Dr Robert L. Dickinson, first described the 'zone of erogenous feeling' in 1944. Because fluid is expelled when this spongy area behind the pubic bone is massaged, early researchers thought the spot was a residual of the male prostate gland. The G-spot is now believed to be its own special female erotic tissue. Like the internal pelvic organs of the body, it feels pressure, but not pain.

The G-spot is located behind the front wall of the vagina along the course of the urethra. The spot can be massaged by placing one or two fingers inside the vagina and pushing against the pubic bone. Hard massage produces pressure that travels by way of the spinal cord to the brain, which perceives a pleasurable sensation. On orgasm, the extra spurt of fluid ejected actually comes from the Skene's glands, which open up on either side of the urethra. (These are the same glands that normally lubricate the vaginal opening.) In volume and colour the fluid closely resembles prostatic fluid, and it's likely that these tiny glands are the true prostate remnant.

Hymen

The vagina is divided into an upper and lower portion. In the embryo the lower portion develops from the outside tissue and the upper portion develops from the inner tissue. Where these two separate tissues meet, about ½ in (12 mm) inside the vaginal opening, a membranous plate forms. This is the hymen.

As the fetus develops, the plate opens in the middle and the membrane shrinks toward the rim. At birth the opening is usually quite small, but by the time a girl enters puberty it is usually big enough to allow menstrual fluid to escape and to accept a tampon. If a young girl does use tampons, the size of the opening is increased a little at a time. When she has intercourse for the first time, there is usually no bleeding and little pain. If she does have trouble, patience and a gently

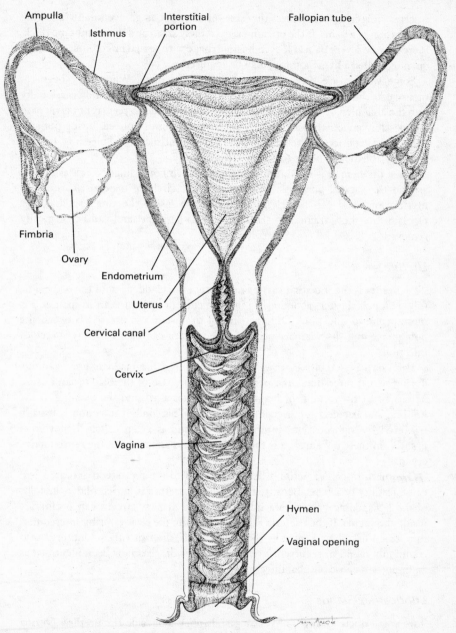

Ampulla

Isthmus

Interstitial portion

Fallopian tube

Fimbria

Ovary

Endometrium

Uterus

Cervical canal

Cervix

Vagina

Hymen

Vaginal opening

The female reproductive tract

inserted finger can increase the size of the opening, eventually allowing penetration of a penis. If the opening is extremely small and the membrane thick, there may be severe pain and even haemorrhage with sexual intercourse. Surgical opening, called a hymenotomy, may be required.

Some women are born with a solid hymenal plate. When they begin to menstruate, blood fills the vagina and goes back into the uterus and occasionally into the abdomen. If undetected, the condition will lead to recurrent pelvic pain and possibly endometriosis. Usually such a condition is noticed during puberty when a girl experiences cyclical monthly pain but no menstrual bleeding. In such an event, the hymen needs to be opened surgically.

Once the hymen is open, remnants of the membrane linger as a fleshy ring around the vaginal opening. This is called the circle of maidens (carunculae myrtiformis) and can be felt as ragged tissue inside the small vaginal lips. Occasionally these fragments are long and bothersome, and can be surgically removed.

Urethra

The urethra is the tube that carries urine from the bladder out of the body. The tube is much shorter, about 1½–2½ in (4–6 cm), in women than in men and is more prone to infection. The open tip of the urethra is pressed between the pubic bone and the vaginal opening. The urethra can be a two-way source of infection.

Bacteria can sometimes travel up the tube into the bladder. For example, during sexual intercourse the penis may hit the base of the bladder and cause irritation. At the same time, vaginal fluid is massaged into the opening of the urethra, and bacteria can escape up the tube. This kind of infection is usually triggered by vigorous and intermittent sex and is often called 'honeymoon cystitis'. In these instances, it is the bladder that is affected, not the reproductive organs.

The urethra can sometimes deliver bacteria to the reproductive organs and cause fertility problems. Because the tip of the urethra is buried under the folds of the labia, some bacteria washing out in the urinary stream can proliferate inside the vagina. If the bacteria are massaged into the cervix during intercourse, they can work their way into the uterus and fallopian tubes. One organism commonly found in recurrent urethritis, chlamydia, has now been identified as an important cause of tubal infection.

Lubricating Glands

Two small ducts known as Skene's glands open alongside the urethra. During sexual stimulation these glands secrete a lubricating fluid. If a woman contracts an infection, such as gonorrhoea, the Skene's glands may swell and the ducts become closed. Pockets of bacteria lodged in the glands can infect the vagina and ultimately lead to tubal infection.

At the lower vaginal opening, buried under the fatty tissue of the labia majora, is another pair of lubricating glands, called vulvovaginal or Bartholin's glands. The ducts of these glands surface on the small lips. Any infection in the area of the vulva can seep through the openings and irritate the glands. The inflamed glands swell, and their ducts squeeze shut, trapping secretions inside. As the secretions accumulate the glands continue to swell, sometimes to the size of golf balls. Generally these cysts are not painful; however, if the mucus becomes infected with bacteria, the cysts can develop into an abscess.

Such abscesses are extremely painful. Any organism can infect the Bartholin's glands, but the most common invader is gonorrhoea. Once an abscess develops, it's likely that the vaginal vault has been invaded and fertility is at risk.

Anus

About an inch below the lower end of the vagina is the opening to the rectum. Like the clitoris and vagina, the anus is sexually sensitive tissue. Usually the skin around the anus is very smooth, but sometimes external haemorrhoids (small varicose veins), which look like pieces of bluish flesh, develop in the area, especially after childbirth. The anus can be a potential source of vaginal infection. Improper hygiene – wiping the rectum from back to front, thus pulling fecal matter into the vagina – can set up a recurrent vaginitis, which can lead to infection of the internal organs. Vaginal intercourse immediately following anal intercourse can also lead to direct contamination of the vagina.

The Internal Reproductive Organs

The lower abdominal cavity is tightly packed with organs, including the bladder, the colon, and yards of intestines. In the midst of these large, vital bodies pulsate the smaller, more delicate organs of the reproductive system: the vagina and cervix, the uterus and fallopian tubes.

The reproductive organs are never completely still. They are always gently flexing, secreting fluids to moisten their soft inner membranes. These membranous linings are as important to conception as are the outer structures of the organs. Eggs are sheltered here and protected from injury. A newly formed embryo finds nourishment within the linings of the tube and uterus.

Vagina

The vagina is an elastic sheath surrounded by muscle. It is the connecting channel between the internal reproductive organs and the outside of the body. As a reproductive organ the vagina guides the penis and holds the pool of semen close to the cervix. It also acts as a channel for menstrual blood flowing out of the body. The vagina is a baby's final passageway before birth.

This astonishingly flexible organ can contract around a penis of any size or stretch to accommodate the head of a newborn baby. With age, sexual activity, and childbirth, the vagina loses some of its remarkable elasticity, but generally women can relax or contract the vaginal muscles at will. Vaginismus, a condition in which the muscles tighten so much that a man's penis cannot enter the vagina, can often be corrected through relaxation techniques.

The vagina is 4–5 in (10–12 cm) long and is lined with surface tissue similar to that found in the mouth. Vaginal length is as myth-laden as penile size. Like the penis, the length of the vagina is determined genetically and has nothing to do with reproductive capability or the ability to enjoy sex.

In young girls the entrance to the vagina is partially closed off by the hymen. This thin membrane may tear a little during initial intercourse, but frequently the hymen enlarges naturally, even without penetration.

A film of moist secretions coats the interior of the vagina and continually cleanses the canal. The normal discharge is odourless and watery; it may be clear or slightly white. During sexual arousal more secretions pour from the muscular coating, and further lubricants are added by the Bartholin's and Skene's glands.

The vagina holds the penis tightly and, when a man reaches orgasm, pulls the ejaculate into the deepest part of the vaginal vault, where sperm can begin their slow, complex journey through the cervix into the uterus and fallopian tubes. Any malformation of the vagina can prevent the semen from being pocketed around the cervix. For example, a relaxed vagina or a rectocele, in which a portion of the rectal wall pushes into the vagina, can cause the semen to spill backwards out of the vagina. Malformations of the vagina also suggest defects in other internal reproductive organs.

Cervix

The cervix is a short, valve-like organ between the vagina and the uterus – about 1½ in (4 cm) in diameter, round and movable, a hard bump with a small depression in the middle. The depression is actually a small hole through which sperm enter the uterus. Blood flows out through the hole during menstruation, and babies push through it during birth.

The cervix connects the uterus to the vagina, usually at a right angle, and allows these two organs to interact. Pain during intercourse is usually caused by the penis hitting against the cervix, which pushes against the uterus. For women with short vaginas, intercourse in the female-superior position may be troublesome. (When a woman sits forward the uterus pushes against the vagina and makes it even shorter.) Intercourse is usually more comfortable when the woman is entered from the rear position or when she lies on her back with her knees against her chest. In these positions the uterus slides back and the full length of the vagina is exposed.

One of the most important functions of the cervix is to defend the body cavity from invasion of bacteria and other microscopic foreign matter. To make entry completely impossible, the tiny portal is blocked by a thick plug of mucus. The behaviour of this mucus plug is crucial to fertility. During ovulation, when the egg drops from an ovary into the fallopian tube, the mucus thins out enough to allow sperm to swim past and reach the uterus and tubes. As soon as ovulation is complete, the mucus returns to its usual impenetrable consistency.

Changes in cervical mucus, like the growth and release of the egg, are controlled by hormones. The complex hormonal system must be working perfectly for ovulation to coordinate precisely with the thinning of the cervical mucus.

To respond accurately, the tissue that secretes the mucus must be healthy. Should this cervical tissue sustain injury, from infection or physical trauma, it may be unable to control the quality or quantity of the mucus. Any infection in the vagina, for example, can damage the cervical tissue.

Uterus

The uterus looks like a hard, flat pear suspended in the pelvic cavity by strong bands of ligaments. Under normal conditions it is no more than 3 in (7·5 cm) long and can hold only a teaspoonful of fluid. But the walls of this vital organ are made almost entirely of smooth muscle cells with elastic and vascular tissue. The uterus is so stretchable that during pregnancy it can expand up to forty times its normal length.

The smooth muscle cells, under the influence of hormones, are constantly in motion, contracting and relaxing throughout the month. During menstruation, the contractions are much stronger, and stronger still during childbirth.

On the inside, the tough muscular organ is coated with a soft lining called the endometrium. Unless a pregnancy takes place, this lush inner layer is shed every month during menstruation. If conception occurs and an embryo is successfully implanted within the uterus, the endometrium becomes a bed for the placenta.

Fallopian Tubes

Branching off from the upper corners of the uterus are the fallopian tubes. These are the vital channels of transport for the ova, and the place where fertilization takes place. The delicate 4 in (10 cm) tubes are densely lined with tall cells with brush-like tips called cilia. The soft, invisible cilia sweep in a uniform pattern towards the uterus, brushing the egg forward while going against any sperm that might be swimming up the tube. This action further contributes to the general downflow of fluids that give sperm their tracking system.

Each thin tube is comprised of four segments. First is the segment braced inside the uterus, called the intermuscular or interstitial portion, with an opening no larger than a pinhead. Next comes the narrow portion called the isthmus. The third portion, called the ampullary, is slightly larger and is the usual site of fertilization. Finally, the tube has a softly flaring trumpet, called the fimbria, at the end.

The fimbria is comprised of hundreds of separate petals. One petal, which is slightly longer than the others and usually tethered to the ovary, acts as a hinge, letting the fimbria swing from left to right, yet holding it within the radius of the ovary. At best, the fimbria covers only 40 per cent of the ovary.

The egg, which has no power of locomotion, cannot track by itself. To find its way into the tube, the egg must drop on to one petal of the fimbria. The petals are blanketed with ciliated cells that curl towards the inside of the tube. As soon as an egg touches one of these flowing petals, the cilia scoop it up and sweep it into the fallopian tube proper.

Fertilization requires optimum conditions. Every portion of the tube must be open, with the millions of cilia sweeping in flawless harmony. The tall cells of the lining, which secrete an enzyme-rich fluid, must also be in perfect condition. These enzymes devour some of the sticky coating around the egg, preparing it for penetration by a sperm. The extreme delicacy of the tubes makes them a major site of fertility problems. If the tubes are blocked on the inside or bound by adhesions on the outside, the egg may not be able to enter. If the tall cells and cilia are damaged, the egg cannot be conveyed into the uterus.

Ovaries

The ovaries, like the testicles, are primary sexual organs. They develop and release eggs and pump out the female hormones oestrogen and progesterone. The ovaries are suspended from support ligaments on either side of the uterus. When a baby girl is born, her ovaries contain about 400,000 immature ova, but only about 400 of these will develop into mature eggs later in life. After puberty,

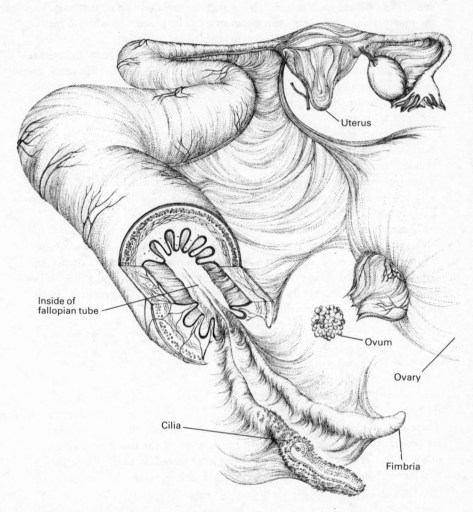

Uterus

Inside of
fallopian tube

Ovum

Ovary

Cilia

Fimbria

A dynamic view of one fallopian tube as it arises from the uterus and sweeps down to capture a ripe ovum erupting from an ovary. The lower cross-section shows one tip of the fimbria lined with millions of tall, delicate cells with brush-like tips, called cilia. The upper cross-section shows the muscle layers inside the tube. Muscle contractions combine with the sweeping motion of the cilia to carry the egg into the deeper recesses of the tube.

one egg is released each month. The ovaries do not alternate consistently, and the monthly egg may come from either ovary. The process by which a mature egg is extruded from the surface of an ovary is called ovulation.

The ovaries of a child are very small and white. During puberty the ovaries grow larger, until they reach 1–2 in (2·5–5 cm) in length. Over the years, the smooth surface of the ovaries becomes pitted from the eruption of mature ova. After menopause, the heavily scarred ovaries shrivel, and in older women they are again quite small.

If one ovary is damaged or missing, the remaining one takes over the entire workload, usually producing one egg each month. It also doubles its production of hormones, so hormone levels remain stable. The onset of menopause, which is determined mostly by genetics, should occur at the normal time for a woman who has lost one ovary. If her mother had a late or an early menopause, she is likely to have a similar biological time clock.

These, then, are the sexual and reproductive organs of a woman's body: the vulva, the vagina and cervix, the uterus and fallopian tubes, and the ovaries. These organs are not static. Every month they perform an elaborate ritual – the ovaries mature and release one egg; the egg drops into the fallopian tube and is transported to the uterus; the endometrium builds a lining and sheds it. All the steps in this gavotte occur within a single menstrual cycle.

3
The Menstrual Cycle

Every woman is born with her own biological time clock. When a girl reaches the threshold of puberty, at about the age of nine or ten, a hormonal trigger releases the gears and springs, and the clock starts ticking. The body begins to grow taller, and the waist slims as the hips grow slightly full. Soft hair begins to grow under the arms and around the vaginal area, and buds of fibrous tissue appear on the breasts. By the time the girl reaches the age of eleven or twelve, a slight milky discharge flows from her vagina, and she begins to menstruate.

Puberty

Puberty occurs about two years earlier in girls than it does in boys, and may take from one and a half to four years from start to finish. During these years the ovaries produce oestrogen in increasing amounts. This female hormone stimulates the development of a young girl's breasts and adjusts the body's contours. Unseen, the uterus also develops. But it is the small secretion of the male hormone testosterone from the ovaries that accounts for the growth of pubic hair, the increased size of the clitoris and vaginal lips, and the new intensity of erotic desire.

Before puberty a little girl has sexual awareness and responses, as all children do. But now, even before major physical changes are complete, the rising tide of sex hormones presses for fulfilment at a time when most youngsters are not yet ready to cope with sexual intercourse. Both boys and girls sometimes find it easier to explore their changing bodies and growing sex drives with friends of their own sex. For the vast majority of youngsters, homo-erotic sex is a stepping-stone to heterosexuality. Nevertheless, these very typical sexual interactions between friends are sometimes a source of guilt and worry later in life, especially among boys.

Throughout puberty masturbation is common in both sexes. It is usually a much bigger secret for girls, again causing much needless worry about being different from everyone else. All these deeply rooted fears about sexuality can loom large in a fertility clinic, when men and women may feel guilt about some early sexual experience that they believe has made them infertile.

Most of us remember puberty as a time of the utmost sensitivity, unexplained moodiness, and disturbing sexual excitement, a clinging to childish behaviour alternating with a fierce longing to be free. For girls, menstruation quite dramatically signals change. The age that a girl begins to menstruate depends on her inherited time clock. If her mother began to menstruate at age eleven, it's likely that the girl will do so also. Ovulation and menstruation are delicate processes that can be affected by nutrition and stress. Almost any upset can delay or speed onset. There is a great deal of leeway in the timing of normal onset; however, a very early or very late menarche may signal a hormonal problem.

Hormones affect the overall growth of the body. Height and sexual development increase together. Some hormones instruct the reproductive and sexual organs to develop, while a growth hormone released by the pituitary gland in the brain tells the bones to grow longer. The growing ovaries release oestrogen. As the tide of oestrogen rises in the bloodstream, the bone growth hormone subsides, then disappears. When sexual maturity reaches an apex, height is fixed.

If a girl produces too much oestrogen too soon, her sexual traits will develop rapidly, but bone growth will stop early. She will be well developed, but short in stature. Likewise, if the ovaries produce only small quantities of oestrogen, she may grow quite tall, yet have minimal sexual development. Height and sexual development are not exclusively dependent on hormones, however. They are also greatly influenced by inherited traits.

Generally, if a girl starts to menstruate before she is eight or after she is fifteen, a hormonal snag should be suspected. Precocious puberty or delayed puberty is sometimes caused by a tumour in the pituitary gland, and a complete medical check-up is called for.

Even though a girl may begin to menstruate at twelve, her reproductive system is still immature. It may take several years for the reproductive organs to reach full size, and for ovulation to occur every month. For all her reproductive years, a woman's biological time clock ticks away the days between menstrual periods. At first the clock is a little erratic, changing the number of days from month to month. It may take a year or more for the clock to find its proper rhythm and settle into a steady, cyclical count. Menstrual cycles vary considerably among women but normally fall into a pattern somewhere between twenty-six and thirty-two days. Once stabilized, the number of days between periods stays roughly the same month after month, although it may be altered by stress or illness.

In general, a girl whose time clock stabilizes quickly and remains steady will have good reproductive function as she grows into womanhood. A girl who begins to menstruate after she is fourteen, and whose cycle is skittish for a year or so, has a slowly developing time clock that could interfere with ovulation and cause fertility problems later in life.

The Cycle

The menstrual cycle is divided into two phases. The first two weeks, called the oestrogen phase, prepares the egg; the second two weeks, called the progesterone phase, releases the egg and prepares the uterus for pregnancy.

A cycle begins with the first day of bleeding. On about the sixth day, just after menstruation has ceased, the endometrial tissue lining the uterus is very thin (no more than $\frac{1}{3}$ in, 0·5 cm). Over the next few days, as the ovaries begin to produce oestrogen, the cells of the lining multiply rapidly, and the endometrium grows thicker. By day 14 of the cycle the endometrium may be ten times thicker than it was the week before.

As the endometrium grows thicker, an egg develops inside the ovary. At the point when the endometrium reaches its full thickness, the ovary releases the egg. This is ovulation. The ovaries stop making oestrogen and begin to produce

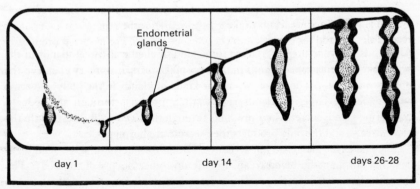

Growth of the endometrium over one menstrual cycle

progesterone. In the progesterone phase the endometrium stops growing, and its cell layers become spongy and wet. If the egg is fertilized, it will pass from the tube into the uterus and bury itself in the plush endometrium on about day 22.

If the egg is not fertilized, it is absorbed by the body and disappears. The blood vessels in the burgeoning endometrial tissue begin to break apart; the uterus fills up with blood and broken tissue. Under this fulsome pressure the muscular walls of the uterus contract and push the debris out. As soon as bleeding begins, the menstrual cycle is completed. In a matter of a few days the complete lining is discharged through the vagina.

Menstruation and ovulation are not synonymous. A menstrual period does not mean that a girl has ovulated. However, if a girl does ovulate and has sexual intercourse during those brief hours, she is fully capable of sustaining a pregnancy.

The growth and release of the egg and the growth and shedding of the endometrium are controlled by hormonal signals from the brain. These hormonal signals, and the glands that control them, are crucial to fertility. Understanding how the hormonal system works has led to the discovery of 'superdrugs' that now make pregnancy possible for thousands of previously infertile couples.

How Hormones Control Fertility

By itself the reproductive anatomy is a perfect machine. The beauty of its function is apparent but not unleashed until invisible chemicals add the fuel to bring the organs to life and release their procreative force. These chemicals are hormones. The word *hormone* is derived from the Greek *horman*, meaning 'to stir up'. Hormones circulate through the bloodstream and arouse cells and organ systems far from their point of origin.

Endocrine Glands

All glands manufacture and release some kind of chemical. Sweat glands in the skin make sweat, lacrimal glands in the eyes make tears, mammary glands in the breasts make milk. There are two major kinds of glands in the body: exocrine and endocrine. Exocrine glands release their products through small ducts. Endocrine glands secrete their products through their cell walls directly into the bloodstream, and the only products they secrete are hormones.

The endocrine glands do not actually use their own hormones, but send them coursing through the bloodstream to 'stir up' other organs of the body. The thyroid gland, for example, sends its hormone to all the cells of the body to regulate metabolism, the rate at which the body uses fuel. The pancreas sends out its insulin hormone to regulate the body's use of sugar. Only in the last hundred years have we even known that hormones existed. Astonishing, then, to learn that these chemical 'messengers' are also the major force behind reproduction.

Although the body has many hormone-secreting tissues, there are six major endocrine glands: the thyroid and parathyroid in the neck; the adrenal glands, one atop each kidney; a portion of the pancreas, located behind the abdominal cavity; the pituitary in the brain; and the testicles or ovaries in the pelvic region. The glands most directly involved in reproduction are the pituitary and the testicles and the ovaries. (Other endocrine glands normally have little influence on reproduction. However, if the adrenals and thyroid glands malfunction, they can interfere with fertility.)

The Brain Connection

Between the eyes and just above the roof of the mouth sits the primitive lower region of the brain, the hypothalamus. This lower brain controls all the essentials of life – thirst, hunger, body temperature, and so on. It also serves as a pathway for electrical messages coming from the higher brain centres and conveys these charged thoughts to the rest of the body. How the hypothalamus converts thoughts into physiology is one of the most exciting and least understood aspects of biological science.

Below the hypothalamus, attached by a stalk of blood vessels and nerve cells, is the penny-sized pituitary gland. The hypothalamus and the pituitary working in conjunction have power over reproduction. Together they are the control centre.

The pituitary gland takes its cue from the hypothalamus. From the brain the hypothalamus directs the pituitary gland to release – or not release – certain hormones to outlying posts. These messages from the hypothalamus are called releasing factors. Until recently it was believed that the hypothalamus used three separate releasing factors to govern reproduction. In 1971 Dr Andrew Schally, of Tulane University Medical School, proved that all three reproductive messages were in fact a single protein, which he named LH-RH. For his brilliant research, Dr Schally was awarded the Nobel prize.

The pituitary gland is divided into front and rear lobes. The rear lobe is linked to the hypothalamus by nerve cells. This portion regulates salt and water retention and smooth muscle contractions during labour and milk discharge from the breasts during lactation. The front lobe, which is joined to the hypothalamus by a bundle of blood vessels, makes up 70 per cent of the pituitary gland, and it is this portion that controls reproduction.

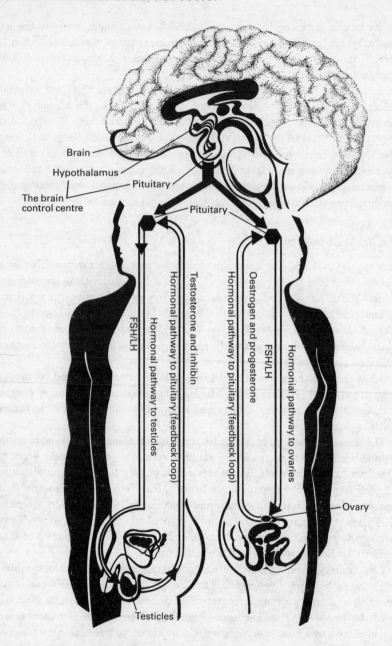

Brain

Hypothalamus

Pituitary

The brain
control centre

Pituitary

FSH/LH

Hormonal pathway to testicles

Hormonal pathway to pituitary (feedback loop)

Testosterone and inhibin

Hormonal pathway to pituitary (feedback loop)

Oestrogen and progesterone

FSH/LH

Hormonial pathway to ovaries

Ovary

Testicles

When the front lobe receives LH-RH messages from the hypothalamus, it secretes several hormones, known collectively as gonadotrophics (*gonad:* ovaries or testicles; *trophics:* nourishment). The two most important hormones for reproduction are FSH (follicle-stimulating hormone), which turns on the ovary and makes the egg follicle grow, and LH (luteinizing hormone), which kicks the ripened egg free of the ovary. The same two hormones that stir up the ovaries also regulate sperm production in men.

The Hormonal Axis

Using hormone messengers, the hypothalamus signals the pituitary, and the pituitary signals the gonads (testicles or ovaries). The gonads use different hormones to answer back. Communication from the hypothalamus to the pituitary to the gonads is called a hormonal axis. Hormone messages flow via delicate blood vessels in both directions along the axis.

For example, the hypothalamus signals the pituitary to send FSH to the ovaries. The ovaries receive the FSH message and begin to develop follicles. They also make oestrogen to signal back. When the control centre detects oestrogen coming along the axis through the bloodstream, it interprets the answer as 'Received enough FSH – stop sending.' It shuts down the FSH service. If no oestrogen comes back along the axis, the control centre picks up a different reply: 'Need more – keep sending.' And it continues to send FSH.

How many hormone messages the hypothalamus/pituitary control centre sends depends on how big a response it gets from the testicles or ovaries. Until the control centre gets a hormonal response that says 'Enough – stop sending,' it will continue to send the same message. Hormonal communication along the axis is the key to the most common cause of female infertility: ovulatory failure.

4
How the Ovaries Work

The way an ovary creates and ejects an egg each month is like the climax of an aria by Mozart – exquisitely intricate and fraught with dramatic overtones. The ovarian system emerges when the fetal ovaries arise from a blurred mass of cells. These embryonic ovaries are empty. In about the sixth week of development ova migrate into the ovaries from the middle portion of the fetal abdomen.

The newly migrated egg cells multiply rapidly and organize themselves into islands within the original mass of support cells. Other cells, called granulosa, cluster around each egg and form a shell. This shell, with an egg resting inside, is a true follicular structure. Thus, the word *follicle*, often used interchangeably with *ovum*, actually refers to a three-part structure comprising a granulosa cell layer, an ovum, and a small cavity of fluid.

When a baby girl is born, each small ovary contains about 200,000 primitive follicles. Surrounding them in the substance of the ovary are stroma, or support cells, and specialized cells known as Leydig's cells. As we will see later, these surrounding cells are crucial to the life of the ova.

None of these primitive egg cells can be fertilized. Only after puberty, when the brain sends out hormones to turn on the ovaries, do the eggs begin to mature. And with maturation occurs one of the most unusual processes in biology.

The Oestrogen Phase

On day 1 of the menstrual cycle, the hypothalamus begins sending short bursts of LH-RH to the pituitary, calling that gland to action. The pituitary immediately releases its egg-growing FSH. As soon as FSH hits the ovaries all the cells in the ovaries begin to pump out oestrogen, encouraging the thin lining of the uterus to build up. Thus begins the oestrogen phase of the menstrual cycle. At the same time, several hundred unripened eggs start to grow. Why a certain group of eggs wakes up in a given month remains a mystery, but once the eggs begin to mature they must either ovulate or die.

The Cell Divides

Just like every other cell in the body, each tiny egg carries forty-six chromosomes. Before it can be fertilized, the egg must somehow reduce its nuclear contents to twenty-three stranded chromosomes. This unique cell division, called meiosis, takes place only in reproductive tissue.

Each growing egg divides and spins off twenty-three chromosomes into a duplicate cell, retaining the other twenty-three for itself. This duplicate cell, called a polar body, shrivels up. It will continue to travel alongside the egg, but it is useless.

Now, in one ovary, one follicle out of the hundreds chosen for that month begins to grow faster than all the others. As this egg burgeons, the rest fall back. The shell around the raw egg cell thickens and separates into four layers. The two inside layers cling tightly to the egg and become its special protection. The two outer layers balloon away from it and the sac fills with fluid.

Ovulation

About fourteen days into the cycle the lead ovum – called the Graafian follicle – reaches its bursting point. Oestrogen pours back to the control centre: 'Enough –stop sending FSH.' The brain gets the message: the follicle is full and the egg is ready to be released. It shuts off FSH.

The mature follicle bulges red on the surface of the ovary, and a slight pitting begins to develop across its smooth outer face. These tiny depressions in the skin of the follicle are LH-receptor sites, the docking place for the new hormone messenger about to be dispatched by the pituitary.

At this point the hypothalamus sends a big pulse of LH-RH to its partner, and this time the pituitary gland releases a hormone called LH to boost the ripe ovum out of the ovary. The LH surges over the outer wall of the follicle and slips into the receptor sites. The chemical reaction causes the two outer layers to rupture, and the egg pops out. The moment of ovulation has been captured in remarkable film footage by Dr Richard Blandau of the University of Washington. The sustaining wall of the follicle weakens, then yields to pressure inside; as the wall collapses, the egg seems to hop out, on to a waiting finger of the fimbria. As the egg rolls out, it carries its two closest shell layers with it for nourishment. This is ovulation.

For the most part, the forty-eight hour period of ovulation in which a woman can become pregnant goes by unnoticed. A woman may feel a small twinge in the lower abdomen when the follicle ruptures. For most women, however, ovulation occurs silently and painlessly.

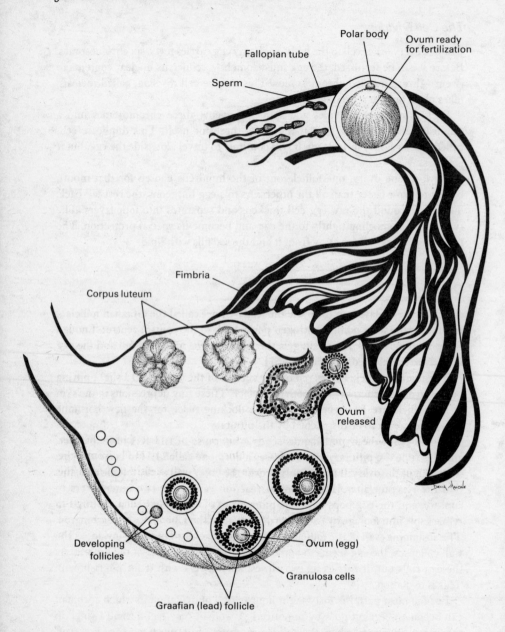

Follicles growing inside an ovary

The Progesterone Phase

The menstrual cycle now enters its luteal or progesterone phase, when it is dominated by the luteal hormone LH. The yellowing outer shell of the egg remains behind on the ovary and continues to receive LH. This empty egg sac forms a knobby cyst called a corpus luteum. Under LH, the dying corpus luteum begins to pour out a new hormone, progesterone (Latin for gestation). Progesterone helps the cells of the endometrium build protein and store sugar. The thick lining becomes lusher and wetter.

Fertilization

The egg is moved along the inner tract of the fallopian tube by the cilia conveyor belt. Each of the twenty-three chromosomes inside the egg has two strands of DNA. Before fertilization can take place, one strand of each chromosome must be eliminated. Nothing happens until a sperm punctures the egg's shell. Then, in an instant, several things happen at once. The egg splits its chromosomes in half, throwing off the excess strands into another polar body. The original polar body imitates the egg, and also splits its chromosomes. This unique cell division called meiosis occurs only in these reproductive cells. The egg now contains twenty-three single-strand chromosomes. Its three withered polar bodies continue to nest alongside.

At that moment, the twenty-three single strands of sperm DNA slip through the opening in the egg's shell and begin to pair up with compatible strands of ovum DNA. The new pairs of DNA immediately generate duplicates of themselves, to create forty-six perfect chromosomes. Fertilization is complete.

Over the next few days the new cell divides into two, four, and then eight cells, and completes its journey into the uterus. Once in the safety of the womb, the embryo clings to the spongy endometrium and derives nourishment from the energy-packed cells.

The fertilized ovum shoots out an early pregnancy signal, telling the control centre to keep the LH coming to support the endometrium. The old egg sac keeps pumping out progesterone for nearly sixty days. Only after the lining develops enough to support the fetus by itself does the corpus luteum finally die.

If the Egg is not Fertilized

If no conception occurs, the early pregnancy signal is not given. The current of progesterone feeds back along the axis to the control centre: 'Enough LH – stop sending,' and LH shuts down. Without LH support, the corpus luteum

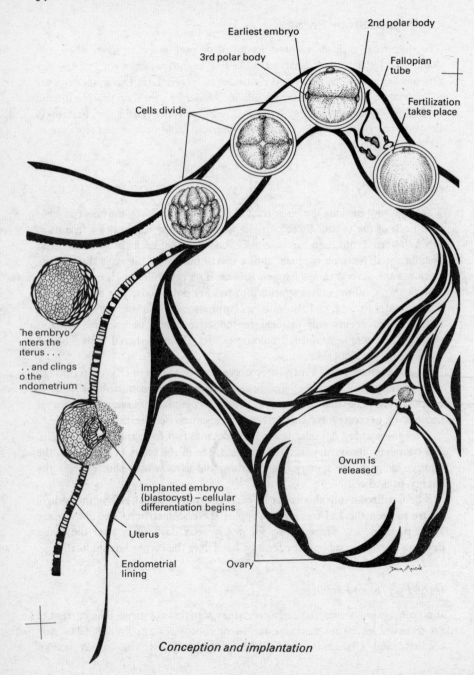

3rd polar body

Earliest embryo

2nd polar body

Fallopian tube

Fertilization takes place

Cells divide

The embryo enters the uterus . . .

. . . and clings to the endometrium

Implanted embryo (blastocyst) – cellular differentiation begins

Uterus

Endometrial lining

Ovum is released

Ovary

Conception and implantation

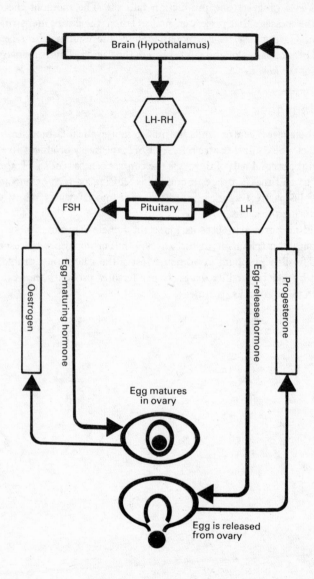

The female hormonal axis

disintegrates and progesterone production falls off. The moment the control centre gets the message that progesterone has fallen, the entire menstrual cycle begins again. Having lost its hormonal lifeline, the endometrium begins to collapse and break apart, sloughing off through the vagina. This is menstruation, the first day of the new cycle.

Shifting Hormones

In women, the control centre sends hormones in a cyclical fashion. In the first part of the cycle the control centre releases FSH; the ovary produces an egg and oestrogen. In the second half of the cycle the control centre sends LH; the ovary ejects the eggs and makes progesterone. This shifting pattern of hormones in women may be partly responsible for the wide mood swings many women experience during the cycle.

These shifting hormonal currents make the female reproductive system an extremely complex mechanism; disturbances in the hormonal axis are responsible for half of all fertility problems in women. Most of these hormonal problems can be solved with modern fertility drugs. Other fertility problems, however, may require much more arduous treatment.

5
When Things Go Wrong: Women

Ovulation is a precise and elaborate system, arranged around four epic events in a woman's reproductive life: her development in utero; her childhood; her prime reproductive years; and menopause, when the door closes to the reproductive cycle. When a woman is infertile, something has gone wrong during one of the first three epochs.

In Utero Development

Sometimes a woman is born infertile. As a female fetus grows inside her mother's womb, some small flaw may occur in the cell groups that cluster into specific bits of tissue. The possibility of error is easy to imagine when we consider that every fragment of the human body, every limb and eyelash, comes from a single pair of fused cells.

Sometimes the cell groups that construct the various organs misread the architect's blueprint. Instead of one vagina, they make two. Instead of one tiny cervical canal, they build two. Where the plan calls for a single roomy uterus, they put up a wall and divide it into two compartments. Sometimes the builders forget to put in an ovary or a fallopian tube.

When the baby is born she looks perfect. No one would know of the few little mistakes on the inside. At least not immediately. These kinds of flaws usually remain completely unnoticed until the baby grows up and enters her prime reproductive years.

Childhood

Most of the time the cell engineers do a flawless job. Generations of exquisitely formed female babies testify to their skill. Once a baby girl is born, however, she is subject to an onslaught of travail from the outside world. If she is lucky, threats to her reproductive function are held at bay throughout childhood. However, even a well-protected child can innocently stumble into trouble. It could be something as simple as falling off a bicycle. If the hard metal frame jams between her legs, her reproductive organs may be damaged. Straddle injuries can be serious for both boys and girls.

Much more traumatic is sexual abuse, an event more common than we previously believed possible. Such acts against a child are usually kept secret. The child victim may feel shame and guilt, and almost never speaks of the crime. The moral implications are only part of the picture.

A little girl has neither emotional nor biological defences against sexual abuse. Her body has not yet developed the cervical mucus that defends the pelvic cavity against infection. Such an infection may go by unnoticed and subside spontaneously; but it can completely destroy the girl's reproductive organs.

The psychological ramifications also may indirectly affect her future fertility. Children who are abused sexually may be so contaminated by the experience that their adult lives are forever haunted by memories and guilt, stress patterns that one way or another can make pregnancy impossible.

Fortunately, most little girls do not encounter such physical or sexual abuse, and come through these years unscathed. Their biological time clocks, which have been quiet through the days of childhood, begin to wind up when they are about ten. Both hands start to sweep erratically around the clock face, stalling here, jumping there. The system seems to be going haywire. Then quite suddenly the hands sweep together at twelve o'clock high, and the girl begins to menstruate. From that moment on, the clock precisely ticks off the cycle of ovulation, and thus begins the third major epoch of her reproductive life, How smoothly the clock starts off plays an important part in the girl's fertility. A quick easy start-up usually means that ovulation will be regular throughout her lifetime.

The Reproductive Years

With the onset of menstruation it is possible for a woman to have a child. This critical epoch is also the time when most fertility problems arise. Something may have happened during fetal development or childhood, but most causes of infertility arise in adult life.

Fertility problems in adult women are divided almost equally into two fairly distinct categories. The first category, called ovulatory failures, has to do with ovulation – the production and release of eggs. Any disturbance in the hormonal axis can cause the system to misfire. Nowadays such problems are almost always treated with the new fertility drugs.

The second major category of problems involves 'mechanical' failures, in which the reproductive organs themselves are damaged. For various reasons, scar tissue or endometriosis can build up all over the organs. Not so long ago this kind of problem was considered hopeless. Thanks to advances in twenty-first-century medicine, microsurgery can often successfully free the tubes and ovaries, making pregnancy possible for thousands of couples.

A third, less frequently seen, group of problems involves the route travelled by sperm as they swim from the vagina through the cervix and uterus, and into the tubes. Problems here may go all the way back to the dim hours of fetal development. Some of these problems can be corrected with clever surgical reconstruction of the reproductive structure.

Ovulatory Failures

At least half the fertility problems in women are related to egg production and release. The egg may not mature properly; or if it does grow, it may not release from the ovary on schedule. The operation of the ovaries is overseen by the hormonal system. If this system is even slightly disturbed, ovulation won't occur.

The hormonal system has two major components: hormones sent by the hypothalamus/pituitary control centre and hormones made by the ovaries themselves. Errors in either part of the system may interfere with egg production.

Birth-control Pills. Some errors occur spontaneously in the timing mechanism of the hormonal system. Others are perpetrated by that ingenious culprit, the birth-control pill. Every helpful modern invention is said to have at least one drawback. We are only beginning to recognize some of the drawbacks of the pill. One that physicians see almost daily is temporary infertility after a woman stops the pill.

Birth-control pills work by interfering with the hormonal axis. Because the control centre receives a constant signal each day to limit its work load, it does not send FSH and LH hormones to the ovaries. The cells that operate the control centre become lazy and dull; they go to sleep at the switch.

The result? When a woman stops taking the pill, the cells grumble and grouse and try to catch another forty winks. Ovulation does not occur in the first month, or the next. Sometimes it does not resume for several months. Time is needed for the cells that run the control centre to reawaken fully and take command of the system. Generally, this condition, called post-pill anovulation (no ovulation) or oligo-ovulation (occasional ovulation), cures itself within six to twelve months.

How quickly the system wakes up depends largely on how easily the woman's periods began when she entered puberty. If she had an instant start-up then, she will usually quickly recover her normal cycle. However, if she had a slow start-up in youth, birth-control pills may have a profound effect on her system.

Serious problems can arise if a woman has delayed pregnancy until her thirties. At that point, she can't afford to wait an extra year for the cell staff to wake up at the control centre. Older women, and women whose systems refuse to wake up after a year, need extra help. The control centre can be booted into action with fertility drugs. At the Omega Institute, we have found that about 25 per cent of patients over twenty-seven years of age who suffer post-pill anovulation need this extra initiation. For the rest, the system usually fires up on its own without medical interference.

Other contraceptives also can affect a woman's future fertility. IUDs have been known to cause secondary pelvic infections, which result in scar tissue around the reproductive organs, so this form of contraception also has some risk to fertility. Abortion does not seem to affect future fertility, unless the precedure is carelessly performed and infection sets in in the pelvic cavity. However, each time a foreign object is introduced into the uterus, there is a chance of infection, and repeated abortions increase the risk.

Polycystic Ovarian Disease (PCO). The most common cause of serious ovulatory problems is a disorder called polycystic ovarian disease. Researchers dispute the exact origin of the disease, but most investigators agree that the ovaries misread the LH/FSH signal from the pituitary and send back the wrong response along the feedback loop. Scientists are uncertain whether the original flaw lies in the control centre or in the ovaries themselves. Some believe heredity may play a role.

Regardless of which came first, the result is the same: ovaries clogged with cysts, and few or no ovulations each year. As with most problems involving hormones, the disease runs in gradations, all the way from very mild to extremely severe. About 75 per cent of the time women with PCO respond well to a three-month course of therapy with superfertility drugs. The pregnancy rate is about 35–40 per cent. In some women, however, the system is completely resistant to drug therapy.

Emotional Disturbances. Few scientists today believe that psychological problems directly cause infertility, but this is still a prime area for research. Too many indicators point to emotional involvement to discount such a possibility. The lower brain (hypothalamus), which is the major thrust behind the reproductive system, can be overpowered by the higher brain (central nervous system). The hypothalamus is sensitive to psychological trauma, which can severely deplete the messenger chemical that it sends to the pituitary gland.

We know that certain drugs, particularly the psychiatric class of tranquillizers and mood modifiers, can override the hypothalamus and disturb the hormonal axis. Usually as soon as the drug is stopped the axis returns to normal. Illness and stress also can interfere with hormone production, and thus temporarily stop ovulation.

The de-emphasis on psychological factors as a cause of infertility is a result of two events. First, it represents something of a backlash against the insensitivity of physicians over the past few decades to the plight of infertile women. Thousands of women were told that their inability to conceive was strictly in their heads. Modern science has shown that the vast majority of these women probably had undiagnosed physical problems that caused their infertility. Second, science has been so successful that 90 per cent of all cases of infertility today can be accurately diagnosed, compared with only 40 per cent ten years ago. Most of the leading researchers in the field are so impressed with these advances that they believe that new, even more sophisticated diagnostic techniques will eventually be able to identify a physical cause for the remaining 10 per cent.

While psychological factors are not often considered a cause of infertility, they are frequently a result. One of the most important discoveries to come out of modern fertility research is the recognition of an infertility stress syndrome. Infertility creates enormous psychological stress for both partners, and the stress increases as the couple goes through the investigation and subsequent treatment. Stress can create problems in the marital relationship and make existing problems worse. For these reasons, professional psychological evaluation is part of many fertility investigations today.

The benefit of this counselling is twofold: couples receive support to help them cope with stress, and scientists gain some insight into stress factors that may, in fact, be putting so much pressure on the couple that treatment cannot succeed. This new knowledge and experience may ultimately help us learn why some couples, for unknown reasons, cannot conceive.

Modern Treatment. Twenty years ago almost no medical treatment was available for women who were infertile because of ovulatory failure. Some physicians tried what is known as the rebound technique. If a woman took large doses of oestrogen orally, the control centre in the brain, detecting the excess in the bloodstream, would completely shut down the ovaries. When she stopped taking the oestrogen supplement, the brain would react powerfully to the sudden hormonal absence from the bloodstream and throw an extra boost of FSH and LH to the ovaries to force them back into production. This new, high-energy start-up would sometimes result in temporary ovulation.

Ovulation is a very precise mechanism. The rebound technique, which involved a general flooding of the system with oestrogen to see if anything happened, did not begin to deal with the complexity of the problem. What was needed was a drug that would directly manipulate the control centre, forcing it to issue correct instructions to the ovaries. That drug was finally made available in the early 1960s when clomiphene citrate came on to the market. Since that time clomiphene (Clomid, Serophene) has been the leading fertility drug in the world (see Chapter 20). Clomiphene acts directly on the hypothalamus, forcing it to boost the pituitary, which in turn drives the ovaries to produce and release eggs.

Clomiphene can induce ovulation in nearly 80 per cent of all women with ovulatory failure. When clomiphene fails, other extremely potent fertility drugs can be tried; these drugs have severe potential side-effects, and must be carefully monitored.

Mechanical Problems

Mechanical problems involve the frailties of the reproductive organs, particularly the egg's transport system. Fallopian tubes may be damaged on the inside or the outside. Even a web of scar tissue tying down the tube can keep it from picking up the ovum. Blockages inside the tube prevent the union of sperm and egg; partial blockages can entrap a fertilized ovum and cause a dangerous tubal (ectopic) pregnancy that cannot implant in the uterus.

The other reproductive organs may also be severely damaged by scar tissue. All the organs should slide naturally and smoothly against one another. Rubbery adhesions on the outside literally paralyse the organs. These are only a few examples of mechanical problems. A woman is not born with these kinds of problems; she catches them.

The Role of Infection. Scar tissue is most often caused by infections inside the pelvic cavity. Such infections, primarily sexually transmitted disease, are the major factor behind the rising incidence of infertility in women. Pelvic inflammatory disease (PID) accounts for roughly 20 per cent of fertility problems in women, and this is a rapidly climbing statistic.

Almost all pelvic infections are venereal in origin, meaning simply that they are transmitted sexually. Women today become sexually active earlier, often in their early teens, and may have a number of different partners during their lifetime. Having multiple partners increases the risk of being exposed to infection.

When a woman contracts even a relatively minor sexually transmitted disease – for example, condyloma (venereal warts) or herpes virus – the tough barrier of mucus in the cervix, which normally protects the pelvic cavity, may be destroyed. Through this open portal, a bacterial infection such as *Streptococcus* or gonorrhoea can travel freely through the uterus and into the fallopian tubes. The body's immune system quickly responds to the invasion. An army of white blood cells swarms over the bacteria and literally eats them up. As the white blood cells destroy the invaders, they excrete a collagen protein that resembles steel mesh. This is scar tissue.

Rapid treatment can stop massive damage, but it doesn't take much scarring to interfere with pregnancy. For example, the fallopian tubes are very susceptible to gonorrhoeal infection and may become permanently damaged after a single 'small case of gonorrhoea'. About 25 per cent of women with any form of gonorrhoea will have significant tubal damage that results in infertility. (Interestingly, because gonorrhoea seldom reaches the ductal system in men, it is not a significant cause of male infertility.)

New diagnostic tests have led to the discovery of other organisms dangerous to women. Some of the so-called non-specific infections ignored in the past have proved to be quite specific. One hard-to-identify organism called chlamydia can invade and silently destroy the fallopian tubes within a few days. Scientists are working hard to develop better detection methods for this elusive organism.

Infection is not the only creator of scar tissue. Even a minor surgical procedure in the abdomen can cause severe scarring in women, particularly if the operation was complicated by infection. Another major cause of pelvic adhesions is endometriosis, dubbed the 'career-women's disease', since it is more likely to occur in women who have never had children. Both endometriosis and pelvic inflammatory disease are sometimes called pelvic adhesive disease (PAD), a general term for adhesions in the pelvis of any origin.

Endometriosis. This is a painful and destructive disease in which tissue identical to the endometrial lining of the uterus begins to grow in the interior of the abdomen. Somehow, endometrial cells implant on the outside of the uterus, on the ovaries or bowel, and continue to grow just as if they were inside the uterus, steadily spreading through the pelvic cavity. Every month, under the influence of hormones, blood flows from this misplaced tissue, just as it does from the uterus. Since the blood cannot escape through the vagina, as it would in a normal menstrual period, it flows into the pelvic cavity, creating scar tissue that ties down the reproductive organs.

No one knows for certain how this tissue gets into the abdomen in the first place. For a while scientists held that some of the endometrial lining, instead of being fully expelled during menstruation, went up through the fallopian tubes into the abdominal cavity. Recently, however, researchers have learned that some women who have their tubes tied still develop endometriosis.

If the endometrium can't go backwards up the tubes, how does it implant itself? One idea is that endometriosis is a birth defect. During fetal development the cell engineers that build the reproductive system misplace tiny endometrial cells in the abdomen, much as carpenters lay down their tools in the wrong place and forget to take them home. The cells may lie dormant for many years, and then, some time after puberty, begin to grow. This neat idea fills several gaps in the old theory. For example, if the error in the blueprint is inherited, it could explain why endometriosis tends to run in families.

Whatever its origin, even a small amount of endometriosis in the wrong place can interfere with fertility. It is a painful disease, especially in the early stages when the cells are tender and burgeoning.

For some reason, endometriosis seldom attacks the flower-like fimbria that picks up the egg. Nor does it harm the delicate cilia. Thus, if the endometriosis can be cleared up, usually with a combination of fertility drugs and new microsurgical techniques, a women has a good chance of pregnancy. After proper treatment of the less severe forms, about 60–70 per cent of women are able to become pregnant. Whether a woman can conceive following treatment for the more advanced stages of the disease depends on how much damage has been done to the reproductive organs.

Twenty-first-century Medicine. Surgical advances have made possible the correction of hopelessly blocked and damaged fallopian tubes. Fifteen years ago the microscope was matched to surgery for the first time, and surgeons were no longer limited to what they could see with their own eyes. With × 10 or × 25 magnification, miraculous repairs could be made on delicate, nearly invisible structures. Surgeons could eradicate problems that had never been seen before, such as small adhesions around the fallopian tubes or 'invisible' implants of endometriosis. Surgeons can today rebuild a fallopian tube, because they can match up, and neatly stitch together, the three separate layers of the tube.

Today microsurgeons can use needles smaller than eyelashes to rebuild reproductive organs. The needle is made by lasers that drill a hole down the length of the steel lash; a technician inserts a thread into the hole and presses the union together, so that needle and thread are one slender strand.

The precision of lasers makes them a natural tool for use in medical surgery. Lasers combined with microsurgery can clear obstructions, rebuild tubes, and free reproductive organs from massive sheets of adhesions. This is done without damage to the surrounding tissue, little bleeding, few sutures, and in half the operating time of conventional surgery.

Microsurgery and laser surgery are recent developments, and are not yet widely available in Britain, however.

Getting There

The last, and usually the smallest, group of infertility problems involves the pathway travelled by sperm on their way to the fallopian tubes – the receptacles of the vagina, cervix, and uterus.

Sperm must be able to penetrate the mouth of the cervix fast enough, and in sufficient number, to reach the egg while it is still in the tube. We have already mentioned that certain birth defects can interfere with this journey. About 80 per cent of such birth defects can be repaired with microsurgery.

Another problem inside the vagina and cervix that can interfere with sperm is a hostile cervical mucus. Typically, the vagina is awash in a highly acidic coating. Once sperm get past this, the cervix is supposed to welcome them and provide a comfortable passageway into the uterus. Not every cervix is so hospitable.

Should even a mild infection set in, for example, the cervix changes its whole milieu. Instead of being a warm, nurturing environment, it becomes a harsh killing place. Chronic infection in the cervix can destroy sperm on contact.

In addition, we now know that some women have immunologic chemicals, called antibodies, in their cervical mucus. Antibodies, like infection, immobilize and kill sperm. They are the focus of intense infertility research today. A woman may be allergic to her husband's sperm, or a man may produce semen with antibodies to his own sperm. One method of treating female antibodies has met with mixed results. For a period of several months, the couple uses a condom during intercourse, preventing any contact between the sperm and the mucus. The antibodies temporarily disappear. For the next few months, the couple engages in unprotected intercourse during ovulation, hoping to get pregnant before the antibodies build up again. A new surgical treatment for cervical antibodies may obviate this approach and prove valuable in curing the disorder.

Once inside the uterus, the sperm encounter few problems, except for rare inflammation of the endometrium, called chronic endometritis. This problem is treated with antibiotics and occasionally a D&C (dilatation and curettage of the uterus) to remove the endometrial tissue.

Menopause

As a woman approaches menopause, the fourth epoch event in her reproductive life, the door begins to close on her childbearing years. The precise, bright countenance of her reproductive mechanism flickers and ultimately fades.

Middle age, which has little effect on male fertility, puts an end to a woman's childbearing years. Our changing views about parenthood have made age a critical issue in the rising incidence of infertility in women. Many women are now postponing childbearing until their late twenties and thirties. They gain the advantage of personal and professional growth, and their children in turn benefit from more mature, stable parents. But the converse of this gain is that a woman's finely tuned reproductive system functions best between the ages of eighteen and twenty-eight, when ovulation is most regular. Also her ova, which are present at birth, are as old as the rest of her body, and older eggs begin to deteriorate and lose some of their capability for fertilization. If her husband has a slightly lowered sperm count, the combination may result in infertility.

Any one of these factors may be involved when a woman finds herself unable to have a child, and each of these components is fully described in the chapters that follow. But an infertility problem may lie with a man as well. We know today that men, for a variety of reasons, have as high an incidence of infertility as women. And in 20 per cent of couples, both partners have a problem. Many women have undergone major surgery for tubal reconstruction only to discover later that their husbands were infertile.

The Fertility Risk Quiz for Women

The following quiz can give a woman some idea of her chances of having a fertility problem. Multiple variables are considered in determining the point value for each question and the entire quiz is computer-verified. The quiz is routinely given to patients at our clinic and has proved accurate 85 per cent of the time. (The only fertility quiz for men is a sperm count.)

Choose the answer that most closely applies and write the corresponding number of points on the appropriate lines in the right-hand column.

Points

1. You first had intercourse when you were:
12 years old (15 points)
13–14 years old (10 points)
15–18 years old (5 points)
19–21 years old (3 points)
22–5 years old (0 points)   _____

2. Your total number of sexual partners to date is:
1–3 (1 point)
4–7 (5 points)
8–15 (10 points)
16 or over (25 points)   _____

3. You started to menstruate at:
10 years old (0 points)
11–14 years old (1 point)
15–18 years old (5 points)
19 or over (10 points)   _____

4. How normal are your menstrual cycles?
Regular (0 points)
Slightly irregular (5 points)
Very irregular (10 points)   _____

5. How many hospital-treated pelvic infections have you had?
None (0 points)
One (5 points)
Two or more (10 points)   _____

Points

6. Have you had gonorrhoea?
No (0 points)
Once (5 points)
More than once (20 points)   _____

7. What is the total number of years you have used birth-control pills?
Never (0 points)
1–3 years (1 point)
4–6 years (3 points)
More than 6 years (20 points)   _____

8. How many years have you used an IUD?
Never (0 points)
1–3 years (5 points)
4–6 years (10 points)
More than 6 years (20 points)   _____

9. Have you ever developed vaginal or vulvar warts?
No (0 points)
Yes (3 points)   _____

10. How many abortions have you had?
None (0 points)
One (3 points)
More than one (5 points)   _____

Points   *Points*

11. For how many years have
you ever tried to become
pregnant without using any
special method for timing
intercourse?
None (0 points)
1–2 years (5 points)
3–5 years (10 points)
6 or more years (15 points) _____

12. For how many cycles have
you ever tried to become
pregnant using any kind of
method to time intercourse to
coincide with ovulation?
None (0 points)
1–6 cycles (10 points)
7–12 cycles (15 points)
13 or more cycles (20 points) _____

13. Do you have menstrual
cramps?
Mild or none (0 points)
Moderate (3 points)
Severe (5 points) _____

14. Do you feel pain with
deep penetration during
intercourse?
Little or none (0 points)
Moderate (3 points)
Severe (5 points) _____

15. Your current age is:
18–24 (0 points)
25–29 (5 points)
30–35 (10 points)
36–40 (15 points) _____

Total points _____

Probability Score

Add up your total points and check below to see what your chances are of having a fertility problem. It is important to keep in mind that your score represents only a *statistical chance* – a high score does not necessarily mean that a fertility problem exists. The result should be used only as a guide. If you are concerned about your score, you may want to consult your gynaecologist

Total Number of Points	Probability of Problem Existing (percentage)
0–10	5
11–19	10
20–29	20
30–39	30
40–49	40
50–59	50
60–69	60
70–79	70
80–89	80
90–99	90
100+	95

The Fertility Risk Quiz, devised by the Omega Institute team, was first published by *Self* magazine.

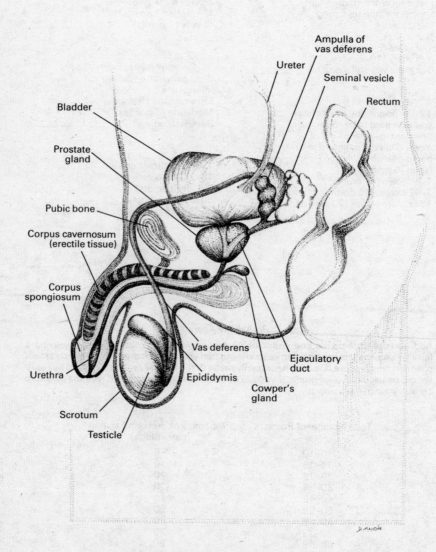

Bladder

Prostate gland

Pubic bone

Corpus cavernosum (erectile tissue)

Corpus spongiosum

Urethra

Scrotum

Testicle

Vas deferens

Epididymis

Cowper's gland

Ejaculatory duct

Ureter

Ampulla of vas deferens

Seminal vesicle

Rectum

The male reproductive anatomy (side view)

6
The Male Anatomy

When a Y-carrying sperm merges with an ovum, a male embryo results. The Y sex chromosome plays many roles, but its premier task is to imprint the new embryo with the reproductive system of a male.

Even though early embryonic tissue looks identical in both girls and boys, the sex imprint is there, waiting to reveal itself. In about nine weeks the special reproductive cells – those few cells in which the two sex chromosomes dominate all the rest – cluster just below the kidneys. As a male fetus develops, the little group of cells migrates down and, together with other support cells, forms the testicles. A small bud of tissue that becomes the clitoris in girls grows into a penis in boys. When a boy is born, his penis is fully formed and his testicles have usually descended from the abdomen into the scrotal sac. All his sexual organs are in place: penis, testicles, scrotum, accessory glands, and a system of ducts. These organs have one major reproductive purpose: to manufacture sperm and deliver them into a woman's vagina.

The Testicles

The egg-shaped testicles are the centre of sperm production. Their position outside the body makes them highly vulnerable to injury. Nature is usually a more cautious caretaker. Yet even in this seemingly irresponsible manoeuvre, biological reasoning can be detected.

Theoretically, the location away from the body cavity helps keep the temperature inside the testicles slightly cooler (93·8° F, 34·8° C) than that of the rest of the body (99° F, 37° C). This coolness is vital for good sperm production. From moment to moment, the temperature is carefully maintained. When the outside temperature is cold, scrotal muscles contract and bring the testicles up closer to the body for warmth; when it's hot, the muscles relax and the testicles drop away from the body.

To offer some cushioning against injury, the testicles are wrapped in membranes and suspended in a pouch of tissue called the scrotum. More help comes from nerve fibres that run through the pouch and make the organs so pain-sensitive that men instinctively try to protect them. During sports or other strenuous activity a jockstrap gives some added protection; even so, any hard blow to the scrotum may damage the sperm production centre and destroy a man's fertility.

The testicles vary in size and weight, depending on a man's overall body build. There is no such thing as a 'right' size, nor does size have anything to do with the number or quality of sperm produced. However, if the testicles fail to mature because of a chromosome abnormality or a severe illness, they will be unproductive and remain quite small.

The testicles are filled with hundreds of tightly wrinkled threads, each one up to a yard long. These are the seminiferous tubules, the birthplace of new sperm. Three or four microscopic tubules coil together into a lobule, and the few hundred lobules roll up into tiny balls that pack the testicles.

Under the influence of hormones, tiny cells planted in the tissue lining of the tubules begin to produce sperm. The initial development of sperm takes about sixty-four days. At that point, the new sperm, which cannot yet swim, drop into the hollow centre of the tubule. These cells have the characteristic head and tail of sperm but none of the power. They are pushed along by muscle contractions and fluid pressure through small canals (rete testis) into another tightly coiled structure, the epididymis.

The Epididymis

The epididymis is a long, hollow length of tissue coiled across the top and side of the testicles. Wound up, the 12–15 ft (3·7–4·6 m) thread is no more than ½ in (12 mm) long. Newborn sperm spend several days passing through this narrow channel; while twisting through its coils, the microscopic sperm mature and learn to swim. This final rite of passage takes anywhere from three to twelve days, with some sperm gaining their full growth before they reach the end of the tube.

The sperm's ability to swim, or motility, is crucial to its success. Immature sperm swim in circles; these spinners cannot fertilize an ovum because they will never get as far as the fallopian tubes. Only fully grown sperm, whose tails lash like whips and propel them straight ahead against the downflow of cervical mucus, can achieve penetration.

Mature sperm use the tail of the epididymis as a holding tank. They can remain stored here for at least a month, but if they are not ejaculated during this time they die. Even though fresh sperm arrive in the holding area every day, a man who ejaculates only once a month will have a high concentration of dead sperm in his semen and subsequently a lowered fertility rate.

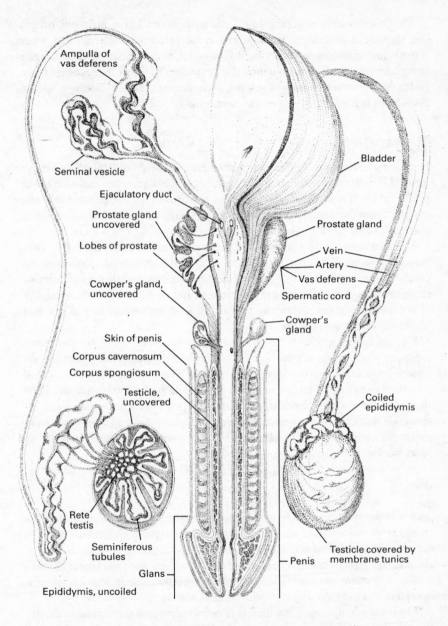

Ampulla of
vas deferens

Seminal vesicle

Bladder

Ejaculatory duct

Prostate gland
uncovered

Prostate gland

Lobes of prostate

Vein

Artery

Vas deferens

Cowper's gland,
uncovered

Spermatic cord

Cowper's
gland

Skin of penis

Corpus cavernosum

Corpus spongiosum

Testicle,
uncovered

Coiled
epididymis

Rete
testis

Seminiferous
tubules

Glans

Epididymis, uncoiled

Penis

Testicle covered by
membrane tunics

The male reproductive anatomy (front view)

The epididymis is vulnerable to infection. Males of all ages, including babies, can develop epididymitis from a variety of infecting bacteria. The most threatening organism, as far as fertility is concerned, is chlamydia, which can scar and partially block the channel if it progresses as far as the testicles. Early treatment, however, usually prevents such damage, and a blockage in the epididymis is not a major cause of male infertility.

The Vasa Deferentia – the Spermatic Cords

Not all mature sperm wait in the holding area of the epididymis. Some move forward into the vasa deferentia, two long, heavy tubes going up each side of the pelvic cavity. These tubes are the main passageway to the penis. Each vas, together with its accompanying network of veins and arteries, makes up a spermatic cord.

The spermatic cords pass up through the scrotum and enter the body cavity through two small openings on either side of the abdominal wall (inguinal canals). Once inside the body proper, the cords continue their course, running along the sides of the bladder, over the ureters, and then down into the substance of the prostate gland. Here the two cords feed into ejaculatory ducts that ultimately empty into the urethra.

Mature sperm entering the vas are gently squeezed along by the tube's pulsating walls; some are pushed all the way to the upper end, where the vas widens into a small pocket known as an ampulla. These sperm will remain stored here until ejaculated. Thus, some sperm are present in the epididymis and along the paths of the vasa deferentia at all times. When a man has a vasectomy, an operation that cuts the vasa near their exit point from the epididymis, some live sperm may remain in his ejaculate from those stored along this pathway for up to six weeks.

Where the Fluid Comes From

Sperm make up only 2 per cent of the total ejaculate. Most seminal fluid comes from the paired seminal vesicles and the prostate gland, and a little more is contributed by the two tiny Cowper's glands located just below and in front of the prostate gland. On orgasm, all these fluids combine with the sperm to make semen. Vasectomy cuts only the sperm duct; therefore, a man who has had this operation will have a nearly normal volume of semen.

The main job of the seminal fluid is to carry sperm into the vaginal vault. But the secretions also contain nutrients whose roles are only vaguely understood. The sugar fructose, vitamin C, proteins, and salts, all present in seminal fluid, may act as fuel. We also know that the overall acid–alkaline (pH) balance of the fluid is crucial to fertility. Fluid that is too acidic can kill sperm.

Volume is also important. Too much or too little semen can ruin a sperm's ability to reach the fertilization site.

Seminal Vesicles

The seminal vesicles are two shapeless pouches adjacent to the upper ends of the vasa deferentia. These membranous glands secrete more than half the bulk of the ejaculate. This fluid is so acidic, however, that by itself it would kill sperm.

Prostate Gland

The prostate gland is a multi-lobed structure that grows out of and surrounds the upper part of the urethra. The vasa, ejaculatory ducts, and urethra all join up inside the prostate. This walnut-sized gland secretes an important chemical that causes semen to liquefy, a process vital for fertility. Its richly alkaline fluid balances the semen and subdues the acids in the vagina.

Ejaculatory Ducts

Each paired vas deferens and seminal vesicle plunge into an ejaculatory duct that courses through the prostate. The two ducts are very close together. In between is a very small blind duct that remains a mystery in the male anatomy. It is a remnant of the female Mullerian system, known as the man's vagina (vagina masculina). The duct serves no purpose except to remind us that men and women, despite their many differences, still have some things in common.

Towards the middle of the prostate gland, both ejaculatory ducts empty into the single narrow channel of the urethra, which will carry the semen out of the tip of the penis. These ducts sometimes become clogged with infection, particularly gonorrhoea and other sexually transmitted diseases. Infections that reach the ducts travel up from the urethra.

Urethra

The urethra is the major channel of transport for both urine and sperm. It leads out of the bladder and down through the prostate gland, where the ejaculatory ducts empty into it, and then exits through the penis. The urethra has two tasks: when the internal muscle of the bladder is open, it carries urine out of the

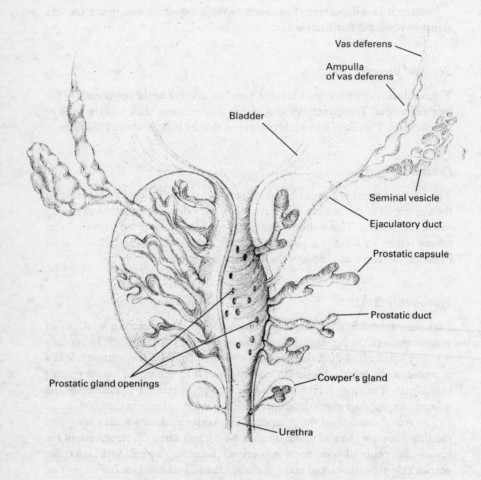

Vas deferens

Ampulla
of vas deferens

Bladder

Seminal vesicle

Ejaculatory duct

Prostatic capsule

Prostatic duct

Prostatic gland openings

Cowper's gland

Urethra

*Cross-section of the prostate gland, viewed from the rear;
here all the semen-carrying ducts empty into the urethra.*

THE MALE ANATOMY · 57

bladder to the penis. When the sphincter muscle clamps shut during orgasm, the semen can use the urethra as a conduit through the penis.

Infection occurs much less frequently in men than in women because the urethra is the only portal of entry into the male reproductive tract. Since the urethra is a much longer tube in men than in women, bacteria need more time to reach the critical organs. All the while, urine intermittently courses down, pushing the infecting organisms back. Sometimes infection may invade the vasa and epididymis, but it seldom reaches into the sperm-producing centres of the testicles. All the intricate mazes and convoluted channels of the epididymis and rete testis restrain it.

Even when the infecting organism is gonorrhoea, the ducts and tubes can escape scarring if treatment is started early enough. Fortunately, because gonorrhoea produces almost immediate symptoms (discharge of pus through the urethra), most men seek treatment quickly, and the disease is usually halted before it damages reproductive organs.

Penis

When a man ejaculates, semen spurts from the opening of the urethra at the tip of his penis. The root of the penis is attached to the pelvic bone. Inside are three cylindrical columns of tissue, abundantly supplied with blood. The lower cylinder, called the corpus spongiosum, is made of soft fibres that cushion the urethra. The two upper cylinders, which lie side by side, are made of erectile tissue. These are the corpora cavernosa. Through the veins of these cylinders, blood circulates continuously. When the penis is stimulated, the outflow veins that normally drain away blood become blocked, and the corpora cavernosa fill with blood. The penis becomes hard and warm, and lengthens and expands.

The size of all the sex organs, including the penis, is determined by genetic inheritance. Large penises seem to run in families, as do small penises. Many scientific studies have proved that penile size has no bearing on either fertility or sexual satisfaction. Men with relatively small penises produce children with the same frequency as do men with unusually large penises.

A normal flaccid penis is anywhere from $2\frac{1}{2}$–$5\frac{1}{2}$ in (6–13 cm) long. When erect, however, penises are remarkably similar. A large flaccid penis gains only slightly in its erect state; a small flaccid penis can more than double in size. As far as sexual satisfaction goes, surveys among women have concluded that it's not the quantity but the quality of the sexual act that satisfies women. In fact, a very large penis may require some adaptation on a woman's part.

Nevertheless, many men continue to be preoccupied with penile size. Increasing the size of penises has become something of a thriving business.

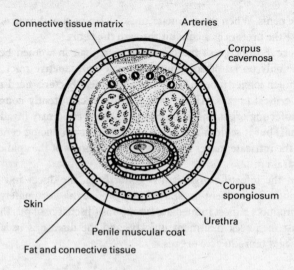

Connective tissue matrix

Arteries

Corpus cavernosa

Corpus spongiosum

Skin

Urethra

Penile muscular coat

Fat and connective tissue

The penis (cross-section)

Numerous gadgets guaranteed to make a penis bigger are sold in sex shops and through mail order companies. Primarily, these devices are rubber or metal rings that are placed around the penis to help a man maintain an erection. They do not actually make the penis permanently longer, although it seems bigger while the ring is in place. Such rings are dangerous and can severely damage the penis.

Men who have lost their powers of erection through surgery or disease may be able to have a flexible silicone rod implanted in the penis. Implants may be rigid, semi-rigid, or inflatable – each has its own advantages and disadvantages. Men whose penises have been partially excised as a result of cancer surgery can use the implants. So can men who become impotent from diabetes or following prostate surgery. These men have a normal sex drive, but the nerves that create the erection are damaged. Implants are almost never recommended for men whose sexual anatomy is healthy but who are impotent for psychological reasons.

Circumcision

Circumcision is another controversial issue for men. The head of the penis, or glans, is dense with nerve endings and particularly sensitive. When a man is circumcised, the fold of tissue over the tip of the penis is cut away. Afterwards, the glans becomes firmer and slightly less sensitive. One myth holds that because a circumcised penis is less sensitive, it sustains an erection longer than an uncircumcised penis. And, according to the same myth, a circumcised man seldom suffers from premature ejaculation. Another theory holds that the same numbed penis offers less sexual excitement for the man to whom it belongs. The idea is that sacrifices, along with choices, must be made. For prolonged erection, a man must give up sensitivity, or vice versa.

Fortunately, neither of these myths is true. Medical observation indicates that both circumcised and uncircumcised penises are exquisitely sensitive, and both can sustain erections equally well. Sexual prowess and circumcision are not kin. Nor is premature ejaculation the *bête noire* of uncircumcised men alone; it occurs just as frequently in circumcised men.

There is yet another medical myth surrounding circumcision. Until recently, it was believed that the foreskin of an uncircumcised penis harboured a dangerous carcinogen. The phenomenon was first noted when physicians observed that the wives of uncircumcised men seemed to suffer a much higher incidence of cervical cancer than wives of circumcised men. New scientific studies have shown that other factors, primarily hygiene, are involved along with circumcision.

The carcinogen is smegma, a soapy discharge normally produced by tiny sebaceous glands under the foreskin. This same discharge is produced by glands in the labia minora in women. Smegma is a chronic irritant, and rubbing it into the skin of the cervix can create cancer. As long as the foreskin is retracted and washed every day, the possibility of the carcinogen being sexually transmitted to a woman's cervix is remote.

If the foreskin is especially tight and difficult to retract, however, it can cause problems. Severe urinary tract infection in men can often be traced to bacteria caught underneath a tight foreskin. In such instances, circumcision is the answer.

When an infant is circumcised, the fold of tissue over the tip of the penis is pulled up, clamped, then cut. The incision is covered with gauze and usually heals within a week. If a man is circumcised later in life, a local or general anaesthetic is needed, and the healing may take several weeks.

The history of circumcision of male infants is shrouded in religious ritual and ceremony. Whether it began as a hygienic practice to prevent infection or as a token 'blood for life' sacrifice is unclear. In Britain, circumcision is performed in the National Health Service only for strictly medical reasons.

Erection and Orgasm

A man's mind and body work together to produce erection and orgasm. Ejaculation is usually, but not always, accompanied by orgasm. A man can think himself into an erection, but physical friction usually brings on the actual orgasm. Even when men have wet dreams and ejaculate in their sleep, it is probably the slight pressure of the sheets on sensitive penile skin that triggers orgasm.

Along the nerves of the spinal cord, fantasy and friction pass back and forth between the erotic zone and the brain. A man sees an erotic image in his mind; the brain turns that image into electrical signals that speed down the nerves of the spinal cord, like electricity along a wire. When the signals reach the erectile tissue of the penis, the blood vessels constrict and engorge with blood. The penis swells and enlarges.

At this point, if the erotic zone of the penis, which lies just under the gland, is rubbed, frictional heat sends new electrical impulses back to the brain along another nerve path in the spinal cord. Sometimes by thinking about something else, a man can temporarily shut off the signals. But if the friction is maintained, the signals eventually build up to a critical level and spill over. The brain cannot contain all the electrical impulses.

A split second before ejaculation, the brain throws off a massive electrical charge. The sphincter muscle outside the bladder slams shut. The two small Cowper's glands squeeze out a spurt of lubricant to moisten the length of the urethra and reduce surface tension along that route.

All the ducts and organs in the reproductive tract violently contract, in a sequence so rapid it seems like a massive shudder. The epididymis and the vasa force millions of sperm into the system. Just ahead of them, the prostate pumps out its fluid. A microsecond later, the seminal vesicles expel another burst of fluid, giving the semen a jet-like mix. A column of ejaculate roars through the urethra: at its head is prostatic fluid, in the middle millions of sperm, and at the rear the forceful burst of seminal fluid.

The ejaculate rushes towards the penis. In a final, powerful thrust, the muscles at the base of the penis contract and the semen spurts through the tip of the urethra. The first massive contraction is the moment of orgasm. A second orgasmic wave empties the remaining portion of the vasa. With each subsequent spasm, the amount of ejaculate lessens. There may be three or four or even five aftershocks.

The first wave contains the highest concentration of sperm. (The very first drop of fluid may contain 80 per cent of the sperm in the total ejaculate.) This is why withdrawing during intercourse is a risky method of contraception. When the rhythmic convulsion ebbs, the blood drains away from the erectile tissue, and the penis relaxes to its normal size.

The typical volume of a total ejaculate is about one teaspoonful (2–4 ml), although it seems like much more. The volume is important to fertility. Enough fluid must be present to bathe the opening of the uterus so the sperm are not

THE MALE ANATOMY · 61

stranded in the recesses of the vagina. But too much semen can 'dilute' the quantity of sperm and spill back out of the vaginal vault, carrying most of the live sperm with it. Thus, too much or too little semen volume can cause infertility.

Ejaculation

On ejaculation, the average man releases 40–150 million sperm into the vagina, each one carrying half the genetic code that can make a new human being. The other fluids in the semen help transport the sperm, providing a slightly alkaline environment to help overcome the acidity of the vagina. Even so, more than 90 per cent of the sperm are killed off by the hostile fluids that cleanse the vagina.

If intercourse takes place when a woman is ovulating, the surviving sperm can swim through the cervical canal within one to three minutes. Only a few hundred will reach the uterus, and many of these swim up the wrong fallopian tube. Those that choose the right passageway may become trapped within the moist folds of the tube. Only a few dozen sperm actually reach the midway point of the tube where the ovum can be successfully fertilized. If the ovum is waiting, the union of sperm and egg can take place within thirty-five minutes of ejaculation. If the ovum is not present, some sperm will find protection within the niches inside the fallopian tube and wait. No one knows exactly how long sperm can survive inside the female reproductive tract, but sperm have been known to impregnate as long as thirty-six hours after intercourse.

The journey of sperm from the testicles into a woman's reproductive system is remarkably difficult. Yet most of the hazards arise within the female system; within the male system the dauntless cells encounter few transportation problems. Occasionally a blockage will arise in one of the intricate tubes of the male system, or the deposit mechanism of the penis may be defective. But these instances are rare. The primary cause of infertility in men is not the delivery system but what is being delivered – namely, the sperm themselves. The vast majority of male fertility problems begin in the sperm production factory inside the testicles.

To understand how infertility occurs in men, and what therapies may help, we must turn our attention to how sperm are made.

7
How Men Make Sperm

Sperm are not born; they are made. And men make millions of them every day. Their ability to do so is one of the great, complex achievements of human biology.

When a boy is born, specialized reproductive cells are deeply buried in the masses of microscopic seminiferous tubules that fill the testicles. These cells arrange themselves in an orderly fashion, dividing one after another until they completely line the convoluted corridors of each thin tubule. Altogether, there are several million of these cells, called spermatogonia, in place. They are sperm cell generators, or mother cells.

In between the mother cells as they march uniformly along the tubule are shapeless Sertoli's cells, which appear to regulate the flow of nutrients to and from the spermatogonia. Whether this system of cells is in place is a matter of genetic inheritance and embryonic development. How effectively some kinds of male infertility can be treated depends on knowing if these cells are in place and functioning.

Analysis of a mother cell under a microscope reveals a cell with a large nucleus and a full complement of forty-six chromosomes, in which the two sex chromosomes are dominant. The job of these mother cells is to generate sperm. Problems can occur anywhere in the complex process of sperm production and can lead to infertility.

The Cell Divides

Sperm production is stimulated by hormones from the brain. These hormones are identical in both men and women, and the hypothalamus/pituitary/gonad axis works in precisely the same way. The difference is that in women the outlying target organs are ovaries, and in men they are testicles.

Sperm production begins when the brain's control centre activates the testicles. The hypothalamus sends bursts of LH-RH to the pituitary, telling the gland to ship out FSH and LH to the testicles. This is the major difference in the hormonal axis of men and women. For women, the axis is cyclical – the pituitary gland sends FSH in the first half of the menstrual cycle and switches to LH in the second half. For men, there is no cycle; the control centre provides a steady level of hormones from day to day, and FSH and LH are released simultaneously. However, only one hormone – FSH – is used to make sperm.

As the two hormones flow along the axis, the FSH message is picked up by the Sertoli's cells and fed to the spermatogonia. As soon as a mother cell gets the hormonal message, it generates a duplicate of itself through mitosis; as a generator of new sperm cells, the mother cell always remains in place, receiving hormonal messages through the Sertoli's cell receptionist. The new duplicate cell, which also has forty-six chromosomes, moves forward.

The duplicate cell, called a primary spermatocyte, now becomes unique. The duplicate divides again – but this time it halves its number of chromosomes. Of all the millions of times cells divide in the male and female body, this unusual cell division, called meiosis, takes place only in reproductive tissue. The two new cells, called secondary spermatocytes, have twenty-three double-stranded chromosomes each – twenty-two plus an X or a Y sex chromosome. Before it can fuse with an egg, each cell must first reduce each double strand to a single strand. Thus, the two secondary spermatocytes divide once more, separating the two strands of DNA. The four new cells that result, called spermatids, have only twenty-three single-strand chromosomes each. At this point cell division ends.

The four new spermatids, which for the first time begin to look like sperm, will grow into mature cells capable of fertilizing an ovum. In the female, the ovum goes through exactly the same process of cell division, but it throws away its three extra bodies. If it didn't, twins, triplets, and quadruplets would proliferate.

The newborn sperm are later transported out of the tubule to mature in the adjacent holding area of the epididymis. The mother cell remains behind, ready to produce four new sperm through this unique process.

A sperm cell cannot develop further unless it meets and merges with an ovum, which also carries twenty-three single-strand chromosomes. When a sperm and ovum fuse, cell division begins again. The forty-six single strands pair up and quickly replicate themselves; each new cell in the embryo carries a full complement of forty-six double-stranded chromosomes.

Leaving the Testicles

The first four stages of sperm production, called spermatogenesis, take approximately sixty-four days. During this time the sperm are passed towards the centre of the tubule at a relatively steady speed of sixteen days for each stage of growth. Viewed under a microscope, the new sperm have the characteristic

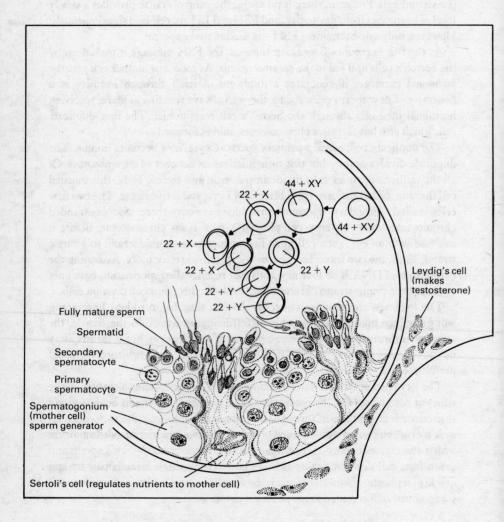

Sperm production (*cross-section of seminiferous tubule*)

head and tail, but the tail merely vibrates weakly and does not yet have swimming power.

Occasionally, a virus or other feverish infection in the body may lead the clock-like mechanism of sperm production to overheat, causing cells to speed up their division and even burn out. Sperm cells that divide prematurely will be deformed and incapable of fertilizing the ovum. When the fever passes, cell division and sperm growth usually return to normal. However, if the fever reaches the burn-out threshold, the mother cells may be destroyed and the damage irreversible.

Poor sperm production also can occur if too few mother cells are laid down during a male baby's early growth in the mother's womb. This developmental error cannot be changed, and sperm production will be low throughout the man's life. Occasionally the mother cells are completely absent, and sperm are never produced. Another cause of sperm deficiency is a low ebb of FSH, the hormone needed to encourage sperm growth from one stage to another. In these instances, sperm production can often be improved if the hormone can be replenished.

The new spermatids spend about twelve days in the epididymis, where they mature fully and gain swimming power. Each mature, healthy sperm has an oval head, a midsection, and a long whip-like tail. A fully grown sperm is invisible to the naked eye, yet it carries a vast data bank of genetic information in its head. Stored there are twenty-three chromosomes, including the X or Y that will determine the sex of a new life when the sperm unites with an ovum.

Capacitation

A small cap called an acrosome sits on top of the sperm's head. This cap contains many enzymes and acts as a warhead to penetrate the egg's shell. Even with all this sophisticated equipment on board, the sperm is still unable to fertilize an ovum. Once inside the female reproductive tract, the sperm must go through yet another process of change called capacitation.

The sperm head is covered by a membranous net that restrains its nuclear material until an egg is in sight. Without this net the sperm would try to merge with every cell it met along the way. Once a sperm reaches the middle of the fallopian tube, the membrane is completely stripped away and the acrosome warhead is bare. The sperm is capacitated and ready to merge with an egg.

For many years the sperm's two-layered membrane was a stumbling block to *in vitro* fertilization. Until recently researchers believed that special enzymes, present only inside the fallopian tubes, could strip away the net and free the sperm head. However, the new *in vitro* successes suggest that different influences may be at work. Test-tube experiments, in which sperm are capacitated outside

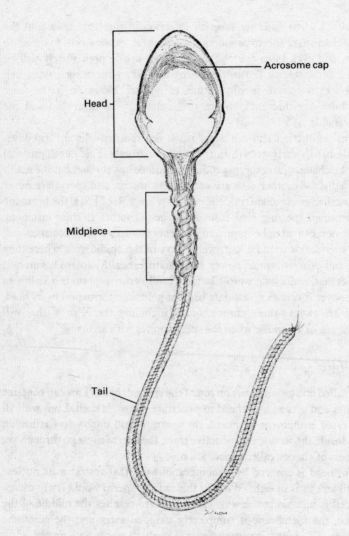

Fully mature sperm

the body, indicate that once the sperm are separated from seminal fluid, the double layers of the membrane fuse and self-destruct. The sperm capacitates itself. This suggests that something in seminal fluid keeps the membrane intact. Even so, the precise mechanism of capacitation is still not perfectly understood.

Within the fallopian tube dozens of tiny sperm swarm over the surface of the ovum, turning the egg over and over. The moment one sperm projectile touches the ovum it binds to the plush outer membrane (cumulus oophorus). The warhead shoots chemicals to puncture a tiny hole through the tough inner membrane (zona pellucida). At that split second the sperm head injects its nuclear chromosomes into the ovum. The egg's shell is instantly transformed into an impenetrable wall, making it virtually impossible for any other sperm cell to enter. The strands of DNA flow through the shell and the nuclei of the two cells fuse.

Unlike women, who produce one egg each month, men manufacture sperm by the millions each day. The hundreds of seminiferous tubules in the testicles produce at a phenomenal rate, so that sperm are present in extravagant millions in each ejaculation. After ejaculation, it takes only about forty hours for the epididymis to fill up again with new volumes of sperm.

Sperm production begins in puberty and continues throughout a man's lifetime, falling off slightly as he grows older. To keep the production line operating steadily, the brain control centre must continuously send FSH hormone in exactly the right quantities. To tell the brain just how much FSH to send, the sperm factory transmits a hormonal message back along the axis in the form of a mysterious substance known as inhibin. The brain matches its FSH output to the levels of inhibin it detects in the bloodstream.

The control centre has another hormonal messenger, called LH, at its disposal, which it uses to make a man's most potent hormone, testosterone.

Sperm, Sex, and Testosterone

Will a big, muscular body-builder have more and better sperm than a small, slender man? Can a hairy chest and bulging muscles predict virility? Are sexual potency, physical appearance, and male fertility related? The answer to all three questions is no.

A smooth-skinned male with a slight build may have both good sperm production and a strong sex drive. So may the man with chest hair and muscles. They may also lack one or both of these qualities. It's impossible to judge a man's fertility – or his virility – by his physical appearance. The highest sperm count ever observed at the Omega Institute belonged to a thirty-four-year-old man who stood about 5 ft 5 in (1·65 m), weighed 9 st 9 lb (61 kg), and had no hair on his chest.

Two facts can help clear up the general confusion over appearance, sexual potency, and fertility. First, physical characteristics are dominated by genetic inheritance, not hormones. Second, sperm production and sex drive originate in two separate cell systems in the testicles. One cell system makes sperm. The other, comprising Leydig's cells, makes testosterone. Testosterone is the potent male hormone that stimulates the sex drive in both men and women.

During puberty, testosterone also creates a beard and a deep voice in men, and makes their penises grow. But it does all this over a genetic framework. A man may have a slight build and little body hair and still be completely virile and fertile. Or he may inherit a big frame, muscles, and a lot of hair and have a subdued sex drive.

And none of this has much to do with making sperm. Sperm are produced from the spermatogonia working in tandem with the Sertoli's cells. These cells, which line the seminiferous tubules, are controlled by FSH; they are fragile and easily damaged. In contrast, testosterone comes from the Leydig's cells tucked in between the tubules. The Leydig's cells respond to LH hormone. They are extremely hardy and almost never fail. That's why it's not unusual for a man to have a low sperm count yet retain all his sexual potency.

All the cells in the testicles are governed by the brain control centre. On orders from the hypothalamus, the pituitary gland continuously sends FSH and LH to the testicles. FSH targets the Sertoli's cells, which regulate sperm production and feed back inhibin along the return loop of the hormonal axis. LH targets the Leydig's cells, which make the testosterone that also feeds back to the control centre. The feedback messages tell the control centre just how much FSH and LH are necessary to keep the cell factories steadily running. Because it is a steady system with two distinct parts, the male hormonal axis is less likely to develop problems than the more complex female axis.

An important question remains: Does testosterone help sperm production? Researchers are ambivalent about the answer. The Sertoli's cells and the Leydig's cells are two separate systems, responding to two different hormones, but they do overlap in some ways. Testosterone seems to play a small, yet vital role in maintaining the sperm production assembly line. But its job description is vague. It is clear that a small amount is needed to do the job – and too much will close down the factory.

What happens to sperm production when a man takes testosterone supplements to build up his body? Nine times out of ten his sperm count falls. The extra male hormone circulating in his bloodstream tricks the brain into thinking that his testicles are overproducing. The brain reduces the supply of both LH and FSH.

Without FSH the testicles cannot make sperm. In addition, the Leydig's cells lose their ability to make testosterone. When a man stops taking the supplements, normal production levels usually resume.

Men and Hormones

Testosterone is present in the blood even before a boy is born. The fetus converts it from oestrogen supplied by his mother. During fetal life testosterone helps the reproductive organs form. And in the last three months of gestation the hormone encourages the testicles to descend by influencing the gubernaculum, a small band of tissue that leads from the testicles in the scrotum.

After birth, testosterone production subsides until about the age of nine or ten, when puberty begins. Puberty and adolescence are not synonymous. Puberty is the biological surge that results in reproductive ability. Adolescence is a psychological response to puberty. Puberty is roughly the same for every boy and girl; the experience of adolescence varies widely among teenagers.

Just before puberty begins, sex hormone levels in boys rise sharply. Changes are felt but not seen. Emotions shift like sand under the increasing pressure of these new chemicals. Like girls, boys begin to masturbate frequently, although they have no sperm in their ejaculate. They also share sexual exploration with friends of the same sex. This is a normal part of sexual development. These early homosexual experiences haunt some boys in manhood, especially if they later discover they are infertile. (Studies show that the psychological profile of some infertile men often shows a latent homosexual pattern, which psychologists believe may be due to anxiety rather than to a true homosexual tendency.)

In boys, the testicles begin to enlarge at about the age of twelve and start producing testosterone about a year later. This new source of male hormone makes the penis develop and pubic hair grow. The prostate gland also grows larger. The voice cracks, and then deepens, as the larynx grows bigger. More protein is deposited in the bones, and boys begin to develop their distinctive musculature. The extra protein also accounts for changes in skin texture. Bones retain more calcium and become thicker. As in girls, sexual development correlates with the 'growth spurt'. When sexual development peaks, the rising tide of sex hormones feeds back to the brain, which shuts off its production of growth hormone.

Puberty occurs about two years later in boys than in girls, and once started it takes about three years to complete. The ability to ejaculate semen with active sperm usually occurs when a boy is about fourteen. This ability to make sperm correlates with a girl's first menstrual cycle. There's a wide variation in the

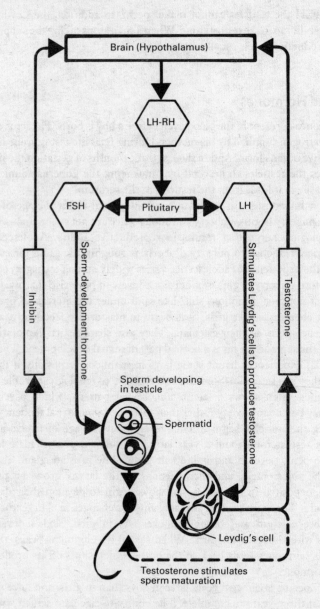

The male hormonal axis

'normal' onset of puberty – anywhere from ten to fifteen. However, very early or very late puberty requires medical investigation.

Sexual organs continue to grow until about the age of twenty. This is a period of intense sexual activity for young men. Their sexual peak, in terms of orgasmic frequency, is between the ages of fifteen and twenty. Testosterone production continues strongly throughout a man's adult life, maintaining his distinctive sexual characteristics and his sex drive.

As he approaches the age of sixty, testosterone production gradually begins to decrease, although the dramatic physical changes that occur in a menopausal woman do not occur in a man. His sex drive and his ability to impregnate are virtually unabated. At about eighty, his production of male hormone falls off significantly, to about a fifth of its peak. This is puberty in reverse. His beard grows scantier, his musculature softens, and his sexual organs seem to get smaller. Even so, the reserves of testosterone circulating through the bloodstream keep many elderly men sexually active for a lifetime.

Hormonal disturbance is only one possible cause of infertility in men, and it is not the most common. Generally, infertility is caused by several different small problems combining to lower sperm count. A multitude of things can go wrong in the sperm production factory, and more problems can arise in the delivery system. Specialists can diagnose most of these problems, but they know very little about many of their causes and can't always treat them. Luckily, however, one of the most common causes of infertility in men is also the most treatable.

8
When Things Go Wrong: Men

When it comes to infertility, men are not nearly so well organized as women. Their reproductive closets are cluttered with a multitude of large and small problems. When the door to the closet is opened, the problems tumble out all over one another and pile up in a confused heap. Each little piece in the jumble is different. One has a funny shape or a peculiar colour, another is chipped on the surface, and another rocks aimlessly from side to side. They look nothing like the well-defined pieces in the intricate reproductive closet of a woman.

It's strange that this should be so, because men and women start off with the same components. Their reproductive organs arise from similar fetal tissue (for every female organ there is a comparable male organ). Further, both sets of reproductive hormones are controlled by identical brain hormones. All that distinguishes the two systems is the final layout of the anatomy.

Apparently that is enough. Because when things go wrong, all comparisons between the two systems come to an end.

Male Infertility: the Newest Science

Three major discoveries over the past thirty years have made the study of male infertility one of the hottest investigative fields in science. The first came when a researcher named J. MacLeod thought about quantifying sperm. The second was the discovery that a varicose vein in the testicle could affect sperm production. Perhaps the most important discovery was that infertility is relative, that a man with a borderline sperm count would be infertile if his wife ovulated irregularly.

In 1951, MacLeod and R. Z. Gold analysed the ejaculate of 1,000 new fathers and compared the results with sperm counts taken from 800 men in involuntarily childless marriages. No one knew why these marriages were childless.

The researchers found that the new fathers had distinctly higher sperm counts than many of the childless men. For the first time, a real difference was measured between men who had fathered children and those who had not. MacLeod and Gold eventually defined the normal sperm count as 125 million sperm per ejaculate. Their work catapulted male infertility into the scientific limelight and opened the door to the future.

Multiple Causes

Once it was known that all men did not produce equal numbers of sperm, a flurry of researchers began to investigate what might cause the difference. They knew that a man might be sterile if he were kicked in the testicles by a horse; they knew that the sperm centres in the testicles might be knocked out if a man contracted mumps after a certain age. But these are rare events. In fact, fewer than 2 per cent of all infertile men are completely sterile.

Faced with hundreds of thousands of men with relatively low sperm counts and no other symptoms, scientists launched a network of preliminary research. Scientists are slowly learning to identify many causes of male infertility. Whereas once it was believed that a low sperm count was just bad luck, researchers now know that specific biological events affect sperm production.

Even so, the science of male infertility remains light-years behind the work that has been done on the female. Research is needed on every level to discover all the variables that might cause sperm levels to drop in some men. The time has come for researchers to give this complex problem the attention it deserves.

The bad news about male infertility is that it's usually impossible to distinguish one single disorder. An infertility problem in a man is usually a mixture of several disorders that overlap, or one disorder that affects several different parts of the reproductive system. Dozens of small problems can arise almost anywhere in the system. In themselves, the problems are not especially destructive, but when they cluster they can reduce sperm count to a point where pregnancy is no longer viable.

The majority of problems fall into the category of sperm production; that is, for a multitude of reasons – some simple and others complex – the testicles do not make adequate quantities of sperm. About 10 per cent of infertility problems turn up in the transport system, that long series of passageways through which sperm must swim to get from the testicles into the penis. Sometimes a passageway gets clogged up; in a few instances the spermatic duct is missing. A few more problems take shape in the final ejaculation of sperm into the vagina. These deposit problems are very rare, but every once in a while a man simply uses the wrong entry point during sexual intercourse.

Because of the clustering of problems, treatment is often difficult and much less precise than it is in women, although the same fertility drugs are used to drive both systems. In men, the fertility specialist usually works with the overall system to improve general conditions in the hope that even a slightly elevated sperm count might be enough for pregnancy.

So what's the good news? The good news is that what some experts consider the most common cause of male infertility – occurring in 30–40 per cent of infertile men – is also the most successfully treated.

The Varicocele

The swollen, hot veins that spell varicocele were the second major discovery that propelled male infertility into the realm of twenty-first-century medicine. In 1952, soon after MacLeod and Gold did their sperm counts, a scientist named W. S. Tulloch tied off a varicose vein in the testicle of a man who had no sperm. Within a few months, the man was producing good-quality sperm and went on to impregnate his wife. This bit of surgical experimentation awakened a new idea: if a man was infertile, something could be done about it. Like MacLeod's earlier surveys, Tulloch's work launched a wave of investigative research.

Today, we know that Tulloch was lucky. When a varicocele causes a complete absence of sperm, as was the case with his first patient, the damage is usually profound; surgery almost never fully improves sperm production.

A varicocele is a small flaw in the anatomy of a vein. One artery and a network of veins carry blood to and from the testicles. The artery pumps blood in, and the little bundle of veins carry it back to the heart. These veins are flaccid. Blood climbs back up to the heart on a ladder of one-way valves. For unknown reasons, these valves may be missing, or existing valves may break down. The blood pools in the veins of the testicle. The question is: Why does a varicocele cause infertility?

Researchers theorize that the warm blood settling around the sperm production overheats the system. Yet every man who has a varicocele is not infertile. In fact, about 10 per cent of all men have a varicocele, and no one knows how many ultimately become infertile. We do know, however, that 30 per cent of men who are infertile have a varicocele.

The size of the varicocele seems to have no bearing on sperm count. A damaging varicocele may be so big that it bulges when a man stands up, or it may be so small that only highly sophisticated sound and heat measurements can find it. The latest thinking is that even a very small varicocele can severely damage sperm production. Fortunately, surgery can be performed to tie off the vein. Indeed, this is the most successful of all infertility treatments for men. After surgery, sperm counts improve in about 70 per cent of all infertile men with varicocele. About half of them go on to become fathers.

As we have said, there are a multitude of other possible causes of male infertility. A few of the most prominent are described below.

Sexually Transmitted Disease

With sexually transmitted disease on the increase, a key issue arises: How does infection affect infertility? Will the man who has several bouts of gonorrhoea wind up sterile?

Venereal disease and other infections are not nearly as dangerous to men as they are to women. The urethra, the only outside entrance into the male reproductive system, is extremely long in men. As the bacteria work their way along the tract, they are flushed back by intermittent streams of urine coursing down the urethra. Therefore, men are usually spared the devastating pelvic infections that destroy the reproductive organs of women.

Gonorrhoea is so easily recognized that men usually seek treatment when they notice any unusual discharge from the penis. The discharge is an early warning sign from the urethra, and early treatment stops the infection from attacking the testicles. However, gonorrhoea can sometimes clog up the tiny passageway of the epididymis and create an obstruction.

One newly recognized source of infection in both men and women is an organism called chlamydia. In men, chlamydia can infect the urinary tract and potentially reach the testicles. Typical symptoms of chlamydia in men are easily confused with those of gonorrhoea, but unfortunately the organism, which is difficult to culture, does not respond to the penicillin-type treatment that so easily eradicates gonorrhoea. Chlamydia can be eradicated only with a tetracycline class of antibiotic.

The true role of infection is still a broad area of research in the field of infertility. Infection does not usually hurt the sperm-producing centres; the real threat is that it can be transmitted to women, in whom it may cause sterility. Many men unwittingly transfer symptomless diseases such as chlamydia to women during sexual intercourse. To prevent such transfers, even mild, innocuous infections of the male reproductive tract should be vigorously treated with antibiotics.

We are also learning that genital infections in men have other, more subtle effects. Many 'unknown' causes of infertility may be the result of infectious byproducts. The so-called antibody problem, for example, in which a man is mysteriously allergic to his own sperm, may be caused by a virus or by bacteria that lurk in the prostate gland or seminal vesicles.

Mumps

If mumps occurs during or after puberty, when reproductive cells are rapidly dividing, there is a substantial danger that the virus will attack the testicles. (Tuberculosis too can invade the testicles, but with the advent of modern antibiotics tuberculosis is rare today.) The mumps virus likes to invade lively cells. Once the virus reaches the testicles it has a devastating effect on the sperm production centres, invading the nucleus of the reproductive cells and multiplying until the cells burst.

If the virus is relatively mild, the testicles eventually recover. If the illness is severe, there is a high chance that the reproductive cells will be completely destroyed. If only one testicle is affected, however, the other one can take over the workload, and the man's sperm count will be normal.

Scrotal Injuries

The same kind of damage done by mumps can be caused by a kick in the scrotum. Men who play rough sports or ride motorcycles are extremely prone to scrotal injuries. Sometimes, for no particular reason, one testicle will twist on its own blood supply. This is called torsion. The testicle swells alarmingly and causes excruciating pain. The one thing *not* to do is put an ice pack on the testicle and wait for the swelling to subside. Any torsion or injury that causes pain and swelling in the scrotum needs emergency care by a urologist. Blood vessels that rupture inside the testicles must be quickly cauterized before internal bleeding scars the delicate microscopic tubules that make sperm. Scar tissue cuts off the blood supply, and the testicle shrivels up and dies.

Hormonal Disturbance

Sperm production, like ovulation in women, is governed by the hormonal system. The hypothalamus/pituitary control centre drives the other gland systems in the body, including the testicles. Therefore, any disturbance of hormones produced in the control centre or the testicles can cause problems. Because the male hormonal axis is a simpler mechanism than the female axis, problems occur less frequently. Only about 15 per cent of all men seen in infertility clinics show a hormonal disturbance.

Chromosomal and Genetic Disorders

Men do occasionally inherit infertility, through either the genes or the chromosomes. A chromosomal abnormality is a defect in a whole chromosome, usually the X or Y sex chromosome. These abnormalities can be discovered only by performing a chromosomal analysis of the blood.

Chromosomal defects may occur spontaneously as the male fetus grows inside the mother's womb. Klinefelter's syndrome is an example of a spontaneous chromosomal flaw. In this syndrome a man is born with at least one extra X chromosome in each cell. Most often a man born with Klinefelter's will have very small and immature testicles, although occasionally all his physical characteristics will appear normal. But he will never produce offspring.

Genetic disorders are flaws in a small section of a chromosome, called a gene. These disorders are difficult to detect and sometimes can be identified only when they repeatedly appear in families.

Genetic and chromosomal disorders that affect sperm production, although rare, are extremely difficult to treat. Usually, sperm production is absent because sexual organs do not develop in puberty. Sometimes sex drive and other male sex characteristics can be stimulated with hormones, but usually there is no way to activate production.

Tubal Blockage

Blockage in the ducts that carry sperm out of the testicles, through the prostate, and out of the tip of the penis occurs in less than 10 per cent of infertile men, thanks primarily to the difficulty infection has in penetrating the male reproductive tract. (Tubal blockage is a major cause of infertility in women.) When blockage does occur, it is almost always lodged in the tiny channel of the epididymis. High-powered magnification has made possible surgical removal of obstructions in this tightly coiled, nearly invisible strand of tissue.

Sometimes a baby is born with his ductal system blocked. Such birth defects in men are becoming more common. Scientists have recently learned that sons of women who took diethylstilboestrol (DES), a potent synthetic hormone used in the 1950s to prevent miscarriage, have a higher than normal incidence of such blockage of the epididymis. A newly discovered chromosomal birth defect may be another cause of blocked tubes. In this disorder, as yet unnamed, cell linings of the tubes produce excessively thick secretions, plugging up the channels and blocking the pathway of sperm. Men who have this mucus disorder also suffer from blocked sinuses and bronchial tubes.

Sexual Problems

Even when a man makes good-quality sperm and has a smooth and clear transport system, he still may have some trouble laying the sperm up against the mouth of the cervix. Most problems concerning sperm deposit fall into the realm of sexual technique.

Impotence is rarely more than a transient problem in young men. When a young man is impotent over a prolonged period of time, the problem is usually psychological. Real impotence can begin to occur after the age of fifty, and it may be either psychological or biological.

For a while, in response to the early stirring of the women's movement, some sociologists and many drugstore philosophers argued that impotence would be the ailment of the 1980s if women persisted in their quest for equal rights. Fortunately, in spite of the warnings, the women's movement went forward. And the incidence of impotence does not seem to be increasing.

One sexual problem occasionally seen in young men is premature ejaculation. A man's genitals are extremely sensitive to tactile sensations, and some men ejaculate the instant their penises touch the surface of a woman's vagina. Not only is this not gratifying to either partner, it fails to deposit sperm near the cervix.

Treatment, which includes both partners, involves behaviour modification training. The idea is to reduce the heightened sensation little by little by touching other parts of the body. The couple begins touching outside the bedroom, away from the conjugal bed. Eventually the exercises progress to genital touching and fondling, without intercourse. By using a squeeze technique (squeezing the penis when he feels he's about to ejaculate), the man learns to prolong the sexual plateau. Finally, when he is able to sustain an erection, the couple begins to have sexual intercourse.

There is one other deposit problem that we seldom associate with infertility. It occurs when a couple simply fails to have sex at the right time. Some couples misunderstand the ovulation cycle and actually avoid sex on the days when the woman is ovulating. Finally, every once in a while we see a couple who has never consummated marriage in the usual way. When the woman is examined, her hymen is unbroken. Explaining the anatomical facts usually results in pregnancy.

In later chapters we will describe these and other causes of male infertility in detail, as if they occurred singularly and affected only one aspect of sperm production. But it's important to remember that most men with low sperm counts have several problems clustered together.

The Future

Because so few records were kept in the past, we cannot tell if the incidence of infertility in men is rising. However, from working closely with men over the last decade, we sense that something is going on. Some surprising new evidence suggests that even if the male infertility statistic is now stable, it may soon begin to climb. Odd as it seems, the concentration of sperm in men appears to be dipping across the board.

Declining Sperm Counts

The decline was first noticed in the mid-1970s, when fertility clinics in Texas and New Jersey discovered that men coming in for vasectomies – that is, men assumed to be fertile – had sperm counts considerably lower than the standard defined by MacLeod and Gold. A significant number of these newly tested men had counts of 60 million sperm per ejaculate or less. Yet these men also had fathered children, and were considered fertile. The researchers double-checked MacLeod's variables, but the dip was still present. Scientists now speculate that some unknown factor is causing sperm production to fall in American and Western European men.

We guess at three possible elements working together: increased population density, stress, and environmental pollution.

All animals have a natural instinct to hold back their numbers when food becomes scarce. When coyotes reach a population density that threatens their environment, they begin to produce smaller litters of pups. If the packs are killed off or their population is otherwise reduced, the litters increase in size. (This theory has lead environmentalists to suggest that sheep ranchers would be better off if they left the coyotes alone.) This environmental balancing act between animals and available food supply is seen throughout nature.

To a great extent humans, because of their ability to control the food supply, have learned to override nature's system. Perhaps, however, humans also have an innate biological instinct. Perhaps sperm concentration dips in response to a denser population. The pathway of this instinct may be stress. Because as the population grows more dense, stress increases.

Stress has become the scapegoat for many illnesses. It is an ideal candidate for the job, since it's virtually impossible to list its components – stress is different for everyone. How stressful a situation is depends on the perception of the individual. Driving a car at high speed may be stressful for one person and stimulating for another. Because stress varies from person to person, it is extremely difficult to trace its effects in illness.

We do know how the body responds when the mind *perceives* stress: it shuts down the oxygen and blood supply to peripheral systems and gathers all its resources to vital organs, primarily the heart and brain. When such stress is constant, the deprived parts of the body begin to suffer. If we could take sperm counts of men on a battlefield we would probably find them to be extremely low.

Modern battlefields can be almost anywhere – behind the corporate desk or in the nuclear power plant, in the classroom or on the motorway, sitting in the courtroom or travelling through outer space. And if the stress doesn't kill you, the air will.

Closely related to stress and population overload is an increasingly toxic environment. Even remoter places are now reeking with invisible pollutants. We are routinely exposed to chemicals unheard of even twenty years ago. This is particularly true in certain occupations. It has been proved that halogenated hydrocarbons, used in the chemical and petroleum industries, carry a high risk of damage to the reproductive organs.

This life-threatening trio – population density, stress, and pollution – could account for the ebb in sperm concentration. If the concentration continues to fall, population may be significantly reduced.

However, most researchers don't believe the dip in sperm concentration is responsible for the present infertility epidemic. They consider the dip a normal fluctuation. Accordingly, they have adjusted the average 'normal' sperm count downwards. Technically speaking, a man is considered probably fertile today if his sperm count exceeds 60 million sperm per ejaculate, about half the original number established in the 1950s. This brings us to the third major discovery in infertility in this decade: The reduced levels of sperm could easily be a part of what researchers call 'subfertility'.

The 'Subfertile' Couple

In men, infertility is a relative condition. At what point below 60 million sperm is a man infertile? Is a man ever truly infertile? Urologists will tell you that as long as a man produces some sperm, and as long as his wife is fertile, there is a chance they can conceive.

But what if a man's sperm count is 60 million per ejaculate or less, and his wife also has a problem that lessens her chances of pregnancy? Perhaps only one fallopian tube is open. Or perhaps she ovulates only six or seven times a year. She is not infertile, but neither is she completely fertile. There may be no such thing as 'a little bit pregnant', but there definitely is such a thing as a little bit infertile. With other, more fertile partners, each person might easily achieve pregnancy. Together, they will have a great deal of trouble.

This recognition of a couple's combined subfertility has changed the face of both research and treatment. It also explains why minor problems, such as the dip in sperm concentration, can be crucial. As the sperm count slips a little lower, a man becomes a little bit more infertile. If his wife is spectacularly fertile, producing one or more eggs each month like clockwork, the lowered count may have absolutely no effect. But even if she has even a slight dysfunction, they will have a serious fertility problem. In other words, any small problem can be very important in the context of the complete evaluation.

A fertility investigation begins with all these thoughts in mind. The major idea today is that the couple must be treated as one. Although each partner requires separate evaluation by a specialist – a gynaecologist for the woman and an andrologist for the man – the fertility team views them as one patient. The specialists try to improve overall physical conditions so that pregnancy has the optimum chance. When a couple is borderline infertile, even small things can make a difference.

Clearly, we still have many things to learn about infertility in men. Above all, we need the cooperation of the male partner, which is not always easy to come by, given the known resistance of men to seek medical help in general and to discuss infertility openly in particular. Infertility is perceived as a threat to masculinity. The recognition that infertility is, in most cases, unrelated to sexuality will hopefully encourage the male partner to participate in a complete medical evaluation when a couple is infertile. Only with such information can infertility clinics accumulate enough data to arrange neatly in the future what now seems to be a tangle of ailments called male infertility.

9
Stress and Infertility

It is now a widely accepted fact that infertility creates stress. The unresolved question remains: Does infertility create stress or does stress create infertility? Psychologists cannot specifically identify which comes first. It's known that the longer infertility persists, the more difficult it is to cure. The term coined by the Omega team to describe the relationship of stress to infertility is *conception stress syndrome*.

Conception Stress Syndrome

When the Omega team first used the surgical laser in women in 1974, we accidentally fell into the trap of treating the reproductive organs rather than the whole person. Women came to us from distant cities in search of the magic 'light scalpels' that might cure their infertility. Many couples had been through several years of unsuccessful treatment and arrived at the Omega Institute in a highly stressed state. We sensed this accumulated stress but did not immediately recognize our obligation to help couples cope with it. Then a dramatic incident illuminated the issue.

Ralph and Emma had been struggling with infertility for seven years. The problem had been diagnosed as badly damaged fallopian tubes, with clubbed fimbriae at the end of both tubes. Emma had undergone two surgical repairs and still had not become pregnant. To make it worse, the previous surgeries probably had added to the damage; her medical surgical history suggested even with laser surgery she would have only a slim chance of pregnancy.

The problem seemed aggravated by the strange relationship that had developed between wife and husband. Emma was as drab as a dustbin; Ralph was as gaudy as a calliope. She wore old clothes; his neck dripped with expensive gold chains. When she spoke, she mumbled and referred to her 'disease'. When he spoke, his black eyes sparkled and he burst with vitality. He also mentioned 'her disease'. If we had never seen a medical record or taken a single test, we would have had no trouble sensing which partner was believed to be infertile.

Over the two days of evaluation that preceded surgery we learned more about their relationship. According to both partners, Ralph was vigorous and healthy; Emma was diseased and abnormal. He was master, she was slave. This notion pervaded every aspect of their lives. Ralph abused his captive in ways both subtle and overt. He took to blaming his wife's disease for everything. Every failure could be palmed off on her infertility.

In the hospital room in which his wife was the patient, he expected her to wait on him. 'Get me a glass of water,' he would command. The telephone rang one evening while Ralph was watching a football game on television. 'Get that, honey,' he said, 'and tell them I'll call back later.' One evening the dinner trays were delivered without cutlery. Ralph sent Emma down the hall in her nightgown to retrieve the missing knives and forks.

She meekly complied with his demands, accepting the treatment as an inherent part of their relationship. We would learn over the next few years that theirs was not an uncommon scenario. Their long search for a cure had distorted their relationship, and the distortion had taken over the marriage. What had begun as little quirks now had become commonplace. At the time, however, we understood little of these interplays.

During the few days they were in the hospital we ran a semen analysis on Ralph and were surprised to learn that his sperm count was marginal. On the morning of Emma's surgery, Ralph watched the operation on closed-circuit television. Along with us, he saw the clubbed ends of the tubes and watched as we opened the fringes and curled them back with the laser. We felt the operation went well, and gave them a much higher chance of pregnancy than we'd originally thought possible.

Back in her room we explained that Emma's reproductive function now looked very good, and if Ralph's sperm count could be improved a little, they would have a very good chance of pregnancy. Were Ralph and Emma happy with the news? One of them was.

Within a matter of hours, Emma went from the 'diseased, abnormal' victim to a healthy and normal young woman. While she was still recovering from the surgery, Ralph asked her to get him another glass of water. She shot back, 'Get it yourself.' That same night the nurses heard loud quarrelling from Emma's room, and the night supervisor had to intervene to calm the patient down.

Ralph was clearly furious. How could Emma be all right and he have a low sperm count? It wasn't possible. He was convinced that bringing her to the hospital was a disastrous mistake. The day they were ready to go home his feelings overwhelmed him. When the attending surgeon stopped in to say goodbye, Ralph grabbed him around the throat, slammed him up against the wall, and socked him in the jaw. Neither Ralph nor the surgeon understood what had happened. One thing, however, was patently clear: For some reason Ralph had blown his top.

This situation points up what therapists believe often happens when one member of a family is emotionally disturbed. As that person begins to get better, someone else falls apart. The healing disrupts the established pattern of relationships in the family.

Ralph and Emma's marriage was a classic example of one person's strength depending on another's weakness. When Emma became stronger, Ralph went to pieces. Three months later Emma telephoned and told us that she was pregnant. All of us on the surgical team knew that the marriage was deeply troubled, and that having a baby wasn't going to make their problems disappear.

It didn't take us long to decide that as specialists devoted to the study of infertility we owed it to our patients to offer psychological support. And it made sense that psychological care should begin at the beginning, before the strain of infertility had severely damaged the couple's marital relationship. For some couples the emotional damage of infertility can be so severe that the marriage never recovers.

In recent years many researchers have noticed the stress that pervades the life of infertile couples and have reached the same conclusion. Counselling should be offered by a psychologist, psychiatrist, or social worker experienced in working with infertile couples. The crises of infertility are similar to those of other stress situations, but infertile couples have unique problems and need the help of an experienced and emphatic therapist.

Stress Components of Infertility

The conception stress syndrome appears to go through predictable stages as a couple begins a fertility investigation, proceeds through treatment stages, and tries to achieve pregnancy. Sometimes the process continues for several years without resulting in the birth of a child.

These elements of stress are similar for every couple, but couples do not always handle them in the same way or with the same degree of success. Even the most stable human beings can be overwhelmed by the stress of infertility. The ability to cope with stress depends on each partner's individual feelings and the nature of their personal relationship. Infertility stress may create discord in the most harmonious marriage; or it may exacerbate an existing problem between the couple. Ultimately, the emotional crisis of infertility can make a marriage stronger. But for this to happen, both partners need to discover their feelings about the situation.

Stress often begins when a couple first realizes that there may be a fertility problem. Months pass without pregnancy; the couple may postpone going to a doctor out of fear or worry. Once the couple decides to see someone, it's hard to know where to turn. Friends offer advice, each recommending a different doctor. There may be too many – or too few – from whom to choose. Many couples turn to the family doctor or to a gynaecologist, who may not be a specialist in fertility. A wrong choice made now, even at this early stage, can create one of the major stresses of infertility – poor medical management of the problem.

Investigation

The first visit to a doctor can exacerbate the problem. The doctor may lead off with intimate questions about the couple's sexual behaviour. Women usually have to cope with a pelvic examination during this visit; and men are told that they will need a semen analysis. All are stress-provoking situations. If the doctor doesn't take the time to explain the tests carefully, the couple may be terrified or mystified by words like *biopsy* and *hormone assay*. Many of these anxieties can be reduced if the doctor takes the time to explain the procedures carefully and describe why he or she is performing each test. But not every doctor does this.

The husband and wife may proceed with the evaluation and do everything the doctor recommends for eleven or twelve months. They take a multitude of tests and perhaps try a variety of treatments. They have sex on all the right days, try baking-soda douches, take a fertility drug just in case it might help, and perhaps even have surgery. In short, they cooperate fully – but they still have not achieved a pregnancy.

At this point, the partners may begin to suspect that the doctor is at fault. And they may be right. The physician may be suggesting whatever comes to mind or recommending any new treatment described in medical journals. The husband and wife may start doing some research of their own and discover that they did not receive the methodical, precise testing they needed. Poor medical management of infertility is responsible for a great part of the conception stress syndrome. The physician's job is to ease the burden of stress, not make it worse. At this point, the husband and wife may decide that everything they have done so far has been a waste. Confused and angry, they may decide to change doctors.

Family and Friends

Family and friends may add stress in a variety of ways, and usually with the best of intentions. Parents may unwittingly remark that they would like to have grandchildren. If the parents are elderly or in poor health, the couple may feel guilty about letting them down. Family gatherings and Christmas celebrations are difficult events for infertile couples; surrounded by infants and toddlers, and pregnant relatives, they find no relief for the anxiety of their own childlessness.

Friends may be embarrassed to discuss the infertility problem openly because of the sexual implications involved, and the couple becomes isolated from the people who could help the most. Or family and friends may become too involved; they may ask for more information than the couple is willing to share with them or offer more advice than is needed. Husband and wife may be torn by the advice of various friends and relatives, feeling disloyal to one person if they seem to favour the opinion of another.

Sometimes their faith in the doctor is eroded at a crucial time in the treatment. Aunt Mary says, 'Dr Smith treated Annie; if you'd gone to him you'd be pregnant by now.' The strain begins to tell on the marital relationship. A husband may casually remark, 'My mum thinks we should see Dr So-and-So,' and be totally dismayed when his wife bursts into tears.

When infertile couples look around, it appears that everyone has a child but them. They are surrounded by brothers and sisters and friends who didn't seem to have any problem getting pregnant. All infertile couples have been told that if they would just relax they would get pregnant. They are reminded that as soon as the Joneses next door adopted a baby, they had a child of their own – because, supposedly, they were more relaxed. (Statistically, there is no proof that infertile couples who adopt conceive more rapidly than those who do not.)

Sometimes couples grow tired of well-meaning advice from friends; they get tired of being asked about their progress. Even when friends are genuinely interested and concerned, the husband and wife may have reached a point where they just can't discuss it any more. The only relief from stress is to isolate themselves so they don't have to think about fertility. The couple, particularly the woman, may begin to withdraw from friends and from people who have children.

Sometimes the opposite happens: friends get tired of hearing about infertility. Some couples are so obsessed with their problem that they can't talk about anything else. As time drags on without pregnancy, the husband and wife lose interest in any other subject and, like all obsessed people, put a great strain on their friends without realizing it.

Sometimes a husband and wife go through both these stages at different times. At one point they are obsessive, wanting to explain every step of the fertility search to friends and family. At another point, they cannot discuss it at all. They may become sensitive to friends who complain that children are a hassle. It's natural for parents to talk about some of the bad aspects of having children. An infertile couple, however, may not be able to tolerate such conversation and may think the parents are ungrateful.

The infertile couple freezes when new aquaintances ask, 'Do you have children?' The question is simply an ice-breaker, but the couple perceives it as a condemnation. One woman commented, 'When I answer no, people always hesitate, and I know they are wondering what's wrong with me.'

For some couples church attendance becomes difficult because it is a family activity, and they may begin to wonder if God is punishing them. They may feel unworthy of having a child. One church member suggested to a young couple that perhaps God had a plan for them that didn't include children, and they should accept God's will.

Infertile couples may resent the fact that other, seemingly much less deserving people have children, sometimes more children than they can care for. One wife commented, 'I knew it was wrong, but I couldn't help thinking about all the women around me who had no business being mothers. How could God give them children and pass me by? It was so unfair, and I couldn't bear it any more.'

Marital Problems

Stress may also be generated within the relationship between husband and wife. A serious problem arises when one partner is more involved in the fertility tests and subsequent treatment than the other. Usually it is the woman who is more likely to be subjected to the batteries of tests; it is the woman who keeps a daily record of her temperature and initiates sex on the right days; it is the woman who goes to the hospital and tries the fertility drugs. Some of these tests are uncomfortable and even painful. After one visit, when he leaves a semen sample, the husband's part may be finished.

If a husband fails to support his wife throughout the investigation, she can become tremendously overstressed. She may feel angry if her husband doesn't seem to share her concern. One woman complained, 'I try to tell him how I'm feeling and what the doctor said, and he's watching television.'

Sometimes a man will start spending more and more time away from home. This happened to one couple when the doctor told them there was no reason for their infertility. Yet the wife continued to complain of painful periods and painful sexual intercourse; she kept insisting that something was wrong with her. She felt that her husband had failed her miserably and resented the fact that he would leave her alone at night and go to a club with friends. For his part, the husband couldn't stand hearing about it any more. 'The doctor says there's nothing wrong with you. What am I supposed to do about it?'

They went on like this for nearly five years, she growing more and more obsessed, he withdrawing until they spent very little time together. Finally the wife went to another doctor who correctly diagnosed endometriosis with tubal blockage. At this point, however, so much anger and resentment had built up between husband and wife that they could barely speak to each other. Even though the fertility problem was successfully treated, the marital relationship had been badly damaged. Both partners agreed that before getting pregnant they needed professional counselling to help them renew their marriage.

Sometimes a husband is more interested in solving the fertility problem than his wife. One man badgered his wife to keep her appointments and fill in her temperature chart. He failed to sense her ambivalence about getting pregnant. Deep down, she wasn't sure that she really wanted to start a family, and she was reluctant to seek treatment. Whenever there seems to be an imbalance in the couple's desire for pregnancy, husband and wife need to talk about it and express their feelings to each other.

Sexual Problems

Many marital conflicts, both small and large, are played out in bed, a common battleground in marriage. This is especially true for infertile couples who try to have sex on schedule. Sex that was once spontaneous and joyful becomes rigid and mechanical.

A couple may try to have sex on the right days and avoid it the rest of the month. A husband may become impotent, or a woman may discover that she doesn't want to be touched, especially on 'fertile' days.

Men, who are much more romantic than many women believe them to be, complain of feeling used. One man said, 'I can't do it like a machine. I had a really rotten day at work, and when I got home I just wanted to relax. My wife said, "Hey, it's 16 May." I said, "So what?" She didn't speak to me for a week after that.' His wife later commented, 'It made me furious. I have tests, biopsies, a laparoscopy, all this stuff. All he has to do is have sex, and he wouldn't do it. How would you feel?'

Blaming Each Other

Part of the problem is that it's physically difficult for a man to have an erection on demand. And should he try to sustain an erection and fail, his confidence in his sexual potency, already eroded by infertility, will be severely shaken. A husband may feel guilty because his wife has done so much, and he can't even provide her with a means of pregnancy. Both partners may begin to blame each other for their troubles. When one person is identified as the guilty party, he or she may begin to fear that the spouse will leave.

When a husband and wife start blaming each other, the stress mounts so severely that all communication between them becomes distorted. Everything carries a double message. Hostility, the silent treatment, cutting remarks become the rule. The doctor sometimes comes in for a share of the hostility. (This can, in fact, be constructive if the physician is skilful enough to turn the confrontation into a positive expression of anger.)

Another likely target for anger and frustration is the unconceived child. Both husband and wife may begin to wonder if they will be able to love a child whose creation has caused so much grief between them. They question whether any baby can make up for the trouble they have gone through. This is a very sensitive area for couples, and most people are reluctant to express such 'terrible thoughts'. Yet these are natural human feelings.

It's not unusual for a husband and wife to cycle in and out of wanting a baby. For a period of time they may fail to keep the temperature chart, miss appointments with the doctor, or throw away medication. They are sick of the hassle and don't want to deal with it any more. A few months later they are ready to work on the problem again. This is a natural coping mechanism. Psychologically, the partners need a break from the infertility obsession. They come back to it when they feel emotionally stronger. But problems arise if husband and wife reach a saturation point at different times.

Losing Heart

Many infertility patients switch doctors at some point and may even see as many as four or five different specialists in their pursuit of pregnancy. When a man is infertile, the possible tests and treatments are limited. When a woman is infertile, however, the struggle for pregnancy may go on for years, partly because most treatments require time to succeed. Therefore, when a couple seeks further consultation after several years of a fertility quest, it is usually the woman who has undergone extensive testing and treatment. At this point, she may be extremely volatile. Her husband may be unable to cope with her angry feelings. 'She acts half crazy most of the time, and she cries over nothing. I don't know what to say to her.' In fact, her emotional outbursts may be completely beyond her control. 'I wish I could be less emotional, but I can't stop myself.'

Sometimes a new doctor exacerbates an already volatile situation by pointing out the previous doctor's mistakes and ordering a fresh battery of tests. The couple, now fairly experienced in the process of an infertility investigation, may think, 'How do we know if this new specialist knows what he's doing? Why should we trust him?' Discouragement becomes layered with doubt. One part of the patient's mind – the optimistic part – wants to keep trying. The other part says nothing will ever work.

For some couples this cycle of hope and disappointment continues for years. Some women have temperature charts that trace seven or eight years of hope and failure. Looking back over those long months of trying and failing is disheartening. It's nearly impossible for couples to remain positive. How can they believe that they will get pregnant in the face of this overwhelming evidence?

Somewhere deep in their hearts, both husband and wife may wish that someone would simply put an end to their quest. Perhaps the most valuable – and difficult – role a specialist can play is to help the infertile couple decide when to give up. The psychologist on the fertility team can also offer help when it comes time to determine whether the saturation point has been reached.

When to Give Up

For all the brilliant advances in fertility research, 10 per cent of infertile couples never succeed in discovering the nature of their problem. Modern drug treatment of infertility can go on almost indefinitely. So can timed intercourse and temperature graphs. So can the disappointment and feelings of grief each month when a woman starts to menstruate. The world seems to stop turning while the couple tries to get pregnant. Jobs stagnate, and marriages disintegrate. Some couples become so enmeshed in the quest for pregnancy that they can lose perspective on the rest of their lives.

Deciding to stop seeking a solution to infertility depends above all else on each partner's deepest feelings. There are no hard-and-fast rules about who should stop trying and who should continue. The following suggestions may offer a framework within which to make a decision. It is time to consider giving up:

- when your marriage and other relationships are suffering;
- when the female partner is over forty;
- when the female partner is between the ages of thirty-five and forty and has a major fertility problem;
- when two medical opinions confirm that your chances are slight to non-existent; if you have any doubts, get a third opinion.

Young couples whose marriages are rocky have the option of taking a year or so off, and then seeking help again when they feel emotionally stronger. Sometimes it helps to spend time concentrating on other aspects of life. Focusing on work and marriage or on making new friends can help put the fertility problem into perspective.

If you do not fall into any of these categories, you can try every fertility option open to you. If a fertility expert tells you that the situation is hopeless, seek another opinion. New discoveries are continuously appearing on the horizon as the intensive research into infertility continues in laboratories round the world. Even experts don't have all the answers; every specialist has had patients who achieved pregnancy against all the odds. As long as a man and a woman have some reproductive function, there's always a chance.

The Investigation

10
Getting Help

Even for the most fertile couple, getting pregnant is a game of chance and mischance. The normal reproductive system has its own built-in population control mechanism and offers only a 20 per cent chance of pregnancy in any given month. With these odds, it can take a year or longer for a fertile couple to achieve pregnancy. Since infertility usually has no symptoms – no pain or headaches, no pulled muscles or broken bones – how can non-pregnant couples know whether the mathematical odds are temporarily running against them or whether something is really wrong? Exactly when should they start to worry about fertility?

When a man or woman first wonders, 'Is there something wrong?' he or she has already crossed the threshold, and it's time to consider professional consultation. Most people have a pretty good idea of whether or not they should have conceived a child.

When to Get Help

In general, couples actively trying to get pregnant for six months or more – or randomly trying for a year or longer – may be candidates for professional counselling. How long couples should try to become pregnant before seeing a specialist also is related to their medical history. A history of pelvic infection, missed periods, or menstrual pain in a woman, or scrotal injuries in a man, can point to infertility problems. Although age is not usually a factor in male fertility, it is important in female fertility. After the age of thirty a woman's reproductive capacity begins to decline.

If you are worried, seek advice anyway. A specialist will give you reassurance if your worries are premature. Usually a visit and a brief discussion will put you on the right track.

Both partners should try to go in for the first visit. It's tempting for a man to say, 'You go for a check-up, then I will.' Stick together. Couples who get off to a good start together, in terms of a fertility evaluation, will have a more productive finish. Even if only one person is worried, both should resolve to get an answer.

Unrecognized problems may worsen and become more difficult to treat as time passes.

Many fertility problems are easily and quickly resolved. However, just as many require careful examination and treatment over a period of several months and sometimes years. Getting help early can save time and stress, and ultimately increase the odds of a successful pregnancy. Even if you should fall into that small group in which no problem can be detected, consulting a specialist will reassure you that you have done everything you can to find an answer.

Having made the point, we add one ironic statistic. In a large population of couples of all ages, about 60 per cent will achieve pregnancy within six months, and 80 per cent by the end of twelve months. If the other 20 per cent all go to a specialist, half of them will get pregnant in another six months – *without any treatment*. Therefore, the length of time a couple has been trying to have children does not specifically indicate the degree of fertility or infertility.

The best advice is that if you are anxious and worried after six months to a year, you should consult a competent specialist. It's possible that the problem is only a matter of mathematical odds and a little more time will solve it. But anxieties and fears can pressure marriages and cause needless unhappiness between husband and wife. When in doubt, seek an answer.

Prenuptial Evaluations

NHS clinics will not give a woman a prenuptial check-up on demand. She would have to have it done privately and a full evaluation would be very expensive. A general practitioner can request a semen analysis at his local laboratory for any of his male patients.

The Fertility Team

The next important question is exactly who – and what – a fertility specialist is. Because the known causes of infertility cross the boundaries of several different medical specialities, a fertility expert may be a gynaecologist, a urologist, an endocrinologist, an andrologist, or even a psychiatrist. Ovulation, sperm production, conception, implantation of the fertilized egg in the uterus, and management of the early weeks of pregnancy all fall within the realm of the fertility expert.

At present, there is no standard approach to a fertility check-up, and no one speciality is devoted exclusively to the problem. Couples entering a fertility clinic must usually consult a number of specialists, each giving different tests and drawing different conclusions. Also mixed into the evaluation are laboratories and hospitals. The whole process may take several months, and after it's all over the couple still may be unable to become pregnant. Thus, when couples seek infertility treatment, they invariably encounter more than one doctor. There is too much scientific knowledge in the field for one doctor – however able – to keep up with it all.

One doctor – in Britain this will be the gynaecologist – acts as the team leader, working with a group of specialists. Ideally, an infertility clinic includes both male and female doctors and counsellors to offer the couple full support through the emotional and physical complexities of infertility. An all-male or all-female fertility team risks missing vital emotional evidence that could make the difference in successful treatment. A team practice treats both partners and should include or have available on a close consulting basis:

- A gynaecologist who specializes in endocrine (hormonal) problems in female reproduction and will carry out any operation which may be necessary.
- A urologist or andrologist who specializes in the problems of male reproduction; this doctor also should be a skilled surgeon or work closely with one.
- A psychological counsellor (psychiatrist, psychologist, or social worker) who helps a couple through the emotional stresses often linked to infertility. Although stress is rarely a cause of infertility, it has been shown conclusively to be a dangerous byproduct of it. With the help of a psychologist, couples can more easily get past the emotional hurdles of infertility.
- A genetic counsellor, either a physician with advanced training in genetics or a non-medical person who specializes in genetic counselling. The need for genetic screening is determined by the couple's family history, physical examination, or chromosome analysis.

Not all of these may be required for your particular tests and treatment. But should they be needed, these specialists should consult together and, at all times, look at the overall picture, not merely at their particular corner of the problem.

The First Step

If you suspect you have a fertility problem, the first person to consult is your family doctor. If difficulties in conceiving are relatively minor, you may not need the help of a specialist. At this point, a woman seeking medical help may assume that infertility is her problem. She shouldn't – nor should the doctor.

Not for Women Only

In the minds of many people, sperm counts and virility are invariably linked. A low sperm count hints at inadequate manhood, just as surely as a high count denotes virility. The fact that these two biological factors are unrelated is almost universally ignored.

When a couple can't get pregnant, it is absolutely essential that both partners receive an evaluation. Causes of infertility are about evenly divided between the sexes: 35 per cent of the time they can be traced to the woman and 35 per cent of the time to the man. In about 20 per cent of cases, both partners have a problem; and in the remaining 10 per cent, no cause is ever found. Clearly, it is pointless to evaluate the female half of the couple alone.

So the first question to ask your doctor should be, 'Do *we* have a fertility problem?' It's extremely important to consider infertility a shared concern. New psychological studies have proved that less strain is placed on a marriage when the woman and man work together to solve the problem. Even when the partners agree to seek help together, it is usually the woman who sees a doctor first, simply because many fertility specialists are gynaecologists. Further, throughout their lives women normally visit doctors more often than men. It seems natural then, when a couple is worried about infertility, for the woman to make the initial inquiry.

After that, several factors conspire to keep her at the centre of the check-up. Many tests in a standard fertility check-up involve the woman alone. If the man's semen analysis or sperm count is normal, he is often relieved of further testing, but it's important for a couple to continue to work together, even when the husband is not being directly tested.

Getting the Help You Need

What a GP or clinic recommends to a couple depends largely on the age of the female partner. If the woman is under twenty-five, the doctor may perform some basic tests, such as asking her to keep a temperature chart for a few months, to discover if she is ovulating. Before seeing a doctor, it's a good idea for a woman to take her waking temperature for one to two months and record the temperature on a piece of paper (see p. 99). A slight rise in temperature will indicate when a woman is ovulating. This record may be very helpful and will probably be the first thing the doctor suggests; the second suggestion should be a semen analysis for the man.

Using these two simple tests, the GP may be able to solve the problem. But if the couple still does not get pregnant within three to six months, consultation with a specialist may be in order. If the woman is over twenty-five, the family doctor should certainly refer the couple to a specialist.

One way to locate fertility specialists is through patient support groups such as the National Association for the Childless (318 Summer Lane, Birmingham BI9 3RL). Sometimes you have to join an organization before you can attend meetings or receive information, but some groups let you attend an introductory meeting. If there is a support group in your area, try to go to a meeting and ask for the names of specialists whom the members favour.

If a major university medical centre is near by, you may want to call and find out if the centre has an infertility clinic. The clinic may be a good one. However, a university label offers no guarantee of quality or advanced technology; many breakthroughs in infertility research have come through private consultants.

Bear in mind that the better known an infertility specialist is, the more controversial he or she will be in the community. When specialists are on the cutting edge of new research techniques, they are bound to attract some criticism. Don't be put off by a doctor simply because he or she is controversial; visit the doctor and make the decision for yourself. Should the doctor have a special surgical unit or clinic where patients are admitted, visit the unit.

Observe the appearance of the unit and the attitude of both patients and nurses. Are the accommodations for fertility patients separate from those for maternity patients, or seriously ill or dying patients? Fertility is more than a physical problem. Your state of mind is crucial to success. Being in a wing where new mothers are cuddling babies can be devastating for an infertile woman. So can the proximity of someone who is seriously ill.

As a patient, you have the right to switch doctors if you wish, at any time.

If you live in a small town, you may have to travel to a city to find a fertility specialist. Although going outside your community will involve travel expenses, you may avoid wasting time on repeat tests and ineffective treatment.

There are no magic doctors. But there are doctors who are up on their research and who pursue their calling with enthusiasm, confidence and, above all, concern for your well-being. Even if you do not achieve the desired pregnancy, you stand an excellent chance of getting answers to your questions. Years later, you won't have to look back and say, 'We never were able to learn why we couldn't have children.'

The Temperature Chart

It's a good idea for a couple worried about fertility to keep a temperature chart for two or three months before seeing a specialist. This preliminary home testing can give the specialist something to work with on the first visit.

A temperature chart is an indirect method of pinpointing ovulation without any tests at all. The charts are used to discover whether a woman is ovulating and record the most fertile days. Making such a chart requires a woman to take her waking temperature every morning, without fail, and to record the reading on a graph.

The chart becomes a daily reminder of both fertility potential and failure to conceive. The prospect of taking their temperature 'one more time' has driven thousands of women across the country to snap their thermometers in frustration. Even so, most fertility specialists rely on the temperature chart as a basic diagnostic tool and support mechanism throughout treatment, primarily because it is easy and inexpensive. Although it is by no means foolproof, a temperature chart can provide valuable information. Here's how it works.

A temperature chart is based on the fact that a woman's basal (resting) body temperature normally rises midway through her menstrual cycle. Progesterone is a thermal hormone, meaning that when it is present in the bloodstream, body temperature rises. Progesterone is elevated in a woman's bloodstream after she has ovulated. Therefore, over a monthly menstrual cycle, a normal temperature chart will be low for the first two weeks of the cycle (the oestrogen phase) and show a decided upward shift during the second two weeks of the cycle (the progesterone phase).

If a woman takes her temperature every morning, beginning on the last day of her period, it should remain relatively low, about 98° F (36·5° C), until about day 14 of the cycle; then it shifts upward to about 98·4° F (36·8° C) and remains elevated through the remainder of the cycle. After her next period finishes, the temperature will drop again, as progesterone falls. If she becomes pregnant, the temperature will remain elevated.

The drawback of this system of measurement is that the shift takes place *after* ovulation has occurred; therefore, to use a temperature chart as a timing device for intercourse, a couple must anticipate the rise. A woman who has fairly regular menstrual cycles will find it easy to predict when the rise is about to occur. Further, some charts will show a noticeable dip in temperature just before the upward shift. This dip, if it occurs, coincides with ovulation.

The key to keeping an accurate chart is to record the temperature first thing in the morning, *before getting out of bed*. Keep the thermometer and the chart on your bedside table, and try to take your temperature at about the same time each morning. If you can't wake up fully, take your temperature and lay the thermometer down afterwards; you can record the numbers on the graph later after you wake up.

A regular thermometer can be used, but an ovulation thermometer that has only the relevant part of the scale, with a mark for each tenth of a degree, is more

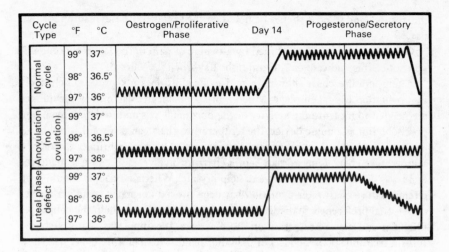

Cycle Type	°F	°C	Oestrogen/Proliferative Phase		Day 14	Progesterone/Secretory Phase
Normal cycle	99°	37°				
	98°	36.5°				
	97°	36°				
Anovulation (no ovulation)	99°	37°				
	98°	36.5°				
	97°	36°				
Luteal phase defect	99°	37°				
	98°	36.5°				
	97°	36°				

Three temperature charts

accurate. Most thermometers take about five minutes to measure basal body temperature accurately. A new easy-to-use electronic digital thermometer, which flashes the degree in numbers, records the temperature in only thirty seconds. Electronic thermometers cost rather more than the others, but they reduce the aggravation component of temperature taking considerably. Thermometers can be purchased at any chemists'.

Making a Graph

Ovulation thermometers come with pre-printed graphs for charting; your clinic can also supply them. Or you can make your own chart with a plain piece of graph paper. Across the top of the page list the days of your cycle. Day 1 is the first day of menstruation. Along the side of the graph write in the degree numbers; begin at the bottom with 97·0° F or 36·0° C, and increase the numbers up the side of the chart by 0·2 until you reach 99·0° F or 37·0° C. Along the bottom of the graph you can write in the days of the month.

Each morning, take your temperature and record the reading by placing a dot in the proper space. Indicate days of coitus (intercourse) by placing a C or an arrow in the space. Indicate menstruation by putting an X through each day of menstrual flow. Body temperature is sensitive to illness and changes in routine. Any obvious reasons for temperature variation – colds, infection, insomnia, indigestion, and so on – should be noted on the graph above the reading for that day.

Ovulation may be accompanied by a twinge of pain in the lower abdomen. If you notice this, indicate on the graph the day when it occurred.

A temperature chart showing a mid-cycle shift does not prove conclusively that ovulation has taken place. Much more sophisticated laboratory techniques are needed to measure the activity of the hormonal axis and to define ovulation precisely. But as a home device, the temperature chart can be useful.

Once ovulation has been established, some women continue to keep a temperature chart. One woman kept a chart for five years 'because it made me feel I was doing something active to help myself'. Whether a couple should keep a temperature chart after ovulation has been proved normal is strictly a matter of personal preference. Statistically, it probably isn't going to help the couple get pregnant and may put a strain on the marriage. It's important that sex should remain free and spontaneous. On the other hand, a temperature chart will show if a woman is having early miscarriages.

11
The Check-up

The goal of a fertility investigation is to provide precise answers within a given period of time. Several tests and examinations are required to provide a complete picture of the reproductive status of a couple. Even though the testing seems to be biased towards the female, the full cooperation of both partners is crucial to a successful outcome. Doctors should approach the case with enthusiasm and optimism, because if they do their job right, they will help make the couple's fondest wish come true.

Some cases are tricky and full of red herrings; the search for answers may lead down obscure alleyways. But if the physician keeps a clear head, he or she will find most of the clues. That is not to say that physicians are not occasionally inspired. Like any good detective, a fertility specialist has hunches that pay off, and like any good detective, the physician will back up hunches with hard evidence.

The timing and sequence of the tests are important. A test performed at the wrong time is useless. The sequence may depend on a patient's age or previously diagnosed fertility problems. Generally, good management indicates that low-risk tests be performed first, and that surgical procedures be reserved for last.

The Five Phases of Investigation

At the Omega Institute we divide the tests into five phases for each partner. Phase I is a fact-finding expedition, gathering information from each person's background, medical history, and physical examination. For a man, Phase I includes a semen analysis. At this stage of the investigation many clues are uncovered that may be confirmed or denied by the diagnostic tests that follow.

Phase II, which follows immediately, includes laboratory studies of hormones and cervical mucus and the ubiquitous temperature chart. To this standard portion of the check-up we have added stress counselling. Stress is rarely a cause of infertility, but it is frequently a serious side-effect. Psychological profiles of infertile couples have proved conclusively that infertility places severe strain on marital relationships. The result is sometimes divorce instead of pregnancy.

The Investigation of Infertile Couples

After a couple has an initial interview with a fertility specialist, each partner enters an individual series of tests designed to uncover any possible infertility problems. The female and male tests are divided into five phases:

Women	Men
Phase I – Fact Finding	*Phase I – Fact Finding*
History	History
Review of previous fertility tests	Physical
Physical examination	Varicocele screening
Phase II – Diagnostic Studies	Semen analysis
Temperature chart	*Phase II – Diagnostic Studies*
Postcoital test	Stress counselling
Hormone blood tests	Hormone blood studies, if necessary
Ultrasound	(If all tests are normal, the male tests
Endometrial biopsy	may end after stress counselling.)
Stress counselling	*Phase III – Surgical Investigation*
Phase III – Surgical Investigation	Testicular biopsy
Laparoscopy	Vasogram (X-ray)
Hysterosalpingogram (X-rays)	*Phase IV*
Phase IV	Chromosome analysis, if necessary
Chromosome analysis, if necessary	*Phase V*
Phase V	Genetic counselling, if necessary
Genetic counselling, if necessary	

Phase III is the surgical investigation carried out in the hospital, which lets the specialist view the reproductive organs directly and take specialized biopsies. In a woman, a laparoscopy reveals the overall condition of the uterus, ovaries, and tubes, and helps the specialist determine whether surgical repair will correct the problem. In a man, a biopsy taken from one testicle may give the final clue to the cause of infertility, and whether it can be corrected.

Phase IV, chromosomal analysis, is used only when the fertility problem appears to be caused by a chromosomal error that affected the development of reproductive organs before birth. In those rare instances when there is some question of sexual identity, a chromosome analysis will reveal the nature of the problem.

Phase V, genetic counselling, is designed for those few couples whose family history suggests the possibility of birth defects or whose chromosome analysis reveals a major defect. Genetic counselling can help such couples determine the chances of passing the defect on to their offspring.

Once a problem is identified and treatment begins, additional tests may be required to monitor the effect of medication.

How Long Do the Tests Take?

The fertility tests can be refined to give a complete picture over two months. In the past, a typical investigation has taken three to six months to complete, and many specialists still prefer such an extended approach, feeling that more time reduces pressure on the couple.

The husband and wife's situation – their age, their commitment to getting pregnant – will affect their desire to go through the tests in a condensed period of time. Many people want answers as soon as possible; others merely want to explore the territory and get an idea of what's going on. Couples in their early twenties with an uncomplicated medical history have time, biologically speaking, to investigate more slowly. But for many infertile couples, time is the enemy.

Does Everyone Need a Full Investigation?

A full investigation requires commitment from the couple and the specialist. The surgical portion of the investigation in Phase III, although simple, may require anaesthesia and an overnight stay in the hospital. A logical question then is: Does every man and woman need every test? For a woman, the answer is usually yes. However, if the male has a normal semen analysis, his portion of the tests will usually end after the stress counselling in Phase II. If the semen analysis is abnormal, he probably will go through the remaining steps.

Infertility often has more than one source. For example, a temperature chart and endometrial biopsy may reveal that a woman isn't ovulating. Her physician prescribes fertility drugs for several months and ovulation begins. Yet after some months the woman fails to conceive. Further tests are then carried out and it is discovered that her tubes are blocked as well. Valuable time could have been saved if the check-up had been completed when the woman failed to become pregnant after three months.

In another common scenario, a woman submits to one or more microsurgical operations to rebuild her fallopian tubes. Several years down the line, when her age is working against her, she learns that her husband has a low sperm count that could have been increased. It seems impossible, but it happens every day. If testing had shown there was no way to improve his sperm count, the woman could have become pregnant using artificial insemination by donor sperm. Or she could have chosen not to have surgery and considered adoption.

For all these reasons, and because of the substantial stress that invariably results from an inadequate investigation, we recommend a full check-up for all our women patients and for men who have an abnormal semen analysis. From the hundreds of couples we have seen over the last ten years, it has become clear to us that it's better to work with all the facts than with some of the possibilities.

Even those couples who elect a piecemeal approach, stretched out over a period of several months, may ultimately undergo all the tests in an effort to nail down the elusive cause(s) of infertility. It is often a matter of now or later. For young couples whose medical history and analyses do not indicate tubal blockage in the woman or a problem in the man, who have biological time to explore slowly, and who do not feel an urgency to get pregnant, Phases I and II of the investigation may be enough to start with. If pregnancy doesn't occur within a reasonable period of time, the couple can complete the tests later, with time to spare.

Do Previous Tests Count?

Many people going for a fertility investigation have already had some tests performed by other doctors. The results of these tests can and should be used again. They are particularly valuable as points of comparison.

If the tests were run by a doctor or a laboratory inexperienced in fertility studies, they may have been misinterpreted. When an expert repeats the tests he or she may discover an inconsistency that puts the investigation on a new track. If a test was run by an expert and a quantity of time has elapsed, the new test will show whether the condition has improved with treatment, whether it is the same, or whether it has grown worse. Occasionally, previous tests will suffice and will not have to be repeated.

When visiting a new clinic the consultant in charge will usually write to any previous clinics asking for copies of your records and all tests done. It helps him or her considerably to know what has already been done, and whether the tests have been done competently.

Hospitalization

Several tests in the male and female check-up are performed in the hospital. A hysterosalpingogram can be performed in an outpatient X-ray department, but a laparoscopy is best performed in a hospital.

If a man's semen analysis is abnormal, a testicular biopsy and evaluation of his sperm transport system may be indicated to show whether the problem can be corrected; these procedures are performed in an outpatient department or a hospital.

After the Investigation

The final phase of a fertility investigation and treatment is a suspected pregnancy. The modern beta human chorionic gonadotrophins test can detect a pregnancy 10–15 days after conception.

At this point, the fertility specialist usually orders a series of tests to check on the weekly rise in hormones; blood tests will show whether the endometrium is getting enough progesterone. Ultrasound can be used to locate the fetus and detect a tubal pregnancy. After the tenth to twelfth week the fertility specialist will place the care of the woman in the hands of an obstetrician. There is reason for this special care. An infertility pregnancy is a 'premium' baby and should be treated as a high risk, since it may be the couple's only chance to have a child.

Cause 'Unknown'

Every once in a while, even after a perfectly designed investigation, a case is 'unsolved'. This does not mean that there is no answer; it means only that scientists have not yet learned everything there is to know about infertility. The specialists have looked at all the possible known culprits, and none is guilty. Every specialist has encountered unsolved cases, where even years of training and sophisticated testing devices do not pay off. It is here that the difficult issues of accepting the facts and considering the alternatives arise.

Before that point, a couple should at the very least be convinced that every step that could be taken has been taken, that every clue that might have led to a solution has been followed and investigated – in short, that everything possible to solve the problem was done, and done correctly. This is the absolute minimum any man and woman should expect from a fertility investigation.

12
How Psychologists Can Help

An interview with a psychological counsellor offers a couple the opportunity to release the stress brought on by their struggle with infertility. The purpose of such an evaluation is not to dig out every secret the husband and wife may share but to give them an opportunity to talk about any worries they may have about infertility. The psychologist is not looking for neuroses that may be causing the couple's infertility. The counsellor assumes that the infertility problem is medical, and his or her job is to help the couple pursue and resolve the problem with the least amount of strain on their marriage and emotional stability.

It is known that infertility causes stress, and that the stress accumulates over the course of treatment. The longer the pursuit, the higher the level of stress. How a psychologist handles the evaluation depends largely on when he or she enters the life of the infertile couple.

Thousands of infertile couples go through months of medical and/or surgical treatment before they receive the benefit of counselling. These couples may desire close counselling from the therapist and may wish to retrace some of the stress events that have accumulated. Ideally, psychological evaluation takes place in the early phases of the investigation so that infertility patients have an opportunity to talk with a counsellor as the testing and treatment progress. In this way they can head off a potential crisis before it gets out of control.

The psychological evaluation is done to help relieve stress, to improve a marriage suffering under the strain of infertility, and to help prevent couples from transferring problems to a child should they succeed in getting pregnant. Should they not be able to have a child, the counsellor can help them cope with this.

There is one more important reason for a psychological evaluation: although it cannot be proved, it's likely that reducing stress helps treatment succeed. The reproductive system is controlled by the hypothalamus, or lower brain. Stress, however, is a function of the higher brain centres, which have the power to override the hypothalamus. We know that when anxiety is present, other biological systems do not function as well as they should. Therefore, reducing stress may well ease the way for both medical and surgical therapies.

The Psychological Evaluation

One of the main things couples feel when they are infertile is a loss of control. For no particular reason, an unknown element has picked them out and taken over, and now rules their lives without permission. This loss of control makes usually confident people feel insecure and agitated. They don't know how to handle their feelings and may take it out on each other, or on the doctor.

If their fertility specialist offers psychological counselling as part of the investigation, the couple will have an opportunity to unleash some of this agitation. The psychological portion of the evaluation usually begins with an interview with each partner alone. There are many sensitive issues that husbands and wives may not wish to discuss in front of each other, such as past abortions or previous children conceived with other partners. Even when both partners know about past histories, talking about them can sometimes bring up old hurts that have been successfully laid to rest.

The stress components of infertility are easily passed off on to other life situations and thus may be deeply hidden. A psychologist may bring out an important issue that is working against the couple's search for fertility. For example, he might ask for a yes-or-no response to the following statement: 'I feel that I'm good with children.' One woman named Carla answered no, and the psychologist asked Carla more about her feelings towards children. Carla described her own mother, who had been a very controlling parent and whose behaviour had made Carla unhappy as a child. Anticipating motherhood herself, Carla was worried that she might be the same kind of mother.

Although she was going through the motions of a fertility check-up, Carla was ambivalent about pregnancy. She decided to complete the tests and treatment, but chose to wait a while before getting pregnant. She spent some time with the therapist resolving this old issue between herself and her mother, and ultimately felt more confident about having a baby of her own. 'It took some hard work to realize that I don't have to be like my mother,' she said, 'but I think now that I can bring a new set of emotions and responses to a child.'

Carla's feeling is unusual among fertility patients. Most often, couples are certain in their desire for a child, and some women are described as obsessive. Women who lose their mothers early in life, through death or divorce, tend to have a single-minded, almost fierce desire to have a child of their own with whom they can create a warm mother–child relationship.

Sometimes this desire becomes so intense that it overshadows everything else in the marriage. Both partners get into the habit of blaming any marital problems on the fact that they don't have a child. Once that problem is solved, they expect all their troubles to end.

In fact, this is seldom the case. Babies do not make marital troubles go away.

Having a baby is high-level stress, and when any kind of stress is applied to a pre-existing problem, the problem becomes worse. A baby changes every aspect of a couple's life, fills every hour of the day with new demands. Much of the experience is exciting and pleasurable, and much of it is exhausting.

Understanding why someone wants a child can sometimes illuminate the depth of a pre-existing problem. The psychological evaluation of a young woman named Lucy indicated that she was very depressed. Lucy said she was picking fights with her husband almost every day, yet she was terrified of losing him. 'I think I want him to leave me, so I don't have to worry about it any more.'

Lucy said that if she could have a child she wouldn't feel so insecure and alone, that she would have someone to love and cherish. Implicit in her desire was the wish for someone who could never leave her. As she talked more, she spoke of her mother, who had died several years earlier, and how this loss still haunted her. Now she had the same fear that her husband would leave her.

There was a danger that if Lucy succeeded in getting pregnant she would use the baby to fill the gap left by her mother. By understanding why she wanted a baby so badly, she was able to look back and resolve the loss of her mother. It was not difficult for her to examine her feelings. Counselling not only helped save her marriage but prevented her from transferring a problem to the child.

These are only a few of the issues that influence a couple's ability to cope with stress. A psychological counsellor is committed to helping both partners discover their feelings and feel comfortable talking about worries; the counsellor can also suggest ways to reduce the stress that quite naturally accompanies infertility.

If the couple seems to be coping with the stress, the counsellor may suggest a monthly session during treatment to talk about how things are going. If the couple feels that additional counselling would help, the counsellor may suggest weekly sessions. If the couple prefers to see someone else, the counsellor will suggest other therapists who work primarily with infertile couples. Sometimes one partner has a special problem that needs to be worked out privately with a therapist; in this case the therapist may suggest individual counselling.

Therapists, like medical doctors, specialize in various fields – child psychology, adolescent psychology, individual therapy, family therapy, and so on. It's important that both partners work with a psychologist who is experienced with stress caused by infertility.

Escaping Stress

When faced with any of the stress points mentioned above, couples can help themselves out of the emotional maze. When relationships seem strained, try to focus on your own actions – not what is being done to you, but what you may be

Checklist for Stress Overload

Hidden stress may accumulate and suddenly cause problems, even among couples who appear to be handling stress well. The best time to deal with stress is before it gets out of control. The psychological team that works with the Omega Institute has pinpointed several danger signs that occur when a couple is reaching stress overload. If you are experiencing one or more of these feelings, it's important to look closely at the stress components in your life. Psychologists suggest that people suffering from infertility stress should try to recognize their feelings and express themselves directly to their spouses, friends, and family. Should you reach a stress point that you cannot work out, it's a good idea to talk with a psychological counsellor. Here are fifteen danger signs that indicate infertility stress overload:

1. Becoming so obsessed with infertility that you can't think about anything else.
2. Feeling that you are being punished because you are infertile; you may put yourself in punishing situations, such as taking a job in a school or nursery where you work around children.
3. Isolating yourself from your normal support system of friends, family, and other people who can help you; you may have changed jobs to get away from people who know you.
4. Sleeping a lot.
5. Drinking to excess; using drugs.
6. Feeling alone.
7. Being unable to talk about infertility, but feeling increased tension and anger towards your spouse.
8. Thinking that your spouse doesn't understand how you feel or doesn't want a child as much as you do.
9. Losing interest in sex.
10. Experiencing impotence during the woman's mid-cycle.
11. Feeling that you are a sexual failure.
12. Sensing failure in your life in general.
13. Feeling that your spouse is to blame for infertility.
14. Feeling that you have no goals or ambitions.
15. Beginning extramarital affairs in which you do not feel the need to 'perform on command'.

doing to others. Insensitivity can fall to either partner: the one who is fertile or the one who is infertile. The infertile partner can become so obsessed that he or she fails to listen to the needs of the one who is fertile.

Ask yourself if you're being fair to friends who want to help you. People under stress send conflicting signals: comfort me, don't talk to me; stay close, go away; why don't you say something, how could you say that. Infertile couples may not want to attend family gatherings because it upsets them to be around children, but they are hurt if they are not invited.

Often a little quiet thinking about other people and their feelings can help a person suffering from conception stress get some perspective on the situation. The best way to alleviate stress is for husband and wife to view the fertility problem as a shared concern. Whenever possible, both should go to the doctor's appointments together.

Some couples have found unique ways to share the stress and enhance their relationship at the same time. One young husband kept his wife's temperature chart for her. Anticipating the rise in temperature gave him such pleasure that he came to view the chart as a playful sex game, rather than 'sex on demand'. His comment was, 'Sex was nice the rest of the month, but when I saw that mid-cycle rise coming up, it was great.'

Other couples trying to escape the effects of mechanical sex say that imaginative love-making can alleviate much of the stress. One women commented, 'We have sex almost anywhere, except the bedroom.' Another said that she and her husband try to think about having an exotic sexual experience, not about getting pregnant.

Sex in marriage is an emotional bond. It is virtually impossible to have a good marriage and a poor sexual relationship. Many unspoken words are communicated through physical desire and fulfilment. However, when a couple is suffering from conception stress, feelings need to be verbally shared. Under stress it is easy for one partner to misread mental signals from the other. The only way your partner knows for certain what's going on in your mind is if you express your thoughts verbally. Good, open conversation between husband and wife is the best way to alleviate fertility stress.

Stress builds up inside some marriages until husband and wife are afraid to talk openly to each other about their feelings. People become afraid that they will hurt their partners irreparably or be hurt by them. Husbands and wives often find it easier to talk together in the presence of an infertility counsellor.

Dr Melvin Taymor of Harvard Medical School and Ellen Bresnick, a fertility counsellor, interviewed sixty-two infertile couples who received counselling. In their book *Infertility*, Taymor and Bresnick note that the couples experienced a significant reduction in guilt, anger, and frustration after only five counselling sessions. Couples who chose long-term therapy (six sessions or more) reported a

70-80 per cent decrease in these symptoms. Most couples said that after counselling they felt less depressed and less anxious; a subsequent study showed that infertility counselling enhanced the quality of life for many who had become victims of the conception stress syndrome.

Help from Other Couples

Many couples find that even though they don't need the continuing help of a professional counsellor, they would like to talk with other people going through similar experiences. Meetings of support groups, where infertile couples get together and discuss some of their experiences, can help alleviate the sense of isolation that haunts infertile couples. Such groups create a sense of normality and friendship, and provide an excellent source of information about new treatment. In America, the best known of these is Resolve, Inc., which began in Boston under the leadership of Barbara Eck Menning, a nurse with a degree in maternal-child health and nursing. She had faced infertility herself and was one of the first to recognize that infertility represented a life crisis. She interviewed many couples who were similarly troubled and concluded that the stress of infertility was similar to the stages of dying first described by psychiatrist Elisabeth Kübler-Ross, author of *On Death and Dying*: a person first denies his or her infertility, then is enraged by it, becomes guilty, and feels grief, and finally accepts the situation. Barbara Menning took her conclusion a step further. She believed that infertile couples might be able to help each other work through these stressful stages. Today, Resolve has grown to include chapters in many major cities in America, and other support groups that function in a similar manner have formed in communities across the USA. In Britain the principal self-help organization for infertile couples is the National Association for the Childless, 318 Summer Lane, Birmingham B19 3RL.

The Female Check-up

13
The History

Day 1 of Phase I is the most important part of the investigation. This is usually the time when the specialist and the couple establish a bond. Most couples welcome the opportunity to review the past in a relaxed, unhurried manner. One young woman who had already been through several years of unsuccessful fertility treatment said, 'I want to know what's wrong with me. Once I know, even if I don't like the answer, I can get on with my life. Not knowing is making me crazy.'

The medical history of both partners is a crucial diagnostic tool. Although the history is not proof of where the infertility lies, it will usually point the doctor in a specific direction.

Talking through the history is an emotional relief. However, many aspects of the history are intensely personal. Both partners may be willing to describe certain episodes to the doctor, but they may be reluctant to speak in front of each other. Abortion, venereal disease, childbirth, sexual encounters – all subjects relevant to the infertility – may be personal secrets. The astute doctor finds a way to protect each person's privacy and still get answers. In general, the doctor talks through the less private aspects of the history with both partners. More private questions are usually reserved for individual interviews.

One thirty-year-old man had fathered a child ten years earlier, when he was an unmarried law student. The mother was a married woman who let her husband believe he was the child's father. The lawyer, ashamed that he had never seen his own child, did not want to tell his present wife. Yet this information was an important clue; it indicated that the husband had been fertile.

Sometimes, letting out old secrets can help a marriage. Partners often carry around guilt burdens that are more imagined than real. Telling their secrets to each other alleviates stress and anxiety. Even so, the doctor never reveals a confidence without permission.

One young woman did not want her husband to know that she had had three abortions before she met him. Obviously, this information was crucial. The previous pregnancies, by another man, indicated that her present partner had a low sperm count or that she had a newly developed mechanical obstruction in her tubes. But again, the doctor did not mention the abortions in front of her husband. The history taking includes many such private areas, and the doctor should approach each with sensitivity.

The history-taking usually begins with routine matters. The doctor first explains the steps of the investigation: what you can expect to happen and when, and what you can expect to learn. A couple should not be surprised each time a new test is ordered, or disappointed each time a test fails to provide an answer.

The first question the specialist asks is, "Why do you think you have a problem?" Most of the time the chief complaint is something like, 'We have been trying for five or six years and haven't become pregnant.' Often, a feeling of frustration and sometimes anger is almost palpable in this early meeting, particularly when the couple has already been through some previous testing. Anger about the problem that has been thrust upon them spills over, and the doctor must try to listen to and accept a certain amount of anger. At this meeting the doctor will ask for any records of previous fertility tests, including temperature charts. Once this information is in hand, the woman's history-taking begins.

The history is an unravelling process, in which each thread needs to be carefully followed. Depending on individual circumstances, the doctor may change the order of the questions. But the eight basic categories are the same, and each is explored across a woman's lifetime:

Menstrual history
Childhood illnesses and injuries
Sexual history
Contraceptive history
Obstetrical history
Infections
Previous surgery
Psychosexual history

From the fertility angle, the four most revealing categories are menstrual history, sexual history, infections, and previous surgical operations. The first will reveal any disturbance in hormonal balance, and the last three will point to possible mechanical obstruction of the reproductive organs.

Menstrual History

In the battery of questions on menstrual history, the doctor takes the woman back to her childhood:

When did you start your menstrual flow, and do you recall having difficulty at this time? When did your breasts begin to develop? (Breast development and growth of pubic hair usually slightly precede or coincide with onset of menses.) Were these early periods regular or irregular? Once you started to menstruate, did you skip any months? These questions may reveal clues to possible complications in the hormonal axis connecting the brain, the pituitary, and the ovaries.

Positive Signs of Ovulation

The normal menstrual cycle is divided into two parts – the oestrogen phase and the progesterone phase, which begins when the egg is released from an ovary. If the cycle doesn't go through these two distinct phases, ovulation (egg release) does not occur.

Onset between the ages of ten and twelve, complemented by pubescent changes in the body, usually means a good menstrual flow and regularity throughout life. Regular periods suggest that ovulation occurs in normal cycles. Almost every woman occasionally has an early or late period, or even skips a period. We also know that the menstrual cycle is affected by emotional stress and illness. For example, it's not unusual for a woman to skip a cycle or have an irregular cycle during the fertility check-up. The irregularity is almost certainly caused by stress rather than by any physical dysfunction.

Some women feel a slight pain (mittelschmerz) midway in their cycle. The pain is caused by a minute amount of bleeding when the egg pops out of the follicle. Pain in this case is a positive sign that ovulation has taken place. The pain is sometimes accompanied by a little spotting, which is not abnormal.

Another positive sign that ovulation has occurred is aching in the legs and back just before menstruation begins, usually accompanied by some discomfort in the breasts. These cramps, called molimina, are caused by the peaking and initial withdrawal of progesterone. The withdrawal of progesterone also triggers menstruation.

Trouble Signs

Ironically, when a woman feels nothing, either before or during her period, she probably is not ovulating. Instead of entering the progesterone phase, her ovaries continue to produce a steady stream of oestrogen through the month and never shift to the progesterone phase.

On the other hand, history of severe menstrual pain is also a trouble sign, pointing to endometriosis. Teenage girls who suffer severe cramping may have early endometriosis. What families and doctors used to shrug off as adolescent dramatizing was often the beginning of a serious disease; if not caught early enough, endometriosis can destroy fertility. Endometriosis tends to run in families. If a woman's sister, mother, or aunts suffer from endometriosis, she may be a likely candidate.

The interval between periods is also important. Normal intervals vary from twenty-four to thirty-two days. Very short or long intervals or, more important, erratic intervals indicate that ovulation is absent or sporadic.

After reviewing a woman's past menstrual history, the doctor asks about her periods now. How the cycle performs today is the primary factor. If she has kept a temperature chart, the pattern of her present menstrual cycle will point distinctly to ovulation or lack of ovulation.

More than half of all female infertility problems fall into the category of ovulatory failure. Thus the doctor will spend quite a bit of time reviewing the menstrual history and temperature chart.

Childhood Illnesses and Injuries

In this battery of questions, the doctor is concerned with past childhood illnesses and injuries and family history. Any unusual medical event in the past can have an effect on future fertility.

The doctor may ask whether you ever had a straddle injury falling from your bike as a child. Did you ever suffer any injury to the abdomen? This kind of injury can damage internal reproductive organs. Even internal bleeding that stops by itself can cause adhesions in the reproductive organs. Surgery to correct such an injury may also create new scar tissue.

You will be asked if you ever received a blow to the head. Head trauma is dangerous because it can damage the delicate balance between the hypothalamus and the pituitary gland, which controls ovulation. A head blow in childhood can interrupt this balance, delay onset of menstruation, and permanently throw off the biological time clock.

Illnesses

The doctor may ask if you ever had a severe case of measles, especially one that caused abdominal pain. Occasionally, inflamed ovaries are a complication of severe measles.

He may also ask if there is a family history of thyroid disease or diabetes. Both diseases can affect fertility. Low or high thyroid production can disturb the axis connecting the brain, pituitary, and ovaries. Too much thyroid shows up in scanty periods; too little thyroid equates with excess bleeding. Evidence of thyroid dysfunction is usually picked up on the physical examination and confirmed by laboratory testing, but a family history is a risk factor.

Diabetes mellitus is associated with rapid weight loss, thirst, and frequent urination. When diabetes is present, the pancreas doesn't release insulin properly and the body's use of sugars is thrown off. As a result, many bodily functions are defective, including ovulation. A woman with undiagnosed diabetes who becomes pregnant has a 50 per cent chance of spontaneous abortion. Urinalysis, a routine laboratory test, will reveal signs of diabetes.

The specialist may ask if your mother took DES during pregnancy. DES is a synthetic oestrogen taken by many pregnant women in the 1950s and 1960s to reduce the risk of miscarriage. Female babies whose mothers took DES were sometimes born with a T-shaped uterus or unusual bands of tissue inside the vagina. Some data suggest that DES daughters have difficulty conceiving in adult life, an increased risk of vaginal cancer, and a propensity to endometriosis. A recent study suggests that DES daughters conceive as readily as other women but are more likely to enter labour prematurely, primarily because of structural defects in the uterus. A poorly shaped uterus cannot expand fully with pregnancy, and the mother has difficulty carrying the child to full term.

Metabolism

The loss or gain of as little as 5 lb (2·3 kg) can throw off a woman's menstrual cycle. Therefore, if your weight has changed recently, be sure to give this information. The appetite control centre is located in the hypothalamus, the part of the brain that releases reproductive hormones. Although the precise relationship is unknown, there is some link between appetite and menstruation. For example, menstruation usually stops with severe weight loss. This may be the body's natural protective instinct: by preventing pregnancy, which makes strenuous physical demands, the body conserves vital resources. Return to normal weight usually causes the menstrual cycle to resume.

Sexual History

The history-taking now enters a more personal realm, crucial to the investigation. The doctor's questions are designed to uncover possible mechanical obstruction of the internal reproductive organs.

It seems obvious that sex and fertility are irrevocably linked, but it's surprising how many couples wish to solve a fertility problem without ever delving into their sex lives. Accept it as a given that when you enter a fertility clinic personal questions will be asked purely in the interest of learning the cause of the infertility problem. Occasionally, sexual timing is off, and merely correcting the days on which sex takes place solves the problem. However, when a couple has not conceived for two or three years, it is unlikely that the cause is purely a matter of timing.

There are three important questions here: At what age did you first have sexual intercourse? How many male partners would you say you've had up to the present time? What types of encounters have you had?

The first question is asked because a young girl is much more susceptible to pelvic infection than an adult woman. The cervical mucus that guards against infection is not fully developed until a woman reaches maturity, usually at about eighteen. A woman who had her first sexual experience in her early teens may have developed a pelvic infection without knowing it, or she may recall being treated for some unexplained infection. The doctor will ask if she remembers any such occurrence, even if no specific diagnosis was made.

The number of sexual partners a woman has had over her lifetime is another critical question. With the high incidence of venereal disease across the country, the number of partners is directly related to the risk of venereal disease and pelvic infection: the greater the number, the higher the risk. Today, a single new sexual encounter carries a 15–20 per cent risk of pelvic infection; two new encounters, 30–40 per cent; three or more new encounters, 60 per cent.

The types of sexual activity are also important. For example, anal intercourse followed by vaginal intercourse presents a good chance of contamination in the vaginal vault. There are other, more unexpected routes of infection. Oral sex, for example, can lead to infection if the man has bad cavities in his teeth.

Infertility due to an allergic reaction – where a woman's body sends out antibodies that destroy sperm – may develop from either regular intercourse or oral sex. The lining of the vagina and the lining of the mouth are made of almost identical tissue. Antibody reaction can result from the presence of sperm in either location.

The doctor may also ask if you are having sexual relations with anyone else. The question is relevant. If a woman has more than one man in her sex life and does not use contraceptives, it's likely that the infertility problem is hers. It's improbable that all her sexual partners are infertile.

The specialist will ask if you feel pain during sex. Pain may have a biological or psychological origin. For example, a low oestrogen level makes the vagina dry and extremely sensitive. The hormones that prime the glands with mucus are under par, which suggests poor ovulation. Therefore, vaginal pain may indicate a hormonal disturbance. A narrow hymenal opening can also cause pain during intercourse. Pain on the right or left side during deep penetration suggests endometriosis. All these conditions need to be treated medically or surgically.

Occasionally pain is caused by a rare condition known as vaginismus, in which the vagina literally closes up during sex, making penetration nearly impossible. Vaginismus is almost always psychogenic in origin. Sometimes a woman really doesn't want to become pregnant or she fears sex for other reasons. The contraction of the vagina is genuinely uncontrollable. The psychogenic reason for vaginismus is usually buried in the past and often can be worked out with psychological and sexual counselling.

Contraceptive History

In line with the sexual history, the specialist will ask about the kind of contraceptives you have used in the past – rhythm method, diaphragm, birth-control pills, IUDs, and so on – and how long each was used. The reason for the question is twofold. First, if you did not use contraceptives or used them erratically and had many sexual encounters, you should have become pregnant. Second, some contraceptives can affect fertility. The rhythm and barrier methods are the least risky in terms of future fertility. The most problematic are oral contraceptives and IUDs.

Women who have used birth-control pills for a number of years typically require several months before their hormonal patterns readjust and ovulation resumes. IUDs that perforate the uterus can set up unseen infections. Even when these infections are detected and treated, they may damage the reproductive organs.

Obstetrical History

The next obvious question is, 'Have you ever been pregnant?' Previous pregnancy shows that you were able to conceive at one time. If so, it's likely that your present infertility problem is due to a new obstruction in the fallopian tubes; or the problem may lie with your partner. A properly performed abortion will seldom damage reproductive function. Today, abortion carries little risk of complications. However, women who have had illegal or improperly performed abortions may suffer infections and scarring that leave them infertile. In addition, a self-induced abortion with a coat-hanger or pencil can cause severe mechanical damage to the cervix and uterus.

If you have had a child before, the physician will ask about your obstetric history. So-called one-child sterility, in which a couple has had a child in the past but cannot conceive again, may be traced to one of two possible causes: either the couple had a fertility problem all along and were lucky once, or something happened in the interim to render husband or wife infertile. The key questions now concern the length of time it took you to get pregnant and any complications that arose during childbirth.

Three or four years of regular sexual exposure before pregnancy, without contraceptives, indicate that you were ovulating erratically or your partner had a low sperm count, or both. However, if you became pregnant easily the first time but cannot conceive now, it is likely that an obstruction has developed in the reproductive system.

Infection following childbirth suggests that the uterus or tubes may now be scarred. Severe loss of blood during delivery can lead to pituitary shock, called Sheehan's syndrome, which may cause both ovulation and menstruation to cease. Any complication arising from an earlier pregnancy can lead to infertility. For example, damage to the cervix during delivery may weaken the cervical muscles or affect the production of cervical mucus. A woman may become a chronic aborter. Damage to the cervix can be surgically corrected.

Infections

Pelvic inflammatory disease (PID) is the single most important cause of the rising incidence of infertility in Western Europe and the United States. The fertility specialist will ask if you were ever hospitalized or treated with an antibiotic for pelvic pain or if your doctor ever suggested that you may have had a pelvic infection. These are crucial questions. A problem serious enough to require antibiotic treatment is a strong clue that some mechanical problem now exists inside the pelvic cavity.

Pain is the main symptom; a pelvic infection may or may not be associated with fever. Any unexplained pain that seemed to abate with time may have been a pelvic infection. A ruptured appendix or other organs that become infected in childhood (bowel operations or hernias) can also cause tubal adhesions.

Venereal infections are particularly virulent in terms of invading the pelvic cavity and setting up a disastrous infection around the reproductive organs. Any past episodes of sexually transmitted disease should be recorded in the history.

Surgical History

If you've ever had surgery for a possible ruptured appendix, ruptured ovarian cyst, or other problem in the abdomen this could cause infertility. A ruptured ovarian cyst, which usually causes sharp, stabbing pain, may bleed into the pelvic cavity and cause scarring. In a recent newspaper interview, Dr Robert Winston, an infertility specialist at Hammersmith Hospital in London, reported that 68 per cent of the women who came to him for blocked tubes had undergone previous surgery in the pelvic cavity. In his opinion, their present infertility was a direct result of the earlier surgery.

Women who have been through surgery for infertility problems have a higher risk of developing internal adhesions. For example, the hysterosalpingogram, a diagnostic procedure that pumps dye through the uterus and tubes, can increase a woman's risk of pelvic adhesions. The chemical itself can irritate the tubes, or a secondary infection may set in. After the third such procedure, a woman stands a 25 per cent chance of developing adhesions. Ovarian wedge resection, a procedure that used to be performed to cure polycystic ovaries, can also cause problems. Women who have had this procedure have a 25 per cent risk of adhesions.

Refined microsurgical techniques reduce scarring, but for some women any surgery on the abdomen will create internal scar tissue. No one knows why. Some women who have had PID or surgical complications, or both, will have a perfectly clean pelvic cavity. Others who undergo minor abdominal surgery or sustain even a minor infection will develop rubbery adhesions all over the internal organs.

Psychosexual History

Emotional problems in themselves are rarely a cause of infertility, but emotions do affect the overall success of treatment. Worries about sex can reduce fertility. The questions the doctor asks concern family beliefs and sexual preferences, sexual assault, and incest.

Sexual Abuse

We now know that many women have been sexually abused in childhood. Many young girls are 'played with' sexually by neighbours, relatives, and even parents. Very often these assaults are kept secret. A woman's adult life may be so contaminated by these early experiences that she cannot derive pleasure from sex. Or sometimes she seeks affection through a multitude of sexual encounters. She may have unrecognized fears about sex and pregnancy. She may also feel guilty about her early experiences, even though she was the victim.

When a woman has been sexually abused in childhood, she is likely to have special emotional needs accompanying the physical problems of infertility. It's also possible that the sexual encounter resulted in an early, undetected pelvic infection. Since sexual abuse is usually a darkly held secret, her parents or GP may not have recognized the symptoms, putting down the infection as stomach ache, flu, or menstrual cramps. The doctor may have prescribed some antibiotics, or the pain may have gone away. The residual effect – scar tissue around the reproductive organs – remains undetected.

Some infertility patients are plagued with unwarranted guilt feelings, convinced that they are being punished for past sins. The guilt may be over a serious event, such as incest, or over a trivial episode, such as masturbation. Women raised in strict religious households often feel guilty if they enjoy sex. Guilty emotions weaken a person's power to cope with the normal stress of infertility, turning treatment into a hopeless cycle of frustration and failure.

When a woman appears to be suffering from such guilt problems, the doctor will ask her to share this personal information with the psychologist. In the ensuing psychological evaluation, the woman may be able to resolve some of her feelings.

Sexual Enjoyment

A woman doesn't have to experience orgasm to become pregnant, and many women have become pregnant under cruel circumstances when sex was a painful and unpleasant act. Even so, lack of sexual pleasure can affect fertility, particularly when a couple has a borderline fertility problem – that is, if the husband has a slightly reduced sperm count and the wife has some ovulatory difficulty. If sex is not pleasurable, there is less chance of having intercourse at the fertile time.

It is not unusual for a couple to experience sexual problems as a direct result of the infertility tests. To discover an underlying problem, the doctor may ask a woman if she usually climaxes during sex, as he needs to be aware of what is going on in the intimate life of the couple. A fertility expert can take tests, perform surgery, and prescribe drugs – but if a husband and wife aren't having sex, they cannot become pregnant.

One woman who had been trying to get pregnant for ten years had never reached orgasm. When asked how often she and her husband had sex, she replied, 'Whenever he wants it.' Clearly even if the physical problem were solved, the woman would have trouble getting pregnant.

With the retelling of past events, the pattern of the infertility problem begins to emerge. A history of irregular menstrual periods points to a hormonal problem. A suspected pelvic infection or any surgery in the pelvic cavity suggests a mechanical obstruction of the reproductive organs. If a woman's history points to neither of these problems, the physician will suspect an infertility problem in the male partner.

The history is not proof, but it is an early indicator of possible problems. The specialist's mind approaches each investigation like a sophisticated computer, taking in a thousand different variables, sorting them, and matching them up until a distinct pattern is perceived. The specialist draws no specific conclusions from the history, but lays the groundwork for the remainder of the investigation.

14
The Physical Examination

A fertility specialist unconsciously begins to make a diagnosis the moment a woman enters the doctor's consulting room. Although first impressions may give significant clues, they should not blind the specialist to other possibilities. For example, such physical characteristics as excess weight, a round face, hair on the upper lip, and acne suggest that a woman's infertility is caused by a hormonal imbalance. On the other hand, a very thin, aesthetic-looking woman with small breasts may suffer from a form of anorexia nervosa, which may upset the balance of hormones and cause menstrual problems. Good breast and hip formation and normal weight suggest normal hormonal function. In this case, the doctor will look for possible mechanical problems or infertility in the male partner.

However, observations of outward physical traits are soft signs that may not mean anything. For the most part, physical characteristics are genetically transmitted. Height, weight, body configuration, and hair growth are all a function of genes inherited from parents.

The External Examination

The medical history provides early clues; the physical examination ensures that nothing has been missed. A woman will be asked to put on a loose gown. The attending nurse checks her height and weight, takes her blood pressure, and collects a urine sample. A urinalysis will determine if her kidneys are functioning normally and may also detect diabetes and other problems.

High Blood Pressure

A slightly elevated blood pressure reading is a common finding, usually related to apprehension over the examination itself. If blood pressure is high, the doctor will repeat the reading at the end of the examination. If the reading remains high, the doctor may want to check it at weekly intervals to determine the cause. The most common form of high blood pressure, called essential hypertension, has no known cause or cure, but it can be controlled with medication. Essential hypertension develops over a long period of time, increasing steadily into a high-risk zone. It is an insidious disease that, left untreated, can lead to complications of heart disease, stroke, and kidney failure.

In rare instances, hypertension is caused by a tumour of the adrenal gland. The tumour causes the gland to overproduce a special class of hormones called steroids. Excess steroids alter salt and water metabolism and affect ovarian function. An adrenal tumour can also cause the blood pressure to rise sharply to potentially lethal levels. This finding, though uncommon, is extremely dangerous. Careful surgical removal of the tumour returns blood pressure to normal, balances hormonal activity, and restores ovulation.

Thyroid Hormone and Infertility

Thyroid hormone is crucial to health because it turns the thermostat of each cell up or down and controls the rate at which the body burns fuel. The gland is located in the hollow of the throat. The doctor will feel its size and shape with the fingertips. People with excessive thyroid production are usually insomniacs. They are always hungry and can eat enormous quantities of food without gaining weight. They are often nervous and irritable. A woman with high thyroid production usually feels hot and sweaty and her menstrual periods are scanty. Low thyroid production has the opposite effect: weight gain, even with low calorific intake, fatigue, sensitivity to cold, and heavy menstrual periods.

Like the ovaries, the thyroid gland is often turned on by the hormones coming from the pituitary. All these hormones are remarkably similar. If the thyroid overproduces, its excess hormone floods the hormonal axis and confuses communication between the brain and the ovaries.

Excess production of thyroid hormone is sometimes caused by a discrete tumour in the gland; or the whole gland area may be overstimulated by the pituitary. By putting a stethoscope over the thyroid, the doctor may hear the blood rushing through the gland, a sign of overactivity. He will also tap your knees; with excess thyroid hormone, reflexes are ultra-quick. You will be asked to squeeze the doctor's hand; a weak grip suggests excess thyroid hormone.

Too little thyroid hormone may be caused by too little iodine in the diet or by eating certain foods, such as rhubarb, that block thyroid production. Most often, low thyroid production is caused by a viral infection in the gland. Sometimes, the body becomes immune to its own thyroid and simply does not respond to the hormone. Goitre, a swelling in front of the neck – a disease that was common at the turn of the century – is a symptom of low thyroid production. Adding iodine to salt and other foods has almost completely eliminated the problem in this country.

Low or high thyroid production can cause the hypothalamus/pituitary/ovarian hormonal axis to go awry. A suspected problem can be confirmed or negated by a blood test.

Skin and Hair

The doctor will look at your skin and the distribution of hair on your body. Any unusual loss of hair may indicate malnutrition or a vitamin deficiency. It may also reveal a hormonal imbalance – low thyroid or excess of male hormones.

Particular attention is paid to the hair distribution on the upper lip, chin, and sides of the jaws. The doctor mentally correlates any facial hair with hair growth around the nipples and abdomen. Again, as far as fertility is concerned, body hair is only a soft sign. Hair growth is largely genetic. Certain combinations must be present before the excess hair is considered a valid clue to hormonal imbalance, and even then they need to be backed up by blood tests.

Facial hair accompanied by marked growth over the abdomen, upper legs, inner thighs, buttocks, and rectal area, plus a receding hair-line points directly to excess production of male hormones. All women produce male hormones; a little extra does not alter femininity, but it can interfere with ovulation.

Face and Throat

The doctor wil look at the nose, ears, mouth, and throat for any unusual discharge or bleeding. Any abnormalities here may be associated with a blood formation problem, such as leukemia or a viral infection.

He will also examine the eyes, which provide many clues to overall health. A slightly yellow cast may indicate early jaundice. Anaemia is indicated by pale lining of the under eyelid. Bulging eyes suggest an overactive thyroid gland.

Neck

A woman's neck is normally smooth and cylindrical. The physician will carefully examine the back of the neck for any thickening or presence of a fatty pad known as a buffalo hump. Like the distribution of hair, such a finding is not conclusive but suggests a possible chromosomal problem. Chromosomal defects are so rare that laboratory tests are not performed unless physical evidence is present or there is a family history of birth defects.

The doctor routinely listens to the lungs and heart. Through the stethoscope, asthma has a whistling sound; bronchitis or pneumonia creates a wet, gurgling sound. If you smoke cigarettes, the doctor is likely to hear a wheezing sound, a sort of combination of asthma and bronchitis.

A surprising new discovery at our clinic has taught us to pay special attention to heart sound during a fertility investigation. We recently observed that many infertility patients who required surgery for blocked tubes or other pelvic adhesions also had a heart murmur known as a mitral valve click. This click is not common in the general population – 5–15 per cent of normal women have it. But we are hearing the click in nearly all our surgical infertility patients.

As the heart contracts and relaxes, it normally makes a boom–boom sound. In these women we heard a boom–click–boom. The clicking sound is caused by a bulging valve, called mitral valve prolapse (MVP), slapping against the heart wall. To investigate the phenomenon, we began to test all new patients with ultrasound, a technique that uses sound waves to visualize internal organs on a screen. Of 125 women who had some form of pelvic adhesive disease, 100 also had a mitral valve prolapse. More important, when patients were under anaesthesia, a high-stress time, the heart appeared to speed up slightly and then slow down and occasionally skip. Normally, as anaesthesia is induced, the heart may accelerate due to the slightly irritating effect of fast-acting gases, but it does not skip unless it is in danger.

Several questions arise: Why did this occur so often in patients with pelvic adhesions? Is there a connection or is it a peculiar coincidence? What, if any, is the relationship between the MVP and infertility?

We believe that both phenomena, MVP and pelvic adhesive disease, may have a common cause – a flaw in the way the body builds connective tissue. Such a disorder may also explain why some women scar badly while others do not. However, this is highly speculative thinking, and conclusions await further studies. We may learn that MVP has no direct bearing on infertility.

Women with MVP appear to have an almost classic physical and personality profile. They are usually slender and very active. Symptoms vary from none at all to chest pain with exertion, unexplained fainting spells, palpitations, and occasional aching joints.

MVP does not appear to be a dangerous condition, and it does not mean cardiac disease. Dr Bruce Iteld, a cardiologist and consultant to the Omega Institute, believes that MVP is a normal variation of the healthy heart. (In fact, because people with MVP are usually athletic, they naturally protect themselves from heart disease and other illnesses associated with lack of excercise.) However, knowing that such a valve eccentricity exists can help the anaesthesia team during any surgery. With previous knowledge they might choose a lower acting, less irritating anaesthetic. Prior knowledge of the MVP also might prevent excessive medical intervention. If the skipping occurs they will know it is a natural function of this heart and does not need treatment.

· THE FEMALE CHECK-UP

Breasts

The physician will notice the shape and colouring of the breasts. As a young woman matures, her breast development responds to oestrogen produced by the ovaries. Full breasts indicate adequate oestrogen stimulation. Any interruption of oestrogen production can slow breast development down; an excess can cause rapid growth.

Sometimes breast tissue does not respond to oestrogen. This unresponsiveness occurs only rarely and is a family inheritance. Likewise, breast tissue may be overly sensitive to hormones and undergo excessive growth. This response is also an inherited trait. It is difficult to know whether very small or very large breasts are caused by too little or too much oestrogen, or by inherited tissue response.

Skin colouring can be important: Purplish streaks, called stria, across the breasts suggest rapid development. The upper skin layer stretches so thin that the underlying blood vessels show through. This kind of streaking is not usually relevant, unless it is caused by excess adrenal hormones. Only blood tests can reveal the precise source of stria.

Behind each nipple are milk glands. During the menstrual cycle these glands are influenced by oestrogen and progesterone, which causes cyclical swelling and occasional tenderness. Breast milk is produced by a special hormone from the pituitary known as prolactin. This hormone is normally released in high levels only during pregnancy and after childbirth. In addition to producing milk, it inhibits ovulation. If something goes wrong and the body releases excesss prolactin at any other time, the hormone will have the same effect – it may stop ovulation.

During the breast examination, the physician palpates each breast and feels under each arm for lumps. He also presses all four quadrants of the breast towards the nipple. A translucent discharge from the nipple suggests excess prolactin release. This is an unusual finding, sometimes caused by intense manipulation during sex. Ordinary sexual foreplay is not strong enough to bring prolactin induction, but rough sex can. Black-and-blue bruises, bite marks, even scars on the breasts are clues that manipulation may have been intense enough to raise the prolactin level. Biting can also result in infection of the milk ducts and may produce breast abscesses. Birth-control pills have been known to occasionally produce small pituitary tumours that can cause prolactin in the blood.

Abdomen

The colour and outer shape of the abdomen are important. Purplish lines across a large, protruding abdomen suggest excess adrenal hormones and are usually associated with similar purple streaking across the breasts. The doctor feels under the rib cage for any enlargement of the liver and spleen. An enlarged liver may be associated with jaundice, tumours, or hepatitis.

The liver is a clearing-house for used hormones. Each month oestrogen, progesterone, and other hormones have to be cleared from the body before a new cycle can begin. If the liver is infected (hepatitis), used hormones stack up in the blood, sending messages to the hypothalamus/pituitary control centre that they are in excess. The control centre responds by reducing production, and ovulation stops. Liver problems can be life-threatening and require the careful attention of a specialist.

The fertility specialist also examines the lower abdomen, the area where the reproductive organs are stored, for any unusual growths, such as fibroid tumours on the uterus. The locations of any surgical scars is noted.

The lymph glands or nodes, which are located in strategic areas of the body, are part of the body's defence system. They catch bacteria and viruses and stop the spread of infection. An enlarged lymph gland that is not sensitive to the touch may indicate past infection or other problems. Tender, enlarged lymph nodes on either side of the groin may indicate an active infection in the pelvis or lower extremities.

The doctor also checks the pattern of pubic hair growth. A diamond-shaped escutcheon growing up towards the navel suggests a higher concentration of male hormones. This is not a dangerous condition, but it may be a sign of hormonal disturbance such as polycystic ovarian disease, a common cause of infertility in women.

The Internal Examination

After completing the examination of the outer body, the doctor asks the woman to assume the gynaecological examining position, with knees up. This is a critical part of the examination.

The physician first checks the pubic hair for any mites or scabies. If a fungal infection on the surface of the vulva is suspected, the area is flooded with an ultraviolet light, called Wood's light; fungi will fluoresce under the light. The physician then carefully separates the labia and looks at the clitoris. An unusually large clitoris indicates a possible excess of male hormones.

Under the clitoris is the urethra, the short channel that drains urine from the bladder. The urethral opening should be clear and free of cysts or other abnormalities. At the same time, the doctor looks for excessive discharge from the vagina and for lesions or growths, such as venereal warts, syphilitic lesions, herpes blisters, or abscesses on the large lips.

He then slips a finger into the vagina and feels the two Bartholin's glands just inside the opening. If infection is present, particularly gonorrhoea, the ducts of the gland become inflamed and swell shut; mucus builds up inside, forming a cyst. If that cyst then becomes infected, it causes extreme pain. An abscessed Bartholin's gland may require surgical drainage and antibiotic treatment.

The Speculum

After examining the outer vulva, the physician opens the vaginal vault to look directly at the walls of the vagina and the cervix. Most women shudder at the sight of the cold metal speculum used to open the vagina. Fortunately, physicians have taken to warming the speculum first by placing it either in a special warming cabinet or in warm water. The new plastic speculums are disposable and more comfortable.

The speculum comes in three sizes: infantile, standard, and large. Insertion should never hurt. If you have regular intercourse the doctor will probably start with the standard-size speculum and decrease or increase the size as necessary. He places a finger on the lower part of the vagina and slides the speculum in over the finger so it will not scratch the walls of the vagina. He then turns the speculum and slowly opens the leaves, just enough to give a clear view of the cervix.

The doctor first observes the configuration of the vaginal vault, looking for two things: any separation or scarring of the vaginal wall, and the shape of the cervix as it protrudes into the back of the vagina. The cervix is normally a smooth mound of tissue that feels like the tip of your nose. In the middle is a small canal leading to the uterus. If the cervical mound does not protrude, but lies flat against the vagina, DES syndrome may be present. DES exposure is also suspected if the walls of the vagina seem to grow up over the cervical mound. Malformations such as these may cause pain during intercourse and may interfere with pooling of the sperm against the cervix. Ironically, previous surgery to correct malformations of the vagina and cervix may have created scar tissue, which also can prevent pregnancy.

Sometimes during childbirth, particularly if the baby is large, an incision called an episiotomy will be made along the bottom of a woman's vagina. If the healed incision lies too close to the rectum, a chronic vaginal infection can set in. The episiotomy can also weaken the muscles of the vagina and allow the semen to pour out after intercourse. If a problem is suspected, the physician will place two fingers in the vagina and ask the patient to contract her muscles. If the vagina does not contract, the episiotomy has interfered with the vaginal muscles. This condition can be corrected easily by surgery.

Minor Infections

Many infections can reside in the warm, moist environment of the vagina. In fact, at one time or another almost every woman experiences some kind of vaginal infection. Moniliasis, trichomoniasis, and gardnerella infection are the most common. These infections are so mild that they often remain comfortably bedded in the vaginal vault. Yet even common, innocuous infections can directly cause fertility problems by wearing down the cervical mucus. As the vagina's normal defence mechanism deteriorates, the stage is set for invasion by more virulent organisms – *Escherichia coli*, chlamydial, streptococcal, and gonorrhoeal bacteria, all of which have a devastating effect on the reproductive organs.

Minor infections can also indirectly kill sperm. As the body fights off the infection, vaginal secretions become more acidic and thus more hostile to sperm. Further, any infection causes white blood cells to proliferate. In the vagina, the same white blood cells that work to clear away foreign bacteria also attack sperm. Therefore even minor infections, which tend to ping-pong between husband and wife, require treatment with antibiotics.

A healthy vagina always has a whitish, clear coating over the pink skin. Red and irritated skin, with unusual discharge, may be infected. When signs of infection are evident, the physician can identify the organism by examining a sample of the discharge through a microscope or sending it to the lab for a culture. Correctly identifying infections in the vagina has helped solve many cases of 'unexplained' infertility.

Moniliasis

Monilia (yeast organisms) look like clumps of cheesy material along the ruffled walls of the vagina. The cervix appears inflamed, and the blood vessels are dilated. These fungal infections, which are usually odourless and not particularly dangerous, can be itchy and uncomfortable. A doctor can confirm moniliasis by taking a swab from the vagina, mixing it with a drop of alkaline solution on a slide, and looking at it under a microscope. Clusters of long rods and small budding spheres of yeast are *Monilia*.

Trichomoniasis

A bubbly, greenish discharge accompanied by a fetid odour is usually caused by *Trichomonas*. When magnified, the cervix will show small blood vessels shaped like antlers. The physician takes a swab of the discharge, places it on a slide, and adds a drop of salt water. Viewed through a microscope, the *Trichomonas* organism has an oval body with two or three tails that whip frantically, beating air into the mucus and giving the discharge its frothy quality.

Gardnerella Infection

Another common vaginal infection is gardnerella vaginitis, sometimes called haemophilus vaginitis. After moniliasis and trichomoniasis, gardnerella is the infection most often seen in the vagina, but it is difficult to identify. It creates a burning sensation and may mimic any of the other infections. It may show up as a grey pasty discharge. As with *Monilia* and *Trichomonas*, the doctor can check for gardnerella by mixing a sample with an alkaline solution. If gardnerella is present, the mixture will usually give off a fishy odour. The microscope will reveal clew cells – large, flat cells affixed with hundreds of tiny rod-shaped bacteria. If diagnosis is uncertain, a sample can be sent to the lab for culture confirmation.

These three infections, which are common in women, do not usually directly attack the internal reproductive organs. Once they are eradicated, fertility is usually restored. Much more dangerous to fertility is the newly identified organism called chlamydia, which invades the pelvic cavity and destroys reproductive function.

Dangerous Infections

Some infections are so virulent that they can eat their way through the cervical mucus and quickly invade the pelvic cavity. Once into the reproductive organs these infections throw off so much scar tissue that adhesions form all over the uterus and ovaries, and the delicate fallopian tubes are destroyed.

Identification is made by observation, microscopic examination, and laboratory cultures. Immediate treatment can limit damage.

Chlamydia

Until recently chlamydia could not be distinguished from an innocuous bunch of infections known simply as a non-specific vaginal irritation, which included allergic reactions to medicated tampons, vaginal sprays, soaps and toiletries. Today we have learned that chlamydia is, in fact, an extremely hazardous organism that directly invades the pelvic cavity. Chlamydia is still difficult to identify. If a physician even suspects that this bacterium is present, he will recommend an immediate course of tetracycline drugs in an effort to spread an antibiotic net wide enough to catch these elusive agents.

The only evidence of chlamydia may be a reddened vagina. Sometimes a woman feels a burning sensation and urgency to urinate. Chlamydia, which will only grow in a special medium, takes between two and five days to grow. A faster diagnostic test, known as chlamydiazyme, which can detect the organism in less than four hours, has recently been developed.

Ureaplasma

The physician should culture for chlamydia and ureaplasma at the same time. Ureaplasma has been implicated in the antibody reactions that some infertile women send out against sperm. Like chlamydia, ureaplasma is a traditional organism between a bacterium and a virus. Because both have fragile coatings, isolating and transporting the culture are difficult. These organisms are usually identified by swabbing the cervix and transporting the samples in a special medium to the laboratory. The samples are easily destroyed in transit, so the transport medium is the critical factor in making a successful diagnosis.

Gonorrhoea

A profuse yellowish discharge immediately suggests gonorrhoea or a bacterial infection caused by *Streptococcus* or *Escherichia coli*. The walls of the vagina will be red and swollen and usually give off a fetid odour. To identify the organism, the physician takes samples from the cervical canal, the vaginal pool underneath the cervix, the urethal opening, and the rectum.

Gonorrhoea specimens are fragile and need to be placed in an appropriate culture medium before they begin to break down. Each of the four samples is separately cultured in the laboratory. A preliminary diagnosis can be obtained by using a special stain on the sample and looking at it under a microscope. If a biscuit-shaped organism appears inside white blood cells, the infection is likely to be gonorrhoea. The lab will confirm the diagnosis.

The Pelvic Cavity

After removing the speculum, the physician places two fingers in the vagina and the opposite hand against the abdomen in order to manipulate the internal organs. It takes experience to read the organs blindly, using only the hands to distinguish the many organs that pack the abdominal cavity. If the patient is constipated, the physician may stop the examination and ask her to return on another day after taking an enema. It is virtually impossible to distinguish an abnormal mass or cyst from ordinary fecal matter in the intestines.

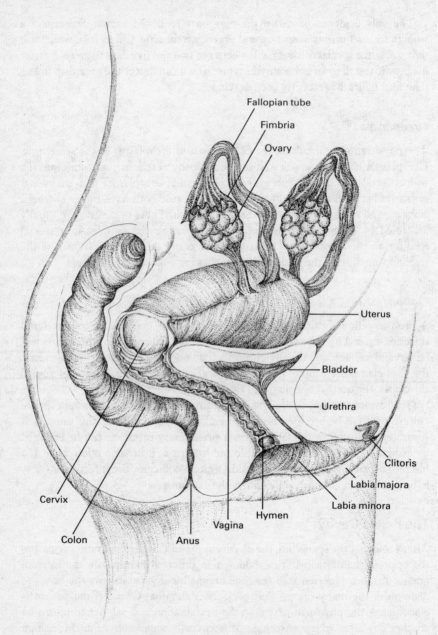

The female reproductive anatomy (side view)

Tilted Uterus

In most women the uterus is in a forward position, tipping at a right angle back into the cervix. Occasionally the uterus is in a mid position or even tilted back the other way in what is called the posterior or retroverted position. It was once believed that a so-called tilted uterus prevented pregnancy and countless infertile women who had a tilted uterus never received a full examination. One elderly woman told us that when she was a young bride she used to stand on her head for thirty minutes after sex. 'My doctor said it would help my tilted uterus.' It didn't. She never conceived. The tilted uterus also resulted in unnecessary operations. Not only did surgery to 'correct' the tilt fail to produce pregnancy, it often created a scar tissue around the troubled reproductive organs.

In fact, the position of the uterus has no bearing on whether a woman can conceive and deliver a baby. The position of the uterus is an inherited trait. If your mother's uterus was tilted, yours probably is too. (And you know your mother had a baby.) It's likely that women who were labelled with this mythological disorder had other, correctable infertility problems, such as blocked tubes.

A tipped uterus may hinder the chances of pregnancy when a couple already has a low fertility potential due to other factors – perhaps the man has a somewhat reduced sperm count and the woman has an erratic menstrual pattern. In that case, a change in sexual position might help. The woman might lie with her hips elevated by a pillow for thirty minutes after intercourse to keep the pool of sperm close to the cervical opening. Intercourse in the rear-entry position also facilitates sperm entry.

After examining the position of the uterus, the physician rotates the organ with the fingers, feeling its size and shape and checking for the presence of any fibroid tumours. Such tumours, which are common in women over thirty-five, can sometimes interfere with implantation of the embryo or cause miscarriage.

Adhesions

The main thing the physician searches for in examining the uterus is adhesions, rubbery bands of scar tissue that remain from old infections or previous surgery. When adhesions encapsulate the uterus, tubes, or ovaries, these organs lose their ability to function. Even light adhesions, if they bind delicate organs such as the fallopian tubes, can cause infertility. The physician will be especially alert for adhesions if a woman has used an IUD in the past or has had previous infection or surgery.

The organs on both sides of the uterus may have adhesions that may be so small that they cannot be felt, but the doctor can recognize any heavy scarring. Thickening on the sides of the uterus, organs that feel immobile, dense, and thick, all indicate the presence of scar tissue. If the organs do not move freely, but seem rigid and tied in place, pelvic adhesions almost certainly are present.

Endometriosis

The doctor will also check for patches of endometriosis, misplaced bits of tissue from the uterine lining. To the fingertips, endometriosis feels like small beading on the surface of the reproductive organs. The normally smooth, supporting ligaments of the uterus feel lumpy and thick, and the examination causes pain.

Small endometrial growths, which are enough to cause infertility, cannot always be detected by manual examination. An accurate diagnosis of endometriosis requires a full review of the pelvic area, possible only by a laparoscopy. Endometriosis may appear on the uterus, inside or outside the ovaries, and around the fallopian tubes.

The slender fallopian tubes branching off either side of the uterus are sensitive to the touch. A sharp pain experienced when the physician examines the tubes may indicate an ectopic (tubal) pregnancy, tubal abscess, or tumour. There is no way to tell from a pelvic examination whether a tube is open. Blocked fallopian tubes, a major cause of infertility in women, can be diagnosed only by surgical evaluation or special X-ray studies (see Chapter 16).

Moving down from the fallopian tube, the physician checks each ovary, examining it for any cysts or enlargements. The ovary, like a man's testicles, is extremely sensitive to pressure. Any large mass on the ovary may be caused by endometriosis, abscess from a pelvic infection, cyst, or other tumour.

The physician repeats the examination of fallopian tube and ovary on either side of the uterus. That completes the vaginal examination. He then withdraws his fingers from the vagina and inserts a finger into the rectum, checking behind the uterus to see if any endometriosis is present between the rectum and the vagina. The rectal examination is also the best way to discover the presence of rectal cancer.

Overall, if the pelvic examination shows that everything is normal, the possibility of physical obstruction to pregnancy is decreased. It is still possible that scar tissue is blocking the inside of the tubes or imprisoning the reproductive organs, or that endometriosis is present. But if the woman has never had a pelvic infection or abdominal surgery and if her physical examination reveals no abnormality, the odds of a physical obstruction are greatly reduced.

The physical examination takes about fifteen minutes to complete. Afterwards the doctor should spend some time with the woman and her husband, going over the preliminary findings and outlining a plan of action. Most of the time the specialist will have an intuitive feeling, based on the history and physical examination, of where the infertility problem lies. The tests that follow in Phase II will provide proof of the presumptive diagnosis and pinpoint the exact cause.

15
Laboratory Testing

A woman's ovulatory system is as intricate and meticulous as a Swiss watch. It functions solely to direct the body to develop and release a mature ovum each month. To achieve this single egg production, the system performs many clever manoeuvres in a precise, orderly manner.

The ovulatory system is so complex that more than 50 per cent of all fertility problems in women can be traced to some flaw in its interior workings. All these problems are lumped together in the general category of ovulatory failure or ovarian dysfunction. (Another 10 per cent of infertility problems in women are related to some byproduct of the system, such as the cervical mucus.) The flaw in the ovulatory system may be slight or it may be major. If even one small component misfires, the whole system may be thrown off. The only way to learn the nature and extent of the problem is to test the entire system systematically.

To produce an ovum, drop it on to the fallopian tube, and prepare a lush, receptive uterus, the female body employs its most important reproductive organs: the brain control centre (hypothalamus and pituitary gland), the ovaries, the uterus and fallopian tubes, and the cervix. Phase II of the female investigation is devoted to testing each of these components and the intricate relationships among them.

Before this testing begins, the husband's sperm is analysed. If his count is hopelessly low, the couple may decide not to pursue the rest of these tests. However, most of the time, even if the man needs treatment, the couple will continue the tests together.

A Brief Review

Each month the normal female reproductive cycle begins with hormonal activity in the brain. Since the hypothalamus is difficult to monitor, hormones sent out by the pituitary gland, measured by blood tests, are used instead. These pituitary hormones – FSH and LH – represent the 'brain hormones'. If they are present in adequate levels, both the hypothalamus and pituitary gland are presumed to be working correctly. If these hormones are not adequate, the problem may lie either in the pituitary or the hypothalamus.

The Menstrual Cycle

The normal menstrual cycle begins when the pituitary sends out a low level of both FSH and LH. FSH is steady, and LH is pulsing. Receptor sites in the ovaries pick out the FSH hormone from the bloodstream, and the ovaries begin to mature their eggs. They also begin to make oestrogen. For the first two weeks of the cycle, the ovaries release oestrogen until the hormone builds to a peak. The rise in oestrogen reflects the rise in FSH.

As the hormones build up, changes occur in other reproductive organs. Inside the uterus, the endometrium grows thicker as cells proliferate. Inside the cervix, mucus continues to hold its thick consistency until oestrogen begins to peak. The mucus is like a thick jumble of straws, a prickly fence that the sperm cannot climb over. The cervix retains this dense quality to protect against bacterial invasion.

When oestrogen begins to skim the hormonal ceiling, several events rapidly coincide. First, the thick cervical plug turns into a watery, saline-rich mucus, and the brittle straws straighten out into clear rods. The sperm can now swim up through the mucus easily. At the same time, the high level of oestrogen in the blood feeds back to the brain. In response, the brain sends a big pulse of LH to the egg follicle; the receptor sites on the follicle are pressured to receive the flood of new hormone, which kicks the egg loose from its follicle. Ovulation occurs.

At this moment, midway through the cycle, oestrogen is at its fullest, progesterone is low. FSH is elevated, and LH should be surging. The endometrium is five to ten times thicker than it was on the first day of the cycle. Within hours of ovulation, as FSH production is reduced, oestrogen begins to fall. In response to the LH surge, progesterone climbs rapidly. This quick rise of progesterone is critical, because it slams the window to the cervix. The mucus quickly returns to its thick, impenetrable state.

The receptor sites on the empty egg follicle (corpus luteum) now pick up LH from the bloodstream and continue to pump out progesterone. The thickened endometrium begins to change its texture. The proliferation of new cells stops; but the influx of progesterone causes the existing cells to change. The cells become 'secretory', filling up with fluid, protein, and sugars. They become wet and plush, highly receptive to a new embryo. As the cycle continues, each cell grows heavier, until its nucleus sinks to the bottom and the rest of the cell fills with fluid.

If the cells do not develop to their maximum, a fertilized ovum cannot cling

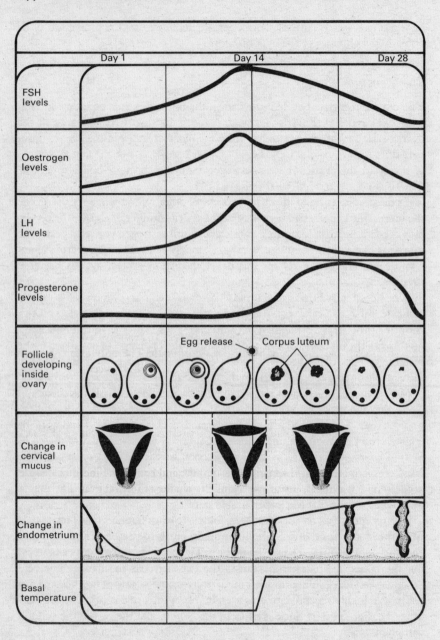

Day 1   Day 14   Day 28

FSH levels

Oestrogen levels

LH levels

Progesterone levels

Follicle developing inside ovary

Egg release   Corpus luteum

Change in cervical mucus

Change in endometrium

Basal temperature

to the inner wall of the uterus. Therefore, if progesterone fails for any reason – weak LH production or early death of the corpus luteum – the endometrium will also fail.

When the endometrium is fully developed, between day 18 and day 21 of the cycle, progesterone peaks. The hormone feeds back to the brain, which cuts off the supply of LH to the corpus luteum. The empty egg sac dies. Progesterone falls rapidly, and the endometrium begins to fall apart. Menstruation begins. (If pregnancy occurs, the corpus luteum survives and continues making progesterone to support the uterus through the first few months of pregnancy.)

For successful pregnancy, all parts of the system must work in consort. Something can go wrong in every one of these processes: in the brain, in the ovaries, in the endometrium, in the cervix. The laboratory tests described below evaluate each part of the system at the three critical portions of the cycle: beginning, mid-cycle, and end.

Timing Laboratory Tests

The crucial factor in getting good information from laboratory tests is timing. The tests reflect unseen events inside the body. The specialist cannot see hormones or watch the egg develop. But hormones can be measured in the blood, and ultrasound can provide a picture of egg growth. The only event that can actually be seen is the change in cervical mucus that usually precedes egg release. To get an overview of the hidden workings of the system, the fertility specialist must look at all the tests together so that any deviation in one test will stand out.

Laboratory tests in Phase II are based on the assumption that a woman's reproductive system is working normally. Each test is designed around a hallmark of the normal system. Three major tests are performed:

Blood tests, performed at the beginning, middle, and end of the menstrual cycle, measure the orderly release of hormones from the brain and ovaries.

The postcoital test, which should be performed 24-36 hours before ovulation, shows whether oestrogen has changed the cervical mucus in preparation for ovulation and whether sperm are compatible with the mucus.

Endometrial biopsy, performed towards the end of the cycle, shows whether progesterone has developed the lining of the uterus to its maximum.

Blood Tests (Hormone Testing)

Hormone testing is usually a matter of compromise. Only daily blood tests can give a fully accurate picture of hormonal action over a menstrual cycle, but daily tests are difficult to perform. Also, not every lab is equipped to perform radioimmunoassays, in which radioactive isotopes are added to the blood samples to follow the hormonal elements. To do these tests well, a lab needs the proper equipment, plus excellent quality control.

Even with such a laboratory, daily tests cost a small fortune. A good compromise is to run blood tests at the three critical points in the cycle: at the beginning, around the time of ovulation, and just before menstruation begins again.

The specialist wants to discover the pattern of hormones over the month – when hormonal production begins, when it rises, and when it falls off. He is looking for a synchronized pattern linking the brain, the pituitary gland, and the ovaries. The test results, plotted over a single month, give a finely drawn blueprint of the hormonal axis running between the brain and the ovaries. If hormones are involved in the infertility problem, the specialist knows which part of the axis is disturbed.

Stress or illness can cause the hormonal pattern to vary from month to month. Therefore, results are most reliable if the three blood samples are taken within the same menstrual cycle. Tests performed out of sequence are useless, as are tests performed at the wrong point in the cycle. (To save money, some physicians perform only one test at the end of the cycle. If something looks out of sync, they go back and take the others the following month. Unfortunately, valuable time is passing; worse, the test results come from two different cycles.)

How the Tests are Performed

Blood tests measure the pattern of the four reproductive hormones – LH, FSH, oestrogen, and progesterone. On day 5, 6, or 7 of the cycle, a woman goes to the lab for a baseline hormone test. The technician takes a blood sample and tests it for FSH, LH, and oestrogen. These three hormones should start off together, in a slowly rising pattern. The results give a baseline to compare with the second group of tests. At this early point, oestrogen is encouraging the endometrium to develop in the uterus and the ovum to mature within the ovary.

The woman returns to the lab around the time of ovulation, on day 13, 14, or 15, and the sample is repeated, testing for LH, FSH, and oestrogen. Now the specialist expects the test to show a higher level in all hormones. FSH and oestrogen should have just peaked, causing LH to surge.

Cervical mucus should also reflect the hormonal changes. A day or two before the test, the rising tide of oestrogen should have made the mucus clear and stringy. If LH has surged, the mucus will have regained its normal, thick consistency. This series of mucus changes suggests that ovulation has occurred. Under LH, the corpus luteum begins to make progesterone.

The final group of blood tests can be run anywhere from day 20 to day 24 of the cycle. This time, progesterone is added to the testing sequence. In the second half of the menstrual cycle, progesterone should reach its maximum level as oestrogen falls off. At this point, the lining of the uterus should have developed enough to receive a fertilized egg. The specialist performs an endometrial biopsy to examine a fragment of tissue from the lining. The biopsy should show that the lining has developed in accordance with the menstrual cycle. Again, timing is everything. Progesterone must build the endometrium in time for the ovum to implant. A delay in maturity of more than thirty-six hours will prevent implantation.

Hormonal Problems

No specialist expects all hormone tests to look alike, but any dramatic deviation from the norm will point to a flaw somewhere in the axis. Any problem, whether it is located in the brain control centre or the ovaries, is called ovarian dysfunction.

There are several possible dysfunctions, but the four seen most often can be described by the acronym PRRP (Prime, Respond, Release, Progesterone):

1. Failure to prime the ovaries: low FSH, no LH surge.
2. Failure of ovaries to respond: low oestrogen production.
3. Failure of egg to release: no LH surge or faulty LH receptor sites on the follicle.
4. Failure in progesterone production: poor development of the follicle, weak LH surge, or faulty LH receptor sites.

Screening for Prolactin

An important new screening test for prolactin has recently been added to the battery of blood tests. The prolactin hormone normally rises to high levels only after childbirth, when it stimulates the milk glands and also inhibits ovulation. For various reasons, some non-pregnant women produce extra prolactin. As a result a little milky fluid may leak from the nipples (galactorrhoea) and ovulation may be absent or erratic.

Excess prolactin can be caused by drugs, breast manipulation, infections, or small tumours in the pituitary gland. Whenever a raised level of prolactin is discovered, skull X-rays and pituitary scans are ordered immediately to detect possible tumours. Depending on the size, tumours may be treated by surgery or by drugs.

The Postcoital Test

The postcoital (after-intercourse) test dates back to the earliest experiments in fertility. In the 1860s an adventurous New York physician, J. Marion Sims, began a series of experiments to find out exactly how the sperm and egg got together.

Naturally, Dr Sims ran up against the same moral strictures that had hampered the earlier researchers, and he was forced to perform many of his experiments in secret. Some of Sim's tests were quite bizarre. For example, in one experiment Sims asked a man to have sex with his wife while she was under general anaesthesia. The wife became pregnant, proving that a woman didn't have to be orgasmic – or even conscious – to achieve pregnancy.

Sims also looked at the mix of male and female fluids after intercourse, the basis of the modern postcoital test. The year was 1869. This test was shunned by the scientific community, and did not become popular until 1913, when another physician, Max Huhner, began to use it. The test became known as the Sims–Huhner test.

The postcoital is a subtle test of compatibility and potential. Primarily, good postcoital analysis reveals the condition of the cervical mucus just before ovulation and the sperm's ability to swim through it. Careful analysis can also reveal other clues to infertility – the presence of infection, the activity of sperm, and the presence of antibodies.

Even though the postcoital gives some information about sperm activity, it is not a substitute for semen analysis. A sperm count tells precisely the number and quality of sperm present in the ejaculate – before they encounter the environment of the vagina. If the sperm are active and healthy in the semen analysis but turn up dead in the postcoital test, the specialist knows that the vagina and cervix are hostile receptacles. Furthermore, if a man's sperm is plentiful on semen analysis but only a few sperm wind up in the cervical canal, either there is some leakage from the vagina or the man's penis isn't reaching the target during intercourse. His sexual technique may need some modification.

A few specialists still believe they can derive enough information from the postcoital alone to evaluate the man's sperm. They are convinced that the postcoital provides the same information as semen analysis, without the embarrassment of masturbating into a plastic pot. If the postcoital is faulty, they go back and take a sperm count later. Again, this is testing out of sequence, starting at the end and working backwards, which confuses the analysis and lengthens the overall testing phase.

What the Test Shows

The postcoital test shows whether enough oestrogen has built up in the bloodstream to turn the cervical mucus watery and set the stage for the LH surge that should trigger egg release. Because the test is performed just before ovulation, it cannot prove that a woman actually ovulates. There is no guarantee that the LH surge will follow, that an egg will pop out of the ovary, or that the cycle will enter its progesterone phase.

However, the postcoital does show whether everything is in position for ovulation and whether the sperm can swim through the cervical mucus. The hallmark of a good postcoital test is a thin, watery mucus without white blood cells or other debris. The mucus pH must be alkaline enough to let the sperm survive up to six hours.

How the Test is Performed

In anticipation of ovulation, the postcoital test is usually performed on days 10 to 12 of a twenty-eight day menstrual cycle. This is a few days before the second blood test. If a woman has kept a temperature chart for the preceding two or three months, the specialist can pick the day more precisely.

Usually the husband and wife abstain from sex for two days before the test. Then, on the morning of the postcoital, they have intercourse without using any lubricants or douches. After sex, the woman remains in bed for thirty minutes to allow the sperm to ascend from the vaginal pool into the cervical mucus.

The couple (or the woman alone) comes into the specialist's clinic usually within two or three hours of intercourse. Some specialists feel that waiting up to six hours will give a better idea of sperm penetration into the mucus, without interfering with analysis. The woman lies down on the examining table, and the doctor aspirates a column of cervical mucus into a thin tube. As the tube is pulled out of the cervix, he immediately makes note of the consistency of the mucus.

Three samples are usually taken – from the opening of the cervical canal, from slightly further into the canal, and from deep inside the canal. The first sample is tested with litmus paper to check the pH. Normal cervical mucus is alkaline; acidic mucus suggests an infection or other problems. The second sample is allowed to dry on a separate slide to check for ferning (the quality of the mucus). The third sample is examined under a microscope to observe the number of sperm and their activity.

Sperm Activity. The specialist needs to determine how many sperm have reached the deeper recesses of the cervical canal. The presence of eight to fifteen active sperm in the small, highly magnified field of the examination slide indicates good sperm production and quality.

Compatibility. If the sperm are dead, there are two possibilities. Either they were dead on arrival or something in the woman's mucus killed them. 'Dead on arrival' can be confirmed by comparing the postcoital test with the semen analysis. If the semen analysis, which is performed on a freshly masturbated ejaculate, shows dead sperm, the problem clearly lies with the man. If the sperm count is good, the specialist must examine the woman's cervical mucus closely. Infection or antibodies in the mucus may be killing the sperm. White blood cells in the sample indicate infection; a clumping together of sperm suggests antibody reaction.

Abnormal Shapes. The specialist also looks for abnormal sperm forms. Distorted shapes suggest that sperm did not develop properly in the male testicles. How well the sperm swim is another clue. On a flat slide, sperm swim randomly in different directions. When the specialist tips the slide, healthy, mature sperm swim upwards, a perfect example of swimming against the resistant flow.

Checking the Cervical Mucus. Two simple tests confirm that the hormonal system has set the stage for ovulation: the spinnbarkeit test and the fern test. Spinnbarkeit measures the stretchiness of the mucus. (A version of this test is actually performed when the specialist draws a column of mucus from the cervix.) A small drop of mucus spun between two glass slides should be thin enough to stretch 8–12 cm without breaking. This threading, caused by a rise in oestrogen, is a good sign of impending ovulation. If the mucus is thick, scant, or greyish, either ovulation is not about to take place or it has already come and gone. Scanty mucus along with a flat temperature chart confirms lack of ovulation. If the temperature has already peaked, the test is too late.

The fern test confirms the change in cervical mucus. Mucus that has undergone proper changes becomes thin, watery, and salty. The sample of mucus on the glass slide that was set aside earlier should begin to dry into distinctive channels edged in salt. Under the microscope the channels form the pattern of a fern leaf. The more salt, the more ferning, and the stronger the evidence that ovulation is pending.

Checking the Cervix. The specialist always takes the opportunity to look directly at the cervix to see if the canal is open. Several factors may keep the cervical canal from opening. The most obvious is that the woman is not ready to ovulate. Or the cervix may have been damaged from previous surgery or infection. Dilated blood vessels on the surface of the cervix may indicate some type of acute or chronic infection.

The Abnormal Test

If any of the results of the postcoital test are abnormal, the test is repeated the following month. This is a standard principle of medicine. If the test is abnormal the second time, and infection is not present, then antibody testing is necessary. The simplest antibody test is to mix the husband's sperm with another woman's mucus. If the sperm are alive and active in a different mucus sample, then the specialist can be pretty certain that the wife is producing antibodies against her husband's sperm. Several other lab procedures can be performed to distinguish the nature of the problem.

In summary, the postcoital shows whether sperm and mucus are compatible.

Ferning: During ovulation the cervical mucus dries to produce a distinctive pattern.

It also shows whether the woman's hormonal system has set the stage for ovulation. The test that follows, the endometrial biopsy, offers more direct proof of ovulation.

The Endometrial Biopsy

The endometrial biopsy – analysis of a few cells scraped from the uterine lining – should reveal a dramatic progesterone imprint toward the end of the menstrual cycle. If cells show the influence of progesterone, the specialist can be reasonably sure that ovulation has occurred. If the cells show only the influence of oestrogen, the specialist can be certain that ovulation has *not* occurred.

Some doctors rely on the blood test for this evidence. However, the biopsy offers additional clues. Besides demonstrating probable egg release, it shows the quality of the endometrium. If the lining is not perfectly developed when the fertilized ovum arrives, the embryo usually cannot implant. Or it may implant and then silently abort within a few days.

Ideally, progesterone has primed the endometrium to its maximum. In the first phase of the cycle, the cells of the endometrium multiply rapidly. Now, in the second phase of the menstrual cycle, the cells stop dividing and change their content. On biopsy, the cells look different on each subsequent day of the cycle.

Failure of the endometrium to develop is usually caused by too little progesterone; sometimes progesterone is completely absent. The temperature chart is flat, and the blood tests show no levels. Ovulation did not occur. Sometimes ovulation occurs, but the progesterone phase doesn't last long enough to prepare the lining. Progesterone may fall off early, a condition known as luteal phase defect, or may be underproduced. In either case, the lining doesn't get enough hormone. Lessened progesterone does not always show up on blood tests and temperature charts, but it's likely to appear as a weakened imprint on the endometrial biopsy.

How the Biopsy is Performed

An endometrial biopsy is an outpatient procedure. The specialist introduces a hollow tube into the uterus, by way of the cervical canal, and strips off a bit of tissue from the endometrium. Sometimes a woman feels some cramping and may have slight spotting afterwards.

The Lab Report. The tissue sample is sent to a laboratory to be analysed by a pathologist. The pathologist reports which day of the cycle the cells appear to be taken from. The fertility specialist later reviews the pathologist's report in relation to all the other tests.

Backdating. To interpret the biopsy, the specialist must know when a woman's next period will begin, and then count backwards to the test day. For example, assume a biopsy is performed twenty-five days after your last period began. Your next period starts three days later. The pathologist knows exactly what the cells should look like three days before menstruation. (They should be fully developed and ready to receive an embryo.) If your biopsy matches, the endometrium has been well primed, and ovulation is presumed to have occurred.

Together with a normal temperature chart and normal blood hormone tests, the specialist has nearly infallible proof of ovulation – short of actually seeing the egg pop out of the ovary. Assuming the biopsy matches up properly, the specialist knows that ovulation has occurred and that the uterus is perfectly prepared to accept an embryo.

Can a Biopsy Interfere with Pregnancy?

Since an endometrial biopsy involves scraping tissue out of the uterus, theoretically it could damage a nascent pregnancy. We usually advise couples to use contraceptives during the test month on the offchance that they might conceive and lose the conceptus to the biopsy.

There is no conclusive proof that a biopsy can cause miscarriage. There is even some notion that biopsy improves the chances of fertilization. This is a strand of thought that runs throughout the investigation – that the fertility tests themselves somehow increase the chance of pregnancy. No one really knows how often infertile couples get pregnant during the investigation. It's true that a certain percentage of all infertile couples will get pregnant without any tests or treatment whatsoever. But until evidence builds up one way or the other, couples are usually advised to use barrier contraceptives (diaphragms, condoms, gels, or foam) during the test month.

Evaluating Phase II

If the laboratory tests are meticulously performed, by the end of one menstrual cycle a woman will know whether a hormonal problem exists. The test will show both the nature and extent of the problem. For the first time, the specialist's hunches will be backed up with evidence. If the system is slightly off, the chances of successful drug treatment are good. The more widespread the problem, the less positive the prognosis.

If all the components of Phase II are normal – and 50 per cent of the time they are – the fertility specialist can be almost certain that the problem does not lie with hormones, egg production and release, or uterine failure. The intricate reproductive system is working.

It's not unusual, however, for the temperature chart to look normal but for the blood tests and endometrial biopsy to show irregularities. Tests may have to be repeated. If the second tests still do not offer a firm diagnosis, the specialist usually proceeds to Phase III, the surgical investigation, which concentrates on the mechanical parts of the system. In fact, since it's entirely possible for a woman to have both ovulatory problems and mechanical problems in the uterus and tubes, Phase III usually proceeds on schedule even if the hormonal system is flawed. Between the two phases infertile couples are generally offered psychological counselling, which has often proved an unexpected boon to both the patients and physicians.

16
Surgical Testing

Phase III of the female investigation is performed in the hospital towards the end of the woman's next menstrual cycle, around days 20–25. This portion of the investigation includes:

1. Ultrasound to observe the shape of the uterus and to look for any tumours embedded in the walls of the uterus (pre-operative procedure).
2. Laparoscopy to view the outside of the reproductive organs.
3. X-ray studies (hysterosalpingogram) to see if the tubes are open and to pinpoint obstructions.
4. Repeat of endometrial biopsy.

These tests are part of the new medicine of the twenty-first century. They are based on such inventions as tiny, flexible microscopes that can enter the deeper recesses of the body through natural openings, and ultrasound, a technique that bounces sound waves off the body to create an image of the organs inside. These procedures are performed primarily to gain information, but they can also be used to correct minor mechanical problems in the reproductive tract.

Crude Beginnings

A few years ago only one test was available to explore the condition of the reproductive organs. This was the insufflation or gas test developed in 1919 by I. C. Rubin, a gynaecologist at Mount Sinai Hospital in New York. Dr Rubin devised a way to pump carbon dioxide gas through the cervical canal to determine if the fallopian tubes were open. He theorized that if the tubes were open, he would hear the gas passing through them. If he heard some hesitancy, something was out of order. And if the gas did not pass through at all, the tubes were blocked. Rubin's test soon became the one hope doctors could offer infertile women.

To perform the test, a doctor blows small amounts of carbon dioxide through thin tubing placed in the cervical canal. He then listens with a stethoscope as gas goes up the uterus and through the tubes. If the woman feels pain in one or both shoulders when she sits up, the tubes are supposedly open. The pain is caused by a gas bubble escaping from the tubes, floating under either side of the diaphragm, and irritating the phrenic nerve, which runs up to the shoulder.

At best, this is a crude test. It detects blockage only when both tubes are obstructed. (If one tube is open and the other is blocked, the test is positive.) And it reveals nothing about the extent of the blockage.

Some doctors continue to use the insufflation test today because it is easy and inexpensive. But it is unreliable and can be painful. One woman experienced such severe pain as the gas was pumped into her tubes that she left the clinic and never went back: 'I figured if it hurt that much right at the beginning, there was no way I could go through with the whole diagnosis.' This woman is still childless and is now past the age when she can get help.

Some gynaecologists still 'blow' tubes with the idea that the rush of air through the tubes may clear out minor obstructions. One of Dr Rubin's first patients supposedly became pregnant following the test. As we learn more about the nature and consistency of such obstructions, it seems unlikely that simply pumping air through the tubes will eradicate blockage. Most specialists today consider the test an archaic method of assessment.

The Rise of the 'Scopes'

From the time of the ancient Greeks, physicians have sought to inspect the inside of the body without cutting it open. The major problem was finding an instrument that was small enough to introduce through natural body openings and that could supply its own light.

In the early 1800s, Phillip Bozzini of Frankfurt built a system of mirrors and tubes that allowed candlelight to be reflected into the body via a long, straight tube. With this device, Bozzini inspected the nasal cavity, the vagina, and the rectum. This was the first endoscope, a general term that encompasses all telescopic instruments used to inspect internal cavities. Later in the same century scientists used similar devices to view the interior of the bladder (cytoscope) and the uterus (hysteroscope). Candlelight eventually was replaced by the electric light bulb.

One problem with all the scopes was finding a way to relax the body enough to introduce the instrument. Soon after the Second World War curare was introduced as a muscle relaxant, safe when used in small enough doses. (Curare, of course, is a deadly poison derived from a South American potato vine.) Introduced into the bloodstream, by way of a dart or spear, curare kills by relaxing all the muscles, including those that control breathing. In a hospital setting, mechanical respirators are used to control the patient's breathing, making the drug both safe and effective.

The greatest stumbling block to perfecting the interior scopes was finding a way to light the dark cavities of the body. By 1900 miniature telescopes with small light bulbs at the tip were in use. These early devices, called peritonescopes, had serious problems. The light was poor, and if the bulb burned out the instrument had to be withdrawn and reinserted. The most serious problem was that the hot light bulb could injure delicate body tissues. These scopes were dangerous and difficult to use.

The breakthrough came in 1952 with the development of 'cold light' – the use of quartz bars to conduct light from an external source to the tip of the endoscope. Soon after came glass fibre bundles, called fibre optics, that could carry light through rigid or flexible optical systems. With the invention of fibre optics, all the scopes were rapidly developed.

Today, different endoscopes can reach many of the hidden recesses of the body without major surgical invasion. The proctoscope and colonoscope can explore the rectum and colon. The gastroenteroscope, which is attached to a long, skinny tube that the patient swallows, offers a full view of the oesophagus, stomach, and duodenum. The hysteroscope lets a physician view the interior of the uterus. And the laparoscope, considered the diagnostic tool of the century, lets the physician view directly all the organs packed inside the pelvis and abdominal cavity.

Little wonder that modern fertility specialists are avid proponents of laparoscopy. It is the only procedure that can reveal obstructions and adhesions around the reproductive organs short of major surgery. It is the only sure way to diagnose endometriosis. It is the only way to actually observe where an ovum was ejected from the ovaries and whether the corpus luteum is in place. In short, laparoscopy is the only sure way to know exactly what's going on inside the reproductive tract of an infertile woman.

Even so, the procedure has its detractors. Some fertility specialists believe that a laparoscopy should be performed only if no infertility problem is found in Phase II. If some ovarian dysfunction is found, that problem should be treated first. If the patient doesn't get pregnant, a laparoscopy can be performed later. These physicians argue that you shouldn't poke around internal organs unless you have a good idea that something is wrong. Laparoscopy is expensive and inconvenient (a hospital stay is required), and like any surgical procedure it carries some risk to the patient.

These are valid arguments. But the fact remains that 40 per cent of infertile women have some mechanical obstruction and 25 per cent of infertile women have both ovulatory failure and mechanical problems. Without a laparoscopy, the specialist might prescribe powerful fertility drugs for a woman whose tubes were completely blocked.

Because it is performed under a general anaesthetic, laparoscopy does carry some risk. (It is usually the anaesthetic, not the surgery, that carries the risk component.) If you live in an urban area, however, it is less risky than getting in your car and driving across town to visit your doctor.

The fact that the procedure must be done in a hospital does make the test more expensive. (Costs can be reduced – and the efficiency of the overall check-up improved – by combining the laparoscopy with two other internal views of the pelvic cavity: ultrasound and X-ray studies.) By performing them in the hospital along with the laparoscopy and a repeat endometrial biopsy, the specialist gets the maximum results and the patient experiences less physical and emotional strain.

At the Omega Institute, the procedures are combined into one and carried out while the patient is asleep. (Ultrasound is performed separately, before surgery.) When the patient wakes up, the specialist usually knows everything there is to know about the condition of her internal reproductive organs. And, if there was an obstruction, the specialist may already have corrected the problem.

A Day in the Hospital

Ultrasound

Ultrasound is performed the evening before surgery. In this test high-frequency sound waves are sent out by a scanning device and transmitted to a small crystal placed on the surface of the body. The sound waves enter the body and echo back when they strike the surface of an organ. The echoes are converted into electrical signals and transferred to a video screen, where internal organs and structures are outlined in detail. The images on the screen are photographed, and the specialist studies them to learn valuable information about the patient's condition. (Sound waves are not related to X-ray and carry no risk to the patient.)

Ultrasound is completely painless, but it does have one awkward aspect. The patient has to drink volumes of water until the bladder feels uncomfortably full. The reason is that sound waves are best conducted through water – and the best way to wrap the reproductive organs in water is to fill up the bladder. It's not as easy as it sounds. One woman likened the process to a bucket brigade: 'The nurse kept bringing it, and I kept drinking it. You have to get to the point where you can't stand up and smile at the same time.'

Fortunately, once the bladder is filled up, ultrasound is carried out within a few minutes. The video-screen images clearly define the internal organs and can reveal tumours or cysts embedded in the walls of the uterus or ovaries. Ultrasound gives the surgeon a working blueprint for the laparoscopy. Even with the laparoscope, the surgeon would need X-ray vision to find these kinds of growths.

The surgical portion that follows is a minor procedure, requiring only short-term anaesthesia. The patient receives a light sedative, followed by an injection into a vein on the back of the hand or arm that makes her fall asleep immediately. After she is asleep, another injection relaxes all the muscles in the body; the anaesthetist inserts a soft tube into the patient's mouth and down her throat to supply a steady flow of anaesthetic gases and oxygen throughout the procedure. The surgeon then runs a catheter through the urethra to expel all the urine from the bladder. (A flat bladder gives a better view of the other organs and also prevents damage to the bladder itself.) The remaining tests are now performed in smooth, rapid sequence.

Laparoscopy

Before the invention of the laparoscope, the only way to view the pelvic cavity was to cut open the abdomen (laparotomy). The procedure required five to seven days in the hospital and a long, slow recuperation. Today the laparoscopy offers the same benefit – direct view of the internal reproductive organs – without a major operation.

With the laparoscope, a host of pelvic problems can be evaluated. The surgeon can trace the source of pelvic pain; diagnose endometriosis and know the full extent of the growth; access pelvic inflammatory disease accurately; examine the outside of all the reproductive organs for adhesions; and look for kinks along the fallopian tubes. As blue dye runs through the fallopian tubes, the surgeon can see if there is blockage and determine almost exactly at what point the obstruction lies. With a direct view of the ovaries, the surgeon can confirm that ovulation has taken place, something that all the other tests can only suggest.

Another tremendous advantage of the laparoscopy is that the surgeon can carry out minor procedures using the instrument itself. This unique instrument has reduced the need for abdominal surgery by about a third. Small cysts and scar tissue can be nipped out and mild endometriosis eradicated. In some hospitals, lasers are fed through the instrument to vaporize tissue.

Unlike the other scopes, which are introduced into the body through natural openings, the laparoscopy requires a tiny incision for entry. The incision, usually made through the navel, requires only a light anaesthetic; post-operative pain is minimal, and recovery is rapid. The incision is small enough to be covered by a Band-Aid; hence the term 'Band-Aid operation'.

The surgeon introduces a hollow needle through the incision and inflates the abdomen with a small amount of carbon dioxide. The gas easily raises the roof of the abdomen and makes room for the instrument, as well as giving the surgeon some manoeuvrability inside the pelvic cavity. Some laparoscopes have special lenses to enlarge the view of questionable areas, but for the most part the view is life-size.

Through the incision in the navel the surgeon inserts the laparoscope – a long, slender telescope with a fibre-optic light source on the end – into the abdomen. The operating table is tilted so the woman's head tips down. The slant causes the intestines to slide away from the pelvic organs.

Some surgeons make a second, tiny incision just below the pelvic hair-line. This second incision lets the surgeon introduce a probe into the abdomen to manipulate the organs. While the surgeon looks through the laparoscope, other procedures can be carried out through this second incision. If necessary, special forceps can be used to pinch off a tiny piece of the ovary for biopsy. The surgeon can cauterize endometriosis, take fluid samples from the abdomen, cut filmy scar tissue, recover lost IUDs that have perforated the uterus, or take cultures to detect infections.

Through the laparoscope the surgeon gets a first look at the reproductive organs. They are smooth-surfaced and glistening. Normally, all the organs are clearly visible and, even though tightly packed together, distinctly separate. The surgeon can move the delicate fallopian tubes easily with a probe. The flared ends of the tubes are dark red and moist. The surfaces of the small, white ovaries are pitted with scars from past ovulations. The uterus looks like a flat pear.

As the surgeon lifts each organ and peers around it and under it, translucent fragments of scar tissue tying organs together may be visible. Such webs are fairly common. In the wrong spot – for example, a tiny web holding down the fimbria so that it cannot pick up the egg – these fragments can interfere with pregnancy.

The surgeon looks for signs of endometriosis on the sides of the uterus, along the ligaments, and around the ovaries and tubes. Mild endometriosis looks like charred ashes – dark flecks scattered across the surface of the organs. Through the laparoscope these small bits of misplaced endometrial tissue can be vaporized with a laser, or the surgeon can use an electric probe to cauterize the spot.

Endometriosis that has spread throughout the pelvic cavity is much more difficult to correct. Often endometrial implants bury into the ovaries and begin to grow. Sometimes the surgeon sees an ovary that looks like a large blue egg, called a chocolate cyst. If the cyst ruptures, a thick, dark brown material oozes out. This is old endometrial tissue and blood. (The blue surface colour is caused by light reflection.)

The fimbriated ends of the fallopian tubes are another common trouble spot. These fringes, which are vital for picking up eggs, are so delicate that they scar easily. Instead of a flower-like opening, the surgeon may see a closed stump. Opening a clubbed fimbria is a major surgical procedure. The surgeon also looks over the length of both tubes; threads of scar tissue wrapped around the outside of the tubes can cause them to kink, trapping eggs on one side and sperm on the other.

Scarring around reproductive organs may cause them to stick together or stick to adjacent organs such as the bowel. Occasionally, scarring is so widespread that all the organs inside the pelvis are welded together. Through the laparoscope the surgeon sees a massive sheet of rubbery white tissue, the lumpy shapes of the reproductive organs barely distinguishable beneath the sheet.

In these severe instances even skilled microsurgery offers small hope of successful pregnancy. To free the reproductive organs, the surgeon must slice through the thick sheets of scar tissue; massive bleeding creates even more scar tissue. New laser techniques have improved the chances for pregnancy, but the odds in these cases remain relatively poor – about 40 per cent.

The surgeon looks at the ovaries to see if an egg has recently erupted from the surface, and if an empty egg sac (corpus luteum) is present. This is proof of ovulation. Occasionally, the egg develops but does not pop out of the ovary. Instead, a large follicle bulges on the surface of the ovary with no sign of rupture. Only 1 out of every 2,000 infertile women has this problem, called the trapped ova syndrome. The hormonal blood test may appear relatively normal. For some reason, however, the receptor sites on the surface of the follicle cannot pick up the LH surge, and the egg is trapped inside the ovary. Sometimes there just aren't enough receptor sites. Treatment involves a course of fertility drugs to provide an extra boost of LH at the time of ovulation.

Dye Studies

After all the organs have been examined on the outside, about three tablespoons of special blue dye are pumped into the uterus through the vagina while the laparoscope is still in place. If the fallopian tubes are open, the physician will see dye pour out of the fimbriae and spill into the abdomen. If dye does not come out – if there is blockage somewhere inside the tube – the surgeon can sometimes identify the trouble spot through the scope. The tube is usually slightly swollen at the point of blockage, and the pocket of dark blue dye can be seen through the skin of the tube. Obstructions can arise anywhere along the length of the tube.

If the surgeon cannot see where the dye meets the obstruction, an X-ray machine is swung over the pelvis to X-ray the organs. Normally, soft organs will not show up on an X-ray. But the special dye, a radio-opaque contrast material, fills up hollow places and shows up on the X-ray. On X-ray the uterus normally looks like a triangle, and the two fallopian tubes float like ribbons from either side; the dye flows out of the ribbons like a puff of smoke. If it meets an obstruction, the dye comes to an abrupt halt. Thus, the X-ray pinpoints the precise point of the blockage.

The dye test, combined with X-ray, is called a hysterosalpingogram. Since the procedure can be performed without anaesthesia, many physicians prefer to do it in the outpatient X-ray department of a hospital, in place of laparoscopy. By itself, however, the X-ray test offers only limited information.

By outlining the interior of the uterus and the fallopian tubes, the dye can reveal polyps, fibroids, and other growths inside the uterus and distinguish any anatomical defects. The dye study reveals nothing about the outside of the reproductive organs. Its primary benefit, one that no other test can offer, is pinning down the point of a tubal obstruction. For that reason, the Omega Institute uses the hysterosalpingogram only in conjunction with the rest of the surgical investigation.

Surgical Risks

Most women recover quickly from a laparoscopy, returning home the same day or the following morning. After the operation there is some minor pain and soreness in the abdomen, caused by the manipulation of the internal organs. One woman said she felt like she had been punched in the stomach. The aching disappears in a day or two. Some women experience slight pain around the neck and shoulders, which is related to the gas used to inflate the abdomen. This also disappears very quickly. Sore throat caused by the soft tubing used to administer the anaesthetic is another common after-effect of any general anaesthesia.

If the procedure is performed skilfully, the risk of bleeding, infection, or other complications is extremely low. (Fewer than three out of every 1,000 women who have the procedure experience complications.) In our view, the information gleaned from the procedure outweighs the possible risk.

Prognosis

As we have seen, some mechanical problems discovered during the surgical investigation can be corrected on the spot. Often, the specialist already knows from the physical examination that endometriosis or adhesions are present inside the pelvic cavity. The laparoscopy will assess the extent of the damage; if the disease is widespread, corrective surgery must be performed through a standard surgical incision.

At the Omega Institute, the laparoscope and the operating microscopes are hooked up to a videocamera so the patient's husband can watch the surgical investigation on closed-circuit television. The camerawork offers a multitude of advantages. It provides a permanent record of all procedures. It keeps the husband involved and eases some of his anxiety. Instead of pacing in the waiting-room, he can see exactly what the surgeon sees. The surgeon and the husband converse via two-way microphone. When the couple has come this far, husband and wife usually agree beforehand that if microsurgery should be required the surgeon will do it immediately, while the woman is still under the anaesthetic. If there is any doubt, however, the husband and surgeon can consider the problem together. If both are not confident in making a decision, they should agree to postpone the microsurgery until the woman recovers from the anaesthesia and can consult with them.

When Phases IV and V are Needed

Phases IV and V of the female investigation, which involve genetic evaluations, are performed only under certain specific circumstances: if any of the couple's relatives were born with birth defects or if there is a history of infertility in the family, if the woman has suffered repeated early abortions, or if any spontaneously aborted fetus was malformed. In these three instances, genetic evaluation is usually carried out before the other steps. If there is a high risk that the couple will give birth to a severely handicapped child, or if chromosomal testing proves that they are biologically incapable of conception, then they can pursue other options, such as adoption, without undergoing the extensive fertility evaluation.

Most women, however, will go through the testing, concluding with the surgical investigation. At this point, the specialist has a total view of the woman's infertility status. The laboratory tests in Phase II have indicated whether there is any ovarian dysfunction. If so, the specialist can try to correct the problem with fertility drugs. The direct view of the pelvic cavity in Phase III has revealed whether any mechanical obstructions block the reproductive organs. If so, the organs can often be reconstructed with microsurgery.

The chances of success in either instance are good, thanks to recent medical advances. It's possible that in a few years the chances will be even better, for fertility science is leaping enthusiastically into the twenty-first century. Only ten years ago, Dr Rubin's insufflation test was the only hope offered to infertile women. Today scientists are making babies in ways almost magical. They use high-powered microscopes and lasers to reconstruct the female reproductive system. They administer potent drugs unknown a few years ago to activate the hormonal system. And if this doesn't work, they can mix up brews of sperm and eggs in test tubes and produce babies out of this nearly invisible solution.

The Male Check-up

17
The History and Physical Examination

Urologists have not yet designed a definitive fertility investigation for men. This is not surprising in light of the fact that until very recently the only test available to men was semen analysis. If the count was sufficient, no further investigation was made. If the count was low, some half-hearted attempts were made to discover why, often followed by a routine dosing with thyroid or testosterone hormones. Doctors administered these hormones with the same medical expertise that travelling pedlars used in selling Chief Red Cloud's Magic Elixir to the pioneers – and with about the same effect.

They had little choice. No one knew why the counts were low, and no treatment was available anyway. Today, although the science of male infertility still requires major research, we are much further along. We now can identify many of the causes of diminished sperm production. And fertility drugs that act specifically on the brain control centre, which governs hormone production, have proved effective for some infertile men. Much of this new knowledge is a result of brilliant advances made in female infertility. By latching on to these female whirlwinds, men have taken a fast ride into modern medicine. The result is that some methods of diagnosis and treatment have been developed without a standard routine investigation. Scientists now are backstepping, to lay a foundation for a partially built house.

We know that male infertility usually results when several problems are combined. A single test, even one as broad-based as the semen analysis, cannot uncover all the problems. Even when a man has an adequate sperm count, he may have other problems that interfere with fertility. Physicians need to develop a routine extensive enough to pin down both direct and indirect causes of infertility. Fertility experts are now comparing the effectiveness of various tests, hoping that careful record-keeping over the next few years will point the way to a well-designed investigation. To chip out an approach and match it to the exacting standards achieved in the female tests, specialists need the cooperation of the male partner.

One burly young man dared the laboratory director to find anything wrong with his semen sample. 'There's nothing wrong with me,' he growled. 'I can have an erection any time of the day or night.' He spoke for a multitude of men who fail to understand that it isn't the delivery system fertility experts worry about; it's what's being delivered.

There is a terrible notion in the minds of men and women alike that an infertile man has lost his virility. Deep down, even the most sophisticated man believes that if he can't get a woman pregnant, he isn't a man. The next question he asks himself is, 'If I am not a man, what am I?' At this point in his interior dialogue, he may begin to wonder if he's losing his sexual potency or if he's a latent homosexual.

In fact, sperm production is not related to sexual prowess or to homosexuality. There is no known biological difference between heterosexuals and homosexuals; only the sexual preference is different. Furthermore, sperm production is a physiological mechanism, unrelated to sexual performance.

The Specialist in Male Fertility

All we know for certain about male infertility today is that about 50 per cent of the time when a couple can't get pregnant, the problem lies with the man. The nature of the problem and possible treatments are major areas of modern research. It's essential, therefore, that his part of the evaluation be performed by a scientist who specializes in male infertility.

Urologists specialize in diseases of the urinary system, including those involving the kidney and bladder. They treat both men and women. Urologists, or other specialists such as endocrinologists, may also specialize in male reproductive problems. These physicians are called andrologists.

The Approach

Male infertility needn't be explored erratically. The specialists at the Omega Institute have devised an approach to the male investigation which is as systematic as that for the woman. Every man begins with Phase I – a history and a physical examination, which includes simple tests to detect a varicocele, and semen analysis. If all systems are normal in Phase I, the man ends his portion of the tests, at least for the time being. However, both partners should meet with a psychological counsellor in Phase II of the woman's tests to evaluate the level of stress the infertility problem may be causing.

If a man has any abnormal findings during Phase I, he proceeds in a methodical fashion through the laboratory and surgical phases of his check-up.

The History

Before performing a semen analysis, the doctor should begin with a history and physical check-up. There are two reasons for this approach. First, more than anything else at this early stage of the evaluation, the doctor wants to establish a bond with the husband, to let him know that the medical team is concerned about his feelings and that his role extends far beyond the number of sperm he can produce for analysis.

The initial time spent with the husband can make or break the fertility investigation. A man may be called upon to contribute several semen samples. Under the best of circumstances, masturbating into a plastic pot is no one's idea of a good time. Letting a man know from the beginning that his physical and emotional well-being are just as important as his sperm count can smooth the way for the next, more arduous portions of the testing.

Second, good background information, combined with data gleaned from other men, may help scientists discover why some men are infertile and others are not. There are many missing pieces in the puzzle of male infertility, and solid background data may eventually uncover causes of infertility that today are completely hidden.

There is one more vital reason to take a history and physical check-up of the husband: to make sure that he'll be around to enjoy the baby when it comes. Many young men have never had a complete physical examination (men usually go to doctors only if something is drastically wrong), and many doctors would argue that such an examination is an unnecessary expense for young, healthy men. However, as an experiment, the andrology team at the Omega Institute performed complete examinations of a hundred young husbands. The wives had come to Omega for surgery, and the husbands, who also stayed in the hospital, generally had time on their hands. The andrology team – Dr Ronald Lewis, Dr Donald Bell, and laboratory director Deborah Bell – took advantage of that time to perform complete investigations of the men, administering sperm counts, blood tests, physicals and histories, semen cultures, and chest X-rays. Surprisingly, thirty of the hundred men, who were checked inside and out, turned out to have major undetected medical problems. These problems ranged from diabetes and high blood pressure to chest tumours and skin disease.

This finding convinced us that a fertility investigation provides a valuable opportunity for both patient and specialist. Evaluating the overall physical condition of a man who is thinking about starting a family can lead to discoveries that increase his lifespan. Many of the problems can be corrected through simple changes in diet and exercise; others can be eradicated by early surgery. If caught early enough, ailments such as diabetes and hypertension can be monitored and controlled before they do permanent damage.

For the time being, at least until a more precise male fertility evaluation emerges, we believe that a complete general medical check-up of the man, performed by an andrologist, is the best way to proceed.

Major Problems

The main purpose of the history is to rule out the big factors: genetic flaws that stop development of the testicles; mumps that occurred after puberty; cystic fibrosis in childhood, which is often associated with an absent vas deferens; undescended testicles that were brought down after the age of six. In most cases, these rare events spell sterility.

Mumps after the age of fourteen occasionally causes sterility, but in many cases the virus does not reach the testicles. If a man had mumps as a teenager, the doctor will ask if one or both of the testicles became swollen or sore. If not, there's a good chance that at least one testicle is still producing sperm. Even when both testicles are involved, some tubules damaged by the mumps virus may recover with time.

At the beginning of the history other broad questions are asked to eliminate gross infertility. These questions concern pain in the testicles, previous surgery, and hospitalization.

Pain in the Testicles. Any pain or swelling in the testicles is a sign of trouble. The pain can be caused by several factors, all of them hazardous to fertility. A sharp blow or injury is one cause. Torsion, a spontaneous event in which one testicle twists on its own blood supply, is another. A man has no doubt when torsion occurs because the testicle usually swells painfully and dramatically. Like any injury that causes pain and swelling, torsion is a medical emergency. Surgery must be performed within six hours to unwind the testicle before it shrivels up from lack of blood.

Many men who have lost one testicle to torsion have been told by their doctor that the other, normal testicle will compensate for the loss. In fact, these men are often infertile, possibly because of an antibody reaction. The theory is that when the first testicle swells up, the body sends antibodies to the rescue that can damage the sperm-producing cells in the other testicle.

Previous Surgery. Any surgery around the testicles, bladder, or penis can impair fertility. Hernia repair, surgery for undescended testicles, or removal of a testicle can sometimes bruise sperm-carrying ducts. Surgical removal of one testicle or removal of a lymph node in the groin can injure the nerves running to the penis and impair erection or ejaculation. Surgery around the aorta also may damage the nerve supply.

Hospitalization. The specialist may ask about other episodes that put the man in the hospital. If he was hospitalized for high or low blood sugar, for example, a malfunction may exist in the hormonal system. Any past neurological problems, such as headaches and muscle weakness in childhood, suggest a link to multiple sclerosis – which is, among other things, devastating to fertility. The specialist needs to know about any medication or treatment administered in the hospital that may be related to fertility. For example, chemotherapy has been known to affect sperm production.

The specialist will probe for congenital problems – particularly for malformations of the kidney and genitals – by asking if the man was ever hospitalized as a child. For example, the vas deferens and the kidney come from the same embryonic tissue. If a man was born with only one kidney, he probably doesn't have a vas deferens on that side.

A personal and family medical history is always taken to reveal a tendency towards diabetes, high blood pressure, heart disease, or other illnesses. From these major events, the fertility specialist works in widening circles, moving into the realm of more obscure problems that may cluster together to hamper sperm production.

Urological History

The urological portion of the history concentrates on the reproductive tract. The specialist asks about any discharge from the penis or pain during erection. Of particular concern is bloody urine, which may indicate kidney stones or kidney diseases involving infections or tumours. Bloody ejaculate is much less serious. These episodes, caused by an inflammation of the seminal vesicles, are usually transient and rarely require medical treatment. Most resolve themselves spontaneously within a day or two.

The specialist also asks specific questions about back injuries, back pain, pain down the legs, and numbness or tingling in the legs. All may be associated with nerve damage, which can extend to the nerve pathways to the bladder and penis.

Any history of urinary tract infection, even a single episode, is important. Because of the length of the male urethra, urinary infections rarely occur in men, unless there is an abnormality in the tract. A urinary tract infection involves the kidneys, ureters, or bladder. Bacteria from the infection can spill back through the urine and contaminate the prostate and other reproductive organs.

Other infections may directly attack the reproductive organs. Bouts of painful and swollen testicles may indicate epididymitis. Any infection that reaches the epididymus can scar and block the small channel, preventing sperm transport to the penis. Fortunately, epididymitis usually occurs only on one side.

Gonorrhoea and other venereal diseases seldom reach the vital internal organs of the male reproductive tract. But they are responsible for the high incidence of stricture disease in the urethra. The channel of the urethra scars down and becomes so narrow that a man may have trouble ejaculating and urinating. Other venereal infections such as non-specific urethritis, chiefly related to chlamydia, may affect the quality of the sperm. The doctor will usually follow this part of the history-taking with a general discussion of the dangers of transferring such infections to the female.

Finally, the doctor may ask if the man was ever treated by a urologist for any reason. If he has answered no to all other questions but answers yes to this one, the man has probably forgotten something important. Even if he can't remember the urologist's diagnosis, he may remember the symptoms and the prescribed treatment. The fertility specialist can work backwards and put the puzzle pieces together. Once in a while an important clue emerges with this question.

The Environment

Modern life seems to have a deleterious effect on fertility. We all take more medications and work in more stressful jobs. In men these activities may decrease both the quality and quantity of sperm.

The next battery of questions concerns drugs, cigarettes, allergies, and the environment in which the man lives and works. Modern drugs – the kind you smoke and the kind you ingest – can be important causes of infertility in men. Certain medications, particularly psychiatric drugs used to adjust mood – tranquillizers, mood elevators, and antidepressants – are known to depress sperm production or render a man temporarily impotent. Some psychiatric drugs will decrease the amount of the ejaculate or cause retrograde ejaculation. These problems are usually reversible when the drug is stopped.

Several studies have shown that prolonged use of cannabis decreases sexual performance and impairs the quality of sperm. The specialist will need to know if, and how often, the man smokes cannabis or uses other drugs. Too much alcohol has a similar effect: poor sexual performance and decreased sperm quality.

The fertility specialist almost always asks about cigarette smoking. Smoking is not thought to be related to infertility, but a man who smokes one or two packs a day may be grappling with a lot of stress, which relates overall to infertility.

This part of the history also includes questions about a man's job and his possible exposure to extreme temperatures and toxic chemicals. It is not yet known if extreme cold has an effect on sperm production, but if an infertile man works in a cold-storage plant, it would be an important footnote to his medical history, one of those little facts that may one day add to the science. Heat is thought to hinder sperm production. Working in a boiler factory or sitting for long hours in the cab of a truck – any prolonged exposure of the testicles to excess heat – may affect sperm. This is still an unexplored area in male infertility; we really don't know how much heat, for how long, would ultimately damage the sperm production centres.

Exposure to toxic chemicals can be dangerous. Men who work in the petrochemicals industry have a high incidence of bladder cancer, especially if they are also smokers. We are just beginning to learn about the side-effects of toxic chemicals, and the list is growing. Life-saving medical treatment may also result in secondary infertility. For example, chemotherapy and radiation treatments can break down the sperm production centres. When a young man receives such cancer therapies, the basic disease can be cured or put into remission, but the man may become infertile.

From a general discussion of occupation and drug use, the specialist may lead the man into specifics about his lifestyle. Regular use of a hot bath, sauna, or steam bath may affect fertility, although little is known about the specific effects of heat on sperm production.

The specialist will also ask if the man travels frequently. Once in a while a husband and wife will fail to conceive simply because they don't get together at the right time. The man may spend one week out of every month away from home; if that week happens to coincide with his wife's fertile midcycle, they won't get pregnant.

The specialist also asks a group of general questions – on athletic activity, weight and diet, whether the man consumes a lot of caffeine in coffee or sodas, whether he feels lethargic or has plenty of energy – to get some indication of his general physical condition and overall well-being. Basically, the goal is to get to know the man better. A man's emotional happiness is often reflected in his answers to this kind of question.

Marriage and Sex

Questions on well-being usually lead comfortably into conversations about marriage. The specialist always asks if the man has been married before and if he ever fathered a child with any other woman. If a man previously had a child, we know only that he had some fertility potential in the past. (Sperm production is a dynamic process; what may have been true a year ago may not be true today.)

As a matter of genetic counselling, unrelated to fertility, some doctors ask if the man has ever fathered a child with birth defects. If he has, and if he and his wife succeed in becoming pregnant, the new baby may have similar problems.

The doctor makes a special point of asking how long the couple has been trying to get pregnant – even though the answer may be known from earlier discussions – in order to assess the man's frustration level and what his feelings are about the infertility problem. He may also ask, 'If you cannot have a child, do you plan to adopt?' There is no 'right' answer to this question. Some couples have sorted out their feelings about adoption; others have not. The response merely gives the fertility team some insight into the man's feelings. Rather than answering a direct question, the man can share some of his thoughts with the doctor.

An effort is made to gauge the amount of stress the couple is feeling in general. Although the wife has answered similar questions, the husband's interpretations are sometimes quite different. Questions like 'Do you feel that infertility is having an adverse effect on your marriage?' and 'Has infertility harmed your sex life?' help the specialist home in on stress related to infertility. Another telling question relates to 'timed' intercourse. Many men feel that timing intercourse takes away spontaneity and drastically reduces sexual pleasure. More than one man has said that he feels like a sex object because he has to perform when his wife says he must, regardless of his own feelings.

Recent psychological studies conducted at our clinic indicate that some couples who feel great stress are unaware of their feelings. It's not unusual for a couple to describe an almost idyllic marriage. Everything is perfect. Husband and wife have ideal jobs, a wonderful sex life, model in-laws, and no arguments about money or anything else. They have only one problem – they're infertile.

For these couples, life's everyday problems get shunted aside as infertility becomes the overriding issue. Difficulties arise when the fertility problem is solved and the couple gets pregnant. Suddenly, all the other problems that were swept under the carpet rush up for an airing. The man and the woman choke in the dust of a thousand conflicts and problems for which they are unprepared.

Questions about stress and emotions will be explored in depth during the psychological evaluation. At this point the andrologist, like the gynaecologist who interviews the woman, is simply trying to prepare the ground and get the man accustomed to thinking about his emotional life.

The specialist may ask if the man believes his wife has any sexual problems. One husband claimed that he enjoyed sex, and so did his wife, although she almost never reached orgasm. This didn't seem to bother him. He said, 'I'm happy – and she's happy enough.' On the other side of the story, the wife said that she felt so distraught over the situation that she was having an affair with another man and was planning to leave her husband. This was the backdrop to the fertility investigation which they both continued to pursue. Fortunately they also chose to work with the psychological counsellor and were at least able to bring some of the underlying issues into the open.

It's easy to see that this kind of information can be crucial. Infertility requires careful, steady, rational evaluation and treatment. A couple under severe stress, struggling with emotional and sexual conflicts, is unprepared to cope with infertility.

The specialist will ask the man if he has any sexual problems. For a variety of reasons most men occasionally have trouble maintaining an erection. It is normal to lose an erection once in a while or to be temporarily impotent. The question is asked to gauge whether the man considers such experiences a problem. In young men such transient episodes are often caused by stress. A history of premature ejaculation, however, is almost always a matter of sexual training. The problem can be successfully treated with behaviour modification counselling.

Other questions relate to ejaculation and to the use of lubricants during intercourse. Painful ejaculation or absence of fluid suggests a blockage in the seminal ducts or a narrowed urethra and calls for careful investigation. Altered sensation during ejaculation – for example, if the penis or thigh becomes numb or if there is no sensation of climax – requires a thorough evaluation of the nervous system. Such findings in a young man suggest multiple sclerosis.

Lubricants used to ease intercourse may also affect fertility. Many seemingly harmless lubricants, even petroleum jelly, can kill sperm. Also, the need for lubricants suggests that something may be wrong with the woman's natural lubrication from the cervix and vagina. If her vagina remains dry during sex, she may be suffering from sexual dysfunction or a biological problem, such as low oestrogen production, or from poorly functioning vaginal glands.

Present Health

The specialist will ask a series of questions about present health. Certain illnesses, when out of control, severely deplete the body's energy, with infertility as one of the consequences. Severe diabetes, severe thyroid problems, and chronic renal disease can drastically reduce sperm production.

Significant weight gain or loss, without any change in diet or exercise habits, may indicate an underlying hormonal disturbance. Weight gain and loss are often caused by emotional anxiety or depression, but they may also have more serious implications. Weight gain suggests a weakened thyroid gland; weight loss suggests diabetes or possible malignancy.

Headaches may indicate sinus trouble – a condition that has a new, unusual connection to infertility related to excess mucus in all the ducts in the body, including those that carry sperm. Headaches or dizziness may also be caused by a tumour of the pituitary gland, which can be associated with infertility. Such a tumour pushes on the optic nerve and may cause a loss of peripheral vision.

Any difficulty swallowing or neck pain may indicate an enlarged thyroid gland. Shortness of breath, coughing up blood, and chronic coughing suggest heavy smoking or bronchitis. Chest pain and irregular heatbeat suggest cardiac problems or thyroid disturbances. Pain in the lower legs may be related to poor blood supply. A history of vomiting blood suggests ulcers; passing blood in the stool suggests haemorrhoids or an infection or malignancy in the intestines; hepatitis or jaundice is usually connected to liver dysfunction. Skin rashes, itching, and ulcerations on the skin that do not heal may indicate underlying disease such as diabetes mellitus. Again, all these questions concern general health and may not specifically relate to fertility.

Previous Sperm Counts

Before concluding the interview, the specialist will ask about any previous sperm counts – how many were performed and when, whether the results were generally positive, consistently abnormal, or erratic. New semen analyses are always performed but earlier counts provide a good basis for comparison.

The Physical Examination

The physical examination is a general assessment of a man's health; only in one place does it specifically focus on infertility.

The examination begins with a check for fever or high blood pressure. The specialist then observes the shape of the cranium and hair pattern – a habit instilled from the earliest days of medical school – and looks at the proportion of the head to the rest of the body. An overly large head suggests a possible pituitary tumour. Bald patches in a young man suggest hormonal imbalance.

The examination proceeds to the man's ears, nose, mouth, and throat. Using an ophthalmoscope, the physician checks the blood vessels in the back of the eyes; their appearance correlates with the blood vessels throughout the body. Peripheral vision is also checked; diminished vision suggests a pituitary tumour. The specialist examines the neck carefully, looking for any signs of enlarged lymph nodes, and runs a finger along the thyroid gland, which sits just underneath the Adam's apple. Any enlargement in this gland suggests thyroid disturbance.

Heart and Lungs

Through a stethoscope, the specialist listens carefully to the lungs to detect any abnormal breathing pattern. Asthma, bronchitis, and smoking all may make abnormal sounds in the lungs. The heart is checked for any abnormal beats. The unusual mitral valve click, often heard in infertile women, also occurs in about half the men examined in our clinic. (It occurs in only 10 per cent of the general population). Whether the valve is involved in infertility is uncertain, but we speculate that it may be connected to another common finding in infertile men: varicocele. At the moment, mitral valve prolapse (MVP) is merely an interesting finding and requires further study.

If a click is observed, the andrologist asks the cardiologist on the team to investigate; if the man later requires surgery for any reason, the anaesthesiologist will be aware of the MVP and govern the anaesthetic accordingly.

Abdomen

With the patient lying down, the physician explores the abdomen through a stethoscope, listening for any abnormal sounds. The intestines should make a gurgling sound each time the man takes a breath. The physician feels for any enlargement of the liver or spleen as well as for any mass suggesting a tumour.

The man stands up for the specialist to check for the presence of a hernia. Hernias occur when internal organs poke through the inguinal canals, the two openings in the abdominal wall. The physician runs a finger alongside either side of each testicle, up to the canals, and feels for the presence of a hernia on either side.

Genitals

The doctor now begins the portion of the physical examination that deals directly with infertility. The penis is checked for any skin lesions or warts, and the tip of the penis is examined to make sure the opening is in the right place. Some men have a rare condition called hypospadias, in which the urethra opens underneath the shaft. This defect occurs during fetal development. If the opening is misplaced, sperm may not be able to reach the desired target inside the vagina. Severe hypospadias, in which the opening is well down the shaft, is usually associated with other congenital defects. Men who have these kinds of problems usually know about them and have received medical advice or surgical treatment in childhood.

The specialist compresses the scrotum between thumb and palm, using the fingers to distinguish each testicle, the coiled epididymis, and the vas deferens, which runs like a cord up the back of each testicle. The testicle feels like a firm, smooth ball. The small coil of the epididymis is softer and slightly tender. If it is exquisitely tender and tense, epididymitis is suspected. Scars suggest previous infections and possible blockage.

Routinely, the physician measures the testicles with callipers and makes a written note of the size and the date of measurement. The main reason is to see if both testicles are approximately the same size – an observation that may prove important later if a varicocele shows up.

The specialist will usually take the time to show a man how to examine his own testicles for signs of incipient cancer. Carcinoma of the testicles is the leading cancer in men between twenty-five and thirty-five years of age. If it is detected early enough, surgery offers a better than 90 per cent chance of survival. Late detection demands treatment with surgery, radiation, and chemotherapy; the survival rate drops significantly. A man should examine his own testicles for lumps or masses, much as a woman examines her breasts. Upon examination, the surface of the scrotal sac should be smooth; when the scrotum is compressed, it should be easy to distinguish the vas and epididymis from the body of the testicle. A lump or hard spot anywhere on the testicle should be checked immediately by a doctor.

Looking for Varicocele

Varicocele, thought to be a leading cause of infertility in men, can usually be detected in the physical examination. A varicocele occurs when the valves inside the veins that carry blood back to the heart break down or are missing. Blood pools up in the lowest portion of the veins. In the case of the testicles, the bundle of dilated veins almost always develops on the left side, but it can occur on the right and occasionally turns up on both sides.

A varicocele is not always easy to find. In some men it bulges dramatically; in others it is completely flat. Its size and shape, however, seem to have little bearing on its effect – and it is imperative that its presence be detected. The doctor asks the man to stand up, hold his breath, and strain down, as if he was having a bowel movement. Blood is pushed down the veins towards the testicles. If a large varicocele is present the veins will balloon up.

But a varicocele doesn't always swell enough for the physician to perceive the change with the fingertips. Since even a small varicocele can affect fertility, the andrologist continues to search, using more sophisticated techniques. The Doppler stethoscope, an ultrasound magnifier used by obstetricians to listen to fetal heartbeats, can help. By listening for the pumping sound of the artery, the fertility specialist locates the spermatic cord. The veins are wrapped around the artery. The artery makes a soft, whoosh-whoosh sound as it pumps blood into the testicle. As the patient holds his breath and strains down, all the blood should go in one direction. If a varicocele is present, however, the physician will hear a loud rushing sound that drowns out the whooshing of the artery. This is blood regurgitating back against the broken or absent valves of the vein.

A new thermogram technique also helps locate a varicocele. The patient places his testicles against a heat-sensitive plate impregnated with cholesterol crystals. The plate measures heat levels and changes colour in response to temperature; colours range from brown (slightly warm) to green (warmer) to bright blue (hot). If one testicle registers 1·5° F (0·8° C) warmer than the other, a varicocele is almost certainly present.

The 3 × 5 in (7·5 × 13 cm) plate, large enough to encompass both testicles, is set into a frame attached to a Polaroid camera, which photographs the colour change. Usually the plate turns brown, clearly outlining the shape of both testicles. If a varicocele is present in one testicle, it will photograph bright blue, while the other testicle photographs light brown.

With all three techniques – physical examination, Doppler stethoscope, and thermography – the majority of varicoceles can be detected. It is not yet known which technique is the most efficient. Some doctors believe that if a varicocele cannot be detected on the physical check-up, it's not big enough to worry about. At our clinic we use all three techniques on every man who comes for an infertility investigation. By doing so, we hope to learn which method gives the best results.

Not every varicocele requires surgical correction. If the semen analysis shows a highly stressed pattern, surgery will usually help.

Rectum

After a thorough exam of the genitals, the doctor shifts to the rectal area. The patient is asked to turn round and bend over, with his elbows on the examining table. The doctor inserts a finger into the rectum and feels the sphincter muscle, just inside the rectal muscle, constrict around it. He also checks the prostate gland, which is analogous to the female cervix and feels very similar, like the tip of the nose. The man can feel the doctor touch the prostate. If the gland is tender and seems infected, he will massage it to try to express a little fluid through the penis for a culture.

The prostate is not a common site of infection in young men, but if infection does set into this gland it can be difficult to treat. Certain prostate infections can be dangerous if they transfer to the female partner. Finally, the doctor reaches the length of a finger into the rectum in search of any masses or other abnormalities that may be developing deep inside the rectal cavity.

After the rectal examination, the doctor runs both hands down the man's legs, checking to see that the legs are the same size and shape. The skin of the legs and feet are examined for any ulcerations. The skin over all the body is checked as well. Since people rarely see their own backs, the back is examined for any unusual warts or moles that may be early signs of skin cancer. Sores that don't heal suggest diabetes; skin changes are associated with vascular disturbances. The physician also taps the knees to check the reflexes. Excess thyroid hormone causes ultraquick reflexes.

Finally, with his fingertips the physician feels the pulse points in the wrists, along the legs, and in the neck to obtain an overall assessment of the blood supply. The pulse should feel about the same in both the lower and upper part of the body. If it doesn't, blockage of blood flow should be suspected. The lymph glands in the groin, the sides of the neck, and the armpits are also checked. Any enlargement suggests infection. A tender enlargement suggests an active infection or inflammation. A growth that is insensitive to touch indicates a possible malignancy or past infection.

The physical evidence must be matched with other facts. If the patient is weak and tired, has recently lost 20–30 lb (9·1–13·6 kg), and has rock-hard lymph nodes, a malignancy should be suspected. If the node is soft and movable and no other symptoms are present, it is almost certain that the node is merely a remnant of a past infection.

The physical examination concludes with a routine chest X-ray and electrocardiogram. Laboratory tests include a complete blood count and platelet count as well as tests for syphilis. A urinalysis reveals the presence of protein, pus cells, or blood in the urine. Other standard lab tests include biochemical screening for a variety of enzymes that provide clues to heart, nutritional, and other abnormalities.

Again, these tests explore a man's overall health. Records are carefully indexed and stored for future computerized analysis using many different variables. For example, in a few years we may discover that a mitral valve prolapse correlates with a varicocele, and that both correlate with infertility.

The final step in Phase I is the semen analysis, the premier diagnostic tool of the male fertility specialist.

18
The Modern Semen Analysis

Male infertility is related almost exclusively to the number and quality of sperm that are released into the vagina on orgasm. Thus, the semen analysis is still the best method of evaluation for the physician who specializes in the male reproductive system.

When expertly performed, the modern semen analysis is much more than a sperm count; it is a group of subtle tests on the seminal fluid. Primarily, the analysis describes the character of the seminal fluid and indicates whether the sperm are moving and how many sperm have a normal size and shape. Semen analysis may also give clues to problems related to the sperm transport system and to outside influences (varicocele, stress, infection) that may be contributing to low sperm production.

How much information ultimately is derived from the test depends largely on the technician who performs it. An expert will wring every possible bit of information from the analysis. An unskilled technician will touch only the surface. Unfortunately, there is no uniform procedure for performing the analysis. Specialists hold many different views on when to collect the specimen, how long to wait before making the analysis, and what indicates trouble in any of the various parts of the test. Since most specialists now agree that semen analysis is more than a sperm tally, the procedure begs for standardization. Until a single standard is defined, semen analysis should always be performed by a laboratory technician who specializes in the technique.

Today, many fertility centres consider the analysis of seminal fluid a speciality in itself. The hallmark for the modern male investigation and semen analysis was set by two pioneers in this field, Drs Richard Amelar and Lawrence Dubin, urologists at the New York University Medical Center. At the Omega Institute two special andrology laboratories are directed by a technical coordinator who oversees all the male testing. The coordinator has the opportunity to meet with each man and discuss the analysis with him. If a man is nervous about the test, the coordinator talks it over with him, explains the various techniques, and answers his questions.

The method of semen analysis described here has been refined in our laboratory over the past seven years. As new tests are developed, the analysis will be further refined. Promising tests will be added, and those that yield inadequate information will be dropped.

Collecting the Sample

The collection process is the foundation of all subsequent testing. If the semen is improperly collected, all test results are invalid.

The specimen is obtained by having the man masturbate into a glass jar or a sterile plastic pot. Many specialists insist that the specimen be produced at the laboratory, so that the semen sample is not exposed to any changes in temperature or other damage in transit. Immediate testing also lets the technician observe changes in consistency that typically occur moments after ejaculation.

Even though the man is usually given a private room in which to produce his specimen, semen collection is an awkward process. We are among those who prefer an on-the-spot specimen; fortunately, one of our labs is located in a hospital where patients have private rooms that they can share with their wives. Even so, some men are extremely upset at the prospect of producing a semen sample. More than one man has fainted dead away when asked for a specimen.

Most doctors recognize the stress factor in collecting a semen sample; if they cannot provide comfortable facilities near the lab, they stretch the rules and let the man produce the sample at home, and deliver it to the lab within an hour. Since emotional turmoil seems to influence the volume of semen produced, if a man has trouble producing a sample, the fertility specialist should make every possible concession to help him.

Sometimes a man simply cannot masturbate, no matter how much privacy he is given. One man tried several times to produce a masturbated sample, but each time the volume was minuscule. When he used a special, non-spermicidal condom to collect semen during intercourse, he produced an excellent full-volume sample. This kind of specimen is not perfect – bacteria on the surface of the penis contaminate the specimen to some extent, and some semen may be lost or damaged in the process – but it is better than no specimen at all. Some men's religious tenets forbid both masturbation and the use of contraceptives; these men may be able to use the special condom with a pinhole made halfway down the sheath so that the condom is not a true contraceptive.

If these alternatives do not meet a man's needs, he can practise coitus interruptus, withdrawing from intercourse in time to catch the entire ejaculate in the container. This is the least desirable collection method because it's virtually impossible to catch that first drop of fluid, and the first drop counts the most. If all else fails, or if for any reason a man simply refuses to contribute a semen sample, the postcoital (after-intercourse) test, described in Chapter 15, will provide a barely passable substitute.

When to Collect the Sample

Because a man's reproductive system is relatively constant, the semen analysis can be performed on any day of the month. A man does not have to save up his sperm before testing. The best analysis will come from a sample taken following a man's usual interval of intercourse. If he usually has sex twice a week, then a three-day interval is best. However, if he ejaculates more frequently than once a day, the specialist will probably ask him to abstain for a day before testing. Or samples may be taken at two different intervals to see if the sperm count is being depleted by too frequent ejaculations. Abstinence for two or three days usually gives the best results.

The Seminal Fluid

The first thing the laboratory technician looks at is the quality and nature of the seminal fluid. Within three to five minutes following ejaculation, the semen turns to a pearly white gel. Biologically, the purpose of the transformation is to help the sperm stay close to the cervix, instead of spilling back out of the vagina. The semen retains this thick consistency for 20–30 minutes, and is then transformed back to a liquid state. As it liquefies, the white semen becomes translucent. A brown stain running through the semen may be traces of blood; a deep yellowish tinge may indicate inflammation or infection.

Viscosity

By examining the semen sample immediately after ejaculation, the technician can observe its transformation from gel back to liquid. The technician draws the semen up into a pipette and watches it drip back from the tip in clear droplets. If it comes out in a thick, viscous string, the sperm may not be able to swim through the semen. Fertility problems can result. The thickness may be a natural condition, or it may be caused by a bacterial infection.

If thick semen proves to be naturally viscous, as it is about 40 per cent of the time, high doses of vitamin C may help, although this treatment has not yet been proved valid. If the high viscosity is caused by bacterial infection, antibiotic therapy should clear up the infection, and the semen should resume a more liquid state.

Volume

The technician measures the volume of semen. A normal volume is 2–4 ml, depending on the length of time between ejaculations. If the man has abstained for longer than forty-eight hours, the volume may be relatively high.

Low Volume. About 95 per cent of the ejaculate is produced by the prostate gland and seminal vesicles, with a little bit more coming from the Cowper's glands. About 2 per cent of the ejaculate is actually sperm. Low semen volume is unusual, unless a man ejaculates more than once a day. In any case, it does not necessarily mean that the sperm count is also low. However, low volume can impair transport of sperm and thus interfere with fertility.

If the volume is low, other tests in the analysis must be matched to the finding to try to pinpoint the cause. The fructose test (described below) indicates whether a blockage in the ducts is impeding the passage of fluid from the seminal vesicles. If sperm are found in the urine sample, the ejaculate is going backwards into the bladder instead of forwards out of the penis. Such retrograde ejaculation is usually caused by impairment of the bladder neck or urethra. Both conditions may be treated surgically or medically.

High Volume. High semen volume can also be a problem because it dilutes the density of sperm and seems to depress their motion. High semen volume cannot be altered, but fertility can be increased by using a split ejaculate or coitus interruptus. Since the first part of the ejaculate contains 80 per cent of the sperm, the husband withdraws from intercourse as soon as he begins to ejaculate. The sperm reach the target before they are flooded out by the excess fluid.

If coitus interruptus fails, artificial insemination may succeed. In this case, the husband is asked to collect his ejaculate in two jars. The first jar holds only the first few drops of the ejaculate; the remainder is collected in the second jar. The laboratory technicians do a complete analysis of both samples. In most instances, the first sample contains the greater number of sperm, with the best structure and swimming ability. The couple then tries artificial insemination by husband, using the first part of the ejaculate (see Chapter 28).

pH

A sample of the semen is measured on a scale of 1–14 for acid or alkaline properties: 1 is the most acid; 14 is the most alkaline; 7 is neutral, the pH of water. The pH of fresh human seminal fluid is usually slightly alkaline, between

7·0 and 8·5. However, wide variations exist and, unless extremely deviant, are not necessarily a factor in infertility.

The Count

Sperm are evaluated on three main points: their travel power (motility), their number, and their shape (morphology). To reach the fertilization site in the female fallopian tube, sperm need to score well on all three counts.

Motility

Motility – the sperm's ability to swim – is evaluated in two ways: by the number of sperm that are swimming and by the quality or grade of their movement. Within one hour of collecting the specimen, the technician examines a drop of seminal fluid under a high-powered microscope. Regardless of how many sperm appear in the drop, the technician notes what percentage are moving. For example, if ten sperm appear in the high-power field and only five are moving, the sample has a 50 per cent motility.

The technician then assigns a grade to their swimming ability, anywhere from 0 to 4: 0 implies no motion at all; 1 implies that only the tails are wagging; 2 implies that the sperm are swimming moderately well; 3 implies active swimming and reasonably straight motion; 4 means the sperm are moving in a straight line with good power.

The technician is looking for a motility index score, arrived at by multiplying the number of moving sperm by their average grade. This index is often used to determine the man's potential fertility. For example, 50 per cent motility multiplied by a grade of 3 gives a motility index of 150. A motility index of 150 or better indicates good fertility potential; 120–150 is a grey zone; and below 120 suggests a low fertility potential.

If there is a problem with motility or grade, a timed motility study is performed to see how rapidly the sperm quality deteriorates over a three-hour period. Occasionally, if a man has abstained from ejaculating for more than ten days he will produce many dead sperm in his ejaculate. More common causes of dead sperm are infection and sperm antibodies, both of which require special testing (see below).

Number

The technician counts the sperm visually with the help of a hemocytometer, a counting plate with four sixteen-square grids. Some technicians use a mechanical counter, which gives a speedier count than the visual method. However, the mechanical counter is less accurate and does not allow the technician to observe the structure and motility of the sperm.

To begin, the technician looks for the total number of sperm per cubic centimetre (cc) of seminal fluid. The semen is diluted by a factor of 100 with a solution of formaldehyde and salt, which fixes the sperm in place so they can be easily counted. The technician counts the number of sperm in each sixteen-square grid, adds the totals together, and divides by four to get an average. This number is multiplied by one million (10^6) and then multiplied again by the number of ccs in the total volume of semen.

How Many Do You Need? A rule of thumb, called the 'rule of the 6os', defines a normal sperm count: 60 per cent motility, 60 per cent normal forms, and 60 million sperm per ejaculate. However, there is a large variation in the norm. Any sperm count of 40 million per ejaculate or more, with good motility, should be enough to produce a pregnancy.

Many couples have achieved pregnancy with counts of less than 40 million. Counts of 20–30 million per ejaculate are considered low, but if all other factors are good and the woman is fertile, pregnancy is still possible. In fact, most specialists believe that as long as some sperm are present and moving, there is always a possibility of pregnancy.

Too Many Sperm. Every once in a while a man will produce too many sperm. The semen is choked with sperm; instead of swimming freely, the sperm clump together. The best treatment in these instances is artificial insemination, using a split ejaculate. Several new insemination techniques may also solve this sort of problem. New sperm enrichment techniques let the technician select the best sperm from the entire ejaculate, suspend them in a fresh medium, and inject these prime sperm into the woman's uterus.

Shape

Definite guidelines regarding size and shape distinguish normal sperm from abnormal ones. Every man produces some abnormal sperm in each ejaculate. In a typical analysis, only about 60 per cent of the sperm are normal in all respects. The technician carefully observes the shape of 100 sperm in the sample. The body of each sperm is assessed, from head to midpiece to tail. A number of variations can be spotted:

Normal

Abnormal midpieces

Cytoplasmic droplets (membrane still clinging to sperm, indicating a sperm that has not matured fully)

Irregular, shapeless heads

Large heads

Small heads

Tapered heads

Double heads

Round, immature forms without tails

Coiled tails

Double tails

White blood cells (these tend to look like immature sperm, so a special stain is used to distinguish between the two kinds of cells)

In the best of circumstances, about 40 per cent of the sperm in a man's ejaculate are deformed – their tails are curled or they have two heads; or they drift sluggishly through the semen. It is interesting that the ejaculate of our near-primate kin, the monkey, has only about 10 per cent deformed sperm.

Do defective sperm make defective babies? Experiments in *in vitro* fertilization, which have cleared up many fundamental mysteries about the life process, have shown almost conclusively that a deformed sperm cannot penetrate an egg. First of all, it swims so poorly that it dies of old age before it reaches the fertilization site in the fallopian tube. Should one such sperm succeed in reaching the thick ovum, its deformed body would be unable to compete with the smooth projectile shape of the normal sperm.

The Fructose Test

Fructose, a sugar produced by the seminal vesicles, is present in all normal semen. If the technician sees sperm in the sample, fructose is invariably also present. If sperm are missing from the semen, a fructose test can help pin down the source of the problem. The technician adds a chemical reagent called resorcinol to a portion of the semen and heats the mixture. If the semen turns brownish red, fructose is present. If the sample does not change colour, it is said to be negative for fructose.

If the test is negative, the technician assumes that the seminal vesicles are blocked, preventing both sperm and fructose from entering the ejaculate. Blockages can be surgically corrected. Sometimes, instead of a blockage, the seminal vesicles and the vas deferens are simply missing. If the test is positive,

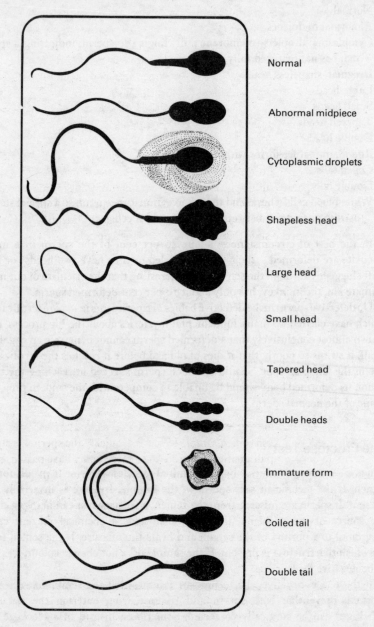

Normal

Abnormal midpiece

Cytoplasmic droplets

Shapeless head

Large head

Small head

Tapered head

Double heads

Immature form

Coiled tail

Double tail

Abnormal sperm

the seminal vesicles are functioning normally. This means that the absence of sperm may be caused by a blockage further down in the epididymis, or that the testicles are not producing sperm.

The fructose test, then, is an indicator. If few or no sperm are present in the ejaculate, the fructose test will eliminate or confirm one possible cause – blockage in the ejaculatory ducts – but nothing more.

Cultures

Before the semen analysis is considered complete, cultures are made for various organisms. One culture is taken for routine analysis of any bacteria present in semen. A separate culture is performed for a micro-organism called ureaplasma (mycoplasma), which will not grow in ordinary media. Another organism, chlamydia, which is very difficult to culture, is usually identified by antibody tests or by a special slide that glows if chlamydia is present.

When present, any of these organisms can cause sperm to clump or die. Such infections are also easily transmitted to women and can destroy the female reproductive organs.

Agglutination

Sperm agglutination – sperm clumping together like bits of iron on a magnet – can occur naturally or can be caused by infection or antibodies. Sperm antibodies can be found either in female mucus or in semen. The effect of antibodies on infertility is still ambiguous, and the problem is difficult to distinguish from infection.

If an agglutination problem is suspected, the technician will run a timed motility test on a fresh semen sample to see how quickly the sperm clump. If the sperm do not clump dramatically until two or three hours have passed, then the good swimmers have had enough time to reach the uterus. If the sperm clump within the first hour, there is a problem. Routine cultures for bacteria will help distinguish the cause of agglutination. If no infection is found, the laboratory analyst will proceed with antibody testing.

Antibody Testing

The existence of antibodies that immobilize sperm is one of the most hotly debated issues in infertility today. Interest in sperm antibodies grew out of research on couples whose infertility could not be explained. The investigation of many infertile couples proved normal in every way, except that the man's sperm grouped together in clusters. Apart from this unusual behaviour, the sperm were normal in appearance.

This peculiar clumping led researchers to speculate that some foreign protein that immobilizes, clumps, or kills sperm is either attached to the sperm or present in the seminal fluid of the man or the vaginal fluid of the woman. Immunologists devised tests to try to identify substances that might account for this bizarre behaviour. But so far the protein structure of antibodies in seminal fluid has not been scientifically isolated. Even so, logic suggests that they do exist, and that the answer to the antibody problem will be found in the near future.

Today several tests are being performed to discover where the antibody is coming from. Most of these tests involve separating the sperm from the seminal fluid and re-suspending them in neutral fluid. If the sperm do well in the fresh medium, it is assumed that the sperm themselves are free of antibodies. The original seminal fluid is then mixed with new sperm known to be free of antibodies. If the fluid causes the test sperm to clump, it is assumed that the semen is defective.

In Britain some laboratories are performing the MAR test (mixed antiglobulin reaction) – to detect antisperm antibodies in semen – as part of the routine

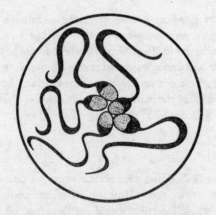

Sperm clumping head to head (agglutination)

semen analysis. Most infertility clinic laboratories are now able to do the Kibrick test to detect antisperm antibodies in the blood of both men and women.

Once antibodies are presumed present, what can be done about them? Andrologists currently use two techniques to reduce antibodies. They attempt to block antibody production in the male by administering steroids, or they try to remove the antibodies by washing the sperm in special solutions. The sperm are then re-suspended in a fresh medium and are used to inseminate the woman

---

How Semen Analysis Identifies Problems

When any of the following problems are observed during semen analysis, the test will have to be repeated at least once. If the problem consistently appears on subsequent analyses, most men will proceed with the rest of the male tests.

Varicocele
The sperm count may show sluggish sperm that appear to have lost their vitality. Typically, the count has many young or immature forms. The motility index may be abnormal for men with a varicocele.

Absent Sperm Production
Absent sperm in the semen may be caused by blockage anywhere in the transport system; absence of sperm also may be caused by failure of the sperm production factories in the testicles.

Blockage in Ejaculatory Ducts
If the blockage is in the ejaculatory duct, no sperm or fructose is present in the semen. However, if the blockage occurs lower in the vas, fructose will be present, with few or no sperm.

Infection
If infection is present, the semen will contain white blood cells (pus cells) and dead sperm.

Antibodies
Antibodies are suspected when sperm appear in clusters, clumped head to head, head to tail, or tail to tail, and no infection is present. Many sperm may be dead.

Low Count
A low sperm count may be caused by one or a combination of factors.

Low Volume
Less than 1 cc of seminal fluid is produced.

High Volume
More than 4 cc of seminal fluid is produced.

---

artificially. Sperm washing appears to be the more successful of the two techniques and is preferred by most clinics.

Some infertility clinics have had considerable success as a result of treating men with a high level of antibodies to their wife's sperm with very high doses of the drug methylprednisolone for seven days at the beginning of the wife's cycle. The old technique of asking the couple to use a condom for three to six months is never successful if the antibodies are on the husband's side.

Repeating the Semen Analysis

A man cannot be considered fertile or infertile on the basis of a single semen analysis. However, if the semen analysis is normal, no further investigation of a man is performed, at least for the time being. If the semen analysis falls within the normal range and the woman's tests fail to turn up the cause of infertility, the analysis should be repeated within four months. If the woman must undergo many months of treatment, the man should have a new semen analysis every six months until pregnancy is achieved.

An abnormal semen analysis should be repeated three or four times. In most instances, when the semen analysis is abnormal, the man will proceed with Phase II to begin to identify the source of the problem.

19
Hormone Analysis and Other Tests

As we have seen, an abnormal semen analysis can involve many problems – few sperm, dead or weak sperm, poorly formed sperm, clumped sperm, low or high volume – and various combinations of them. When a semen analysis is abnormal, special tests are ordered to define the source of the problem. Cultures are taken to check for infection; if no infection is present but the sperm are clumping, antibody studies are performed.

Once these causes are discounted, a man with a low sperm count usually enters Phase II, in which his blood is tested for the hormones vital to sperm production. Hormone testing can help the specialist figure out which part of the man's reproductive system is responsible for the poor semen analysis. Invariably, a problem exists either in the brain control centre or in the testicles.

Although researchers believe there are many subtle interplays among the hormones that travel back and forth along the axis between the control centre and the testicles, the hormonal system in men is a relatively simple mechanism. The hormones sent by a man's control centre are identical to those sent by a woman's control centre, FSH and LH. The major difference between the two systems is that instead of a monthly combination of on-and-off signals, a man's brain sends out hormone messengers in a fairly steady stream every day.

As the testicles receive the hormone messengers from the brain control centre, they make sperm and testosterone. To keep their sperm production factories going, the testicles continue to place orders for FSH and LH by sending hormone messengers back to the control centre. The messengers used by the testicles to carry the orders are testosterone and the mysterious hormone known as inhibin.

The brain receives the orders and keeps shipping out FSH and LH. The brain must send just enough FSH and LH to keep the sperm factories running efficiently. Although scientists recognize this concept, they still understand very little about the amount of brain hormones needed and precisely which cells in the testicles respond to the LH/FSH messengers.

Generally, the Leydig's cells pick up the LH message and produce testosterone, which build a man's sexual characteristics. The Sertoli's cells appear to pick up the FSH messenger and help distribute the vital hormone message to the spermatogonia. To some degree, both hormones are needed to make good-quality sperm, but the levels of these hormones vary widely throughout the day.

When a man has a persistently low sperm count or no sperm at all in his ejaculate, a hormone evaluation will show whether the control centre is faulty or whether the sperm production factories in the testicles are crippled. Most of the time, the problem will be traced to some sort of breakdown in the sperm production factories.

Testing the Hormone System

A man's hormone levels can be tested on any day of the month with one blood sample. Although levels usually vary considerably throughout the day, the variations fall within certain acceptable limits established by testing hundreds of fertile men. Blood samples are tested for FSH, LH, and testosterone.

A glance at the hormone chart tells the specialist the condition of the hormonal axis. The hormone levels may be normal, low, or high. If the sperm count is low and the hormones are also low, the control centre is not working. If the hormones are high or normal, the control centre is working but something may be wrong with the testicles.

Low Hormones: The Control Centre

If the blood tests show low FSH and LH, the problem probably lies in the brain control centre. The next thing to figure out is which partner in the control centre – hypothalamus or pituitary – is at fault.

It's not easy to separate the glandular partners from one another. The hypothalamus issues instructions to the pituitary via a special releasing factor called LH-RH. When the pituitary receives this releasing order, it sends FSH and LH to the testicles. Thanks to new research, LH-RH can be re-created in the laboratory. To test the control centre a man is given an injection of synthetic LH-RH. Blood tests are taken again. If the hormones have risen, the pituitary is healthy enough to respond to the synthetic LH-RH. The specialist infers that the fault lies in the hypothalamus. If the hormones do not rise, the pituitary is assumed to be sick and unable to respond to the LH-RH.

Problems in either part of the control centre can be treated with drug therapy. The idea is to correct the problem as high up in the system as possible. As we have seen, the hypothalamus signal can be artificially induced with synthetic LH-RH. The difficulty is that the LH-RH has to be given by injection on a daily basis. Scientists are experimenting with a LH-RH capsule that can be embedded in body fat and supply a steady portion of LH-RH to the system.

If the pituitary isn't working, the control centre can be bypassed and hormones administered directly to the testicles in the form of Pergonal or HCG (human chorionic gonadotrophin). Pergonal is a combination of FSH and LH; HCG is the equivalent of LH. Although their use in men is still speculative, these fertility drugs have proved highly effective in women.

High Hormones: The Testicles

If blood tests show high FSH and/or LH, the problem probably lies in the testicles. The hormonal messengers are working extra hard to drive the testicles, but the sperm factories aren't getting the message.

The sperm production factories have two separate cell systems working on the assembly line: the Leydig's cells are in charge of testosterone, and the mother cells (spermatogonia) are in charge of sperm. One or both systems may fail.

If FSH is high, the spermatogonia aren't working, and the sperm count will be low. If LH is high, the Leydig's cells aren't producing any testosterone, so testosterone levels will be low. If both hormones are high, then probably neither cell system is working. This indicates a primary failure of all systems within the testicle, both sperm and testosterone. When hormone testing points to a flaw in the testicle, the man will need a testicular biopsy to show exactly what is going on in the sperm production factory.

Normal Hormones: Blockage in the Transport System

If all hormones are normal, yet a man has a persistently low sperm count, the fertility specialist will suspect that a blockage in the transport system is preventing sperm from reaching the penis. At this point, only surgical tests – Phase III of the check-up – can identify the source of the low sperm count. These tests, performed in a hospital setting, include a testicular biopsy and a vasogram.

Surgical Tests: Testicular Biopsy and Vasogram

A testicular biopsy provides a blueprint of the sperm production factory in the testicle. In the bit of tissue taken from one testicle, a pathologist can view the inner workings of the entire factory and explore the efficiency of the assembly line that manufactures sperm. Although testicular biopsy is 'same-day surgery', it is usually performed in association with a vasogram, using a general anaesthesia. The vasogram outlines the sperm transport system with dye and an X-ray reveals any obstructions.

The Testing Procedure

The skin of the scrotum is opened with a quarter-inch incision and pushed aside so that the surgeon can see the smooth surface of the testicle, the epididymis, and the lower part of the vas deferens. The surgeon inserts a small needle into the vas and slowly injects a radio-opaque dye into the transport system. The X-ray material fills all the internal cavities, from the epididymis, up the vas deferens, into the seminal vesicles and the ejaculatory ducts. X-rays are taken at this point. If any blockage is present, the contrast material stops at the obstacle.

When the vasogram is complete, a small wedge of tissue is removed from the testicles and placed in a special protective medium. The tissue must be handled more carefully than other biopsy specimens. If fragile testicular tissue is improperly excised or placed in regular fixing solution, its readability may be blurred beyond comprehension.

The surgeon closes the testicle with two or three small stitches, then uses three or four more small skin sutures to close the scrotum. An ice bag to the scrotum, plus aspirin, will usually take care of any post-operative discomfort; the man usually goes home the same day and wears an athletic supporter for a few days until the incision is completely healed.

What the Biopsy Shows

The biopsy is sent to the lab, where it is read by an expert pathologist. The bit of tissue, which encompasses a cross-section of many tubules, is like a book of sperm production. Under the microscope the pathologist should be able to see the mother cells in place and a generation of sperm cells being born. All stages of growth should be present – from immature spermatocytes to mature sperm.

The worst finding on a biopsy is complete absence of the mother cells (spermatogonia) that produce sperm. In this case, the Leydig's cells, which make the male hormone testosterone, may be present. The Sertoli's cells, which regulate the flow of nutrients to the growing spermatocytes, may or may not be in place. But absolutely no sperm are being produced. This is a hopeless situation. Sometimes the biopsy will show some tubules that are scarred and others that are still active. Such damage may have been caused by mumps or scrotal injury. In this case, there is some hope.

Other possibilities exist. Sometimes the primary spermatogonia have not been stimulated by the brain hormones and produce sperm cells that are unable to mature. In such a case, even though brain hormones are low, the mother cells are present. Treatment involves supplementing the missing hormones, which usually results in increased production of mature sperm.

If the mother cells are intact, and the various stages of sperm production are in progress, the biopsy is normal. It is then assumed that the low sperm count is due to an obstruction somewhere in the transport system. The vasogram X-rays will reveal the location of the obstruction. Most obstructions occur at the junction between the vas and the epididymis; however, blockage sometimes occurs inside the epididymis. Blockages anywhere in the epididymis require careful microsurgery. A blockage seldom occurs in the vas deferens proper, unless the man has suffered a major infection or severe scrotal injury.

At the end of Phase III of the male investigation the andrologist should have a definitive diagnosis and be able to recommend therapy. The physical examination has shown whether a varicocele is present. If so, the approach will be surgery. Hormone tests have indicated whether there is a problem in the brain control centre. In that event, the andrologist can try to help the control centre with fertility drugs. The vasogram has outlined the transport system, and the biopsy has tested the integrity of the testicle. A blockage in the transport system can usually be surgically corrected. A faulty sperm production centre is less promising, but in some cases hormone therapy will increase sperm production.

In certain cases, the andrologist will recommend that the man go into Phase IV of the investigation, which involves an analysis of the sex chromosomes inside each cell.

Chromosome Analysis

A chromosome analysis is indicated when the biopsy reveals that all the spermatogonia are missing. Such an analysis is also performed when there is any question of sexuality – for example, if a man has no sperm in his ejaculate and his sexual characteristics are undeveloped. In these instances, the analysis is performed to see if a chromosomal error is responsible for the man's infertility. When a chromosomal defect does show up, it is usually a spontaneous birth defect rather than an inherited trait. Very seldom is infertility caused by an inherited defect, simply because men with such defects usually don't have children.

Sometimes a chromosome analysis is performed at the beginning of the investigation when the family history suggests that one or both partners may be carriers of a birth defect that could be passed on to the children. Couples may choose to have genetic counselling, which usually includes chromosome analysis, to figure the odds of passing along a defect such as Tay-Sachs disease or sickle-cell anaemia to their child.

A technician performs a chromosome study by drawing a blood sample and growing the white blood cells in a special culture medium. After seven days, a chemical is added to the cells to stop cell division. The white blood cells are placed on a slide and crushed, spreading out the chromosomes. The chromosome pairs of 100 cells are counted to determine the chromosomal constitution (karyotype) of the person. Normally, a man's cells have an XY sex chromosome. The normal female cells have an XX. Abnormalities arise when there are too many – or too few – sex chromosomes. Any chromosome abnormality is extremely rare. Fewer than 2 per cent of all infertile men display a chromosomal flaw. (Klinefelter's syndrome is the most common of these abnormalities.) But when such a problem does occur, it is genetically locked in for ever. In only the rarest of circumstances, when the chromosomal flaw is mixed with some normal cells (called a mosaic Klinefelter's), is there some potential to improve fertility with hormone therapy.

Reviewing the Completed Tests

As much as possible, a woman and man are evaluated in parallel testing sequences. After all the evidence has been gathered, the fertility team meets with the couple and reviews the results of the completed tests. An infertile couple may be facing a single problem, such as blocked tubes, or several problems involving both partners. The fertility specialists should describe the treatment they recommend for each problem and the probability of success. Sometimes, even after all the testing, the best the experts can come up with is an educated guess. Given the frustration couples feel on coming up empty after they have spent two or three months being tested, the experts may suggest a course of treatment on the offchance that it will help. However, they should make it perfectly clear that the recommendation is guesswork.

For the vast majority of couples, however, the fertility experts should have firm answers. They should be able to tell you what is causing the infertility and how the problem can be treated.

Causes and Treatment: Women

20
Ovulatory Failure

Ovulatory problems of one sort or another account for more than half of all infertility problems in women. Until recently these problems were unsolvable and were often considered mind over matter. The doctor simply told the woman, 'Everything seems to be fine. Why don't you relax?' In the vast majority of these cases, however, the infertility was not some sort of mental lapse on the part of the woman. It was caused by a small kink in the hormonal axis that prevented an ovum from maturing and releasing on schedule each month. Today, 90 per cent of these problems can be successfully treated with fertility drugs.

Two primary segments of the hormonal axis work in consort to produce and release a single ovum each month: the brain control centre (hypothalamus/pituitary gland) and the ovaries. If either segment fails, ovulation may cease. Sometimes the brain control centre malfunctions and the messages between the hypothalamus and pituitary gland are distorted. Or the hormonal axis between the control centre and the ovaries may break down. Sometimes ovaries themselves are flawed and cannot respond to proper signals from the control centre. Occasionally secondary hormones from another gland, such as the thyroid or adrenals, feed into the axis. These excess hormones can jumble up the messages travelling between the brain and the ovaries.

The result is the same in every case: an ovary fails to produce and release an ovum on schedule. It may fail some of the time or all of the time. The only outward sign may be an erratic pattern of menstruation. A woman may have no periods at all, or she may menstruate only two or three times a year. She may even have periods every other month or every 28–40 days. A surprising number of women who are not ovulating still have regular menstrual cycles. But if the temperature chart remains flat throughout the month, showing no mid-cycle rise, the bleeding is caused by a fall in oestrogen and is usually not a true menstrual period.

When a woman fails to ovulate, it isn't always easy to know which part of the hormonal system is at fault. A battery of tests needs to be performed to pin down the source of the problem; some of these tests may have to be run over a period of two months or longer to provide a specific diagnosis.

Recovery from Birth-control Pills

The most common ovulatory problem is caused by oral contraceptive pills. The pill temporarily jams a wrench into the biological time clock, stopping ovulation. Hormones in the pill take over for the hormones normally produced by the brain control centre and the ovaries. The hormonal axis goes to sleep. When a woman goes off the pill and the wrench is removed, the natural system does not always wake up immediately – 10–15 per cent of all women coming off the pill have some trouble ovulating. These problems usually resolve themselves without treatment. About 5 per cent of post-pill women, however, need help from fertility drugs.

Three factors influence the ease with which ovulation resumes after the pill is stopped: the strength of oestrogen in the pill, the consistency with which the pill was used, and the woman's menstrual history.

The higher the dose of oestrogen, the bigger the wrench and the greater the impact on the hormonal axis. Side-effects are also more pronounced; blood clots and coronary artery disease and other ageing processes have all been associated with the high-dose pill. Modern birth-control pills are much less potent than their predecessors, and side-effects are fewer. Today's low-dose pill is less risky than driving your car – or being pregnant.

The length of time a woman stays on the pill doesn't seem to affect the recovery of the hormonal axis. But erratic use does. A woman can take the pill indefinitely with little risk to her fertility if she uses it consistently, stopping only when she wants to get pregnant. When a woman initially takes the pill, the brain control centre is shocked. Stopping and starting the pill repeatedly jerks the system on and off, until it loses its buoyancy. After such a series of shocks, treatment with fertility drugs can usually help the ovulatory system start up again.

A woman who has a regular, well-established menstrual cycle before going on the pill will usually resume normal ovulation quickly after stopping the pill. A woman who has an erratic menstrual cycle, suggesting an immature reproductive system, typically needs more time. Many people have the mistaken notion that the pill straightens out menstrual problems; in fact, the pill masks problems by turning off the regular hormonal axis and substituting a false chemical signal. Underneath that false signal, the true menstrual problem still exists.

This is particularly true for young women who were late developers. A girl who begins to menstruate in her late teens and who has scant or irregular periods and immature breast development needs more time to develop a normal reproductive cycle. If she takes birth-control pills to 'regulate' hormonal flow at this time – something that was often recommended when the pill first come on the market – her immature ovaries will be held in limbo. When she stops taking the pill at the age of twenty-five or so, it may take several years for her reproductive system to catch up and come to full maturity. Today, doctors seldom prescribe oral contraceptive pills for young girls unless they have regular and well-established menstrual patterns.

Occasionally, putting the regular system to rest gives the body time to correct the problem. Most often, however, the irregular pattern starts again after the pill is stopped. The only way to straighten out a menstrual cycle is to identify the cause of the problem and correct it.

The Diagnosis

Again, the three keys to how quickly the hormonal system fires up after stopping the pill are dose, consistency of use, and menstrual history. Age is not especially relevant, although ovulatory function seems to come back faster in young girls than in older women.

The obvious symptom of a fertility problem is failure to become pregnant after stopping the pill. A woman may have no menstrual periods, irregular periods, or even normally occurring periods but without ovulation. The best treatment is time. If a woman who wants to conceive has not become pregnant after a year, she may fall into that very small percentage of women who require treatment with fertility drugs to fire up the system.

How long to wait before starting drug treatment depends on the age of the woman. Some women wait two years for the system to come back. A young girl has time to wait, but for an older woman time is the enemy. As a woman approaches thirty the problem becomes more urgent. If she wants to get pregnant, she should wait no longer than six months before starting treatment with fertility drugs.

Before drugs are prescribed, blood tests are necessary to identify which segment of the axis is out of commission. Blood tests may show that some oestrogen is being manufactured by the ovaries over the whole menstrual cycle. (In normal women, oestrogen is produced in the first half of the cycle, and progesterone is produced in the second half.) In this case, the ovaries are working, receiving messages from the brain control centre, but the control centre is still sluggish. The best way to wake up the control centre is to stimulate the hypothalamus.

A sluggish control centre is the most common and the most easily treated post-pill problem. The drug of choice is clomiphene citrate (Clomid, Serophene), discussed later in this chapter, which acts directly on the hypothalamus. The drug is taken for only five days each month and is usually given for three months, over which time a woman keeps temperature charts to track the rise in temperature midway through the menstrual cycle. Blood tests to measure hormones should also be used to document ovulation; occasionally a physician will recommend an endometrial biopsy to confirm that ovulation has resumed. In the vast majority of cases clomiphene will do the job; it is used when blood tests show that at least some oestrogen is being produced by the ovaries. If the blood tests show very low oestrogen, the ovaries may be shut down. Then, no matter how much the brain is stimulated with drugs, the ovaries will not work. In that case, a more powerful drug called menotropins (Pergonal), which supplies hormones directly to the ovaries, is needed to get the system going again.

With treatment, 99·9 per cent of women coming off the birth-control pill resume normal ovulatory function; there is that very rare instance, however, in which ovulation never returns.

Fine-tuning Problems

About 25 per cent of all ovulatory problems involve the fine-tuning mechanism of the hormonal axis. These problems are called non-specific anovulation. The menstrual cycle may appear to be perfectly normal, but tests show that the biological time clock occasionally skips a beat. A woman may be ovulating at random only five or six months out of the year. Although the woman may inadvertently get pregnant, the erratic clock makes it difficult for her to conceive when she chooses.

Usually the temperature chart appears normal for some cycles; at other times it may be completely flat or show a gradual rise in temperature instead of a clear upward shift. Blood tests provide the main clue: a slight idiosyncracy in the FSH/LH ratio, just enough to disarm the egg release mechanism.

Of all ovulatory disturbances, fine-tuning problems are the easiest to treat. With clomiphene citrate the system usually regulates itself in three to six months; and once the brain control centre adjusts, ovulation remains normal.

Polycystic Ovaries

Another common, and extremely complex, cause of ovulatory failure is a set of circumstances called polycystic ovarian disease, also known as Stein–Leventhal syndrome. In 1935, Dr I. F. Stein and Dr M. L. Leventhal observed several events that occurred together too often to be coincidental: absent or infrequent periods, excessive hair on the face and breasts, obesity, and finally the characteristic large ovaries with multiple cysts. Women with these seemingly unrelated characteristics were often infertile.

Interestingly, when Stein and Leventhal surgically cut a large wedge out of the ovaries, the woman's menstrual cycle and subsequent fertility improved. Today polycystic ovaries (PCO) can usually be successfully treated with fertility drugs, but ovarian wedge resection may be used if drug therapy fails. There is great confusion about what causes PCO in the first place.

A Flaw in the Hormonal Axis

If the blood hormone levels of a woman who has PCO were measured on almost any day of the month, they probably would show this distinctive pattern:

Constant low to low-normal FSH
Constant high oestrogen
High-pulsating LH
Low progesterone
Elevated weak male hormones

Normally these hormones seesaw back and forth in a cyclical pattern over a single menstrual cycle. When PCO takes over, the hormone levels are constant, maintaining the same ratios to one another over the entire cycle.

When PCO is present, something is wrong with the hormonal axis between the brain control centre and the ovaries. Either the brain is sending the wrong signals to the ovaries or the ovaries are sending the wrong replies back along the feedback loop. No one knows where the problem begins – whether the pituitary gland goes awry or whether the ovaries cannot respond to hormonal signals. Since the distorted pattern is firmly entrenched before the symptoms of PCO show up, the origin of the problem becomes obscured.

Once started, the syndrome has a snowball effect. Because the follicles never release an egg, they swell and turn into cysts inside the ovaries. The support cells around the cysts begin to produce excessive amounts of weak male hormones, which are less potent than testosterone. These hormones stimulate hair growth on the face and the breasts, across the abdomen, and along the inside of the thighs. Women with PCO tend to gain weight through the waist, while the hips remain narrow. Inside the body, the weak male hormones cause the thin single-cell membranes around the ovaries to thicken into capsules, like the tunics that surround the testicles.

The weak male hormones are picked up in tissue and converted by fat cells into oestrogen. This conversion creates the sustained, high level of oestrogen that floods the feedback loop to the brain. Although FSH, which normally stimulates oestrogen production, is low, oestrogen is still high.

When the brain control centre senses all this oestrogen in the bloodstream, it assumes that the ovaries are functioning beautifully and that a big, ripe egg is ready to be ejected. But the elevated oestrogen messenger, which tells the brain to stop sending FSH, is an impostor. The oestrogen is coming not from the ovaries but from the converted male hormone. The brain falls for the message. The control centre reads the signal this way: 'Enough FSH; stop sending. Egg is mature.'

The control centre slows FSH and starts pumping out LH in an effort to eject the egg from the ovary. But there is no mature egg inside the ovary; the egg follicles swell but cannot release an egg. The swollen follicle becomes a cyst.

The situation grows steadily worse. In its effort to eject the egg, LH overstimulates other cells around the cysts, which produce more weak male hormones. The disastrous circle is complete:

1. More male hormone leads to more oestrogen conversion from body fat.
2. Oestrogen leads to more LH production from brain.
3. LH leads to more cysts.
4. Cells around cysts make more male hormone.

The major problem with PCO is that the constant high oestrogen level overstimulates the lining of the uterus. Since the endometrium doesn't shed during menstruation, it can develop abnormal growths and possible malignancy. Also, a woman who doesn't ovulate cannot get pregnant.

Theoretically, the false hormonal messages can start anywhere in this circle of events. The object of therapy is to break into the circle with an anti-oestrogen drug. Before treatment, however, it is essential that PCO be accurately diagnosed – and diagnosis of this disease is not easy.

The Diagnosis

Many physicians assume that PCO is present when a woman's menstrual history shows erratic periods and her temperature chart is sometimes flat. But PCO comes in many degrees, and with several variations. A battery of tests is needed to make an accurate diagnosis. The history, physical examination, and temperature chart will provide the first clues.

A woman's medical history often reveals that she has scant or absent menstrual periods. The problems may have started when her periods first began or soon afterwards. PCO is usually established by age eighteen or twenty.

The woman may or may not have pronounced physical symptoms. Acne and excess weight are common. Typically, pubic hair grows up towards the navel; some hair may also grow on the chest and down the inside of the thighs. Since inherited family traits can also produce this pattern of hair growth, excess hair is considered a soft sign of PCO.

When the doctor performs a pelvic examination, the ovaries feel two to three times larger than normal. On those months that the woman ovulates, her temperature chart looks normal, with the characteristic upwards shift in the middle of the cycle. If the charts are normal three months in a row, it's unlikely that she has PCO.

An abnormal temperature chart, however, is not necessarily proof of disease. Every woman skips ovulation occasionally as a result of stress or illness. Only blood tests to measure hormone levels can confirm the diagnosis. All hormones are measured: FSH, LH, testosterone, oestrogen, weak male hormones, and adrenal hormone (cortisol).

When the doctor reviews the blood test taken initially, the main theme will be a steady supply of oestrogen; the tip-off will be the elevated male hormones. Before making a firm diagnosis or starting treatment, he needs to pin down the source of the male hormones, which may be coming from the ovaries or the adrenal gland. A special suppression test does just that. The woman takes a drug that shuts off, or suppresses, the adrenal gland. If male hormones are still present, they are coming from the ovaries.

A laparoscopy is then performed to make certain that no scar tissue or adhesions are clogging the reproductive organs. Usually, the laparoscopy will also reveal that the ovaries are enlarged and full of cysts. No woman should take powerful fertility drugs to get pregnant until damaged tubes and ovaries have been repaired.

The Superdrugs

The initial aim of all treatment for PCO is to start menstrual bleeding so that the endometrium is shed before it becomes malignant. The hormone progesterone will usually start periods. If pregnancy is a goal, however, ovulation must be induced with more complex fertility drugs.

In the 1960s several different scientists involved in unravelling the intricacies of the hormonal axis discovered both birth-control pills and fertility drugs. Birth-control pills interrupt the normal axis to prevent ovulation. Fertility drugs do the opposite – they interrupt a faulty axis to encourage ovulation.

As noted earlier, there are two major fertility drugs on the market today: clomiphene citrate and menotropins (Pergonal). The safest and most commonly used is clomiphene, an anti-oestrogen drug. Pergonal, which is an extremely potent drug, is normally used only when clomiphene fails or when the ovaries are not working.

Clomiphene

Clomiphene works by stopping up the oestrogen receptor sites in the hypothalamus and tricking the brain into thinking that there is no oestrogen in the blood.

A woman begins to take clomiphene on day 4 of her menstrual cycle. As the drug blocks the oestrogen sensors, the brain tells the pituitary to pump up FSH production and get some oestrogen. This new flood of FSH reaches the ovaries and stimulates egg production. As the egg follicle develops, increasing amounts of oestrogen enter the bloodstream. Oestrogen is now higher than ever, but the brain doesn't know it.

After five days, clomiphene is stopped. Suddenly the receptor sites on the hypothalamus open up and detect the massive level of oestrogen. To counteract the oestrogen, the hypothalamus sends a quick-releasing factor (LH-RH) to its partner, the pituitary. The pituitary responds by sending a whopping message of LH to the ovaries. The LH burst kicks the egg free from the ovary, and progesterone production begins. Ovulation has now been artificially created by clomiphene.

Testing the LH Surge. Fertility drugs are very good at getting the egg follicle to grow, but they don't always come up with the LH surge needed to boost the egg out of the follicle. As ovulation approaches, the specialist will test to see if the LH surge is beginning.

Until recently the only way to measure LH was through a series of expensive blood tests taken on days 11, 12, and 13 of the cycle. Now a fast, inexpensive, and remarkably accurate urine test can do the same job. A small plastic stick impregnated with chemicals is dipped into the urine sample. If the LH surge is present, the stick turns dark blue. During the next 32–36 hours the woman should be ovulating.

If the surge is not present by day 13, a drug called human chorionic gonadotrophin (HCG) can be given on two consecutive days to create the boost of LH artificially. HCG is a chemical derived from a hormone produced by the placenta of a pregnant woman. This chemical so closely resembles LH that it can trick the ovaries into thinking that LH is present. HCG is given in injectible form to encourage the egg to leave the primed follicle.

Clomiphene works 75–80 per cent of the time. It is used to induce ovulation in women suffering from PCO, post-pill amenorrhoea, minor fine-tuning problems, and luteal phase defects (discussed below). Once ovulation occurs, the hormones balance and physical symptoms of PCO disappear.

As soon as ovulation occurs, pregnancy is possible. When all other factors are equal – when the fallopian tubes are not blocked and when the male partner is fertile – a woman has about a 65 per cent chance of pregnancy. Sometimes three or four cycles of clomiphene are needed before the drug works; and the dosage may have to be adjusted upwards. About 33 per cent of women who have PCO conceive within the first six months of treatment.

Sometimes treatment completely cures PCO; once the faulty system is shocked into a normal pattern, some women continue to ovulate. The response depends on the severity of the disease. If the imbalance is slight, treatment followed by pregnancy may cure it. If the problem is severe, the woman will probably have to use a fertility drug every time she wants to ovulate. In that case, she takes the drug only when she wants to get pregnant.

Even a woman who doesn't want to get pregnant needs to menstruate at least four times a year to shed the lining of the uterus and protect against cancer. She doesn't need fertility drugs to menstruate; instead, she can take birth-control pills or progesterone every three months to create an artificial menstruation. Like clomiphene, these drugs also decrease the levels of weak male hormone in the system. Acne clears up and body fat is easier to control. New hair growth is suppressed, although the hair that has already developed can be removed only with electrolysis. Because the biological time clock is not working properly, intermittent use of birth-control pills is not problematic for these women.

Twins. Because the rejuvenated ovaries sometimes work extra hard, women taking clomiphene may produce more than one egg in a given cycle, and one clomiphene pregnancy out of every fifty will produce twins. (The incidence of twins in the normal population in Britain and America is one in 100.) Clomiphene twins are non-identical (fraternal), meaning that the babies develop from two different eggs and are separate individuals sharing a common uterus.

Identical twins, which occur in one in every 300 regular pregnancies, result when a single unfertilized egg cleaves into two portions before undergoing regular cell division. Identical twins share the same genetic pattern. Women who take fertility drugs do not produce identical twins any more frequently than women who do not take such drugs.

Side-effects. Clomiphene is a safe drug. Sometimes cervical mucus becomes scanty and thick just before ovulation, which makes sperm penetration difficult. The condition can be corrected by small doses of oestrogen given in combination with clomiphene.

Bloating and nausea occur occasionally and usually disappear when the drug is stopped. Every once in a while the ovaries enlarge, and the drug has to be stopped immediately. Acute pelvic pain is the main symptom.

Clomiphene is not responsible for birth defects greater than those found in the normal population. However, the incidence of spontaneous abortion following clomiphene treatment is twice as high as that of the normal population.

Most women take clomiphene with few or no side-effects. Nevertheless, before starting treatment, both partners should complete the fertility tests to make sure that other factors are not involved that would make treatment futile. A woman should never take fertility drugs unless her husband has first had a semen analysis.

Clomiphene doesn't work for everyone. Nor does it solve every case of ovulation failure. For more stubborn problems the answer may be Pergonal.

Pergonal

Pergonal (menotropins) is an equal combination of LH and FSH obtained from the urine of menopausal women. Hence the drug is sometimes called human menopausal gonadotrophin (HMG). After a woman reaches menopause, levels of LH and FSH soar in an effort to prime the sinking ovaries. The body clears these excess brain hormones through the urine.

This interesting discovery was made by an Italian biologist, P. Donini Serono, who later concluded that the best place to collect quantities of menopausal urine was a convent. Today HMG is routinely collected from the urine of nuns over fifty years of age. Serono Pharmaceuticals Company of Italy also sends vans round to numerous Italian villages to collect the urine of elderly ladies in exchange for soap powder and other household items.

Clomiphene acts on the hypothalamus. Pergonal, however, bypasses the brain control centre and supplies LH/FSH directly to the ovaries, encouraging them to develop eggs. This direct push is the reason Pergonal can be dangerous. The drug can overstimulate the ovaries and cause them to rupture. A woman takes Pergonal for five to ten days each month. To avoid complications, a blood test should be run each day the drug is taken to measure oestrogen levels, which reflect the degree of stimulation. Without this close monitoring, a woman risks losing her ovaries.

Pergonal is responsible for the multiple births so lavishly reported in the press because it stimulates the ovaries indiscriminately, so that several ova often mature and release simultaneously. Even with Pergonal, however, there is an 80 per cent chance of bearing a single baby. When a multiple birth does occur, there is a 75 per cent chance it will be twins. The chance of having quintuplets is less than 1 in 5,000 (without the drug, it's 1 in 41 million). In the United States, Pergonal has produced thirteen sets of living quins and one set of sextuplets.

Careful monitoring by ultrasound reduces the chance of multiple births.

Ultrasound provides an image of the eggs maturing; when the physician sees that one egg is big enough to release, the woman is given an injection of an early pregnancy hormone nearly identical to LH. When the imitation LH hits an ovary, the mature egg pops out and ovulation is complete.

An improved version of Pergonal, called Metrodin (urofollitrophin), has recently been issued by the makers of Pergonal and is in use in clinics in Britain.

Variations of PCO

PCO is an extremely complex syndrome, and the disorder often appears with one of several possible variations attached to it. When this happens, additional drug therapy may be needed to solve the ovulatory problem.

PCO with Adrenal Hormone Interference

In PCO with adrenal hormone interference, the adrenal gland contributes weak male hormones to complicate the faulty hormonal axis further. Low doses of synthetic cortisone hormone given daily will usually suppress the gland. At the same time, clomiphene is used in the first part of the cycle to stimulate ovulation.

Cortisone carries some risk because it reduces the efficiency of the immune system. Therefore, as soon as a woman gets pregnant, she stops taking the drug. Over the long term she can take birth-control pills to manage this form of PCO.

PCO with Elevated Prolactin

In PCO with elevated prolactin (discussed below), the pituitary gland produces a slight excess of the hormone prolactin, which blocks ovulation. About 25 per cent of the time this rise in prolactin can be traced to a small tumour of the pituitary gland, which can be surgically removed. If no tumour is present, the drug bromocriptine (Parlodel) will block the prolactin. Bromocriptine is taken daily throughout the cycle, combined with clomiphene on days 5–9. After three or four months, prolactin levels usually return to normal, and the drug is stopped.

PCO with Thyroid Problems

Any sort of thyroid problem must be cleared up before PCO can be treated. If the thyroid gland is overactive, a woman takes suppression drugs; if thyroid is low, she can take synthetic thyroid hormones to increase production. Once the thyroid is under control, clomiphene is used to treat PCO.

Elevated Prolactin

Prolactin is a hormone that stimulates milk production in new mothers. When prolactin levels are above normal, the hormone jams the feedback loop to the brain control centre and ovulation stops. Prolactin levels sometimes rise even when a woman is not pregnant and may contribute to infertility. At the Omega Institute, about one out of every twenty-five infertile women shows elevated prolactin on blood tests. Elevated prolactin may prove to be an important underlying cause of 'infertility unknown'.

Prolactin, like other hormones that affect reproduction, is controlled by the combined efforts of the hypothalamus and the pituitary gland. In the case of prolactin, the hypothalamus normally sends out an inhibitory factor that prevents the pituitary from releasing the hormone. When a woman is pregnant, the hypothalamus stops the inhibitory factor, and prolactin floods into the system. Scientists have recently learned that many events other than pregnancy may interfere with the inhibition of prolactin. Intense research into the workings of the nervous system is helping scientists identify the control/release mechanisms of the higher and lower brain. This is an important new phase of infertility research.

Stress and Transient Factors

Some outside events that affect prolactin, such as stress, are transient. The prolactin level rises for a few hours or even a day, then returns to normal. If the stress is prolonged, the body seems to adjust to it and prolactin eventually comes back to normal. Breast stimulation, sexual intercourse, and strenuous exercise can have a similar temporary effect on prolactin. So can minor surgery and anaesthesia. These are transient episodes of elevated prolactin and do not usually lead to infertility.

Drugs

Drugs can also affect the hypothalamus inhibitory factor and cause prolactin levels to rise. Antidepressants, antihypertensives, hallucinogens, painkillers, and alcohol may all be responsible for ovulation failure traced to elevated prolactin. When the drug is withdrawn, the prolactin levels fall. Sometimes changing to a different drug eliminates the side-effects. If the prolactin doesn't fall within two weeks, the physician must look for more dangerous causes of elevated prolactin, specifically brain tumours, which raise the prolactin permanently and must be treated medically or surgically.

Brain Tumours

If a doctor discovers an elevated prolactin in the blood tests, the first job is to eliminate the possibility of a brain tumour.

About half the women who show an elevated prolactin on blood tests have some type of pituitary tumour. Large tumours are easily diagnosed by a Computerized Axial Tomography (CAT) scan. A tumour big enough to be identified on this X-ray can be surgically removed. Such tumours, left untreated, will impair vision and ultimately lead to blindness or even death. Early discovery and removal of the tumour will return the pituitary gland to normal.

Some tumours are so small that they do not show up on X-ray. Left alone, such tumours will eventually grow until they can be picked up with diagnostic CAT scan. Most physicians, however, feel that any suspected tumour should be suppressed with drugs as soon as possible. The doctor first eliminates all other possible causes of the elevated prolactin. If the high prolactin level continues to show up on blood tests taken at two-week intervals, he assumes that a small tumour is present and begins medical treatment.

Other Causes

Very rarely a tumour may appear on the hypothalamus, and today these tumours can be surgically removed. Other rare tumours located in distant parts of the body may also occasionally elevate prolactin.

Another dangerous and life-threatening cause of elevated prolactin is encephalitis, an infection involving the hypothalamus, which is treated medically. Strangely enough, an underactive thyroid gland can also create an excess of prolactin. Thyroid-stimulating hormone (TSH), usually working overtime to drive the impaired thyroid gland, also stimulates the cells that make prolactin. The prolactin blood levels improve when the woman takes supplements of thyroid extract.

Bromocriptine

The major new drug being used to suppress prolactin production is bromocriptine, which interferes with the receptor sites on cells that produce prolactin and keep the pituitary gland still. The drug is given daily in varying doses until prolactin levels fall. Should pregnancy occur, the drug is stopped immediately. A woman may have to take bromocriptine for three or four months, or longer. If the prolactin level doesn't fall, the doctor should keep looking for possible brain tumour. A new, long-acting version of bromocriptine (Pergolide) is now being used in trials.

Luteal Phase Defects

Any time the endometrial lining of the uterus fails to develop properly after ovulation, it is said to have a luteal phase defect. An egg may ovulate properly and be fertilized in the tube, but when it tries to implant inside the uterus there is no lush lining to cling to. The fertilized ovum aborts.

There are three major types of luteal phase defects: defective LH signal from the pituitary gland, faulty LH receptor sites on the empty egg follicle (corpus luteum), and premature death of the corpus luteum.

A luteal phase defect is usually suspected when the menstrual cycle is short, although sometimes short menstrual cycles are perfectly normal. An endometrial biopsy taken on days 21–25 of the menstrual cycle is the best way to make the diagnosis. If the endometrial tissue does not match the normal criteria (for example, if the tissue looks like day 17 on day 22 of the cycle), then the specialist assumes there is a luteal phase defect.

Before a luteal phase defect can be treated, the specialist needs to precisely trace the cause. Hormone studies in Phase II will show the activity of all three hormones. If LH is low, the treatment of choice is HCG, which supplies the missing hormone directly to the ovaries. If FSH and oestrogen are low, the physician assumes the receptor sites on the empty egg sac (corpus luteum) are poorly developed. In that case, clomiphene is used to correct the FSH signal.

Low progesterone means that the corpus luteum, which is supposed to pump out this hormone in the second part of the menstrual cycle, has died. Premature death of the corpus luteum can be treated with vaginal pessaries of progesterone. The progesterone is directly absorbed by the endometrium.

Luteal phase defects are common in female infertility, and they are among the easiest of all problems to correct. Treatment of any luteal phase defect is 80–85 per cent successful within three to six months.

21
Mechanical Obstructions

Twenty years ago, blocked tubes, pelvic adhesions, and other mechanical obstructions accounted for only about 25 per cent of infertility in women. Today, that figure has leaped to more than 40 per cent. Obstructions may be caused by endometriosis or surgical scarring in the abdomen. But the major reason behind the soaring incidence of mechanical infertility is infection of the pelvic cavity.

Pelvic Inflammatory Disease

Each year about a million women in the USA are treated for pelvic inflammatory disease (PID), sometimes called pelvic adhesive disease. The complications of PID cause many severe health problems, especially infertility.

Almost all pelvic infections are venereal in origin, meaning that they are sexually transmitted. The invading organism, whatever its type, reaches the pelvic cavity via sexual intercourse. The skyrocketing increase of VD among all segments of the population, especially teenagers, may make PID the dominant cause of infertility for women in years to come.

A woman who has had one episode of PID has a 15 per cent risk of becoming infertile, and the rate increases with each subsequent infection. After two infections, there is a 50 per cent chance of infertility. After three infections, the risk of infertility is 75 per cent.

The Invaders

Any bacteria, under the right circumstances, can cause PID. The bacteria invade the pelvic cavity through the cervix by first breaking down the mucus barrier that protects the portal. The most common and most dangerous invaders are gonorrhoea, *Streptococcus*, *Enterococcus*, and chlamydia. A host of other organisms that fall into anaerobic and aerobic groups can also invade the pelvic cavity. (An anaerobe is an organism that grows without oxygen; an aerobe must have oxygen to survive. Either kind can cause PID, and it is important to identify which kind is doing the damage, since different antibiotics are used to eradicate them.)

216 · CAUSES AND TREATMENT : WOMEN

Bacteria, the smallest of the one-celled animals, excrete toxic chemicals that destroy tissue. Gonorrhoeal bacteria, for example, excrete endotoxins inside their cell walls. When the walls rupture, the toxins pour out. The bacteria can travel harmlessly into the fallopian tubes; but when the bacteria burst, the endotoxins spill out and dissolve the tube's lining. The tube collapses; its walls stick together and fill with excretions (a condition called hydrosalpinx). The ends of the fallopian tubes can also collapse and seal over.

Streptococcal bacteria, in contrast, excrete exotoxins through their cell walls. These bacteria tunnel their way directly through muscle and tissue, using chemicals to eat holes in the tissue. The dead tissue left behind is ripe for invasion by anaerobes. Unchecked, a dangerous aerobic/anaerobic infection may spread steadily until all the reproductive organs are wrapped in sheets of rubbery scar tissue.

Standard textbook teaching has been that the first episode of PID is always caused by gonorrhoea, which paves the way for future invaders. However, recent studies show that most women with PID have several invading organisms present at the same time, and the most dangerous of all is a newly recognized organism called chlamydia.

Chlamydia. Chlamydia, a hitherto little-known and often misdiagnosed infection, is now increasingly being diagnosed and treated in clinics in the United Kingdom. Little attention was paid to chlamydia until researchers began to speculate that some unidentified, 'non-specific' organism was partly responsible for the high incidence of PID in infertile women. Finer diagnostic tests developed in the 1960s eventually identified one such elusive organism.

Since that time, chlamydia has revealed itself as the most dangerous of all organisms that invade a woman's pelvic cavity. Chlamydia insidiously destroys the inside of the fallopian tubes and builds extensive scar tissue through the pelvic cavity. The worst part of the disease is that its symptoms are deceptively mild. A 'silent' chlamydial infection can ruin the reproductive organs without a woman even knowing she has it. Swedish studies have shown that a single attack of chlamydia is about three times more likely than gonorrhoea to cause sterility in women. If a pregnant woman contracts chlamydia, the newborn infant can develop eye infections and pneumonia from chlamydia during passage through the birth canal.

Chlamydia is a special animal; by definition it is a bacterium, but it closely resembles a large virus. Like a virus, chlamydia lives and multiplies inside other cells. The host cells eventually fill up and explode; the chlamydia bacteria escape to invade new cells. Because the bacteria like to invade epithelial (lining) cells, the inside of the fallopian tubes is an ideal target.

Research on chlamydia as a leading cause of pelvic infection has been severely hampered by the fragility of the organism. Chlamydia has a soft outer cell wall, in contrast to the thick coating of a regular bacterium, and breaks down rapidly when removed from its own territory. To test for chlamydia, a sample of the infected tissue, usually taken from the cervix, must be placed in a special medium and carefully transported to a laboratory to identify the culture. If the tissue sample survives, it takes five to six days for the culture to grow.

Recently a new, faster test for chlamydia has become available. A swab of the suspected material is spread on a chemically impregnated slide that glows in blue light if chlamydia is present.

Other Infections. Not all pelvic infections are venereal in origin. There can also be an invasion from inside the pelvic cavity. Appendicitis is an example. A bout of appendicitis in childhood may be responsible for badly scarred reproductive organs in adult life.

Tuberculosis is another example. In countries where the disease is still rampant, pelvic tuberculosis is known to cause pelvic adhesive disease. Tuberculosis may invade the reproductive tract through the lungs. If a man has tuberculosis of the prostate gland, he may pass along the infection to a woman's vagina, where it can invade through the cervix and uterus. Pelvic tuberculosis causes profound scarring, and chances for reconstructive surgery are almost nil. Fortunately, tuberculosis is seldom seen in the United States or Britain today.

Viruses. A virus is the smallest living molecular structure, a molecule that is alive. Instead of a nucleus, it may have only a single strand of DNA. Sexually transmitted viruses include herpes simplex, papovirus or condyloma acuminata (venereal warts), and the virus associated with AIDS (Acquired Immune Deficiency Syndrome), first identified in the Pasteur Laboratories in Paris. Unlike bacteria, viruses do not directly invade the reproductive tract to create mechanical obstructions in the pelvic cavity. But they do seem to lead the way by breaking down the cervical mucus, so that bacterial invasion is facilitated. Viral infections also change the chemical milieu of the vagina, altering the pH and shifting the balance of bacterial flora. These environmental changes may be lethal to sperm.

The Trouble with PID

The most worrying aspect of PID is that it is difficult to diagnose. The primary symptoms – fever, abdominal pain, perhaps some bleeding through the vagina – are the same as those of half a dozen other diseases. Sometimes there are no symptoms at all, and the infection eventually clears up on its own. The only remaining evidence is a badly scarred pelvic cavity – and infertility.

If PID is diagnosed accurately and proper treatment is begun immediately, the chances of preserving fertility dramatically increase. With each subsequent episode, however, the chances diminish. Each infection reduces the body's defences and makes recurrence more likely. Also, scars left by old infections are ideal sites for a new infection. The new infection gets such a good foothold around the pockets of scar tissue that it takes off and quickly spreads through the pelvis.

Sex and PID

Sexually inactive women almost never contract PID. A woman who becomes sexually active in her teens and who has several different partners during her adult life runs a high risk of contracting PID. The more partners a woman has, the wider the variety of bacteria to which she is exposed. Only recently have researchers focused on the man's role in PID. The greater the variety of bacteria in a man's semen, the more likely his partner is to develop PID. Men who have several female partners seem to have a greater variety of bacteria isolated in their semen. So do men who have had past bouts of gonorrhoea.

The reservoir for seminal bacteria appears to be a chronic infection of the prostate gland. Rarely does a man know that he has such an infection. The most common symptom – mild lower back discomfort – is usually attributed to poor posture, lack of exercise, or back strain.

The Role of Sperm. Apparently, bacteria attach themselves firmly to a man's sperm and travel high up into a woman's reproductive organs on the backs of this sperm transport. Wives of sterile men – that is, men who produce no sperm – seldom develop PID. Teenage girls, who have a longer oestrogen phase during their menstrual cycle than adult women, appear to have an extended time in the middle of their cycle when the window of the cervix is open to sperm. The mucus stays watery and permeable from three to five days longer, making young girls especially vulnerable to PID.

The Role of Contraceptives. The type of contraceptive a woman uses can affect her risk of contracting PID. The diaphragm and condom block the entry of sperm into the cervix. The birth-control pill, which sustains a tough cervical mucus all month long, helps block sperm penetration. These contraceptives offer protection against some, but not all, bacterial invaders.

In contrast, the IUD, which permits normal changes in cervical mucus, leaves a perfectly clear runway for bacteria-laden sperm to travel. A woman using an IUD who has never had a baby is especially prone to pelvic infection because her uterus is small and easily irritated by the foreign IUD. The irritated tissue sets up ideal conditions for infection to take hold. Such a woman is seven to ten times more likely to develop PID than a woman who uses other forms of birth control.

The plaited strings used in the old-style IUDs were especially hazardous because bacteria could climb up between the threads. A recent landmark court decision awarded $4·6 million to seven women who had suffered infection, PID, infertility, spontaneous abortion, and birth defects from using one brand of IUD (Dalkon Shield). New IUDs have a single, monofilament fibre that is resistant to bacteria.

One of the mysteries surrounding the PID is the fact that oral contraceptives protect against some types of bacterial invasion but not others. For example, chlamydia infections occur most frequently in sexually active teenage girls who use birth-control pills. Dr Sebastian Faro, director of the Infectious Disease Section at Baylor College of Medicine in Houston, believes that even though chlamydia attaches to sperm, it also has some other mode of invasion. In his view, the idea that oral contraceptives protect against PID has proved a false hope. To stop chlamydia, we need to discover how the organism invades.

Making the Diagnosis

Modern microsurgical and laser techniques, where available, have made it possible to rebuild damaged reproductive organs. Nonetheless, the pregnancy rate following such surgery is best when the damage is least, so it's imperative that physicians diagnose PID accurately and begin treatment as soon as possible.

For most women, the symptoms of PID belie the seriousness of the disease. The early phase of PID, when the infection is lodged in the vagina and cervix, often passes unnoticed or creates only slight discharge and light fever. Fever and discomfort in the lower abdomen are sometimes explained away as a 'stomach virus' or a cold. It is not unusual for a doctor to prescribe a mild painkiller and bed rest for a woman with these symptoms. A week later, the medication has somewhat obscured the pain, but now the woman is weak and has a profuse discharge from her vagina. The gynaecologist puts her in the hospital and begins aggressive treatment for PID, but it is often too late to save her reproductive function.

Today, a doctor should become suspicious whenever a woman complains of any discomfort in the lower abdomen. Other classic signs – fever, tenderness around the ovaries, tubes, and uterus, and painful swelling in the lower abdomen – may or may not be present. Major symptoms, such as severe pain on both sides of the lower abdomen, usually occur only after the infection has invaded the reproductive organs. At this point, the abdomen is extremely tender, and sexual intercourse or routine pelvic examination is very painful.

Fever and occasionally vaginal bleeding are seen more often when the infecting organism is gonorrhoea. Overall, the symptoms are much sharper and arise much faster with gonorrhoea than with more insidious infections such as chlamydia. Typically, when the infection is gonorrhoea a woman will experience severe enough symptoms to see her doctor within three days, whereas a week or more may go by before she notices a chlamydial infection.

About half of all women who contract PID have swelling in the ovaries and tubes. Occasionally other symptoms occur: nausea and vomiting, inflammation in the rectum, pain in the upper right side of the abdomen. These symptoms are typical of many other serious disorders and make diagnosis difficult.

Preliminary Assessment. It's easy for a doctor to mistake PID for acute appendicitis and vice versa. Other possible diagnoses are blood clots (pelvic thrombophlebitis), ruptured corpus luteum cyst, and leaking ectopic pregnancy. These are all dangerous, life-threatening conditions in which blood can seep into the abdomen. They require immediate diagnosis and medical and/or surgical treatment. Symptoms may also be caused by endometriosis or a simple viral

---

Symptoms of PID

Mild to moderate None (50–70 per cent of cases)
Low-grade fever (25–50 per cent)
Slight cramping in lower abdomen (25 per cent)
Pain with intercourse (25 per cent)
Irregular spotting (25 per cent)
Mild vaginal discharge (20–40 per cent)
Pelvic pressure (20–40 per cent)
Diarrhoea or constipation (10–20 per cent)

Severe Rapid pulse (90–99 per cent)
Abdominal pain (80–99 per cent)
High fever (80–90 per cent)
Severe pain with intercourse (80–90 per cent)
Acute pain, left or right, or both sides of the pelvis (75–95 per cent)
Pressure in rectal area (25–50 per cent)
Swollen genitals (25–50 per cent)
Sweating, shortness of breath (20–50 per cent)

---

infection of the lymph glands. These are not emergency situations and do not ordinarily require surgical intervention.

The doctor can make an initial diagnosis in the surgery by looking at a sample of vaginal secretions under a microscope. A PID smear will often be loaded with white blood cells and bacteria. This test is not infallible, but it does prove accurate in about two out of three cases. The gonorrhoea organism – a pair of biscuit-shaped bacteria found inside a white blood cell – will retain a red colour when red and blue Gram's stain is applied.

If few white blood cells are present, the doctor will suspect something other than PID. The location of the pain will point the way to an accurate diagnosis. Isolated pain around the lower right abdomen usually points to appendicitis. Pain on both sides could be viral infection or PID. General pelvic pain radiating into both legs could be thrombophlebitis. Cyclical premenstrual pain is probably endometriosis.

All of this is still not enough for diagnosis. Many doctors will also sample the abdominal fluids indirectly, placing a speculum in the vagina and puncturing the back of the vagina (cul de sac) with a long, hollow needle. The needle passes into the abdominal cavity, behind the uterus, and sucks up enough fluid for microscopic examination. The difficulty with this test is that the fluid can change as an infection progresses. In one young woman the fluid was a light straw colour, indicating a simple viral infection. Her doctor prescribed bed rest. Forty-eight hours later she was in severe pain, and a new test showed thick, pus-laden fluid. The infection was rampant throughout the pelvic cavity, and the woman was in danger of becoming sterile.

Such indirect approaches are notoriously fraught with error and carry a 50 per cent chance of misdiagnosis or delayed diagnosis. In the case of PID, a delayed diagnosis can spell the end of a woman's potential fertility.

Laparoscopy. The one infallible way to accurately diagnose PID is by direct visualization – laparoscopy – plus fluid cultures taken from inside the fallopian tubes. The laparoscope, a long, telescope-like instrument inserted through a small incision in the belly button, affords the doctor a panoramic view of all the internal pelvic organs. Using a special operating channel, the surgeon can remove samples of fluids and bits of tissue for laboratory analysis.

Treatment

The hallmark of good medical care is accurate diagnosis and appropriate medical or surgical management. It is imperative to diagnose and treat PID before it scars the reproductive organs seriously. Sometimes this means that the doctor will prescribe medication before the infecting organism has been identified by laboratory culture. Before the introduction of antibiotics, pelvic infections were often fatal. Even today, a woman may die if the infection is not quickly treated.

Mild Symptoms. If symptoms are mild, the doctor should take cervical cultures for gonorrhoea, chlamydia, and aerobes and anaerobes, and should prescribe a protective course of doxycycline. Most researchers agree that all patients who have gonorrhoea should also be treated for chlamydia. Among women with gonorrhoea, 30–40 per cent are simultaneously infected with chlamydia. The usual brief treatment for gonorrhoea – administration of a penicillin-type antibiotic – does not eradicate chlamydia. The broad-spectrum doxycycline can eradicate both organisms. When either organism is suspected, both should receive antibiotic treatment.

If the symptoms do not subside within twenty-four hours, the patient should be admitted to the hospital to receive antibiotics intravenously until the results come in from the laboratory cultures. Test results may show that a different, specific antibiotic is needed to eradicate the infecting organism. If the patient fails to respond to antibiotic treatment, a laparoscopy should be performed to take tissue samples from the infected organs and make an accurate diagnosis.

Moderate to Severe Symptoms. When symptoms are more pronounced, the doctor should take cervical cultures for all possible infecting organisms and admit the patient to the hospital at once for intravenous antibiotic treatment. Later, the drug therapy can be adjusted according to results of the cultures. If symptoms do not subside within twenty-four to forty-eight hours, a laparoscopy should be considered.

Rampant infections usually involve a combination of bacteria. At least two, and sometimes three, types of antibiotics are needed to cover the whole range of aerobic and anaerobic organisms. The chances of protecting the fallopian tubes in these instances are dim. The surgeon normally assumes that the tubes are ruined and focuses on preserving the ovaries.

After the infection subsides, the surgeon considers a second-look laparoscopy to assess the damage. Depending on the extent of the damage, a skilled microsurgeon may be able to rebuild the tubes.

Occasionally, a pelvic infection fails to improve, or even worsens, in spite of antibiotic therapy. A life-threatening pelvic abscess develops; immediate surgery is required to remove the diseased organs and wash out the peritoneum, the membrane lining the walls of the abdomen. In these extreme cases, reproductive function will be irretrievably lost.

Protecting Fertility

PID is one major cause of infertility that can be prevented. The best means of prevention is judicious choice of sexual partners. It's a good idea, for many reasons, to be cautious about having sex with a man until more can be learned about his sexual habits. A man who has many different sexual partners is clearly not a good candidate. As the army training films suggest, you can't tell if the man has VD by looking in his eyes.

If a woman thinks she has contracted an infection – or even thinks she has been exposed to one – she shouldn't wait for symptoms to appear. She should go to a Special Treatment Clinic, or Genital Medicine Clinic immediately and tell the physician why she has come. The woman should ask for a pelvic examination and gonorrhoea tests – not merely a check-up.

The physical examination should be followed by both a slide analysis of the vaginal discharge in the surgery and a culture of the discharge at the lab. The physician examines a few drops of the discharge under a microscope to check for infecting organisms. Full-blown infections will show up immediately on the slide test. Even if the slide analysis shows nothing, it is important that the laboratory culture be performed, since early infections may become apparent only when bacteria are allowed to grow in the proper laboratory environment for twenty-four hours. If a woman feels certain that she was exposed to venereal disease, she should emphasize this and ask about a protective course of antibiotics until the results are in from the lab test.

Repairing Tubal Damage

If the fertility specialist knows that a woman has had PID, the extent of the damage is assessed with laparoscopy and dye studies. These procedures complement one another. Chapter 15 describes fully how these diagnostic procedures are used together to evaluate the internal reproductive organs. A surgeon should never plan full-scale microsurgery until the damage has been assessed by laparoscopy. In some cases, the damage can be repaired through the laparoscope, without a major incision into the abdomen.

Laparoscopy offers a full outside view of all the organs within the pelvic cavity. Scar tissue and adhesions wrapped around the organs are clearly visible. The dye study (hysterosalpingogram) will show whether the tubes are open; if the tubes are blocked, an X-ray of the dye inside the tubes will show exactly where the blockage is.

Four things can happen to the tube. First, and most commonly, the fimbria will scar over and 'club'. Rather than resembling a flowerette, the fimbria will look like a round stump. Nothing can get in – or out – of the tube. Second, scar tissue builds around the fallopian tube and attaches the organs together. Third, the tube may puff up with excess fluid that cannot escape through the clubbed fimbria. This is called a hydrosalpinx.

Finally, as infection works its way through the narrow segment leading out of the uterus, it may break down the lining of the tube. The walls of the tube then cave in and stick together. In this case, the infection literally cuts itself off from the rest of the tube. After the infection is cleared up, the obstruction remains. It may be fairly thin, or may be so thick that it intrudes well into the middle portions of the tube.

Today, adhesions and scar tissue can be cut away and damaged tubes 'reconstructed' by microsurgery, but at present this is only available at a few centres in Britain. The problem with any kind of surgery, of course, is that the surgery itself often lays down more scar tissue. Success depends on the extent of the damage, the skill of the surgeon, and the surgical technique used. For example, a scalpel yields poor results on the narrow cornual end of the tube because even the sharpest blade cannot cut without damaging surrounding tissue. Laser microsurgery, which minimizes scarring, can vaporize obstructions lodged in this spot; the surgeon then stitches the tube back into the uterus.

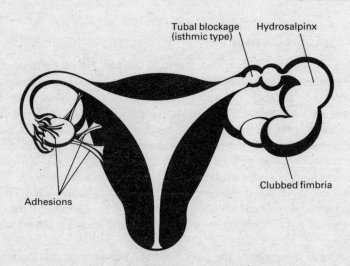

Tubal blockage
(isthmic type)

Hydrosalpinx

Clubbed fimbria

Adhesions

Common sites of tubal obstructions

The fimbria presents a much more complex challenge. The fimbria's job is to pick up the egg from the surface of an ovary. To do this, it relies on millions of cilia brush tips, which act as a conveyor belt. If the cilia are crushed in the process of opening the tube, they cannot do their job. Instead of being sucked along into the tube, the egg will simply roll off into the abdomen. The tube may be opened with either conventional microsurgery or laser surgery. Again, the extremely precise laser seems to offer new hope for these cases.

22
Endometriosis

The second major cause of scarring and blockages inside the pelvic cavity is endometriosis, one of the most pervasive and least understood diseases of the female reproductive system. About 15 per cent of all women have endometriosis, and the incidence of infertility among these women is nearly 50 per cent. Although endometriosis can occur at any age, it occurs most frequently in women over thirty who have never had children.

As more and more women delay childbirth, infertility related to endometriosis is likely to rise. If a woman with endometriosis can succeed in getting pregnant in her early twenties, she may avoid the worst repercussions of the disease. (Pregnancy clears up endometriosis for a time because hormonal fluctuation temporarily stops.)

In this painful and destructive disease, tissue identical to the endometrial lining of the uterus begins to grow in the abdomen. Somehow, these endometrial cells implant on the outside of the uterus and on the ovaries or bowel, and continue to grow just as if they were inside the uterus. Every month, the implants are stimulated by the same hormones that build the endometrium of the uterus: the misplaced tissue grows and spreads through the pelvic cavity. At the end of the monthly cycle the tissue bleeds just like the endometrium. Bleeding creates scar tissue. Remnants of the tissue burgeon again the following month and spread through the pelvic cavity until the ovaries and tubes are smothered in scar tissue.

Origins

Despite considerable speculation and research, the origins of endometriosis remain elusive. The most popular theory is that bits of endometrial tissue go up the fallopian tubes and escape into the abdomen. During menstruation the misplaced tissue is trapped in the abdomen and cannot slough off through the vagina with the rest of the endometrium. The problem with this theory is that some women who have had their tubes tied, a procedure that blocks any exit into the abdomen, still get endometriosis. If the endometrial tissue can't spread back through the tubes, how does it get into the pelvic cavity?

One possible explanation is that endometriosis is a birth defect. Young endometrial cells are misplaced during fetal development. They may lie dormant for years, then begin to grow after a woman reaches puberty. This may explain why endometriosis tends to run in families. It's also possible that loose endometrial cells travel through the lymphatic system or blood vessels, because endometriosis is sometimes found in organs far from the pelvic cavity, such as the lungs or the rectum. Whatever its origin, even a small amount of endometriosis in the wrong place can interfere with fertility.

How Endometriosis Affects Fertility

Endometriosis seems to affect fertility in several ways. The endometrial implants take little tucks in the surface of the organs, kinking and puckering the skin so that egg pick-up and transport become difficult. Monthly bleeding from the implants irritates the surfaces of all the organs. When two raw, irritated surfaces come into contact, they fuse and are bound together by scar tissue. Also, as the endometrial cells divide, rupture, and burn out, they leave massive dead scar tissue around reproductive organs. For some reason, the open ends of the fallopian tubes are usually spared from endometrial attack, but the ovaries and uterus are highly susceptible.

Several new theories about the effects of endometriosis are under investigation. In some women even a tiny amount of endometriosis, with minimal scarring, appears to cause infertility. Researchers theorize that the body's defence mechanism recognizes the misplaced tissue as a foreign substance and sends out antibodies against it. The same antibodies may kill sperm or in rare cases reject a fertilized ovum (see Chapter 29).

Another theory states that women with endometriosis have a higher level of prostaglandins, a chemical byproduct of the disease. Prostaglandins are hormones that cause blood vessels to narrow and smooth muscles to contract so that the level of oxygen is decreased. The resulting pain is similar to a heart attack, except that it occurs in the uterus. Increased prostaglandins may make the tube contract sharply and prevent pick-up of the egg.

A third possibility is that endometriosis shortens the second half of the menstrual cycle. If this luteal phase is too short, the lining of the uterus doesn't have time to prepare for a fertilized ovum. Even if fertilization takes place, the uterus will reject the implant (spontaneous abortion). Nearly half of all pregnant women with mild endometriosis will abort.

Symptoms

The major symptom of endometriosis – consistent, severe cramping before, during, or after menstruation – is often associated with lower back pain, leg cramps, and discomfort around the inner thighs. The pain is caused by the excess tissue pressing on the nerves and seems to worsen on the second and third days of the menstrual cycle. In addition, the extra prostaglandins cause contraction of the smooth muscles. Bleeding between periods and pain during sexual intercourse are other common symptoms.

Doctors used to believe that menstrual pain was a normal and perhaps largely imagined event. Generations of doctors told their female patients who suffered menstrual pain that there was nothing wrong. Drugs could relieve the cramping somewhat, but according to medical science there was no real physiological reason for the pain.

Even though endometriosis is most prevalent in women between thirty and forty, it also occurs in younger women. Years ago, teenage girls who sometimes fainted from menstrual pain were told they were having an 'emotional response' to puberty. The pain, along with the fainting spells, would supposedly pass when they got older. For these young women, pain became a normal monthly event. Sometimes, if they succeeded in getting pregnant, the symptoms disappeared for a while. But many women never became pregnant, and the symptoms endured for a lifetime.

Emotional Side-effects

Depression is a common byproduct of endometriosis. A woman's feelings of self-worth diminish when she is ill with a mysterious, hidden disease that causes pain during normal sexual intercourse. Women often say: 'I feel sick inside.' 'Everything churns on the inside.' 'I'm just a shell walking around.' Some older women feel they are being punished because they didn't have children when they were young. One thirty-five-year-old woman said, 'I'm paying a terrible price because I'm a lawyer instead of a mother.'

When women don't feel right about themselves physically, they don't feel right about being someone's sexual partner. Endometriosis poses an especially difficult problem for a single woman trying to form new attachments. The association of sex with pain removes all pleasure from the encounter. The pain also heightens any existing guilt feelings about sex. Sex drive decreases, and a woman may begin to doubt her sexuality. Some women cease to achieve orgasm and even fail to lubricate during sex.

Medical treatment can produce unpleasant side-effects that exaggerate all the negative feelings a woman is already experiencing. Even more disturbing than the physical changes are the quick fluctuations in mood – angry one minute, sad the next – triggered by drug therapy.

Women who haven't had time to discover their sexual identities may be especially troubled by endometriosis. One young woman became so confused that she began to wonder whether she was a normal woman with a physical problem or a crazy, frigid, neurotic woman who hated sex. When she was seventeen, Libby eloped with her school sweetheart. The marriage ended in an annulment a few weeks later, primarily because Libby discovered that she was frigid. Petting was all right, but intercourse made her feel that she was doing something wrong. Besides, intercourse was uncomfortable.

A few years later Libby had an affair with an older man who offered her a much more polished sexual relationship than her teenage husband. Libby recognized the difference, yet still experienced pain during intercourse. The relationship ended within a few weeks. Libby consulted her doctor, but was too embarrassed to be explicit. Her doctor told her that everything seemed fine and that unless she was concerned about her ability to bear children there was no need for a medical check-up.

Libby dated a few men, and each intimate act had the same unpleasant result. Either the men dropped her or she withdrew from the relationship. By the time she was twenty-four, Libby had sworn off men. 'I knew it was me,' she said, 'that I was frigid or something, and I just couldn't deal with it.'

Then she met Jack, and for the first time in her life felt a physical response to a man. She was elated. After a few months, they set a wedding date. But even as they planned for the future, things began to go wrong. Libby became withdrawn. Jack, who was in love with her, put it down to prenuptial nerves. Libby did not tell him that every time they had intercourse she was in pain.

Jack and Libby were married on schedule, and things went from bad to worse. Their relationship deteriorated so rapidly that Libby finally told Jack about the pain. He seemed to think it was an excuse to avoid sex with him and felt rejected. Libby grew less affectionate.

Finally, Libby went to a doctor, who performed a laparoscopy and discovered the endometriosis. He explained that endometriosis, not Libby's imagination, was causing the pain. Libby was given danazol, a new drug that has proved especially effective against the disease. The drug is also known to have disturbing side-effects in some women, but Libby's doctor did not warn her about that.

As soon as Libby started taking danazol, her personality changed radically. Her moods shifted violently – she would weep uncontrollably one minute, then attack aggressively the next. She experienced double vision. She gained weight, her voice deepened, and hair started to grow along the sides of her face and over her upper lip. The physical changes frightened her and made her feel ugly and undesirable. Although Jack now understood about the pain, the alteration in mood completely mystified him.

They started fighting every day. Libby wouldn't let Jack touch her, and he felt more rejected than ever. After ten months of misery, the doctor took Libby off danazol, and recommended surgery to erase the remaining endometriosis. Following the surgery, the physician told Libby and Jack that if they wanted a child they should have one as soon as possible. If the endometriosis recurred, as was likely, Libby's reproductive organs could be damaged beyond repair.

The demand for pregnancy put even more pressure on the marriage. Libby and Jack had been married less than two years, and it had all been terrible. Now they were supposed to have a baby. Jack felt they should work out their problems before having children. Libby's response was, 'You don't love me.' And when they had sex, Libby still felt pain, even though the endometriosis supposedly was gone. She could not separate the illness from their sexual relationship.

Eventually, Jack began to see other women. He felt so guilty about the affairs that he confessed to Libby and moved out of the house. Surprisingly, as soon as Jack left, Libby was filled with remorse; she begged him for another chance. He agreed, but only if they sought marital counselling. Fortunately, the counsellor they chose was experienced in working with infertile couples. He explained that the stress and sexual confusion Libby was experiencing was common for women suffering from endometriosis.

At this point, however, the endometriosis had so tangled up their relationship, and caused so much bad feeling between them, that a lot of emotional repair work had to be done before they could get back on solid footing and feel any sort of affection for each other. The marriage survived, though it took a long time for Libby to lose her fear of sex. They also postponed trying to have a baby until they resolved their marital problems. As their doctor had warned, there was a possibility that the endometriosis would recur, and it eventually did, although in a relatively mild form. Libby and Jack still have hopes of having a baby.

One thing seems certain – Libby and Jack might have been saved much of the trauma in their marriage if they had received psychological evaluation when Libby first visited the doctor. Clearly this is an extreme case, but it demonstrates the serious emotional repercussions that can arise when a woman suffers from endometriosis.

Frequently, women with the greatest amount of endometriosis have the least pain, and those with the smallest amount have the most pain. The pain seems to be worse in the early stages of the disease, when the cells are burgeoning, rupturing, and spreading. After the disease has progressed and created thick sheets of scar tissue around the organs, the pain lessens, since scar tissue causes less pressure than active cells. However, if the scarring is on a critical site, it can still hurt, especially during sexual intercourse.

Not every woman who has endometriosis suffers pain. In fact, in 30 per cent of infertile women with the disease, infertility is the only symptom.

Making the Diagnosis

Endometriosis is diagnosed by a combination of three tests: history, pelvic examination, and laparoscopy. Laboratory studies offer no diagnostic evidence for this disease.

If present, physical symptoms of pain often resemble those of chronic pelvic infection. To distinguish between the two, a doctor should perform a pelvic examination while the patient is actually experiencing the pain, usually just before her period begins. If endometriosis is present, a bluish cyst may appear on the cervix and the doctor may feel tender nodules or some thickening of the ligaments that support the uterus. Endometrial implants around the uterus and ovaries feel like clumps of tiny beads.

Often, however, he will feel nothing unusual on physical examination. The diagnosis can be confirmed, and the extent of the endometriosis assessed, only by laparoscopy.

A laparoscope inserted through a tiny incision in the umbilicus allows a full view of the uterus, fallopian tubes, and ovaries. Laparoscopy should be performed after ovulation, on days 20–25 of the menstrual cycle, when hormonal stimulation is at its height. At this point, any implants will be swollen and easy to detect. This simple and necessary procedure requires an overnight stay in the hospital and is usually performed under general anaesthesia (see Chapter 16). A laparoscopy is a standard part of a good fertility investigation.

Stages of Endometriosis

Endometriosis changes in appearance as the disease progresses. In the early stages, it may look like little tucks on the surface of the ovaries or like scattered bits of ashes or charred tissue paper. In the more advanced stages, cysts form. As the tissue bleeds each month, the cysts swell with blood, and over a period of time they can become extremely large. Sometimes the endometriosis burns out and leaves behind massive patterns of dead plaque.

Endometriosis is classified according to what the surgeon sees through the laparoscope. Stage I is early, minimal disease. There is some puckering, little mounds of tissue with blue dots in the crater, and tobacco-coloured stains where implants have died. The implants are confined to the back of the uterus and around the supporting ligaments.

Stage II is still considered a mild form of the disease. Now the little implants have spread to the bladder and ovaries, and even the fallopian tubes, with some scar formation between the uterus and ovaries. The cysts are up to $\frac{1}{4}$ in (8 mm) in diameter.

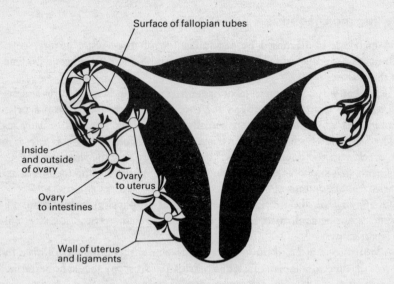

Common sites of endometrial implants

Stage III is moderate disease. The cysts now may be up to 3 in (7.5 cm) in diameter, taking over the bowel and ovaries. A cyst full of old blood (chocolate cyst), classically involving an ovary, is common. On laparoscopy the whole ovary looks like a huge, dark blue cyst.

Stage IV is severe endometriosis. The cysts may be very large; or the disease may have progressed to the point where the cysts have burned out, but massive scar tissue remains throughout the abdomen. The fallopian tubes may be twisted and buried in scar tissue. In extreme cases, all the organs are buried beneath rubbery sheets of scar tissue, and the surgeon may not even be able to distinguish one organ from another.

In these very serious cases, laser surgery is quite successful. If the tubes can be freed from the scar masses, the fimbria will still be open and able to pick up an egg. For some mysterious reason, endometriosis spares the fimbria, the critical portion of the egg transport system.

Treatment

Treatment of endometriosis is controversial. The disease may be treated with drugs or surgery, or a combination of the two. Some surgeons feel that medical treatment with drugs, which takes several months, prolongs the condition and does not always work. They believe it is more expedient, and therefore ultimately less stressful, to clear out the endometriosis surgically as soon as possible. Surgery ensures that the endometriosis is cleared (with drug therapy it is hard to tell). And, following surgery, the woman has those extra months in which to get pregnant. This approach makes particular sense for older women whose biological time clocks are running down.

In Britain drug teatment is usually tried initially unless chocolate cysts are extensive, in which case surgery is necessary. Modern drug therapy with danazol to shrink endometrial implants is often successful. With the help of drug therapy, the body usually does a much better job of cleaning up the disease than surgery can. Drug therapy also saves the patient the trauma of major abdominal surgery and the risk of more scar tissue forming.

There are good arguments for both medical and surgical treatment. The mode of treatment selected should depend on the woman's age and the extent of the disease.

Drug Therapy

Danazol is a synthetic weak male hormone that stops ovulation by inhibiting the brain control centre, which in turn suppresses the ovaries. Without hormone stimulation from the ovaries, the endometrium cannot develop. Likewise, endometrial implants scattered through the pelvic cavity are deprived of hormones. The implants shrink and ultimately disappear. Although danazol acts primarily on the control centre, some medical evidence suggests that it may also directly suppress the endometrium.

The drug is usually taken over a period of several months; it is the best possible medical therapy for endometriosis known today. A prime benefit is that ovulation resumes within six weeks after the drug is stopped.

Side-effects. As we have seen, a small percentage of women experience serious side-effects with danazol. Not every doctor prepares patients for the possibility of side-effects. Some doctors believe it's better to wait and see if side-effects occur, so that a woman's imagination doesn't play tricks on her. Also, if she knows about the side-effects, she may be unwilling to take the drug.

In fact, severe side-effects are rare: only about 5 per cent of women who take danazol experience side-effects severe enough to warrant complete withdrawal from the drug. Still, every patient should know what to expect from a drug. A patient who does experience the sharp swings of mood that may accompany treatment with danazol may be able to recognize those swings as a result of the drug, not her own personality. A reduction in dosage may diminish the effect.

Other side-effects include muscle cramps and nausea, weight gain, facial hair, acne, and increased sex drive. If a woman experiences any breakthrough bleeding during the month, her physician should measure the oestrogen level in her blood. A high oestrogen content means that danazol isn't working, and the woman should receive another form of therapy. Severe headaches, personality changes, and depression all indicate that the drug should be stopped. All side-effects are usually completely reversible as soon as the drug is stopped.

Alternatives. When danazol doesn't work, other hormone drugs can be used. Overall, the alternatives are less effective and more likely to induce side-effects. The combination oestrogen/progesterone birth-control pill can be used to suppress the endometrium. However, for the pill to work as treatment for endometriosis, menstrual bleeding must be completely stopped. This usually requires such high doses that the side-effects of nausea and vomiting and the risk of blood clots are increased. Oral progesterone, which blocks only one part of the hormonal axis, can sometimes be effective. However, the necessary dosage is so high that it may take six months to two years after the drug is stopped for ovulation to begin again.

When all else fails, the doctor may suggest a trial course of testosterone. Given daily in low doses, this male hormone stops ovulation and seems to suppress endometrial implant directly. Testosterone is very rarely used, however, because of its masculinizing side-effects, such as heavy hair growth and changes in body configuration.

Advances. The newest medical therapy, which can be used either to induce ovulation or to stop ovulation, is a synthetic form of LH-RH, the releasing factor produced by the hypothalamus. When LH-RH is given as a supplement, an excess builds up in the blood and overdoses the pituitary gland. The pituitary gland doesn't know how to read the constant signal of LH-RH and shuts down its production of hormones.

LH-RH therapy is still in the experimental stages; the major problem to overcome is administration. At this time the drug must be injected daily. Ultimately, it may be used with a small plastic tube embedded into body fat so that the hormone is released in a constant dose over the whole monthly cycle.

Stages I and II

Some physicians feel it is unnecessary to treat minimal endometriosis because the disease may not interfere with pregnancy. They prefer to wait and see if the patient gets pregnant without treatment. Unfortunately, while the patient is waiting, the disease can get worse, and damage to reproductive function may be irreversible. Also, even a small amount of endometriosis seems to interfere with pregnancy in some women. For these reasons, we think that even the smallest amount of endometriosis should be eradicated.

Women with minimal (Stage I) endometriosis will usually respond to medical therapy alone. Danazol is prescribed for three months, and then stopped. Generally pain and tenderness are completely relieved, and within six months of stopping the drug 65 per cent of women will become pregnant. If they are not pregnant within six months, a second-look laparoscopy is in order to see if the endometriosis is still present.

Women with mild (Stage II) endometriosis should respond to similar treatment, with the drug therapy lengthened from three to six months. If a woman is resistant to danazol or if the endometriosis is cleared and then comes back, surgery with a laser will erase all remaining signs of endometriosis. After proper medical treatment of the less severe forms (Stages I and II), 60–70 per cent of women become pregnant.

Stages III and IV

Treatment for Stages III and IV should be adjusted to a woman's age. If the woman is under thirty-two, danazol is usually prescribed for nine months, after which a second-look laparoscopy is performed. Over 75 per cent of women with extensive disease will still have scar tissue after medical therapy. Surgery can be used to clean up the remainder.

Where available, the laser can perform some remarkable feats in advanced endometriosis without damaging existing organs. For example, if the endometriosis has invaded the ovaries, a huge chocolate cyst filled with old endometrial blood and tissue will take over the entire ovary. Using the laser, the surgeon can split open the ovary and let the thick, dark blood and tissue spill out. The inside of the ovary may be blanketed with endometriosis. After the old blood is emptied out, the surgeon skims a laser back and forth across the inner surface of the ovary, vaporizing the endometriosis without disturbing the delicate underlayer of egg cells that impregnate the lining. When the endometriosis is cleaned out, the surgeon stitches the ovary back together; it is a hardy organ and fully regenerates itself. As long as the egg cells are undisturbed, the ovary will revive and function normally.

After surgery, the patient takes danazol for another three months to make sure that any endometrial remnants are damped down. After the third month, she stops the drug.

Over the following year, as the patient tries to get pregnant, the doctor should monitor her menstrual cycle at random to make sure that she is ovulating. This is a critical phase: after medical treatment and surgery, the patient cannot afford to have medical oversight delay or impede pregnancy. Temperature charts and progesterone levels taken every three or four months, plus a check of mid-cycle cervical mucus, will confirm that ovulation is occurring on schedule.

If the patient is not pregnant within twelve months, the doctor should perform a third laparoscopy. Endometriosis may have recurred or previous surgery may have created new scar tissue. Because of the potential for even more scarring, there is considerable controversy about performing three laparoscopies. But if a woman isn't pregnant within a year, something is wrong; the only way to discover the problem is to look. If everything appears normal on the laparoscopy, the patient must wait a little longer. But if the endometriosis proves highly drug resistant, every effort should be made to destroy it surgically.

If the woman is over thirty-two years of age, there are two major differences in treatment. First, after three months of post-operative danazol, a third laparoscopy should be performed immediately, before the woman embarks on a year-long quest for pregnancy. It is imperative to make sure that the combined surgery and drug treatment has left her with a clean pelvic cavity and that the next twelve months will provide an optimum opportunity for pregnancy. The reason is obvious: the patient is running out of time. About half the time, a few filmy adhesions are left between the tubes and uterus. Even this transparent tissue can tie the tube down and prevent pregnancy. Where available, laser surgery or microsurgery through the laparoscope can remove these adhesions. Some physicians believe the adhesions do not have to be removed, but results indicate an excellent pregnancy rate when they are.

The second major adjustment is a monthly check of ovulation during the year the woman tries to get pregnant. Again, this continuous watchfulness on the part of patient and physician is essential to ensure every possible opportunity for pregnancy.

Success Rates

The combined medical and surgical approach described above offers excellent chances of success even in Stages III and IV of the disease. At the Omega Institute we treated and kept track of 159 women with extensive endometrial disease for three years. Their average age was thirty-two. After the variables unrelated to treatment were taken into account, the rate of conception was 80 per cent – which is exactly the probability for normal, fertile women.

Surprisingly, researchers are finding a better pregnancy rate with Stages III and IV endometriosis than with milder stages of the disease. With the more advanced stages, the disease has often burned itself out. The new surgical techniques can clear away the dead scar tissue, and as long as the disease is inactive, chances of pregnancy are good. The fact that the disease is active in the early stages, even though scarring is mild, suggests that some other problem – perhaps an unknown chemical reaction from the active disease – is causing the infertility.

Complications

Tubal (ectopic) pregnancy is fairly common after treatment of Stage III or IV endometriosis. Some researchers report an overall figure of around 16 per cent (compared with 1 per cent in normal, fertile women). With medical and laser treatment combined, the ectopic rate is only 4.4 per cent. An ectopic pregnancy can be life-threatening, and many women lose their fallopian tubes along with the pregnancy. However, conservation is the byword of modern surgery, and it's essential to try to preserve the tube if an ectopic pregnancy occurs. A laser can remove the ectopic pregnancy without major damage to the fallopian tube. Among fourteen patients who had this procedure done at our clinic, eight became pregnant again and went on to deliver normal babies. To date, not one of the fourteen has suffered a second ectopic pregnancy. (Note, however, that laser microsurgery is not yet available in most British hospitals.)

Sometimes the pain caused by endometriosis is incapacitating; in severe cases certain nerve fibres within the pelvic cavity can be cut. If all the pelvic organs are bound and pain continues to increase, a hysterectomy and removal of both ovaries may be the only relief. Clearly, this is a major decision and any woman who is considering hysterectomy should have a second, and perhaps third, opinion.

There is one important fact to remember about endometriosis. So far, it cannot be cured. Treatment is aimed at controlling the disease. Even after a woman has a child, endometriosis can still come back and begin to grow again.

23
Problems in the Cervix and Uterus

The Cervix

At the end of the vaginal tunnel lies the cervix, a small pink valve that leads to the uterus. The smallness of the mound of flesh, with its pinpoint centre, belies the enormity of the task it performs for the female body. The cervix receives those sperm that survive the rigours of a journey through the vagina. The tiny glands that line the cervical canal secrete mucus, which protects the sperm and supplements the seminal fluid. Little crypts within the cervical canal act as way stations for sperm to rest and pace their ascent into the uterus.

In addition to providing many benefits for sperm while a woman is ovulating, the cervix protects the pelvic cavity from invasion by foreign bacteria over the rest of the cycle. During pregnancy, the round valve also acts as a retaining ring to hold the fetus inside the uterus.

Because of the vital nature of its task, even minor problems in the cervix can lead to infertility. Between 10 and 15 per cent of fertility problems in women can be traced to a poorly functioning cervix. Most of these problems involve the cervical mucus.

Hostile Cervical Mucus

Normally, the great quantities of mucus produced by the glands of the cervix during ovulation provide an inviting, slightly alkaline milieu for sperm. Should the mucus turn acidic for any reason, sperm stop in their tracks or die instantly. A hostile cervical mucus can be created by infections, trauma to the glands, or antibodies.

Infections. When the cervical glands become infected, they secrete infected mucus. As the sperm reach the cervix, they are killed or immobilized by the infected mucus. Either bacteria or viruses can infect the cervix. Antibiotics will cure most infections. Occasionally, small polyps within the cervical canal irritate the glands so that they produce a similar type of mucus. Once the polyps are removed, the infected condition subsides.

Trauma. Cryosurgery (freezing) or electrosurgery to remove growths on the cervix sometimes scar the glands and block mucus secretions. Glyceryl guaiacolate, the active ingredient in cough syrup, is effective medical therapy in some cases, because it increases the secretion of all mucus glands in the body.

Antibodies. Occasionally, during examination cervical mucus will look normal, but the postcoital test, which examines the activity of sperm in the mucus, reveals immobilized sperm. This immobilization may be caused by antibodies in the cervical mucus. Checking for antibodies in women involves serum assays, a sophisticated and relatively expensive series of tests.

Antibodies are sticky protein substances produced by the body's defence (immune) system. These proteins travel in body fluids; whenever a foreign substance appears, the antibody protein sticks to it. Foreign cells covered with sticky antibodies clump together and are unable to spread through the body. The antibodies clinging to the surface of foreign substances are like little flags that attract killer cells known as phagocytes. The phagocytes swoop down on the foreign substances and literally eat them up.

When antibodies have once been called to action by the body's immune system, they learn to respond quickly the next time a similar foreign substance shows up. Antibodies attach instantly and in great numbers.

For unknown reasons, some women send out antibodies against sperm. A woman may be allergic to all sperm or only to her husband's sperm. Some physicians have prescribed low-dose steroids to reduce the woman's allergic response, but the results have been mixed. The best treatment seems to be eliminating contact between the sperm and cervix for a long period of time. If the husband wears a condom during intercourse, the antibody reaction eventually subsides. When antibodies are in remission, the couple can have free intercourse during ovulation, in the hope that the woman will become pregnant before the antibody reaction re-establishes itself.

Laser Treatment for Antibodies. When no other medical management succeeds, we have found that the cervical glands can be eradicated with the laser and new growth stimulated with oral oestrogen therapy. Such surgery was performed on the cervical glands of eight women with chronic infection or suspected antibodies who did not respond to antibiotic therapy. The glands grew back and began to produce healthy cervical mucus, without a sign of infection or antibodies. Over the last sixteen months, all eight women have become pregnant. This small series is encouraging, but cervical factors need much more investigation before we can routinely recommend laser therapy for 'antibody problems'.

Artificial Insemination. When all else fails, and the cervical mucus continues its hostile activity towards sperm, the cervix can be bypassed with a special form of artificial insemination. This is usually performed by depositing semen into the cervical mucus rather than directly into the uterus, to reduce the risk of infection. The sperm then make their own way through the cervical canal and into the fallopian tubes. In this variation, however, the sperm are first washed and suspended in fresh media. The doctor gently inserts a straw-like catheter through the cervix and injects the sperm directly into the uterus. This type of insemination is a last resort because there's always a small risk of pushing bacteria into the uterus.

Cervical Incompetence

Occasionally infertility is caused by a cervix that is too weak to support a developing pregnancy. With this condition, called an incompetent cervix, the cervical ring dilates prematurely and the pregnancy falls out. The only symptom is a painless spontaneous abortion after twelve to twenty weeks of pregnancy. The condition is very difficult to foresee and is usually diagnosed only after a woman becomes pregnant and miscarries.

When an incompetent cervix is suspected, the doctor should watch a woman closely as her pregnancy develops. If the cervix begins to dilate in early pregnancy, a suture should be placed around the cervix to give it added support. The woman may need intermittent bed rest throughout the pregnancy.

When a woman has had two or more spontaneous abortions and her cervix can be easily dilated, the physician can be certain enough of the diagnosis to make the surgical correction before pregnancy. To spare further trauma to the cervix, the baby can be delivered by caesarean section.

One woman who had seven spontaneous abortions was told to have a hysterectomy. Instead, she chose to have surgery performed on her cervix. She subsequently gave birth to two healthy babies by caesarean section.

The Uterus

The uterus is a remarkably sturdy organ and is rarely a source of infertility problems. Problems that do occasionally arise are caused by developmental defects, infections or surgery that scar the lining, or fibroid tumors that distort the inner walls and prevent the embryo from attaching or growing.

Developmental Defects

Once in a while a female baby is born without a uterus; in some instances, the vagina is also missing and defects arise in the urinary system. These are very rare events. Most developmental defects in the uterus are slight structural modifications and do not necessarily lead to infertility.

Women whose mothers took DES in the first and second trimesters have a propensity to structural defects in the reproductive tract. DES abnormalities include a T-shaped uterus and unusual bands of tissue within the vagina. Sometimes there is a narrowing at the juncture where the fallopian tubes open out of the uterus. Many women who have a slight distortion in the shape of the uterus are still able to bear children.

The most common of all developmental variations is a heart-shaped uterus (uterus cordiformis). When the heart shape is pronounced, a septum (wall) may divide the middle of the uterine cavity. A few women are born with two separate uteri, two cervices, and even two vaginas; the embryologic Mullerian tubes that normally fuse into a single reproductive organ system remain separate and develop into two half systems.

Infertility problems correlate with the volume of the uterine cavity. If the

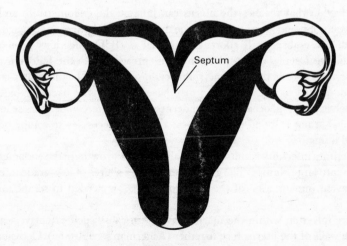

Heart-shaped uterus with septum

deformity makes the cavity too small, the uterus cannot expand enough to retain a pregnancy and abortion occurs.

Diagnosis. A double vagina and double cervix are easily identified on the physical examination. However, a deformed uterus may require X-ray, dye studies, and laparoscopy to determine the nature and extent of the problem. The more distorted the shape, the easier the diagnosis.

Whether surgery is needed depends on the severity of the defect. For example, a heart-shaped uterus rarely causes a problem. A septum in the uterus may require surgical correction if a woman has been unable to carry a pregnancy to term. Two different surgical approaches may be used to remove a septum. If the septum is thin, it can be removed through a hysteroscope, if available. The surgeon inserts long, thin scissors through the operating channel of the hysteroscope, snips around the wall, and pulls out the septum with forceps.

A thick septum requires major surgery. The laser is exceptionally effective in reducing operating time and blood loss in this procedure, and allows the surgeon to remove the septum through a small opening in the roof of the uterus. Other problems, such as double uterus, vagina, and cervix, require more inventive surgical corrections. Again, the goal is to create a single uterus big enough to support a pregnancy. If a woman does not wish to have a child, the uterus is left alone.

Infections

Any infection that reaches the uterus can inflame the endometrium and scar inner walls. Should a woman become pregnant while the endometrium is infected, the embryo will abort. Chlamydial or IUD infections need quick antibiotic treatment to prevent them from spreading into the fallopian tubes. Chronic infection of the endometrium (endometritis) is diagnosed by culture and endometrial biopsy. A woman may have symptoms of irregular bleeding, lower pelvic pain, and occasionally tenderness during intercourse. If these uterine infections do not respond to antibiotics, a D&C is necessary to scrape out the infected lining.

Sometimes infertility results when small polyps or growths in the endometrium develop into large clumps. The growths are often a source of low-grade infection and prevent implantation of the embryo. A D&C is needed to scrape out the polyps.

Severe infection within the uterine cavity can cause such extensive scarring that the walls of the uterus fuse together (Asherman's syndrome). Occasionally, an overzealous D&C may strip away so much of the endometrium that the walls stick together. If damage is minimal, a woman's menstrual flow may remain relatively normal; if it is severe, she may cease menstruating. X-ray and dye studies will reveal the scar tissue. In such cases there is little that can be done.

Fibroid Tumours

The most common of all uterine problems are fibroid tumours. These benign tumours of the uterus occur in approximately one woman in four aged thirty to fifty. Fibroid tumours are growths of fibrous connective tissue that develop at varying depths within the uterine wall, and sometimes interfere with implantation of an embryo. In these cases, a woman is able to conceive, but may suffer repeated spontaneous abortions (see Chapter 29). The most damaging location to fertility is in the inner wall of the uterus, between the muscle and the endometrium. Occasionally, a tumour deeper in the uterine wall will compress the passageway into a fallopian tube and create a natural tubal sterilization.

Fibroids are stimulated by oestrogen, so they may enlarge during pregnancy, when high-dose birth control pills are being taken, or when hormone supplements are taken after menopause. However, growth is usually slow and they shrink when hormone stimulation is reduced.

Uterine fibroids usually have no symptoms, and they are almost always benign. A doctor can feel them during the pelvic examination and discover their exact size and location by using ultrasound. Ultrasound is also an excellent way to observe the growth or regression of the tumour. Unfortunately, tumours cannot currently be shrunk without causing a chemically induced menopause.

Treatment is not needed unless the fibroids cause chronic or severe pain or bleeding, grow rapidly, or if the tumours appear to interfere with conception or implantation of the embryo. New microsurgical and laser techniques are being developed for removing fibroid tumours in an operation called a myomectomy.

In the past, when clusters of large fibroids caused frequent menstruation and pain, many women were subjected to hysterectomies, and fibroids are still the most common reason for hysterectomy today. Yet for many women the procedure can be avoided unless severe haemorrhaging is threatening the woman's life. Sometimes the tumours are so close to the uterine blood supply that the entire uterus must be removed. Also, if multiple fibroids completely take over the womb or if extensive adhesions make removal of tumours impossible, the uterus must be removed.

When an infertile woman has fibroid tumours that are not causing her pain, she and her husband should complete the tests before resorting to a myomectomy. Recently, a woman was referred to us for laser surgery to remove fibroids from her uterus so she could become pregnant. Her physician assumed that the fibroids were interfering with conception. When we took a routine semen analysis from her husband, we discovered he was sterile.

Only when the specialist is certain that the fibroids are causing a fertility problem, and only when all other factors have been corrected, are fibroid tumours removed. A major abdominal incision is necessary, and the tumours are cut out of the uterine wall. The wall is carefully repaired, to maximize the size of the inside cavity and avoid damage to the delicate fallopian tubes.

24
Microsurgery, Lasers, and the Twenty-first Century

Lasers are hot, lasers are cool. Lasers are used to make records, develop colour film, and saw James Bond in half. Apparently there is no limit to what the ingenious light beam can achieve. In the hands of a skilled microsurgeon, the laser (for *L*ight *A*mplification by *S*timulated *E*mission of *R*adiation) is nothing less than a magic wand. The instrument has justified the brilliant claims made for it by performing delicate surgery on the brain, eye, hands, and throat. In these surgical specialities the laser is a miracle worker. For the gynaecologist, the laser offers hope to thousands of infertile women.

All these advances have taken place in less than twenty years, and they have revolutionized surgical techniques in operating rooms around the world. We have come a long way from the days when the best-known surgery was whacking off injured limbs with an axe or drilling holes in a person's skull to let disease leak out. Skull drilling, or trephining, is perhaps the oldest-known form of surgery. Ancient skulls recovered from archaeological digs lead us to believe that cavemen saw some merit in the technique. Certainly the Mayas and Aztecs were known to perform it routinely, apparently with some delicacy. Whereas most cave skulls show only one blunt hole, Mayan skulls often have four or five neatly drilled holes.

As civilizations progressed, surgeons became more sophisticated in their techniques. The Greeks and Romans recorded many marvellous operations – amputations, tumour removals, even eye surgery. Over the less enlightened centuries that followed, surgery was advanced through techniques acquired through warfare and torture. As knowledge of human anatomy grew, so did surgical skills. Modern surgery came into existence when physicians learned that instead of simply chopping into limbs and organs, they could tie blood vessels and close up cuts.

Towards Constructive Surgery

All surgical techniques took a great leap forward with the advent of sulpha drugs and modern antibiotics, yet surgery remained an essentially destructive process, based on the principle that any organ that was diseased should be removed. Early attempts at constructive surgery (repair of organs) were limited by the surgeon's ability to see, and operate between, small blood vessels and nerves. A few surgeons tried to operate on the brain and other critical organs, but these attempts at microsurgery (surgery of small structures) were dismal failures.

In 1886 a Dutch surgeon tried using binocular glasses for surgery on the eye, but the technique did not catch on. In 1921 Dr C. O. Nylen performed ear surgery under a microscope, but again the operation failed to attract attention. It wasn't until 1961, when neurosurgeon H. P. House described how he had removed tumours around the auditory nerve, that surgeons began to show interest in operating magnification. Other specialities followed suit, and surgeons soon were able to operate successfully on small areas throughout the body. Today some form of magnification is used in all microsurgery, including vascular, plastic, hand, brain, ear, nose, and throat. Magnification of the actual structure may range anywhere from × 4 to × 25.

The microscope changed the face of surgery throughout the world. For the first time surgeons saw the damage that conventional scalpels and sutures did to delicate tissue surfaces. They saw sutures tear through tissue and blood spill out of microscopic blood vessels. This bleeding, caused by ordinary handling of the organs, led to the formation of adhesions as the wound healed. As a result of these new visions, manufacturers began to develop much finer thread and much smaller surgical instruments. Surgeons learned new techniques to handle tissue gently and lessen trauma.

Today, sutures are made from delicate strands of non–irritating synthetic plastic. Surgical needles are a fraction of an eyelash in length, so small that it is difficult to find one in the palm of the hand.

Gynaecologists were especially receptive to the new microsurgical techniques. In 1967 Swedish gynaecologist Dr Kurt Swolin used an operating microscope to perform microsurgery on a blocked fallopian tube. The operation set off a chain of events that are still being felt throughout medicine. Over the next few years microsurgical techniques developed by Dr Victor Gomel of Vancouver, Dr R. Palmer of France, and Drs J. Rock, C. R. Garcia, and L. Mastrioanni in the United States transformed the way surgery was performed on the female reproductive organs. At the 1974 meeting of the World Infertility Society, Robert Winston, an infertility specialist at the Hammersmith Hospital in London, described another landmark; operating under a microscope, Winston was able to obtain consistently excellent results in rebuilding fallopian tubes that had been severed during tubal sterilization.

Today, gynaecologists achieve a better than 60 per cent pregnancy rate with tubal reversal. The same technique is used to rebuild the fallopian tubes of infertile women. Under a scope, the extremely delicate and thin tube can be reconstructed by cutting out the obstruction, and separately stitching the tubal layers back together.

The microscope is responsible for many other advances made in infertility in the last two decades. 'Invisible' endometrial implants show up clearly under the microscope. Surgeons can put a normal-looking fimbria under the microscope and see filmy adhesions that retard egg pick-up. The microscope also allows the surgeon to operate between critical blood vessels that carry blood to the fallopian tube; if these vessels are inadvertently cut by surgery, the tube will wither and die.

Today, all pelvic surgery on young women, including removal of an ovarian cyst, should be performed using the basic principles of microsurgery: gentle handling of tissue, small sutures, moist tissue, minimal operating time, and magnification when indicated.

Light Scalpels and the Future

At the same time that Drs Gomel and Winston were performing tubal reversals under the microscope, the surgical laser was first used in gynaecology.

In its precision, the surgical laser exceeds all known forms of surgery, including the scalpel and the electric needle. The laser allows surgeons to reach inaccessible tissues, even if it means reflecting the beam around corners with mirrors. More important, as it cuts, the laser damages only seven red blood cells on either side of the impact site. By comparison, electrosurgery damages 100 to 1,000 cells, and the scalpel literally tears tissue apart.

A laser produces a very particular kind of light energy. Unlike the diffused light from an ordinary bulb, laser light is highly concentrated. To illustrate its intensity, imagine taking all the light waves produced by a 100-watt bulb and distilling them into a thin, highly energetic rod; that same 100 watts would now be powerful enough to burn through a quarter-inch plate of solid steel.

Lasers were put to surgical use soon after their initial industrial development in the early 1960s. Most of these light scalpels operate on the principle that laser light, on impact, turns into heat. When the beam touches a cell, the fluid inside boils over and the cell is 'vaporized'. The laser is so precise that it can vaporize a few cells at a time, without damaging surrounding tissue.

There are several different kinds of surgical lasers. Some have deep penetration; others barely glide on the surface of the skin. Some are blue-green, others are red, and still others, in the infra-red spectrum, are invisible.

Colour allows the laser to beam through some tissue without damage and

248 · CAUSES AND TREATMENT : WOMEN

reach a target organ behind it. For example, the first surgical laser, the ruby laser, was initially used by eye surgeons to repair detached retinas. The red beam passes harmlessly through the transparent cornea covering the eye, but once it strikes the pigmented layer at the back of the eyeball, it is instantly absorbed and converted into heat. The heat is so intense that the peeling layers of the detached retina are 'spot-welded' back into place. Today, ophthalmologists use a variety of lasers to treat and repair delicate parts of the eye.

In the beginning there was one major drawback to laser surgery. Since the laser beam is uncompromisingly straight, it was impossible to use a laser on tumours deep inside the body without major surgery by scalpel to expose the target site. This problem was brilliantly solved for many procedures with the invention of flexible optical fibres, the revolutionary communications medium that conducts light waves (instead of electricity) along thin strands of glass.

By threading optical fibres through the body's natural openings, laser surgeons can reach into the recesses of the body. The laser beam, travelling inside the sheath of a fibre, enters the body, turns corners, and slips into places that scalpels cannot fit. More than 90 per cent of the laser's energy comes out at the target site. Heart surgeons predict that bypass operations will soon be outmoded by a procedure that clears blockages by pumping a laser beam along fibre optics threaded through the arteries.

In gynaecology, fibre optics are used to beam lasers through the laparoscope, allowing the surgeon to make minor repairs without a major incision. Most infertility surgery, however, does require an abdominal incision and an exposed operating field.

During abdominal surgery, the exposed organs are packed with wet gauze, which protects them from accidental penetration by the laser beam. The surgical carbon dioxide (CO_2) laser, which is powerful enough to cut through steel, cannot penetrate a wet handkerchief because CO_2 laser energy is absorbed by water.

The CO_2 laser is the most versatile laser used in surgery. It was the brainchild of Dr Thomas Polanyi, project director of American Optical Company, and Dr Geza Yako of Boston University. The first CO_2 laser was tested in Boston, and the second was brought to the Ear, Nose, and Throat Hospital in New Orleans through the efforts of Dr Ronald French.

Since the CO_2 laser can be tuned to penetrate or merely prick the surface of the skin, it is used to particularly spectacular effect in surgery performed on the ear, nose, and throat. For example, in the narrow regions of the throat, growths on vocal cords are extremely difficult to remove. But the CO_2 laser can slip into the confined space of the voice box and vaporize the growth – without touching the cord itself and thus saving the power of speech.

It was just such a procedure that attracted our attention to the possibility of using the surgical laser on the extremely fragile tissues of the female reproductive system, which bear a remarkable similarity to the tissues of the mouth. The first laser microsurgery on the female reproductive tract was performed by Dr Joseph Bellina in April 1974. The patient was a twenty-one-year-old woman with a pre-cancerous lesion on the cervix. Using the laser, Bellina erased the lesion with the same technique used to erase pre-cancers in the mouth. Encouraged by the precision, lack of bleeding, and exquisite healing in this initial case, Bellina applied the same technique to twenty similar patients, with the same excellent results.

In the past these lesions, which are increasingly common in young women, were usually removed by cryosurgery or electrocautery; both methods cause pain and scarring, and cryosurgery often has a high recurrence rate. Today, laser surgery, a brief procedure, is an excellent treatment for cervical lesions. The cure rate is dramatic: 96–8 per cent.

These early successes helped develop the laser technique. In September 1974 Bellina and Dr Janos I. Voros became the first surgeons in the world to use the laser to operate on blocked fallopian tubes. The patient, a twenty-two-year-old infertile woman, conceived six months after surgery and subsequently gave birth to a healthy baby boy.

The laser systems used today would make Buck Rogers turn green. In the laser surgeon's operating room, a high-powered, double-faced operating microscope is mounted on a massive floor stand and suspended above the operating table. The balance of the microscope is so delicate that it can be adjusted with the light touch of a finger. Surgeons on either side of the operating table can look through the microscope and share the same view.

The laser is housed in a three-foot metal box supported on a hydraulic lift. At the base of the lift is another box that contains the laser's power source. By adjusting the knobs and switches, the surgeon can select an infinite array of power, time, and beam parameters.

Through long tubes and gold mirrors the laser light is fed into the surgical microscope. The surgeon pilots the laser like a plane – if he can see the target, he can beam the laser into the tissue and vaporize it. The surgeon pinpoints the target through the microscope lenses, lines up the beam with an ingenious joystick, and fires the laser. Sometimes the surgeon directs the beam around corners by bouncing the light off a hand-held mirror. At the speed of light, the beam cuts through the tissue and seals the vessels with utmost precision.

In the last ten years the use of the laser in gynaecology has grown rapidly. At the Omega Institute the laser has replaced the scalpel in 90 per cent of microsurgical procedures. Surgeons use the light scalpel to cut adhesions, open blocked segments of the fallopian tube, remove dividing walls from the uterus, cut away infected tissue, remove fibroid tumours, and destroy even the smallest amount of endometriosis.

Operating time is reduced considerably. In conventional surgery much time is used to cut tissue with a scalpel, cauterize each bleeding vessel with an electric needle, and then repair the damage with sutures. The laser cuts the tissue, seals vessels, and repairs the area in one smooth motion, without trauma to the tissue. For example, when tubal blockage is performed with conventional microsurgery, the surgeon needs twenty minutes to an hour to repair each tube before it can be sewn back together. The laser surgeon needs only one to three minutes to vaporize the blocked segments before proceeding with the fine microscopic suturing of the layers of the fallopian tube.

Because total operating time is reduced, less anaesthesia is needed, and recovery time is shorter. Most people who have laser surgery on the abdomen leave the hospital within four days and return to normal activity within ten days. Because there is so little trauma to surrounding tissue, new scarring is minimal, and tubes and other organs remain free.

The medical community at large has been slow to accept the surgical laser. It is a complex, expensive instrument that requires special training to use. Just as every doctor does not have the skills needed to perform surgery, so every surgeon does not have the special talent required to use the laser. Laser surgeons operate without touching the patient. Yet their eye, hand, and foot reactions and coordination must be excellent in order to control an instrument that functions at the speed of light. Today the laser is the instrument of choice in much brain, throat, and eye surgery. And its uses are expanding daily in the fields of gynaecology and urology.

Lasers and microsurgery are slowly coming into use in Britain and an increasing number of young gynaecologists are learning the technique. Unfortunately, high technology techniques are slow to spread because of shortage of funds in the NHS.

Causes and Treatment: Men

25
Varicocele and
Other Production Problems

Infertility in men is almost always caused by a collection of overlapping problems. It is virtually impossible to pin down one without another popping out. Organizing the causes in an orderly manner is like trying to line up a gaggle of schoolchildren the day before the summer holidays.

For those of us working in the science of infertility, the 'male factor' is a new and unfinished jigsaw puzzle. Many pieces are still missing, and those that are present often fit into more than one spot. A single disease may affect several different facets of the male reproductive system. For example, a hormonal defect originating in the brain may have its ultimate effect in the testicles. A man may be born with the defect, or it may be caused by an illness later in life. A kick in the scrotum can have the same result: poor sperm production. At present, there is no neat way to fit these pieces together.

The andrologists who work so diligently in this field have been able to identify many male infertility problems, yet treatment is not always possible. Most problems fall into three broad categories. The first, and biggest, category is sperm production. The second is sperm transport. The third is impotence and other problems associated with depositing sperm in the woman's vagina.

Sperm production is like a symphony: many instruments must play in perfect harmony to make the music. The brain control centre must be perfectly coordinated with a well-developed sperm factory in the testicles. Many male infertility problems can be traced to a flaw in one of these systems. One of the few exceptions is varicocele, the most curious and most prominent of all causes of male infertility. Varicocele is a category unto itself.

Varicocele

Varicocele may turn out to be the most common cause of male infertility; fortunately, at this time it is also the most treatable. Between 30 and 40 per cent

254 · CAUSES AND TREATMENT: MEN

of all infertile men have a varicocele – a varicose vein of the testicle – as their only symptom. Yet andrologists disagree heartily about the significance of a varicocele.

Varicose veins usually occur in the legs and lower parts of the body, where there is the greatest fluid pressure. For the same reason, they also occur in the testicles. About 10 per cent of all men have a varicocele, and most of the time it is harmless. But in a significant number of men, the varicocele seems to cause infertility.

Here is how a varicocele develops. The heart is like a water tower. It pumps blood into the circulatory system by way of the arteries to the organs; from the organs blood returns to the heart by way of the veins, which are flaccid tubes. Since the veins have no pump, muscle pressure creates a squeezing action, which literally pushes the blood back to the heart by a series of one-way valves.

A ladder of these valves lines the return pathways of the veins. If the valve leaflets are defective, as they often are in the lower extremities, blood falls back. When one valve falls apart, pressure builds on the valve below; eventually all valves give way and the valve ladder is destroyed. This creates a heavy pool of stagnant blood. The more valve damage, the higher the reservoir of blood, until a point is reached where the vein begins to swell. This is a varicocele, or varicose vein of the testicle.

Most of the time the varicocele occurs in the left testicle, probably because of a slight difference in anatomy between the veins draining the two testicles. (In the left testicle, the spermatic vein enters the renal vein at a right angle, allowing for pressure. In the right testicle, the vein enters at a more oblique angle, moderating the pressure and putting less strain on the valves.) Sometimes there is so much pressure that the other testicle is affected. Rarely does a varicocele occur only on the right testicle.

Exactly how a varicocele leads to infertility remains a mystery. Of the several theories advanced, the most credible is that the pooled venous blood overheats the sperm production centres of the testicles. Excess heat can kill sperm. Heat can also speed up sperm production, causing the primary cells to divide so fast that sperm are forced rapidly through development without enough time to mature in each stage. The result is immature and deformed sperm.

If the theory is correct, why doesn't every varicocele cause infertility? Neither the size nor the location of a varicocele seems to have any bearing on its effect. Another theory suggests that the damaged veins allow chemical toxins normally cleansed through the kidneys to drift down into the testicle. But this possibility seems remote and also does not explain 'selective' infertility. The only certainty about a varicocele is that if it is surgically tied off, sperm production often improves.

Diagnosis

A varicocele may be discovered for the first time during a man's physical examination, when he is asked to stand up and bear down or cough. If a varicocele is present, the extra pressure will usually make the vein bulge, and the specialist can feel it in the scrotum. Sometimes, however, the varicocele is so small or so hidden that it can't be felt.

Two devices can help the specialist detect a hidden varicocele. One is thermography, which can detect pockets of heat in the testicles. The other is the Doppler stethoscope, which magnifies sound so much that the specialist can listen to the blood flowing through the veins (see Chapter 17).

If a varicocele is discovered, the specialist will compare the finding with the semen analysis. A varicocele that causes fertility problems presents a distinct pattern on the semen analysis – typically, a great number of immature sperm, with tapered or 'stressed' heads. Many more sperm are dead or dying.

Treatment

If a varicocele is present and the semen analysis shows a stress pattern and a low sperm count, surgery is usually recommended. Either general or local anaesthesia can be used in this operation. The surgeon makes an incision in the groin, locates the spermatic cord, and isolates the veins from the artery and vas deferens. The surgeon then ties off the main trunk of the veins above the varicocele.

New pathways will open up to carry blood to and from the testicles. The man usually remains in the hospital for the day or overnight and can resume his normal activities, including sex, within a week.

New surgical techniques have been developed to allow the surgeon to correct the varicocele without a major incision. One technique uses a tiny balloon inserted into the vein through a skin puncture. When the balloon is inflated, the vein is blocked. The technique has the same effect as tying off the vein.

Another new technique, developed by Dr Joel Marmar of North Carolina University Medical School, involves making a small incision in the groin, then using a microscope to separate the vein from the pulsating spermatic artery. The surgeon ties off the main trunk and injects the smaller veins with a sclerosing agent to block them. Marmar's technique offers the advantage of magnification, which reduces the risk of damage to the critical artery to the testicles.

After surgery, a man must wait three months for new sperm to develop and find their way into the ejaculate. This is a stressful period, since the first post-operative semen analysis will not be taken for ninety days. Some improvement is

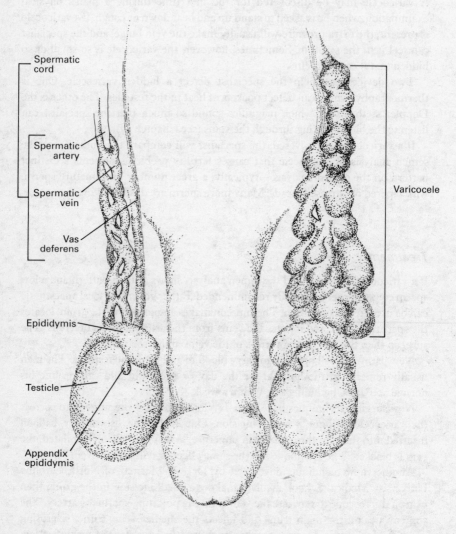

Spermatic
cord

Spermatic
artery

Spermatic
vein

Vas
deferens

Varicocele

Epididymis

Testicle

Appendix
epididymis

Varicocele

usually seen at that time; but maximum recovery of sperm usually doesn't show up until the next analysis, at the six-month mark.

Semen quality and/or sperm count improves in 80 per cent of infertile men who have surgery, but only half of these men go on to impregnate their wives. The number of successful pregnancies is higher for those men whose sperm counts were relatively high (10–20 million per cc) before surgery. The pregnancy rate is somewhat lower when the sperm count is under 10 million per cc before surgery. Even so, the overall high success rate makes surgical correction of varicocele the most effective of all fertility treatments available to men.

If the sperm count doesn't improve following surgery, some physicians recommend a course of drug therapy with either clomiphene or HCG (human chorionic gonadotrophin). HCG is similar to the brain hormone LH, which helps the testicles produce testosterone.

Other Factors

Why doesn't every man whose sperm count returns to normal succeed in impregnating his wife? We suspect that extenuating circumstances are involved in many cases. Here's where all the other tests in the male and female fertility investigation come into play.

Careful history-taking may show hidden psychological factors at work. Not every infertile couple really wants to have a child, and some couples may unconsciously avoid sex during the fertile period. Or something may be off in the woman's ovulation pattern. Surgeons can correct the varicocele, but if the fertility team misses the other, more subtle causes of infertility, the couple will not get pregnant. Careful evaluation of both partners can pick up additional causes and improve the pregnancy rate.

One difficult question is whether a varicocele poses a threat to fertile men. Should a fertile man with a varicocele have surgery to tie off the vein? Does an infertile man who doesn't want children need surgery? The answer seems to depend on the size of the varicocele.

A large varicocele can be dangerous. Sluggish blood flow has the potential to create a blood clot, known as thrombosis. Any blow to the scrotum can cause the clot to break loose and travel to the heart or lungs. A man who has a varicocele should wear a scrotal support, similar to a support stocking for varicose veins. The support presses the stagnant blood out of the vein and lessens the risk of clotting. The bigger the varicocele, the greater the risk of a blood clot, and the more vulnerable the varicocele is to injury. The specialist should document the size of a varicocele when it is first discovered and measure it again three to six months later. If the varicocele is large and growing, surgery is probably indicated.

Although a varicocele affects sperm production, it is not, strictly speaking, a sperm production problem. Sperm production problems are primarily divided into those originating in the hormonal system (brain control centre) and those originating in the sperm factories of the testicles.

Hormonal Problems

The hormonal system is so complex that it seems easy for something to go wrong. Yet in men it is a superior system, rarely faltering. The reason for its durability is that a man's control centre supplies hormones in a steady daily rhythm rather than in the cyclical, on-off system required for women. The system does fluctuate slightly throughout the day in response to stress, illness, frequency of ejaculation, and other yet-to-be-identified factors. Even so, in men hormones are implicated in only 15 per cent of infertility problems (compared with 40 per cent in women).

Sperm production is directly controlled by the brain control centre, which is comprised of the hypothalamus and the pituitary. These work closely together, and both can be damaged. The hypothalamus can be damaged by tumours, infections such as encephalitis, and drugs. When the hypothalamus fails to supply the LH-RH signal to the pituitary gland, the pituitary does not send hormone signals to the testicles. Sperm and testosterone production cease.

Kallman's Syndrome

A primary example of trouble in the hypothalamus is Kallman's syndrome, which is probably congenital. In Kallman's syndrome, the cells of the hypothalamus are defective and cannot release the LH-RH signal.

The little that scientists know about Kallman's syndrome indicates that the central nervous system does not develop properly in the embryo. Men born with Kallman's never complete puberty. In their late teens they are tall and skinny with small, soft testicles and no sense of smell. The inability to smell is a classic symptom of Kallman's, because along with other vital cells the olfactory nerves fail to develop. Men born with Kallman's may also be deaf and possibly colour-blind. Cleft lip or cleft palate is common.

Generally, a man with Kallman's syndrome will have no sperm in his ejaculate. Blood tests show that all hormones are very low. When a biopsy is taken from the testicles, the seminiferous tubules that produce sperm are immature, and the mother cells are poorly developed. No Leydig's cells have developed in the testicles and the man makes no testosterone. Chromosome analysis is normal. All the tests together point to a weakness in the hypothalamus. Long-term treatment with HCG may at least help testosterone levels rise to normal, so that a man's sexual characteristics will develop.

The drug that holds the most promise for this disorder is synthetic LH-RH, which supplies the missing signal from the hypothalamus. The pituitary gland receives the signal and begins to produce its hormones, which will start the testicles going. This drug is still highly experimental and is given by daily injection. Researchers are experimenting with a long-acting LH-RH capsule that can be implanted in fatty tissue and release the signal over a period of time. Preliminary studies report that when men with Kallman's syndrome receive LH-RH they achieve full sexual maturation and begin to produce sperm in normal quantities.

The Fertile Eunuch

Sometimes the hypothalamus sends the proper signal, but the pituitary gland fails to fully respond. One example is the 'fertile eunuch', a rare condition in which only one pituitary hormone, LH, is low. Because the pituitary gland does not send LH to the testicles, the Leydig's cells do not produce enough testosterone. The man has a small penis and no sex drive. His body is feminine in shape and usually shows some breast development.

Blood tests show that FSH is normal, which means that the man may actually produce some sperm. A man with this problem usually responds superbly to supplemental LH, in the form of HCG. Regardless of the man's age when he begins taking the drug, the testicles will be encouraged to produce testosterone. As the testosterone level rises in the blood, sexual characteristics develop and sperm production increases. If neither of these hormones works, a testosterone supplement may be needed to increase the man's sex drive.

Other Pituitary Problems

No one knows why the pituitary gland fails in some men. If the failure occurs before a boy reaches puberty, sexual characteristics will never develop and his testicles will remain small. If failure occurs after puberty, a man will develop more breast tissue, his testicles will soften, and he will become impotent. Failure of the pituitary occurs about equally in men and boys. Semen analysis shows no sperm or a very low count.

The pituitary gland seldom ceases to function completely. Most often it fails partially, and both FSH and LH subside together. By far the most commonly known cause of a failed pituitary gland is a small growth within the gland that compresses or destroys the hormone-producing cells.

Such a tumour usually shows up long before a man recognizes a fertility problem. In women, a pituitary tumour is quickly revealed because of menstrual irregularities. In men, the tumour must grow quite large before symptoms appear. As the tumour grows it compresses the optic nerve, causing loss of vision. Hormone studies show that both FSH and LH are low. Prolactin, a hormone that keeps a low profile in men, is usually high. Elevated prolactin in itself is not proof that a tumour exists, because stress, drugs, and other outside influences can cause this hormone to rise. Pituitary tumours are diagnosed by CAT scan and can be removed surgically.

When pituitary hormones are low for unknown reasons, a physician will sometimes try fertility drugs to stimulate the testicles. Clomiphene, which stimulates FSH, acts by blocking the oestrogen receptor sites on the hypothalamus. Theoretically this drug, which is highly successful in women, should have little effect on men, since men produce very little oestrogen. Yet some researchers have reported encouraging results. Others find that clomiphene actually depresses sperm counts. To date, Pergonal, which supplies FSH and LH directly to the testicles, has shown the most promise for infertile men. However, all hormone therapy for men is highly speculative and requires further study. The prevailing opinion is that it doesn't hurt to try, but a man shouldn't get his hopes up.

Problems Outside the Control Centre

Sometimes excess hormones coming from other endocrine glands can enter the pathway of the axis between the control centre and the testicles. When this happens the axis becomes jammed with erratic signals.

Adrenal Gland. A fault in the adrenal gland is a rare, but important, cause of male infertility. The adrenal gland produces identical male hormones in men and women. Should the adrenal begin producing excess male hormones, the pituitary responds just as if these hormones had come from the testicles. The excess hormones feed back to the pituitary, and LH and even FSH are suppressed.

In young boys, excess adrenal testosterone causes rapid hair development and growth of the penis and scrotum at the expense of sperm production. Sperm production requires both FSH and LH in a balanced system to complete the maturation of sperm. If the gland acts up after puberty, the man will have normal sexual characteristics, although his sperm count will be low. If the adrenal gland interferes before puberty, his sexual characteristics will be advanced for his age.

Hormone studies will show a normal to low FSH, low LH, and a high level of testosterone. To figure out where the excess testosterone is coming from, the physician administers a steroid to suppress the adrenal gland. If testosterone has subsided when the blood levels are measured again, the physician knows it originated in the adrenal gland. If the testosterone level is the same, the excess hormone originated in the testicle. An ailing adrenal gland is treated with adrenal steroid (cortisol), which slows testosterone production.

Thyroid Gland. Years ago when a man had a low sperm count he was automatically given thyroid hormones. Today thyroid is given only if a disease state – too much or too little thyroid – exists. The thyroid gland regulates cell metabolism, the rate at which cells burn up protein and sugars. If there is too much or too little thyroid, the cell thermostats respond by increasing or decreasing their metabolism. Sperm production, like all other cell systems, may be affected. However, by the time a man's sperm count is affected, he usually has many other physical symptoms. The diagnosis is made with blood tests.

With hyperthyroidism (too much thyroid), the man is agitated, can't sleep, and feels muscle fatigue; he is irritable and his reflexes are ultra-active. His hands shake, and occasionally there is a swelling in the neck. Hyperthyroidism seldom causes infertility because the symptoms are so pronounced that the man receives treatment before sperm production is affected. Treatment may be in the form of drugs that reduce thyroid production or radiation of the gland.

With hypothyroidism (too little thyroid), the man is sleepy and frequently constipated. His reflexes are poor, and his speech is slurred. He may begin to lose his hair and there may be a swelling in his neck. The treatment is to give thyroid supplements.

Problems in the Testicles

A man is born with a certain number of mother cells (spermatogonia) in place, and no treatment in the world will increase that number. Sometimes fertility drugs will temporarily stimulate the existing cells, but this is short-lived. Anything that destroys the mother cells will reduce fertility. When cells are lost to infection, illness, or injury, it's as if they never existed. If half the spermatogonia are knocked out, the man will have a 50 per cent decrease in sperm production.

A variety of events can conspire to directly destroy the spermatogonia, and together these causes account for about 15 per cent of all male infertility. A low or absent sperm count may be the only symptom. Various tests are used to diagnose testicular failure, including semen analysis, chromosome and hormone analysis, and the fructose test. The chances of improving sperm production in these instances are dismal.

Mumps

Mumps – that seemingly innocent swelling of the salivary glands in the neck and jaw – can be dangerous to both boys and men. In a child, mumps that leads to pneumonia can be lethal.

The mumps virus does not usually attack the testicles in boys. A virus looks for cells that are turning over rapidly, it invades the nuclei of these cells and starts dividing along with them. In a child, the reproductive cells are at rest and therefore relatively safe from the mumps virus.

After the boy reaches puberty, however, these reproductive cells begin to divide rapidly. A mumps virus will now settle into the cells of the testicles and divide millions of times, until the cells explode. This is mumps orchitis – a disease that can destroy the mother cells.

Only 18 per cent of all cases of mumps occur in men past the age of puberty. And 70 per cent of the time in adult men the virus affects only one testicle; the other testicle continues to function normally and produce adequate numbers of sperm.

Fortunately, when mumps does affect both testicles, the disease is often halted before the testicles are completely ruined. The nuclei of the mother cells may be in shock, but they have a good chance of recovery. Sometimes it takes a year for sperm production to come back to normal. Less than 5 per cent of men who contract mumps are left sterile.

The diagnosis of infertility caused by mumps is made from the history, semen analysis, and blood tests. On the physical examination the testicles are usually small. A typical finding on a blood test is a high FSH. When the testicles stop working, no hormones feed back to the brain. The pituitary gland beefs up FSH in an effort to stimulate the testicles. Thus, hormone tests will show a high level of FSH in the bloodstream.

If sperm are absent, there is no treatment. If a man has some sperm, there is always a chance he will respond to hormone therapy. In this case, he should receive the complete check-up, and all attempts should be made to increase sperm production with fertility drugs.

Venereal Disease

Years ago severe gonorrhoea infections could lead to meningitis and even death. Today, with modern antibiotic treatment, gonorrhoea seldom gets past the urethra; and only 2 per cent of the time does the disease reach the epididymis and cause infertility.

The signs of gonorrhoea are thick, yellow-white pus discharge and pain on urination. Repeated gonorrhoea infections may lead to a stricture of the urethra. Scarring narrows the opening and a man may have trouble ejaculating and urinating. Scarring can be corrected surgically, but there's always the chance that surgery will create new scar tissue.

Treatment consists of penicillin and probenecid or a tetracycline class of drug. A few strains of gonorrhoea are resistant to routine therapy and require antibiotics such as spectinomycin. A new strain of gonorrhoea, which became prominent during the Vietnam war, has resisted all forms of antibiotics. In rare cases this highly dangerous organism can lead to death. A man who has any sign of venereal infection should never assume that it is innocuous; he should seek prompt treatment from a urologist.

Gonorrhoea does not usually cause infertility in men, but it is dangerous when transmitted to women, since it can completely destroy the female reproductive organs.

Prostate Infections

Prostate infections, which occur only rarely in young men, can pose fertility problems. The man's sperm count will be depressed while the infection is rampant, but will return to normal after the disease has subsided. Prostate infections are notoriously difficult to treat because of the interior design of the gland. Even after antibiotic therapy, bacteria can remain hidden in multiple lobes of the prostate, causing recurrent flare-ups.

The man's sperm count will fluctuate as flare-ups recur and subside, but the real danger is in transmitting the infection to a woman. Certain types of prostate infections are readily transferred during intercourse. If a woman's pelvic cavity is invaded, the infection can permanently damage her reproductive organs. For this reason, prostate infections need to be monitored vigorously. To protect his sexual partner, a man who has had a prostate infection should have continuous antibiotic treatment for a period of two years to make sure the prostatic fluid is clear of infection.

Other Illnesses

Many other viral and bacterial infections can alter sperm production. A primary symptom is discharge from the urethra; a man may notice a slight discharge of pus or mucus in his underpants or jockstrap. Sharp twinges or dull aches around the testicles can also be warning signs that infection is present. Should the prostate be infected, a low, dull backache may be the only symptom. All these signs and symptoms should be thoroughly evaluated by a urologist.

Measles and other viral infections that cause high fever can be severe enough to alter sperm production temporarily. Any virus that invades the body has the potential to enter the testicle. Whenever a man has a general infection accompanied by swollen or painful testicles, he should consult a urologist.

Many illnesses that do not directly involve the reproductive organs may still temporarily halt sperm production. Infection anywhere in the body or any illness associated with persistent high fever, such as hepatitis and mononucleosis, can dramatically depress sperm production. Flu virus and dental abscess have also been associated with low sperm production. Once the underlying infection is cleared up, sperm production will usually return to normal within three months.

Testicular tumours can displace and smother spermatogonia. Tumours that originate in the testicles or that migrate into the testicles from other parts of the body have a strong tendency to malignancy.

Any illness that affects the metabolism of the body (such as diabetes mellitus) can have an adverse effect on sperm production. A classic example is a diseased liver that can no longer clear used hormones. The chemicals stack up in the blood and block the hormonal axis between the control centre and the testicles.

All these illnesses require careful diagnosis and treatment. When they are controlled or cured, sperm production usually resumes.

Trauma

Some men have been rendered partially or totally infertile by injury to the testicles, which are especially vulnerable because of their location outside the protective body cavity. Moreover, like the eye, the testicle seems to have a sympathetic response to injury in its partner. If one testicle dies, the other, healthy testicle may reduce its production of sperm.

Sports Injuries. Straddle injuries or direct blows to the testicles during vigorous athletic activity can have devastating effects. The organs swell dramatically because the tissue inside is inflamed and bleeding. Ruptured vessels may reduce the flow of oxygen to spermatogonia and cause the cells to die. Applying ice packs and waiting for the swelling to go down can result in irreversible damage. Ruptured blood vessels may heal, but scar tissue can block the ductal system. Such injuries demand immediate surgical treatment.

The surgeon opens the testicle and removes the damaged tissue, then sews the rind of the tunic back together. If the repair is clean, little or no scarring occurs. Such injuries are relatively rare, and they are the one form of male infertility that is preventable; risk of injury is lessened when a man wears a sports cup during strenuous sports activity.

Torsion. Torsion is a rare, spontaneous event in which one testicle twists on its own blood supply. The event is painful and sudden. If the testicle is not released within six hours, it will die. To save the testicle, a urologist first unwinds the organ, then stabilizes it with sutures to adjacent tissue.

Surgical Injury. Some kinds of surgery can threaten the blood supply to one or both testicles. Surgery to repair a hernia or to release undescended testicles comes treacherously close to the spermatic cord. Either the vas or an artery may be accidentally damaged. Vas injuries can be repaired; injury to the artery, however, usually leads to permanent death of the testicle.

Congenital Defects. There are some problems in the sperm production centre of the testicle that a man is simply born with. During fetal development the testicle arises out of a cloudy, amorphous cell mass that pushes its way through the abdominal wall and comes to rest outside the abdomen in the scrotum. Any minor lag in this amazing journey can result in a major problem in adult life.

Sertoli's Cell-Only Syndrome. In extremely rare cases, the spermatogonia are missing, probably from birth. During fetal development the mother cells do not migrate properly with the rest of the cells that eventually make up the testicles. However, the Sertoli's support cells, which are thought to help regulate sperm production, are present.

Semen analysis shows no sperm, but fructose is present, indicating that the transport system is open. A hormone study shows a high FSH. The testicular biopsy is normal, except for one thing: absence of spermatogonia. There is no possible treatment for Sertoli's cell–only syndrome.

Klinefelter's Syndrome. A few congenital disorders are caused by spontaneous defects in the sex chromosomes. In Klinefelter's syndrome, first described in 1942, a man will have at least one extra X chromosome in his cells, and sometimes more. Chromosomal disorders of any kind are extremely rare. Even Klinefelter's, considered the most common, occurs in only 0·2 per cent of the male population; 1–2 per cent of infertile men have Klinefelter's.

The disorder is sometimes noticed when a boy's testicles fail to mature during puberty. But in many instances the slightly feminine look to the body – small testicles, slightly enlarged breasts – is still well within the range of what is considered a normal outward appearance. Most men who have Klinefelter's are unaware of it. They are comfortable with their masculinity and their sexual identity. They seek medical advice because they have an infertility problem. Unfortunately, there is nothing that can be done to alter the XXY pattern, and these men will never be able to produce sperm. If the sex drive is diminished because of low testosterone levels, as sometimes happens, a testosterone supplement will usually stimulate the sex drive.

Some men with Klinefelter's have what is known as a mosaic pattern, in which some of the cells in the body carry the XXY chromosome and others carry the normal XY. Men with this mixture of normal and abnormal sex chromosomes may produce some sperm. Infertile men with a mosaic pattern may be helped with drugs. If a man with mosaic Klinefelter's succeeds in impregnating a woman, the fetus should be normal.

Hidden Testicles. The testicles are formed behind the abdominal cavity near the kidneys of the male fetus, and by the time the child is born they have descended into the scrotum. For some reason, about one out of every 200 male babies is born with one or both testicles still inside the body proper. When the child reaches puberty he will develop all the masculine characteristics, but the warm environment of the abdomen will have destroyed the ability of the testicles to make sperm. Hidden testicles are responsible for about 5 per cent of male infertility.

At one time physicians advised waiting until puberty to see if the testicles descended spontaneously. But once the damage to the sperm factory is done, there is no treatment. Today the testicles are brought down through microsurgery into the cooler environment of the scrotum early enough to preserve fertility.

The diagnosis of undescended testicles is usually made as soon as the baby is delivered. Between six and eighteen months the infant is given HCG to increase testosterone levels. If the testicles don't descend naturally after drug therapy, microsurgery is recommended as early as possible. The younger the boy is when surgery is performed, the more likely his sperm-producing capacity will be intact. Two years is considered the optimum age.

If only one testicle is hidden and the other is in the scrotum, the boy will probably be fertile after he reaches puberty. However, the hidden testicle can become cancerous and should be routinely examined along with the normal testicle.

'Cause Unknown'. Most of the time we don't know why the testicles fail to develop normal sperm-producing cells. The sperm count is less than 10 million per cc, and no traceable cause can be found. The testicles are normal or somewhat small; the transport system and all other sexual characteristics appear normal.

The cause is probably related to something that happened when the fetus was developing in the uterus. For example, we know that male babies of mothers who took DES, a form of oestrogen, may have abnormal semen analysis (thick, viscous semen, low volume, or poor movement). This is uncharted territory for fertility researchers.

Environmental Stress

Many elements outside the body influence what is going on inside. Stress, heat, altitude, and drugs, to mention only a few factors, can all affect sperm production. As sperm cells grow and mature, they become increasingly sensitive to toxic agents from the environment. Therefore, a man suffering from environmental stress may continue to produce sperm, but the cells will be sluggish or deformed. Often, only some of the sperm-producing tubules are affected, while the others remain relatively free from environmental toxins. Further, the Leydig's cells can sustain almost any abuse without losing their ability to make the male hormone testosterone. A man's sperm may be affected without affecting his sex drive.

Stress. In general, stress, anxiety, and tension have a deleterious effect on sperm production. Emotional stress alters the functioning of the hypothalamus, which in turn affects all the signals passing back and forth along the hormonal axis. This phenomenon has been proved conclusively in both human and animal studies. In 1933, in a rather bizarre study, testicular biopsies were performed at various times on prisoners waiting on death row. Severe depletions were seen in sperm production, and in some cases sperm production completely ceased.

Stress produces similar effects in animals. Overstressed male rats show diminished fertility, and young mice in crowded cages show inhibited and delayed puberty. Even though these effects are well documented, most researchers believe that only severe and prolonged stress, not the ordinary wear and tear of daily life, will affect fertility. The trouble with this view is that stress events accumulate in modern life, with subtle and compounded effects. It is difficult to say with certainty that stress is not involved in a man's infertility.

Diet. The consensus of the medical community is that good nutrition is important to sperm production, though this position is hard to prove. Severe crash diets seem to lower sperm production, but production returns to normal when a regular diet is resumed. As in women, this phenomenon may be traceable to the hypothalamus. The appetite control centre is located in the hypothalamus, and may interact with reproductive signals to the testicles and ovaries. Women who lose weight rapidly often stop menstruating.

Some research has been performed to learn whether specific vitamins have any effect on sperm production. Vitamin E deficiency damages the testicles in rats, but the effect has never been observed in humans. Vitamin C may help men whose infertility is related to sperm clumping, if there is no other identifiable cause.

Radiation. Scientists have been fully aware of the effects of radiation on sperm production since the turn of the century. In the 1950s, shoe salesmen who used fluoroscopes to demonstrate correct fit became infertile. Since then, the effects of X-rays on sperm production have become well known among the general population.

Radiation appears to affect only the spermatogonia, or mother cells. All the support cells of the testicles escape damage. If some of the mother cells survive and continue to produce sperm, the sperm themselves may suffer from the radiation. They may be incapable of fertilizing an ovum, or they may carry defective chromosomes.

Even when all the spermatogonia are damaged by radiation, they have the ability to revive. In June of 1958, a radiation accident at a nuclear plant in Oak Ridge, Tennessee, rendered five men sterile. Their semen was examined at intervals, and within twenty-one months of the radiation exposure sperm were present. Within forty-one months sperm production returned to levels high enough to be regarded as fertile. However, if the DNA code of the spermatogonia has been rearranged, they will always produce sperm with abnormal DNA coding. Birth defects are directly related to abnormal sperm DNA.

All men should be guarded from unnecessary exposure to sources of radiation. Doctors, dentists, and X-ray technicians are most obviously at risk. Radiation shields placed over the testicles can protect against exposure. Young men receiving radiation treatment for tumours of the testicles will find it difficult to avoid exposure. Although the unaffected portion of the testicles is shielded, the high dose necessary to kill the tumour exposes even the shielded portion to considerable radiation. Even if the spermatogonia recover, the sperm DNA may be damaged.

People who work with radiation should be monitored with radiation badges to show what and how much they are exposed to each day. Anyone going for X-rays should have the reproductive organs shielded with lead plates.

Chemicals. Chemicals may have similar effects on the testicles. Such toxic industrial compounds as polychlorinated biphenyls (PCBs), agent orange, lead, mercury, and other heavy metals, appear to lower sperm production; more important, they increase the risk of birth defects. The list of industrial waste products is so long that it is impossible to determine the number of chemicals that might affect sperm production in men. The sources of these compounds include landfills, municipal incinerators, and factory spillage.

Chemicals affect sperm production in three ways. First, they may directly attack and kill spermatogonia. Second, they may invade the nucleus of the spermatogonia and rearrange DNA. The spermatogonia may die or may produce sperm. These sperm may appear normal, but most will be unable to fertilize an egg. Should they fertilize an ovum, birth defects could occur. Finally, and most dangerous of all, the spermatogonia may begin to divide into sheets of abnormal cells without definition. This is cancer.

Heat. In some occupations that appear related to infertility, heat may be the culprit. Heat interferes with sperm production. Lorry drivers, for example, who sit for long hours literally on a 'hot seat', may have a low sperm count. Welders working inside boilers or storage tanks exposed to the sun may have surrounding heat of up to 120 degrees. In these cases sperm production is often severely depressed. Likewise, the man who regularly takes a long soak in a hot tub or sauna may show a depressed sperm count. Tight briefs that hold the testicles close to the body all day can also contribute to overheating. When humidity is excessively high, the body cannot effectively evaporate its heat through perspiration. As a result, the body retains heat, with deleterious effects on sperm production.

Heat, however, has to be continuous over a long period of time to affect sperm production in any important way. Heat exposure should be taken into consideration in an overall evaluation of an infertile man, but should be specifically targeted only when no other cause can be identified.

Altitude. High altitudes may affect sperm production. Spermatogonia require very high levels of oxygen to continuously produce sperm. When deprived of oxygen, the cells seem to go into a resting state. Historical documents show that the Spanish conquerors of Bolivia who founded a city 14,000 feet above sea level did not produce a single living child for over fifty years. The native population continued to reproduce.

Relocation to significantly high altitude – say, from sea level to 5,000 feet or higher – may result in a transient reduction in sperm production. The higher the altitude, the more pronounced the effect. Conversely, divers working below 100 feet also may have depressed sperm counts and loss of libido. High saturation of oxygen in red blood cells may account for this phenomenon. In addition, for every 110 feet of descent, 50 pounds per square inch of pressure are placed on every cell of the body. The brain and spermatogonia respond by decreasing sperm production and testosterone.

Alcohol and Drugs. Drugs may affect male infertility in two ways: by interfering with sperm production or by causing impotence.

Alcohol contributes to liver damage, and if the liver is unable to clear used hormones, ordinarily small amounts of female hormone accumulate and depress both sperm production and potency. Alcohol also causes inappropriate release of prolactin, which has deleterious effects on sperm production.

Anti-hypertensives, antidepressives, and hallucinatory drugs can act on the brain control centre and depress the hormonal messengers that signal the testicles to make sperm and testosterone. Narcotics such as morphine and opium derivatives are known to cause elevated prolactin, which can also block the hormonal messengers.

Cannabis too may cause an inappropriate release of prolactin. The substances in cannabis are known to remain for weeks, and even months, in body tissues, including the testicles.

Another cause of impaired sperm production is therapy with anti-cancer drugs. These drugs work by interfering with critical vitamins necessary for DNA production. The drug takes the place of the vitamins during cell synthesis and jams the system. As a result, the malignant cells die. Because spermatogonia are rapidly dividing cells, their systems are likewise jammed. Fortunately, not all spermatogonia succumb to these drugs, and some sperm production may resume after the drug therapy is stopped. Today research is under way on the use of synthetic, modified LH-RH to turn off the cell division of spermatogonia while a man is receiving chemotherapy. Once the drug therapy is completed, synthetic modified LH-RH is discontinued and, theoretically, sperm production will resume in full force.

A host of medications taken on a regular basis – including aspirin in large doses – has the potential to hamper fertility temporarily. A man should always tell his fertility specialist about any drugs that he is taking.

26

Blocked Ducts and
Other Transport Problems

Once sperm are produced in the testicles, they are pumped through the system of long ducts that are fed at various posts by glands that contribute seminal fluid. Sometimes obstructions occur and block the passageways. Sometimes the semen ejaculates backwards into the bladder. The glands that dump fluids into the ejaculate along the way may contribute too much or too little fluid. Sometimes previous surgery has inadvertently bruised or scarred the ducts. And sometimes these passageways are missing completely. All these factors can interfere with the sperm's ultimate fate.

Blocked Ducts

Only about 5 per cent of infertile men have a blockage in the transport system. Sometimes transport ducts do not develop, or develop incompletely. Most often, however, blockages occur later in life as a result of injury or infection. Fortunately, this is one area in which microsurgery offers hope.

An obstruction can arise in any of the passages through which sperm travel – the epididymis, vas deferens, or ejaculatory ducts. Infections usually invade through the urethra and set up housekeeping in the prostate gland, from which they can spearhead an attack anywhere along the length of the transport system. Obstruction occurs most often in the tightly twisted corridor of the epididymis because bacteria become trapped in its narrow coil.

Infection can be caused by any bacteria. Gonorrhoea seldom reaches as far as the epididymis, however, because the infection produces immediate symptoms and treatment is readily available. Chlamydia may produce a mild urethral discharge and slight burning, or may be totally asymptomatic.

Other infections can and do invade the ducts. Tuberculosis, rarely seen today, goes directly to the epididymis and destroys its passages or invades the vas deferens. Ureaplasma, which has now been linked with urethritis, may result in ejaculatory duct obstruction. This organism also can enter the seminal fluid and affect sperm.

Previous Surgery

Surgery to correct a hernia, undescended testicles, or a pocket of fluid in the testicle (hydrocele) – operations that are typically performed in infancy or childhood – can bruise or accidentally cut the vas deferens and cause infertility later in life. The vas can be successfully repaired, but a better solution is to avoid the problem in the first place through improved surgical technique.

A surgical blockage may also be deliberate – vasectomy involves cutting the vas in the scrotal area and is theoretically 100 per cent effective for contraception. In rare cases a channel may re-form between the two cut ends, enabling sperm transportation to resume. In modern society, however, few things stay the same, including the wish for permanent contraception. Numerous men have divorced, remarried, and wished to start new families. In some tragic circumstances, children have died and parents who thought their child-rearing years were past have decided to have another child. The tides of life make us wish to change the unchangeable. Reversing a vasectomy – called a vasovasostomy – is, in the hands of a skilled microsurgeon, a successful operation.

Reconstructing the Vas Deferens

The most influential factor in reconstruction of the transport system is the skill of the surgeon performing the operation. Blockages in the vas deferens are corrected in the same manner as reverse vasectomies. A vasectomy is a simple operation that takes about fifteen minutes under local anaesthesia, but the average reversal requires two or more hours of surgery under general anaesthesia and a four-day hospital stay.

Reconnecting two segments of the vas can be as complex a procedure as reconnecting the fallopian tubes in women. A cross-section of the interior vas is about $\frac{1}{70}$ in (0·35 mm) in diameter. The lining of the inner canal is only three cells thick. Techniques vary, but in the most frequently performed operation the surgeon cuts out the blocked portions under a microscope, then lines up the small inner canals of each segment with a suture and stitches together the outer muscular wall. This two-layer sewing gives the best chance of alignment between the segments.

The laser has a unique ability to re-attach severed ends of the vas. The vas is so thin that the laser can weld the segments together, rapidly reconnecting the vas without sutures. This is still an experimental technique, but it offers tremendous promise for blockages and reversals. It's quick and effective, requires no sutures, and creates minimal scarring, so there is an excellent chance of success.

Success rates for vas reconstruction, in terms of the presence of viable sperm in the man's ejaculate, vary from 60 per cent to 80 per cent. Pregnancy success rates are usually between 30 and 35 per cent.

Blocked Epididymis

Blockages can occur in the epididymis as a result of infection or birth defect. A blockage caused by infection is usually easier to correct because most often it is located in the tail of the epididymis, near the entry point into the vas.

Because the epididymis is so thin and so tightly coiled, it is impossible to unravel the structure, find and remove the blockage, and sew the ends back together. Instead, the surgeon slices across the tail of the epididymis and finds an opening from which live sperm can be recovered. The surgeon then makes another opening in the wall of the vas and attaches the two openings with sutures.

Obviously this is an extremely delicate surgical procedure because the structures are incredibly small. Men undergoing this operation have about a 20 per cent chance of producing a pregnancy when the blockage is in the tail of the epididymis; the chances are minimal if the blockage is in the head of the structure.

Ejaculatory Ducts

Blockage in the ejaculatory ducts is rare, but may be caused by gonorrhoea infection. Because these channels are buried in the prostate gland, the urologist works through the urethra. A cystoscope is used to place a narrow tube into the ejaculatory ducts and dilate the blockage.

Problems with Seminal Fluid

Seminal fluid, like sperm, is continually being produced. Each normal ejaculate contains about one teaspoonful of fluid; the body can replenish the ejaculate once or twice a day. If a man ejaculates more frequently, fluid volume may be low. Too much or too little volume can cause fertility problems.

On ejaculation, the semen goes through two stages. The moment it is pumped out of the penis, it coagulates. The theory is that this thickening process helps the sperm pool up around the entrance to the cervix. Within minutes the semen liquefies again. The liquefied semen is still thick enough to pour out in droplets.

Thickening, followed by liquefaction, is crucial to sperm transport. Occasionally, something goes wrong with the process (see Chapter 18).

Infections

Infections in the seminal vesicles or the prostate gland, the two major sources of seminal fluid, can make sperm miserable. Pus cells inhibit their ability to swim, and many sperm die. Any bacteria or virus in these glands can alter semen. The prostate particularly is a reservoir for bacteria, and infections in this gland can affect the transport system in several ways. Bacteria can leak into semen and kill sperm. From the prostate bacteria can travel into the ductal system and cause blockages.

Certain infections harbouring in the prostate gland are readily transmitted to women. And infections can reduce nutrients to the seminal fluid. The fluid may become thick, and sperm may clump together. Prostate infections are notoriously difficult to treat, but most infections eventually respond to antibiotics.

High Viscosity

The pourability of a fluid is called viscosity. If semen does not liquefy into droplets, it is said to be too viscous. We don't really know what causes this condition, nor can we measure the effect of high viscosity on fertility. If the semen analysis is good in every other respect, high viscosity is probably not a problem. If infection is present, the semen may liquefy better after a course of antibiotics.

If a man has naturally viscous semen that seems to be impairing sperm transport, he can try vitamin C to thin the fluid. Sometimes semen will liquefy better if a woman uses vaginal suppositories made from alpha amylase, an ingredient in cocoa butter. These treatments, however, may prove fruitless, because so far high viscosity is not a proven cause of infertility.

Agglutination

Sometimes, instead of swimming individually, sperm cells clump together. This clumping is called agglutination. Although semen is usually thick when sperm clump, agglutination is different from simple high viscosity.

Clumping may be caused by infection or by sperm antibodies; or it may be a 'natural' phenomenon, with no particular cause. When sperm continue to clump after any infection has been cleared up, the best treatment is sperm washing (discussed below), followed by artificial insemination. A man is said to have an immunologic factor when he produces antibodies in seminal fluid or antibodies attached to sperm. Antibodies are sticky proteins that cause cells to clump together. This factor in men is elusive, however, and researchers disagree about its validity as a cause of infertility.

Low Volume

Sperm need a substantial quantity of semen to reach the cervical canal. Too little volume, and sperm are stranded in the vaginal vault. Sometimes low volume can be corrected simply by extending the hours or days between sex. If the low volume is caused by infection, antibiotics can be used. Stress too seems to affect the volume of seminal fluid a man produces. Occasionally, there is no traceable cause. A successful pregnancy can still be achieved by artificial insemination of the husband's sperm directly into the uterus. If this doesn't work, sperm can be removed from the husband's semen, suspended in an adequate volume of synthetic fluid, and then transferred by artificial insemination.

High Volume

Too much seminal fluid can be as harmful to sperm as too little. Too much fluid dilutes the concentration of sperm. The sperm literally get lost swimming through the flood of seminal fluid. Treatment for too much volume involves splitting the ejaculate. The technique is based on the fact that the first part of the ejaculate contains 80 per cent of the sperm and is also more alkaline. A natural way to split the ejaculate is to stop intercourse as soon as the man begins to ejaculate (coitus interruptus). Or the man can masturbate the first part of his semen into a glass jar; the semen is then used for artificial insemination.

Absent Vasa or Absent Seminal Vesicles

Less than 5 per cent of infertile men are born without vasa deferentia. Sometimes the seminal vesicles that supply the fluid that carries the sperm are missing. In this case the volume of seminal fluid will be low, but sperm count will be normal.

When vasa are missing, the surgeon may create a little pouch in the testicle to trap sperm; the sperm are then withdrawn with a needle and used for artificial insemination. This technique is still highly experimental, and to date no pregnancies have been achieved.

Sperm Washing

Many infertility problems associated with seminal fluid can be solved using the new sperm-washing techniques. One technique, which can be used for men with low sperm counts or counts with only a few good-quality sperm, involves separating the sperm from the seminal fluid by centrifuge. The sperm are then placed in a special medium. Poor-quality sperm will sink to the bottom, and good sperm will swim to the top, to be collected for artificial insemination. The results, however, are so far very disappointing.

Special Techniques

To boost a low sperm count, batches of sperm have been collected, washed, and frozen until the sperm is concentrated enough to be used for artificial insemination. The freezing process reduces the mobility of the sperm however, and the technique is unlikely to prove successful.

27
Impotence and Other Deposit Problems

Sometimes all parts of the sperm production and transport system work perfectly, yet the sperm fail to reach the cervix. Problems concerning the deposit of the ejaculate high in the vaginal canal are usually simple to correct and can be very effective if a man has a low sperm count but otherwise normal sperm.

Frequency of Sex

Ejaculating too often – or too seldom – may lead to fertility problems. A man with a moderate to low sperm count will be relatively infertile if he ejaculates every day because he depletes his volume of stored sperm. On the other hand, if he abstains for two weeks or longer, the sperm in storage are likely to die.

Surprisingly, researchers still do not know if it's better to have sex every day, every other day, or every third day to maximize a man's fertility potential. One study of fertile men showed a high rate of pregnancy in couples who had intercourse every day. However, daily sex for men with lower counts may not be so helpful.

It seems logical that if daily sex doesn't lead to pregnancy, switching to every other day may help. Likewise, a man who 'saves up' to match ovulation may be inadvertently compounding the problem by producing dead sperm. A careful look at the sexual history of the couple will provide some clues. Changing the interval between sexual intercourse sometimes helps solve fertility problems.

Sexual Technique

When a man's sperm count is high, with good motility, his sexual technique is usually not a factor in infertility. Sperm deposited anywhere inside the vagina will find their way to the cervical canal.

Sexual technique becomes important when a man has a low sperm count or low motility. In this case, sperm need every advantage. The optimum position for pregnancy is the missionary position, with a pillow under the woman's hips. It helps sometimes for the woman to stay in bed for thirty minutes afterwards, to give sperm a chance to reach the cervical opening. These small adjustments in sexual technique can help a 'sub-fertile' couple conceive.

Creams and jellies used to lubricate the genitals during intercourse can kill sperm. Even petroleum jelly, which is not considered a spermicide, can interfere with fertility by creating an impenetrable barrier. The best lubricant is saliva, which not only eases penetration but produces a safe environment for sperm.

Sexual Problems

Changing sexual technique is easy. Solving sexual problems is more difficult. Occasionally, an 'infertile' couple has never had intercourse. Sometimes very infrequent sex takes place between them; and sometimes orgasm and ejaculation take place outside the vagina. Sexual education usually solves the problem.

Premature Ejaculation

Premature ejaculation is a much more complicated problem. When ejaculation is on a hair trigger, any stimulation to the penis causes instant orgasm. Premature ejaculation is almost always psychogenic, and the best approach is behaviour modification, in which a man slowly learns to control his erection. These adaptive techniques, which have become widely accepted in recent years thanks to the landmark work by Masters and Johnson, are very successful in helping men who ejaculate prematurely.

Impotence

Impotence is the inability to carry out sexual intercourse because an erection cannot be maintained. Impotence is emotionally threatening to both the man and woman. A woman tends to see a man's impotence as a personal rejection of her; a man feels it is a failure of his masculinity.

True impotence may be physical, psychological, or a combination of both. The incidence is about evenly distributed among these three possibilities. In a young man impotence is usually transient, the result of stress or other psychological factors. Potency resumes when the man resolves the emotional conflict or alleviates the stress. Older men tend to have a combination of problems that lead to impotence.

Because impotence is medically complex, a man who is consistently impotent over a period of three months or more should receive a thorough physical examination. Thirty per cent of all cases of impotence can be traced to physical causes. The habitual use of narcotics, tranquillizers in the phenothiazine class, drugs in the monoamine oxidase inhibitor family, and some anti-hypertensives can lead to impotence. Alcoholism is a recognized cause of impotence. A man who is impotent may require medical treatment, sexual counselling, or both.

Sex and Diabetes

Diabetes ranks as one of the most sexually destructive diseases in men. It frequently causes impotence because of progressive damage to small blood vessels, which ultimately destroy fine nerve endings around the penis.

Impotence occurs in 27–55 per cent of all diabetic men. Occasionally, the impotence is transient, caused by an acute episode of excess acids in the blood. Potency returns when the disease is under control. However, for some diabetics, irreversible impotence may occur. Even when a diabetic man loses his power of erection, he retains his sex drive, sensation of orgasm, and power of ejaculation. If he can masturbate into a glass jar with the help of a vibrator, his sperm can be used for artificial insemination. Some diabetic men have splints surgically implanted in their penises. Penile implants may be permanently stiff, semi-rigid, or inflatable.

Diabetic men may need sexual counselling as well as medical treatment. When a diabetic man becomes impotent, the physician's job is to distinguish between the effects of the disease and psychological stress. Because diabetics are subject to the same emotional stress and strains as non-diabetics, they may be able to regain some of their potency by solving emotional problems.

Retrograde Ejaculation

A man suffering from retrograde ejaculation experiences a normal orgasm, but nothing comes out: instead of the semen squirting out of the tip of his penis, it is ejaculated backwards into the bladder. The next time the man urinates, his urine will be milky white and full of semen.

The site of the problem is the point at which the ejaculatory ducts empty into the urethra. Normally, as the ejaculate spurts forward, the muscle at the base of the bladder closes off to allow sperm an open pathway into the urethra. Certain conditions can weaken the nerves that control the muscle, so that the bladder entrance fails to close and sperm are forced backwards into the bladder.

Diabetes is one common cause of retrograde ejaculation. As the disease progresses, there is a slow degeneration of the sympathetic nervous system. Often the nerves can be stimulated by medication. High doses of drugs that override the sympathetic nervous system can occasionally be effective in correcting retrograde ejaculation in diabetic men.

Certain drugs, particularly anti-hypertensives, may also weaken the sympathetic nervous system. The system is restored when drug therapy is stopped or changed. Occasionally the nerves are damaged by previous surgery around the bladder neck or by prostate surgery. These mechanical faults can sometimes be corrected with special surgical techniques.

If medical treatment doesn't work, it is still possible for a man to make his wife pregnant through artificial insemination. The man drinks quantities of sodium bicarbonate to neutralize his urine; then the urologist inserts a catheter into the penis and washes out the bladder with a sterile solution that is hospitable to sperm, leaving a small pool of the solution in the bladder. The man masturbates to orgasm and immediately voids into a glass jar. The sperm recovered from the jar are washed, suspended in a fresh medium, and then used for artificial insemination.

Malformations

The normal urethra ends at the tip of the penis. Some men are born with hypospadias, a urethra that opens farther down the shaft of the penis. If the hypospadias is anywhere near the tip of the penis, sperm deposit probably will not be affected. If a hypospadias is located well down the penile shaft, the problem is usually corrected surgically when a man is quite young.

Altogether, deposit problems account for less than 7 per cent of all fertility problems encountered by men. It's important to remember that each of the various causes listed in this chapter and in preceding chapters represents only a very small percentage of infertile men. An infertile man may have one problem or several; his sperm count may be improved to some extent through therapy or not improved at all. In a few instances, particularly if he has a varicocele, there is a good chance that fertility will be fully restored.

Fertility drugs are still experimental in men. However, new surgical techniques are effective for those whose infertility can be traced to blockages in the transport system. New sperm-washing techniques offer hope in the future for men whose fertility potential is hampered by unexplained thick semen, antibodies, sperm clumping, or too little volume. Much more work remains to be done. The field of male infertility is wide open and ready for the entrance of high technology and applied science.

Special Considerations

28
Artificial Insemination

Artificial insemination is the oldest, least complicated, and most successful alternative to natural conception. In artificial insemination from the husband (AIH) or from a donor (AID), sperm are implanted into the cervical canal or uterus by means other than intercourse. AIH is an effective way to fertilize an ovum when a man has a low sperm count. Sperm that would be normally lost to the hostile environment of the vagina during natural intercourse are saved and placed closer to the cervix. The success rates for both forms of artificial insemination are generally equal to the natural pregnancy rates of fertile couples.

In the mid eighteenth century the Italian scientist Lazzaro Spallanzani recorded the first artificial insemination of a viviparous animal when he inseminated a female spaniel with fresh semen from a dog of the same breed. Today, artificial insemination is widely used to breed cattle and prize bulls. The technique is popular among animal breeders in general since the male doesn't have to be physically moved to the female. Seventy per cent of calves born today are the offspring of frozen semen, sometimes shipped to remote and impoverished areas throughout the world.

The first pregnancy and delivery of a child conceived by AIH was recorded in 1790 by John Hunter, the great English anatomist and surgeon. In America, Marion Sims began experimenting with artificial insemination in the 1860s, using a rather startling technique. A couple had intercourse while Dr Sims and a nurse, armed with warm speculums and syringes, waited outside the bedroom door. The minute the husband leaped from the bed, the nurse and Dr Sims rushed in, aspirated the contents of the vagina into a warm syringe, and injected it into the cervical canal. Since Sims believed that pregnancy occurred just before and just after a woman's period, it's surprising that he ever obtained a pregnancy. However, he did report one success out of fifty attempts.

Artificial insemination with donor sperm was first used in 1890 by the American Robert L. Dickinson, one of the most innovative gynaecologists of his time. In those Victorian times, Dickinson's work was carried out in the greatest secrecy.

Artificial insemination is accomplished by using a small plastic tube to implant the sperm at the neck of the cervix. Often, a silicone cup is used to hold the semen in place for several hours, until the sperm can penetrate the mucus and swim through the cervical canal into the uterus. Occasionally, the physician bypasses the vagina and implants the semen directly into the uterus to reduce the chance of sperm rejection. Most physicians advise against direct uterine implantation, however, because the procedure carries a risk of infection.

The insemination is performed just prior to or on the day of ovulation, anywhere from day 10 to day 16 of a woman's menstrual cycle. During this time her cervical mucus is most receptive to the semen. Ovulation can be pinpointed most accurately by placing a dipstick in the woman's urine sample. If the LH surge is present, indicating pending ovulation, the stick turns dark blue. This method is relatively inexpensive, simple, and accurate. Some doctors monitor ovulation through ultrasound and blood tests to measure changes in the hormones. Women who do not ovulate properly may need drug therapy to help develop and release the egg before they receive artificial insemination.

Artificial Insemination with Husband's Sperm (AIH)

AIH is used primarily when a husband has a low or abnormal sperm count. Since artificial insemination reduces the distance the sperm must travel, it increases the chances of fertilization. In other words, it can get the most use out of the quantity of sperm the man produces. By using special washing and separation techniques, AIH can also be used when semen is too thick, when semen contains only a few good-quality sperm, or when sperm clump for no apparent reason. It can also be used in those rare instances when a man makes too many sperm.

Most doctors prefer that the semen be collected in a private room at their clinic. If collection is done at home, the ejaculate has to be kept warm and delivered within the hour.

The Clinic Technique

The husband masturbates into a sterile glass or plastic jar and a small portion of the specimen is screened under a microscope to assess the quality of the sperm. Once it has been determined that live sperm are present, the implantation procedure begins, usually within thirty minutes.

The doctor inserts a warm speculum into the woman's vagina and uses a syringe to push the semen into the cervical os. Next, a Silastic cup is inserted directly over the cervix to hold the semen close. Any additional semen is inserted into a little tube in the cup. The woman lies quietly for 15-30 minutes. There is no more discomfort than with a routine Pap smear. The woman leaves the cervical cup in place for at least six hours, and then removes it herself.

The At-Home Technique

Couples can also perform AIH at home, without the assistance of a doctor. The woman puts the soft rubber cup in place over the cervix. The husband then masturbates into a sterile glass jar and waits 10-20 minutes for the semen to liquefy. He draws up the semen into a plastic syringe, inserts the tip of the syringe into a slot in the cervical cup, and slowly depresses the pump. The cup is left in place at least six hours. For best results, the AIH procedure should be repeated two or three times during the woman's mid-cycle.

A recent investigation of this at-home method, conducted by Michael Diamond and his associates at Vanderbilt University Medical Center in Nashville, Tennessee, revealed a 53 per cent overall pregnancy rate – somewhat less than the success rate when AIH is performed in a clinic. In his book *Fertility and Sterility*, Dr Diamond noted several advantages of the home method: fresh semen, less psychological stress, and reduced costs. The reduction in psychological stress is especially important. Stress may cause delay in ovulation or failure to ovulate and may also affect the quality of the sperm.

Artificial Insemination by Donor (AID)

Artificial insemination by donor (AID) is a more controversial technique than AIH because the semen used to impregnate the woman comes from a man who is not her husband and whose identity is probably unknown. Still, if the husband's semen contains little or no sperm, AID is a viable means to pregnancy. A small percentage of couples who attempt AID are fertile but have Rh incompatabilities or some history of genetic defect, such as certain forms of Down's syndrome, blindness, Tay-Sachs disease, or Huntington's chorea. Suspicion of such hereditary disorders frequently leads a couple to seek help from the AID process. Soldiers who were exposed to agent orange in Vietnam may resort to AID if they are worried about the chemical's effect on their children. Currently, 10,000 to 20,000 children are born in the United States each year as a result of the AID procedure.

Advantages of AID

Many fertility experts believe that AID is a favourable and successful alternative to adoption. Waiting lists for newborn adoptive children are long and slow-moving. Scrutiny by the adoption agency may be intrusive, and regulations may be restrictive. Further, with AID there is no other 'natural' mother who may appear or whose existence would later pique the interest of the child. Nor would a so-called biological father intrude into the relationship, since donors are not informed about any use of their sperm. The experience of pregnancy itself is an advantage for many couples. And, of course, the child can resemble, both physically and genetically, at least one of the parents – the mother. Finally, AID offers a perfect opportunity to reduce birth defects by genetic screening.

Disadvantages of AID

The couple must sign an informed consent agreement to accept responsibility for the child regardless of its mental or physical condition. Although the incidence of abnormalities with donor sperm does not appear to be greater than that of children born by natural insemination, as the technique becomes more popular, this type of problem may arise more often. In Britain, an increasing number of clinics are doing AID on the NHS.

The Technique

AID has been used for nearly a century in Britain. The procedure employs the same implantation method as AIH, but the preliminaries are more complex and certainly more controversial. Donor sperm comes from a sperm bank, which screens potential donors, collects their semen, and analyses it for possible venereal disease. If the donor is approved, he is paid a nominal fee. A record is kept of various donor characteristics so that the traits can be matched to those of the husband as closely as possible.

Matching of the donor is left to the discretion of the doctor, and the couple agrees to absolve him of responsibility for any abnormalities the child may have. There are three important questions for a couple to ask when considering AID:

1. Does the sperm bank do genetic counselling?
2. If not, where do donors come from? For example, medical students are frequent donors, but donor requirements vary.
3. How often is one donor allowed to provide sperm for AID?

Like AIH, chances of success with donor sperm are similar to those of natural pregnancy. Within six months about 50 per cent of women using donor sperm become pregnant.

Frozen Sperm

The AID insemination technique differs from AIH in one important way: frozen sperm, common in cattle breeding for many years, is always used in British clinics. The freezing of human sperm became popular in the early 1950s, when scientists discovered that adding glycerol to semen before freezing enhanced the sperm's ability to survive. Recent research indicates that newer agents may work even better than glycerol.

Sperm banks usually take time to screen donors for diseases or genetic defects. Each specimen can be cultured for infection before freezing. Frozen sperm, which can be ordered from banks around the world, allows a wide choice of donors. This lessens the possibility that two children fathered by the same donor might meet later in life and marry.

Finally, freezing sperm allows for donation from men with characteristics that prospective parents might desire in their children – mathematical wizardry, business acumen, musical talent, and so on. But remember that it is said that a showgirl once wrote to George Bernard Shaw, rhapsodizing on how a child of theirs would be extraordinary, with her beauty and his brains. 'But suppose,' he replied, 'that the child inherited my beauty and your brains?' Intelligence is not a single genetic trait. Intelligence is formed by the interplay of numerous genes from both parents, plus the overlying effect of the environment.

The long-term effects of using frozen sperm have yet to be thoroughly researched, and there is speculation that prolonged frozen storage of sperm could lead to genetic damage and birth defects. However, one recent international report showed that 5,000 children conceived by AID with frozen sperm were as healthy as normally conceived children.

Currently, the major problem with frozen sperm is that its success rate at achieving pregnancies is somewhat less than that of fresh sperm. Freezing appears to lessen the motility of sperm, thus reducing its ability to reach the fertilization site. Also, whereas fresh sperm can live for about forty-eight hours in the woman's reproductive tract, thawed sperm live for only half that time. Thus, timing of insemination must be calculated to a much finer degree with frozen sperm, so that egg and sperm are active and ready at the same time. Numerous studies indicate that when timing is precise, there is no difference in the fertility rate for fresh or frozen sperm.

How Long to Keep Trying

AID, like natural pregnancy, does not promise immediate success; even fertile couples have only a 20 per cent chance per month of achieving pregnancy through normal intercourse. Still, it is probably not wise to continue indefinitely with AID. Costs mount (it is more commonly done privately in Britain), and it's not easy to drop everything once or twice a month to see a physician for insemination. After six months of trying to achieve an AID pregnancy, a couple should discuss the situation with the doctor. Poor timing of the insemination may be at fault, in which case the doctor should consider blood or urine tests and/or ultrasound to pinpoint the exact time of ovulation. Or the wife may have an undetected fertility problem and need further testing. Success rates with AID vary widely. A current medical journal reports that the times for pregnancy with AID treatment vary from 2·5–9·5 months.

Legal Problems with AID

If the donor's sperm is responsible for fertilizing the egg, who is the real father? Before contributing semen, each donor must sign a form waiving all parental rights to any child conceived with his sperm. The donor will never know who is impregnated with his sperm or be held responsible for the care of the child if the husband and wife refuse to accept it.

In Britain, the husband is the legal father of the child, as with adoption. In a divorce case, the husband may be awarded custody, even though he is probably not the child's biological father.

AID is an Emotional Choice

Before any couple chooses AID, a complete fertility investigation should be performed to be certain that the cause of infertility cannot be treated. One sperm count is not enough to make a decision. With treatment even a man with a repeatedly low sperm count has a good chance of having a child naturally.

Even when AID seems right for physical reasons, the time to go forward depends on emotional considerations. Many doctors suggest a waiting period of about six months after male infertility has been firmly established to give the couple time to absorb the fact emotionally. The decision to use AID should not be made in haste. Husband and wife need to talk over their feelings about the procedure, and a man may want to discuss his feelings with a psychologist or counsellor.

The couple should agree wholeheartedly before going ahead with AID procedure. A husband shouldn't agree to AID simply to satisfy his wife's desire for a child or to prove how much he loves her. Both partners should agree to AID because they individually and together want to achieve the goal of parenthood.

Both women and men worry about the effect on the marriage if a child is created with another man's sperm. One way round this is to ask the doctor to mix the donor sperm with the husband's sperm, so there would always be some possibility that the husband's sperm fertilized the ovum. However, current statistics show that mixing sperm can militate against the pregnancy by decreasing the donor sperm's ability to fertilize the ovum. Some doctors suggest that the couple make love the evening after the insemination; this creates a bond between husband and wife while the donor sperm is reaching the fertilization site.

Most couples who choose AID are happy with the procedure and its results. In fact, in wide surveys couples with AID children said almost unanimously that they would have another child in the same way.

Choosing Baby's Sex in Advance

Eventually couples may be able to choose the sex of their baby through a new artificial insemination technique that separates sperm into male and female cells. However, since the techniques discard at least 50 per cent of the sperm cells, this technique would rarely be appropriate for infertile couples. However, predetermined sex selection could be important to some couples, especially those who are carriers of certain sex-linked hereditary diseases such as haemophilia and muscular dystrophy.

29
Spontaneous Abortion

Spontaneous abortion, or miscarriage, is a disastrous event for a couple trying to have a child, an event filled with grief and loss. Yet it is so common that many doctors do not consider miscarriage a serious medical problem.

There is much confusion about the meaning of abortion, often compounded by misconceptions that have been portrayed in the movies: a woman runs down the street, or falls down a flight of stairs, or has an argument with her mother-in-law, and loses the baby. The doctor comes out of her room solemnly shaking his head, and tells the husband, 'I'm sorry, your wife won't ever be able to have a child.' In films, of course, no one ever explained why; the inability to have a child used to be a fateful mystery, laid at the doorstep of a higher being. Often, it was understood that the woman was being punished for past sins.

In fact, spontaneous abortion is usually a single occurrence, often followed by successful pregnancy. It is almost never caused by physical exertion, unless there is already something wrong with the pregnancy. The fetus is well cushioned and firmly attached to the inside of the womb, and is virtually impossible to dislodge. Running, jogging, swimming, and other sports have not been shown to initiate abortion. And, to the best of scientific knowledge, abortion is not caused by sin.

Spontaneous abortion is usually caused by the same problems that interfere with fertility. When abortion occurs repeatedly, a full fertility investigation is needed to help identify the problem. After the loss of a single pregnancy, the statistical chance of another loss is only 20 per cent. Women who have given birth to one child and abort their second pregnancy have an even better chance of successful future childbearing. After two losses, however, the chance increases to 38 per cent; after three spontaneous abortions, the chance increases to 73 per cent; and after four abortions the possibility of having another loss jumps to 94 per cent.

Abortion is the technical term for expulsion of a fetus before it is big enough to survive. Miscarriage and spontaneous abortion are synonymous and refer to loss of the fetus before the twenty-sixth week of pregnancy. (When a woman aborts after the twenty-sixth week, it is called a late abortion or a premature birth, depending on the weight of the fetus.) Between 10 and 15 per cent of all pregnancies abort naturally within the first eleven weeks, and many of these go by completely unnoticed. Recent studies suggest that the figure is as high as 30–50 per cent.

Women who abort early three or more times are termed chronic aborters. The cause may lie with the woman or with her husband. Any couple who repeatedly abort need to find a fertility specialist who is willing to pursue the problem until it is solved. This is not to say that fertility experts agree on the causes or treatment of chronic abortion. Far from it. The problems associated with chronic abortion are numerous, complex, and only partly understood.

When Abortion Threatens

Most miscarriages begin with bleeding from the uterus through the vagina. Sometimes the bleeding is slight spotting, and sometimes it is severe haemorrhaging. Spotting and cramping before the twenty-sixth week are signs of 'threatened abortion'. In this instance the woman may be put to bed for a few days in the hope that the embryo will settle itself into the womb. The cramping may halt, and the pregnancy may proceed normally.

Whether or not a threatened abortion stabilizes has more to do with the nature of the problem than with physical exertion. Recent scientific studies show that with few exceptions physical stress plays a minor role in miscarriage. The question of bed rest was tested by Dr Edward C. Mann, director of the Recurrent Miscarriage Clinic at New York Hospital. One group of pregnant women who started to spot or experience mild cramps was put to bed. Another group was allowed to continue with a normal daily routine and was merely asked to avoid over-exertion. The same number of miscarriages occurred in both groups, demonstrating that factors other than physical activity were probably responsible for the abortion.

If a threatened abortion does not occur and the pregnancy successfully reaches full term, the odds are greatly in favour of a normal delivery. The mother needn't worry that she has saved a defective embryo. When a threatened pregnancy does go on to full term, the chances of having a normal baby are approximately the same as if no threat had occurred.

In rare instances a woman's uterus is extremely irritable and the cervical muscle is so weak that it cannot support the pregnancy. The physician will try to strengthen the cervix by placing a stitch round it, but sometimes the uterine contractions are so severe that the stitch cannot hold when the woman is on her feet. Bed rest seems to be the only way to stop the contractions. A woman may need to stay in bed for a few months or even for the entire length of her pregnancy to avoid miscarriage.

Inevitable Abortion

A threatened abortion may advance to an inevitable abortion that cannot be halted. There is frank bleeding, with intense cramping and a dilated cervix. The neck of the womb opens up, and the conceptus (fetus and placenta) passes out. This is a complete abortion. If any bits of tissue remain inside the uterus, the abortion is termed incomplete – a serious hazard to the woman – and requires a D&C within a few hours of the event to scrape all remnants of the tissue out of the uterus. Should any tissue be left in the uterus, there is a serious risk of infection, or 'septic abortion'. Before antibiotics, such infections were frequently fatal. Today these infections are not usually life-threatening, but they may destroy a woman's future fertility.

Sometimes a woman will have a missed abortion, in which the fetus dies in the womb but is not expelled. Labour can be induced or, in the first three months, a D&C can be performed to evacuate the uterus. A missed abortion occurs once in every hundred pregnancies.

Causes of Spontaneous Abortion

Many of the same problems that lead to infertility also cause spontaneous abortion. The most generally cited causes of any spontaneous abortion – isolated or chronic – are faulty development of the embryo and incorrect implantation of the embryo in the lining of the uterus.

Defective Embryos

When abortion threatens, a woman is usually put to bed to see if the pregnancy will stabilize. However, more than half of all spontaneous abortions in the first trimester are due to genetic defects in the embryo, and these pregnancies cannot be saved. The problem may be caused by deteriorating chromosomes in the ovum or in the sperm, or both. The flaw may be minor or major, but even small flaws may result in early death of the embryo. In these instances a natural, spontaneous abortion prevents the development of a severely defective conceptus.

The defective embryo usually stops growing at about six weeks, but the expulsion may not occur until a few weeks later. Occasionally the fetus does not abort, and a surgical removal by D&C is required. Subsequent pregnancies are usually perfectly normal. However, if spontaneous abortions occur frequently, the husband or wife may have an underlying chromosome abnormality.

Genetic testing may reveal why the miscarriages are occurring. About 7 per cent of couples who sustain multiple abortions have a chromosome problem. If a woman consistently aborts, or if there is a family history of birth defects, a chromosome study should be considered. This test, called karyotyping, consists of growing white blood cells from both partners in specialized media, crushing the cells, and examining the chromosomes under the microscope.

If the chromosome pattern is seriously flawed, genetic counselling is in order. Counselling will give the couple enough information to decide whether to attempt another pregnancy. If the chromosome pattern is normal, the fertility specialist must look for other causes of the consistent loss of pregnancy. The aborted fetus should also be tested for genetic defects. Specialists in birth defects believe that every miscarriage or stillborn fetus should receive meticulous laboratory evaluation, includiing X-rays and karyotyping. Some hospitals routinely perform genetic testing on aborted fetuses.

Implantation Problems

A variety of problems can prevent the embryo from successfully implanting on the lining of the uterus.

Underdeveloped Endometrium. If too little progesterone is produced in the second phase of the menstrual cycle, the lining of the uterus may not develop enough to sustain an embryo. This is known as a luteal phase defect and accounts for 35 per cent of all abortions in the first trimester.

Luteal phase defects are diagnosed by hormonal studies and endometrial biopsy (see Chapter 18). Such defects can be corrected by supplements of progesterone or by clomiphene. Progesterone bolsters the second phase of the cycle, and clomiphene normalizes the overall menstrual cycle. Both drugs seem to work equally well, but progesterone is a more direct, less complicated approach. In 95 per cent of cases one of these drugs will solve the problem. Sometimes, however, there are other problems in addition to the luteal phase defect.

Uterine Growths. Another problem that can cause habitual miscarriage is the presence of uterine growths. The most common of these are endometrial polyps, small growths of tissue on the lining of the uterus, which are easily removed by D&C.

Fibroid Tumours. Fibroid tumours, which are benign growths in the walls of the uterus, sometimes can prevent the implantation of a fertilized egg. These tumours are diagnosed by ultrasound and confirmed by laparoscopy.

Fibroids are often found in clusters, and even when they are surgically removed others may take their place. Conventional surgery on fibroid tumours causes tremendous bleeding and tissue damage. For this reason, hysterectomy may be recommended, even for young women. In the future, however, these tumors will be removed by laser surgery without performing a hysterectomy. The laser affords such precise removal of tumours in strategic areas that critical reproductive organs are not damaged. Thus a woman's reproductive function is preserved, even though the tumours may recur. Surgical removal of a fibroid tumour is called a myomectomy.

Placement. The exact place the embryo attaches inside the uterus can affect how well it clings. A favourable spot for nesting is the back wall of the uterus. If the embryo implants in the lower part of the uterus, near the cervix, the placenta may detach as the pregnancy grows, causing the mother to abort. This kind of abortion usually occurs in women who have had many children; because of the repeated pregnancies, the lining of the uterus becomes scarred. There is no treatment for this rare disorder.

Misshapen Uterus. Rather than having a pear-shaped uterus that expands as the baby grows, some women have an irregularly formed uterus that cannot enlarge enough to accommodate a growing baby. Such malformations include a uterus divided by a wall (septum) and a double or heart-shaped uterus. These abnormalities are present from birth and are diagnosed by X-ray studies (hysterosalpingogram). Treatment is surgical reconstruction. A dividing wall can be removed through a hysteroscope, if available, or through open surgery. A double uterus usually requires major surgical reconstruction.

Ectopic Pregnancies

Sometimes the fertilized ovum does not complete its journey to the uterus and implants in one of the fallopian tubes; or it may start to grow within the mother's abdominal cavity. This is called an ectopic pregnancy, an extremely dangerous condition that will ultimately result in the loss of the embryo and risk to the mother's life.

Ectopic pregnancy can be caused by endometriosis or by some mechanical obstruction inside the fallopian tube. An ectopic pregnancy can happen to any woman of childbearing age, even one who has been sterilized by a tubal operation. (In a few cases of tubal sterilization, the tubes reopen or grow back together, permitting fertilization but not normal movement of the fertilized egg.) The risk increases with age, from about 4·5 per 1,000 pregnancies among women between the ages of fifteen and twenty-four to a high 15·2 per 1,000 among those thirty-five to forty-four.

The number of reported ectopic pregnancies has tripled in the last ten years, reaching a peak of 52,200 in 1980. One outstanding factor accounts for this dramatic rise: the tremendous increase in pelvic inflammatory disease (PID) in recent years. Inside the fallopian tubes PID can lead to strictures and scarring that block entry of the fertilized egg into the uterus. Women with a history of tubal infections are seven times more likely than others to have ectopic pregnancies, and one pregnancy in fifteen is ectopic after tubal infection.

An ectopic pregnancy begins like any normal pregnancy; there is little to indicate that a life-threatening condition is developing. However, because of the location of the pregnancy, symptoms of spotting and pelvic cramps usually arise around the eighth to tenth week of pregnancy. These symptoms may be overlooked as the woman simply assumes she is starting a late period. The next warning sign is more spotting accompanied by severe pain. This usually brings the woman to her doctor. If the pregnancy ruptures at home, her life is at risk.

Physical symptoms are easily confused with other diseases, such as appendicitis and pelvic inflammatory disease. A pregnancy test at this time may be positive or negative, depending on whether the embryo is still alive. If a woman has a positive pregnancy test but ultrasound shows no embryo inside the uterus, a diagnosis of ectopic pregnancy is nearly certain. If the pregnancy test is negative, ultrasound may reveal the misplaced embryo, and in some cases laparoscopy is needed to confirm the diagnosis.

Once an ectopic pregnancy is located, it must be removed quickly. Delay can result in rupture, followed by severe haemorrhaging. Surgical intervention can save the mother's life and also preserve the reproductive organs. The traditional treatment has been to remove the entire tube. An ectopic pregnancy may implant anywhere along the length of the tube. Sometimes it lodges in the open fimbria, and begins to attach to an ovary. In these instances, both tube and ovary are removed.

New laser technology can remove the embryo and preserve both tube and ovary. The precise laser enables a surgeon to slit the tube, remove the embryo, then reconstruct the tube, barely touching the fragile cell layers inside. If an ovary is involved, the surgeon can detach the embryo with minimal damage to the ovarian surface (but, as with all ectopic pregnancies, the embryo is lost). At present, this can only be done in a few hospitals in Britain, but the situation should improve slowly.

If an ectopic pregnancy is caused by an obstruction in the fallopian tube, the risk of another ectopic pregnancy is high unless the tube is reconstructed. When the ectopic pregnancy is caused by other factors, the event may never recur. If

296 · SPECIAL CONSIDERATIONS

the fallopian tubes can be preserved, a woman has a good chance to have a normal pregnancy in the future. Among fourteen women who had laser surgery to remove ectopic pregnancies, eight conceived again within six months and went on to normal pregnancies. None of the women has had a repeat ectopic pregnancy.

Generally, if a woman experiences repeated ectopic pregnancies in the same tube, the physician should consider removal of the tube in order to keep the ovary from becoming damaged. In that case, fertilization can still take place in the other tube, or the woman may be a candidate for *in vitro* fertilization.

Incompetent Cervix

A major cause of a second trimester spontaneous abortion is a weak or incompetent cervix, a condition in which the cervix is not strong enough to support the growing pregnancy. As the weight of the fetus increases, the cervix dilates and the pregnancy falls out. An incompetent cervix may be related to previous cervical surgery, damage during childbirth, or developmental defects. The classic symptom is repeated, painless abortion after the twelfth week of pregnancy.

When a woman has a known history of such abortions, she needs to be closely watched during her next pregnancy. If the cervix begins to dilate prematurely, the physician usually can support the pregnancy by placing a stitch around the cervix to tighten it. If this procedure, called Shirodkar suture, is performed early enough, the woman has an 80 per cent chance of a successful pregnancy.

Other Causes of Abortion

Infections

Infections that involve the lining of the uterus (endometritis) can prevent implantation or lead to early abortion. Infections may be caused by *Streptococcus*, ureaplasma, chlamydia, and a host of other infectious agents. Diagnosis is made by performing cultures on a tissue sample from the lining of the uterus. Antibiotic treatment usually cures the infection.

Allergic Reactions

Occasionally, a woman's immune system perceives the fetus as a foreign threat and rejects it. There are four major forms of immune rejection: blood type rejection (ABO); Rh factors; fetal tissue rejection, or human leukocyte antigens (HLA); and defective early pregnancy factor (EPF).

These reactions are very rare and, with the exception of Rh factors, are considered only after all other possible causes have been eliminated. Sophisticated laboratory testing of both partners is needed to make a diagnosis. Treatment is directed towards reducing the allergic reaction in the mother and requires highly specialized laboratory work, such as giving the mother transfusions from her husband or other people with a different blood or tissue type.

Psychological Problems

Psychological factors are not considered a direct cause of infertility or spontaneous abortion. Yet we know that mental stress can override the hormonal axis and create menstrual and ovulatory problems. Stress may also influence abortion. Some researchers have noted that neurotic women tend to conceive easily and abort more readily than a comparable group of emotionally stable women. Fear of pain during labour, misgivings about motherhood, or anxiety over an insecure marriage may contribute to abortion.

Before a doctor tells a woman that repeated abortions are being caused by psychological stress, all physiological causes should be ruled out. A complete fertility check-up will take everything into consideration, including the stress components.

Smoking and Alcohol

Women who smoke have a 25 per cent greater chance of aborting than non-smokers. Chronic smoke inhalation prevents oxygen from getting from the lungs through the blood and to the baby. As a result, the fetus is deprived of oxygen during its critical growth phase. Smoking is also associated with serious birth defects, including malformations of the central nervous system, cleft palate, and facial defects.

Daily alcohol intake, likewise, is associated with a high percentage of birth defects. Beer and wine, however, which have a low alcohol content, do not appear harmful in small amounts. Children born of alcoholic mothers may have minimal brain damage, such as learning defects, or such severe defects as mental retardation and deafness. Alcohol is also associated with facial and other defects.

Drugs

As a rule drugs do not affect the quality of the ovum, because egg cells, complete with their DNA, are in place before the woman is born. However, some drugs, such as hormones, antibiotics, and anti-hypersensitives, can interfere with the implantation of the fertilized embryo, and chemotherapy and certain hormones such as DES actually attack and mutate the embryo in the uterus. In men, chemotherapy reduces the number of good-quality sperm. Should an egg be impregnated with poor-quality sperm, the probability of abortion is high.

There is some controversy about the effects of cannabis and other psychogenic drugs on developing embryos. However, to date there is no conclusive proof that these drugs increase the risk of abortion.

Environmental Pollution

Women today are increasingly exposed to environmental toxins and waste products from high-risk occupations.

Women who work in operating rooms, particularly anaesthetists, have a high rate of abortion because of the anaesthetic gases. Women who work in the textile and clothing industries may be affected by inhaling toxic fabric 'dust'. Hairdressers and cosmetologists who routinely work with chemicals and solvents are also extremely vulnerable to toxins that may cause abortion.

Certain metals, such as methyl mercury (found in water and fish), have been directly linked to high abortion rates in Japan and Iraq. The mercury from factory waste pollutes the water, which is ingested by small organisms, which are eaten by small fish, which are eaten by bigger fish, which ultimately are eaten by human beings. Each step results in a magnification of the mercury content. The ingestion of lead in high concentrations is also known to cause spontaneous abortion and produce serious bone defects in small children.

In the town of Kokkola, Finland, many of the women in a heavy-metal factory and a sulphur factory were hospitalized because of spontaneous abortion. The sulphur factory was shut down in 1977.

Hazardous Occupations

The following industries have been linked to an increased frequency of spontaneous abortions. At risk are women who work in:

Metallurgy plants: exposure to copper, lead, arsenic, cadmium.
Radio and television manufacturing: exposure to solder fumes.
Chemical laboratories: exposure to solvents and other chemicals.
Plastics factories: exposure to polyvinyl chloride and other chemicals.
Hospital operating rooms: exposure to anaesthetic gases.

The possible effects of pesticides on human reproduction have not been fully verified, but one Finnish study has shown that women gardeners often bear children with muscle and skeletal deformities. Much more research is needed in this area because almost all human beings are exposed to small residues of pesticides in food.

Today, it is known that the environment is definitely related to many abortions. Industry and medicine owe an obligation to future generations to study and eliminate environmental hazards that may mutate the species.

Diseases That Affect Pregnancy

Some diseases can make pregnancy difficult and may even be life-threatening. Diabetes, heart disease, endometriosis, kidney disease, thyroid problems, and herpes virus all need to be well controlled before pregnancy begins. These serious diseases can be dangerous to both mother and child, and in every case a woman should have careful medical evaluation before considering pregnancy.

Diabetes

Diabetic women need special management to complete a pregnancy successfully. In 25–50 per cent of pregnant women with out-of-control diabetes, the fetus will abort or die in the uterus. The hormones of pregnancy, plus physical stress, will cause the mother's blood sugar to rise and the diabetes to escalate. If the disease is not well controlled, there is a substantial risk that the fetus will try to produce extra insulin to assist the mother; the result is massive fetal growth. Such babies may weigh up to 15 lb (6·8 kg) at birth. The newborn baby may also have cleft palate or other malformations. More dangerously, some infants will be born with extremely low blood sugar, which may cause death.

Heart Disease

Pregnant women with congenital heart disease have a 50 per cent risk of spontaneous abortion, possibly because the blood supplies inadequate oxygen to the placenta. If a woman with severe heart disease succeeds in carrying a baby to term, her life may be at risk during the delivery should heart failure develop. A woman with heart disease should never contemplate pregnancy without the close collaboration of a cardiologist.

Endometriosis

Endometriosis has also been associated with a high rate of spontaneous abortion, particularly in the mild phase of the disease. Nearly half of all pregnant women with mild endometriosis will abort, compared with about 25 per cent of those with moderate to severe forms of the disease. The reason for this perplexing twist lies in the nature of the disease. In the mild early stages, endometrial implants give off potent prostaglandins, which constrict blood vessels and make smooth muscles contract. These contractions are thought to increase the incidence of abortion.

As the disease advances, the active cells burn out and scar tissue takes over. If a woman does manage to become pregnant at this advanced stage, her risk of abortion is less. Generally, women with endometriosis have trouble getting pregnant and usually require treatment by a fertility specialist.

Kidney Disease

Kidney or renal disease, when associated with severely high blood pressure or protein loss in the mother's urine, can lead to spontaneous abortion. Mild hypertension, however, does not usually affect the fetus.

Thyroid Problems

Low thyroid production is also associated with spontaneous abortion. The ailing thyroid may not be able to meet the increased demands of pregnancy. A battery of thyroid and pituitary tests can help the physician rule out this easily corrected hormone deficiency.

Genital Herpes

The herpes virus is a sexually transmitted disease. Once begun, the disease comes and goes in sporadic outbreaks of genital lesions that may vary from a slight red bump to clusters of blisters. If a woman gets herpes for the first time during the early weeks of pregnancy, she has a 25 per cent greater chance of abortion than the unaffected woman. The first infection is usually more virulent than recurrent episodes, and is therefore more dangerous to the fetus.

If herpes is active at the time of vaginal delivery, the child has a 50 per cent chance of contracting the disease; a child who does contract herpes during delivery has a 95 per cent chance of brain damage, blindness, or death. If a woman knows she has herpes, careful observation, appropriate blood tests, and Caesarean delivery may prevent the virus from being passed on to the child.

Caesarean section carries some risk to both mother and child, as does any surgical operation. To avoid unnecessary Caesarean delivery, as a woman with a history of herpes approaches term, the physician should examine the woman carefully and perform a weekly culture. If symptoms appear, a caesarean delivery should be performed. The problem with this sort of evaluation is that the test for herpes is slow – between two and six days. In that time, an active herpes lesion may disappear and reappear. To avoid any possible contamination, some physicians routinely recommend caesarean delivery for any woman who has a history of herpes virus infection.

Testing the Man

Abortions have traditionally been considered a female problem. Today we know that two important causes of recurrent abortions can be traced to the male partner. The DNA inside the sperm may be faulty, even though, on semen analysis, the sperm look completely normal. Diagnosis is made by chromosome analysis when no apparent reason can be found for repeated miscarriages. There is no treatment. In these cases, artificial insemination by donor sperm is the answer.

A chronic infection of the lining of the womb that causes the pregnancy to abort can sometimes be traced to sperm that carry bacteria from the male semen. Semen cultures, taken during routine semen analysis, will detect the presence of bacteria, which can be treated with antibiotics.

Stillbirth

A child that is dead at the moment of delivery is called a stillbirth. There are three major causes of such a catastrophe, and all involve loss of oxygen. First, knots of blood clots can form in the umbilical cord and cut off critical oxygen to the child. Second, the placenta may prematurely separate from the embryo, cutting off the flow of oxygen from the mother to the baby. Both of these events usually occur within the last three weeks of pregnancy. The classic symptom is that the mother no longer feels the infant moving inside her womb. Once the obstetrician confirms that the baby is dead, labour is induced as quickly as possible to reduce emotional stress and potential medical complications.

Finally, the air supply may be cut off if the umbilical cord becomes trapped around the baby or compressed against the pelvis during delivery. Today, such

302 · SPECIAL CONSIDERATIONS

entanglements are detected with fetal monitoring, and the child can be delivered by Caesarean section or another emergency obstetrical manoeuvre.

Premature Babies

A newborn baby who is not developed enough to survive without the help of life-support systems is called premature. In the past a baby born before the twenty-eighth week of pregnancy had little chance of survival. Today, however, chances of survival are excellent, and babies weighing less than two pounds can be saved. Uterine tumours, loss of oxygenated blood to the placenta, infections in the placenta, weakness in the cervix, and deformities in the uterus are the principal causes of early delivery.

When a woman suffers a premature delivery, it's important to discover the reason. Some of the problems can be corrected so that future births will be normal. Fibroid tumours can be removed surgically, a weak cervix can be strengthened, and deformities can be reconstructed. Problems of the placental blood supply may be caused by diabetes or other illnesses that can be medically treated during pregnancy. Infections of the placenta are very difficult to treat during pregnancy. However, placental infections that lead to premature delivery rarely recur, and subsequent pregnancies are usually normal.

The Emotional Aftermath of Lost Pregnancies

The death of a child before birth is a loss whose severity is rarely recognized by family and friends and sometimes not even by the couple themselves. The loss is difficult to describe, because the child was anticipated and desired but never actually seen. The couple grieves for a loved one whose existence was evanescent and whose duration on earth may now be marked only in the mind. There is nothing to remember except anticipation. When a man and woman repeatedly sustain such a loss, every new day becomes disheartening. Because of the ambiguous nature of miscarriage, the couple often is not able to resolve one such loss before being faced with another. People who are not allowed to express their sorrow become trapped in grief and find it difficult to carry on with their lives. Trying to get over it quickly usually makes the process more difficult.

But how can a couple mourn alone, with few people around them to acknowledge their grief? Psychologists feel it helps to recognize the universal stages of grieving. The first stage is a feeling of numbness, which may last a few weeks or a few months. Friends will remark on how well the couple is 'handling the situation'. In fact, numbness is nature's way of letting time pass before the full impact of the loss is felt. It is a built-in protective mechanism of the mind.

Grieving is more complicated for couples who have suffered an early abortion because there is no tangible loss. They have never seen the child whom they mourn, and there is no funeral to symbolize the loss. If the fetus is aborted early, laboratory tests should be performed, particularly chromosome analysis, to try to identify the cause of the miscarriage. Learning the facts gives the couple something real to hold on to in a very unreal situation. The couple may find it helpful to hold a private funeral and actually see the child. Hospitals should assist the man and woman in obtaining the autopsy report so they will know exactly what happened to their infant.

When the feeling of numbness begins to pass, many couples sink into serious psychological difficulties. By the time that they are ready to express their grief openly, family and friends assume that they have got over their loss. In fact, the sorrow is just beginning.

The next stage is one of anger and emotional turmoil. The couple, especially the wife, may not be able to socialize when babies or children or even pregnant women are present. This is a common response. Helpful friends who recognize the signs can offer assurance by sharing their own feelings and similar emotional experiences. Help may also come from other couples who have lost a baby. The best thing a couple can do is to express the anger and emotion. Friends and family may be dismayed and uncomprehending, but the rage doesn't last for ever.

Anger is usually followed by a period of deep depression, when the real meaning of the loss has penetrated the surface of defensive anger and been absorbed into the life process. It seems as if the despair will never cease. This stage is the most uncomfortable for other people, and friends often stay away. Grief is a constant, tormenting presence – but at least this is the end of the road.

A year or more may pass before despair subsides and the couple can begin to think about the future. Ideally, only after these stages of grieving are complete should a couple think about getting pregnant again. Unfortunately, many couples must move on hastily and try again, even while they are mired in mourning, to stay ahead of the biological clock ticking against them in their search for parenthood. Compassion and support from the fertility team will help them work through the loss and decide when enough time has passed to try again. Such couples need the reassurance that following one or two spontaneous abortions there is a 70 per cent probability of successful pregnancy.

30
Pregnancy after Thirty-five

A 1983 report from the Bureau of the Census showed that the number of women bearing their first child after the age of thirty-five had risen dramatically since 1980 – from 3·6 to 5·2 per 1,000. The report also showed that childbirth has increased across the board for women between the ages of thirty and thirty-four – from 12·8 per 1,000 in 1980 to 13·8 in 1983.

These statistics reflect the trend in recent years of women postponing marriage and childbirth until they have finished their education and launched their careers. After working a few years, women then decide to have children. There's often a sense of urgency attached to these pregnancies as the women recognize that time is running out.

In modern society delayed childbirth offers some important advantages. Love and marriage are not as simple as they once were. Relationships are complex in a complex society; and professional roles are equally difficult. Many couples want time to make sure that their marriages are stable and their careers are established before taking on the responsibilities of parenthood.

For them, having children late in life means being less torn between work inside and outside the home. Most women who become mothers after thirty feel that they have more patience and more 'quality time' with their children; most fathers feel the same way. Statistically, the home environment differs sharply for women over thirty. It is likely to be more secure financially, and while no one would argue that money guarantees a happy family the statistics do suggest that financial security is one reason why many women are delaying childbearing.

The difficulty with delayed childbearing is that the advantages do not always match the biological facts. For a variety of reasons, some women over the age of thirty will have difficulty becoming pregnant; and if they do achieve pregnancy, they have a greater likelihood of complications than younger women. Childbearing is still relatively safe for women between thirty and thirty-five. After thirty-five, however, medical problems occur with greater frequency.

The most fertile time for a woman is in her late teens and early twenties. When no contraceptives are used and a woman has sexual intercourse on a regular basis, she has more than an 85 per cent chance of becoming pregnant within twelve to fifteen months. As a woman grows older, events may combine to decrease the chances of pregnancy: there is greater likelihood of extensive damage from endometriosis and a higher incidence of fibroid tumours in the uterus and reproductive tract diseases (pelvic infections); ovulation may be less regular and the quality of the ova will gradually diminish.

The Ageing Ova

A woman has approximately 400,000 ova in place when she is born, and each small reproductive cell has a limited time span. When a woman is between eighteen and twenty-eight, the ova are at their best and her ovulation cycle is regular. From twenty-eight on, the cells begin to wind down. After thirty-five, as ovulation becomes less reliable, a woman has less chance of becoming pregnant. More important, if she does succeed in becoming pregnant, she carries a higher risk of a miscarriage.

Chromosomes

Inside older ova, chromosomes begin to deteriorate and stick together. Before an egg can be fertilized, its twenty-three double-stranded chromosomes must separate into single strands. The egg discards twenty-three single strands into a polar body that eventually disintegrates. It retains twenty-three single strands, which will match with an identical number provided by sperm. In older eggs, when the time comes for the double strands to part, the chromosomes don't always separate properly. One notoriously troublesome chromosome is No. 21.

When chromosome No. 21 tries to part in an older egg, it often pulls its mirror image along with it. The egg then carries twenty-two single strands of all other chromosomes, plus a double strand of No. 21. When the ovum is fertilized, it gains twenty-three single-stranded chromosomes from the sperm. The result is a new cell union in which the twenty-first chromosome has three strands of DNA. This is known as Down's syndrome or mongolism. Down's syndrome babies are usually born moderately retarded. Although most live well into adult maturity, their mental development does not grow past age five or six. Down's syndrome is only one of many birth defects that can result from a mismatching of chromosomes. Other chromosomes may stick together and drag along extra pieces.

Testing for Birth Defects

New data on birth defects have revealed that the incidence of Down's syndrome increases steadily as maternal age advances, rather than rising dramatically at about the age of thirty-five, as was previously thought. In the past it was also generally assumed that the increased incidence of Down's syndrome was due solely to increased maternal age. It is now thought that an older father may also be responsible.

The Options

Medical science has made major strides in recent years in understanding diseases with significant genetic components. Scientists look forward to the day when these defects can be corrected while the fetus is still developing in the womb. For the time being, sophisticated testing, such as amniocentesis, can detect many severe genetic defects in the early months of pregnancy, which allows couples time to abort the pregnancy if they choose.

Because abortion is an option, women who wish to become pregnant after thirty-five need to first resolve some pressing issues. Will they have amniocentesis to detect Down's syndrome? If the test indicates that the child will be defective, will they choose abortion? The likelihood of having two abnormal pregnancies in a row, even in older women, is extremely small. If the fetus does have Down's syndrome, the odds greatly favour a second normal pregnancy. There is only a 4·0 per cent chance that Down's syndrome will recur. For some reason, mothers at highest risk for recurrence seem to be those who had a Down's syndrome child when they were younger than twenty-nine. Here the chance of having another child with Down's syndrome is 1 per cent.

The question of what to do about a defective fetus should be resolved before the woman becomes pregnant, and husband and wife need to make the decision together. If they are unable to face a possible abortion, yet feel unable to cope with the stress of bringing up a retarded child, they should probably decide against pregnancy.

Amniocentesis

Between the fourteenth and eighteenth week of pregnancy the obstetrician will offer amniocentesis. In this test, ultrasound is first used to locate the baby inside the amniotic sac. Then a thin needle is slipped through the abdomen into the uterus. The procedure is painless, although occasionally a woman feels very slight uterine contractions. The needle pierces the sac of fluid surrounding the baby. About 1 oz (30 ml) of fluid is withdrawn and transferred to a vial for delivery to a laboratory.

Amniocentesis is a safe and accurate procedure when performed by a skilled physician. The risk of spontaneous abortion or damage to the fetus is slight, approximately 0·05 per cent. Withdrawal of fluid takes about three minutes. While the mother rests for a few minutes afterwards, the physician checks the baby's heart rate, then repeats the ultrasound to make sure there is no leakage from the amniotic sac. In big cities amniocentesis is usually an outpatient procedure.

The fluid withdrawn from the sac contains cells with the baby's genetic make-up. It takes between three and five weeks for these cells to grow; some cells may take an additional week or two. After the cells grow and reproduce, they are washed and fixed; the chromosomes are then counted. A normal test will show forty-six matched chromosomes in each cell. Down's syndrome will show that chromosome No. 21 has three strands of DNA instead of two. Amniocentesis is accurate about 90 per cent of the time, although there are rare instances when the laboratory analysis is in error.

If an abnormality is present, a decision must be made. By now a woman is well into her second trimester of pregnancy. If she chooses to have an abortion, the procedure will usually require a chemical induction. Such inductions, given in a hospital setting, are safe and carry only minimal risk to reproductive function or health. A woman who chooses to abort such a pregnancy stands an excellent chance of having a normal child if she can become pregnant again.

The test for Down's syndrome is only one of a hundred possible tests that can be run on the fluid withdrawn during amniocentesis. If a couple has a family history of genetic defect, such as Tay-Sachs disease, sickle-cell anaemia, or certain forms of muscular dystrophy, the physician can order additional tests on the fluid. Since each of the possible tests is different, physicians must know what they are looking for before they can order the right test.

There are about 700 additional birth defects that amniocentesis cannot identify. However, Down's syndrome is by far the most common, comprising 70–80 per cent of spontaneous birth defects.

New Tests

Chorion Villus Biopsy. A new test, called a chorion villus biopsy, can detect birth defects much earlier than amniocentesis. However, there is greater risk to the fetus. With this test the physician inserts an endoscope through the mother's cervix up to the placental bed, guides a pair of special scissors through the endoscope and snips off a piece of membrane (chorion) surrounding the baby.

Some experts predict that the chorion villus biopsy will replace many of the current uses of amniocentesis within the next few years. The prime advantage of the new technique is the simplicity and speed with which it can be applied.

Another key advantage is that it can be done as early as the ninth or tenth week of pregnancy, far sooner than amniocentesis. The disadvantage is that since the test directly interferes with placental integrity, it holds greater risk of miscarriage. The miscarriage rate with chorion villus biopsy may be as high as 8 or 9 per cent, a much higher rate than amniocentesis, which is only 0·05 per cent.

Fetoscopy. Another new procedure, called fetoscopy, can detect birth defects and will also allow surgery to be carried out on the fetus *in utero*. A fetoscope is a long, thin telescope with a diameter about the size of a large needle. Using ultrasound as a guide, the surgeon makes an incision in the mother's abdomen and passes the instrument through the uterus and into the amniotic sac. The surgeon can look into the scope and have a limited view of the fetus. The telescope has special attachments so that the doctor can take tiny samples of the baby's blood and tissue. Cleft palate and limb abnormalities can be detected. Blood samples can be tested for such inherited disorders as haemophilia, thalassaemia, and sickle-cell disease.

Two surgical procedures can also be carried out on the fetus. The first is a blood transfusion for a fetus that is severely anaemic due to Rh antibodies in the mother's blood. The other is to help a baby with abnormal build-up of fluids, for example, a blocked urinary tract, which causes a build-up of urine in the bladder. A catheter can be passed into the bladder of the fetus so that the urine drains into the amniotic fluid. After the baby is born, the catheter is removed, and the blockage is corrected by surgery.

Fetoscopy is a delicate procedure that carries a higher risk of complications than other antenatal tests because the fetus is touched directly. However, it is the only test that can determine the presence of certain crippling blood diseases or other severe birth defects, and the only procedure which permits *in utero* surgery. All the antenatal tests will reveal the baby's sex, but they will not be performed simply to tell parents the gender of their child.

In Vitro Fertilization for Older Women

An older woman's natural conception rate is still higher than that obtained by the best *in vitro* programme in the world. The *in vitro* process cannot detect a chromosome abnormality in an ovum; nor can it overcome any of the special problems faced by older women wishing to become pregnant. But women whose fallopian tubes are irreparably damaged have no other means of achieving a pregnancy (see Chapter 32).

Menopausal Babies

Women over forty-five who are approaching the menopause do occasionally ovulate. Should both an egg and a sperm be in the right place at the right time, and should the uterus be adequately prepared, a pregnancy can occur. However, the probability is less than that of being hit by a bolt of lightning. If it happens, the precautions are the same as for any woman over the age of thirty-five, but the obstetrical care is more intense. A woman in this age group requires careful monitoring and delivery under the strictest controlled conditions.

31
Contraceptives That Protect Fertility

Just as human beings have tried since the dawn of history to discover how babies are made, so have they tried to prevent pregnancy. The ancient Egyptians, as confused as anyone about the origins of life, nevertheless showed some understanding of the process when they tried to avoid pregnancy by spooning a mixture of honey and crocodile dung into the vagina before intercourse. Egyptian women were using spermicides before anyone knew such a thing as sperm existed.

Lint soaked in honey and acacia juice, a primitive form of the sponge contraceptive, was used in 1500 BC. In the sixth century the hollowed-out half of a pomegranate served as a diaphragm. Casanova supposedly offered his numerous lovers half of a squeezed lemon for the same purpose.

Desert nomads may have invented the first IUD when they placed pebbles in the uteri of camels to prevent pregnancies during long treks across the desert. In the Bible, Onan practised coitus interruptus when he spewed his semen on to the ground, and thus committed a sin. Today, *onanism* means interrupted intercourse, and the word is often used interchangeably with masturbation.

Hundreds of years ago women developed their own oral contraceptives in the form of various drug concoctions, such as strychnine and arsenic; these drugs were extremely dangerous, and often prevented pregnancy by killing the users. Abortions were induced by dilating the uterus with various herbs that absorbed moisture and gently expanded until the uterus went into spasms. In the 1880s an English chemist named Walter Rendell mixed together cocoa butter and quinine to create a best-selling spermicide.

Throughout history the search for fertility has gone hand in hand with the attempt to control the time when children were conceived and brought into the world. In modern times this quest is more vital than ever. Population control is a major issue around the world. Further, in countries like the United States and the United Kingdom, where infertility has taken a sharp upswing, women are asking whether some contraceptives permanently interfere with the ability to bear children.

Just how dangerous to a woman's health and future fertility are various forms of contraceptives? Is the contraceptive a woman used as a teenager still the best choice as she grows older? What kinds of contraceptives should a woman use when she hopes to postpone childbearing until her thirties, or has one child and decides to wait a few years before having another?

Contraceptives need to be selected according to a woman's age, her health, her present fertility status and hormonal balance, and her lifestyle. The best contraceptive for a woman is one that offers the most protection with the fewest side-effects. Failure rates, typically given in percentages, refer to the number of women out of every 100 who get pregnant while using a particular contraceptive for one year. Therefore, a failure rate of 10 per cent means that ten women out of every hundred get pregnant within one year.

Each of the many forms of contraceptives comes with its own set of advantages and disadvantages. Long-term use of a certain type of oral contraceptive pill has been linked to some forms of cancer. Birth-control pills also may affect future childbearing potential. The IUD has received unfavourable publicity because of the high infection rate, which may lead to infertility. The barrier methods (condoms and diaphragms) are the safest in terms of protecting fertility but have other drawbacks. And the spermicides have a high failure rate.

All in all, we are striving for reproductive freedom, so that a couple can choose the appropriate time to bear children according to their circumstances.

Oral Contraceptives

Most contraceptives attempt to keep a sperm and an egg from meeting. Of all the contraceptives available, only the pill accomplishes this feat by stopping egg production, which accounts for its remarkable success rate.

When it was introduced in the early 1960s the pill revolutionized contraception. It was easy to use, highly effective, and reversible. Hundreds of thousands of women immediately began to use it. Then, in the 1970s, the news broke that the pill caused cardiovascular damage and any number of other dangerous side-effects. These side-effects were primarily associated with the high doses of oestrogen in the pill, which interfered with the blood-clotting system. Studies indicate that the modern low-dose pill, which combines oestrogen with progesterone, is much safer than the old pill. Still, every woman taking the pill should know its positive and negative effects, and the fact that ovulation does not always resume immediately when a woman stops taking the pill.

The pill acts by jamming a wrench into the hormonal axis between the brain and the ovaries. The control centre and the ovaries shut down, and the pill takes over the hormonal supply to the body. Instead of the cyclical shifting between oestrogen and progesterone, the pill creates a steady supply of hormones all month long. Eggs do not develop in the ovaries and therefore are not released into the fallopian tubes. The cervical mucus remains thick and impenetrable all month long.

The smooth supply of hormones has some beneficial effects on the rest of the body. Acne usually clears up, mood shifts are less noticeable, and menstrual cramps and premenstrual tension subside, because even though a woman will bleed every month these are false periods.

The Right Pill

Birth-control pills are derived from male and female hormones. Not only do they stop women from getting pregnant; they may also carry additional hormonal signals to the body that affect menstrual pattern, breast size or tenderness, and hair development. There are four main types of birth-control pills: oestrogen-dominant, progesterone-dominant, equal ratio of oestrogen/progesterone, and male-derived hormone. Which pill to take should be based on a woman's menstrual pattern and body configuration.

The pattern of menstrual flow may be scant, normal, or excessive. Body configuration may be extremely female, with very large breasts and hips; average, with normal breast-to-hip ratio; and what doctors call masculinized – small breasts and narrow hips with a tendency towards acne or excessive hair growth.

Masculinized means only that a woman has more than usual amounts of male hormone in her system. All women have some male hormones, which influence the sex drive of both sexes. Patterns of hair growth and body build are also governed by genetic traits. So you can't tell the hormone content of a woman just by looking at her.

Any combination of menstrual pattern and body configuration can exist together. However, scant periods usually accompany the average or masculinized body configuration. Excessive menstrual periods usually go with the average or extremely female configuration. A doctor's job is to help the woman choose the most effective pill with the fewest side-effects. Most women can use the evenly balanced, low-dose oestrogen/progesterone pill, which throws off the feedback loop just enough to prevent ovulation. It has minimal side-effects and a low failure rate.

A woman who has acne and excess hair may do better on an oestrogen-dominant pill, in which the effect of progesterone is minimal. Usually with this pill hair growth diminishes, skin clears, breasts fill out, and periods are slightly longer.

Women who have excessive bleeding during menstruation usually respond best to a progesterone-dominant pill. This version of the pill is also ideal for women who suffer from premenstrual tension. If a woman has acne, however, and takes a birth-control pill with dominant progesterone or with a weak male hormone effect, the acne is likely to become worse.

The male-hormone-derived pill is reserved for women who have very large breasts and heavy periods. Their reproductive system is so highly oestrogenized that it needs something to slow down the hormones speeding between the pituitary and the ovaries. If these women take the regular birth-control pill, they frequently have breakthrough bleeding.

Side-effects

Severe side-effects seldom occur with the new pills, but every woman who takes contraceptive pills should be screened by her doctor twice a year for any sign of high blood pressure, heart disease, or other problems.

The pill is safe for most young women but becomes less safe after the age of thirty. Women between thirty and thirty-five who use the pill do not run a significant risk of serious complications unless they are obese, smoke cigarettes, or have pre-existing diseases, but after the age of thirty-five, side-effects of the pill become more dangerous for all women, regardless of their weight or blood pressure or whether they smoke.

Women with the following conditions should never use birth-control pills at any age:

Serious liver disease or impaired liver function
Thrombophlebitis (blood clots), stroke, or coronary artery disease
Severe migraine headaches
Breast cancer
High blood pressure
Sickle-cell anaemia

Most side-effects reported with the pill are temporary and disappear as a woman's body adjusts to the new hormonal pattern. However, a few women do not adjust to side-effects and have to stop taking the pill. Possible side-effects include nausea, weight gain, water retention, breast enlargement and tenderness, skin pigmentation, headaches, and spotting or breakthrough bleeding.

The chances of getting pregnant on the pill are about 1 per cent. In these cases the chemical blockade is not strong enough to hold back the hypothalamus and pituitary. If a woman does become pregnant while on the pill, there is a risk of congenital malformations in the fetus. The woman should discontinue the pill immediately. Today, there are no tests that reveal conclusively whether a birth defect is present in such a fetus. Less than 1 per cent of babies conceived on birth control pills are defective; the defects are usually in the heart and blood vessels, which if severe can cause death.

Although medical evidence is inconclusive, women who stop taking the pill and then become pregnant immediately seem to have a higher rate of miscarriage than those who never use the pill or those who wait for two or more years to conceive. This may be due to a vitamin and mineral deficiency, particularly of the B-complex group. Many doctors recommend that women wait for at least three months after menstruation returns to normal before becoming pregnant.

The Pill and Fertility

The pill has both good and bad effects on future fertility. Past studies indicated that women who take the pill are protected against the risk of pelvic inflammatory disease because the thickened mucus barrier prevents the transmission of disease during sexual intercourse.

However, recent investigations suggest that some newly discovered venereal organisms, namely chlamydia and ureaplasma, can get past the mucus barrier and invade the pelvic cavity. Dr Sebastian Faro, of Baylor College of Medicine, suggests that birth-control pills may lower a woman's immune system, allowing some organisms to gain a foothold in the reproductive tract. The actual method of invasion is still unknown, but for now the protective nature of oral contraceptives is questionable.

One major problem, as far as future fertility is concerned, is that it takes time for ovulation to resume after a woman stops using the pill. Normally, natural menstruation and ovulation resume three or four months after the pill is stopped. About 20 per cent of women, however, need a year's time to regain their fertility. This can be a serious problem for a woman who has delayed pregnancy until her thirties, when her fertility is in decline. A very small percentage of women never regain their fertility after taking the pill.

How Long to Take the Pill

In the early days of the pill, most women used it for only two or three years because no one knew precisely what the long-term effects were. Today, many women begin using the pill in their teens and continue up until the time they decide to have children. Studies suggest that length of use does not affect future fertility, but consistency does. A woman who goes on and off the pill will have more trouble regaining regular ovulation and menstruation than a woman who consistently uses the pill.

The age at which the pill is begun is another factor. A very young girl with erratic menstrual cycles usually has an immature reproductive system. She needs more time for her biological clock to establish a regular pattern before going on the pill. Women who recover normal menstrual function quickly after stopping the pill usually had normal cycles before they started taking the pill. Those who had erratic cycles when they started the pill take the longest to recoup.

For the most part, then, considering the side-effects and the risk to fertility, a woman should not use the pill after the age of thirty. If she does not want to get pregnant, she can safely use the pill until she is thirty-five, unless she has a pre-existing medical condition that would be worsened by the pill.

The Morning-after Pill

DES (diethylstilboestrol) is no longer used in the UK as a morning-after pill. There are now two methods of morning-after contraception: special doses of a contraceptive pill or the fitting of an IUD. The pill must be started within seventy-two hours of intercourse, and as it involves a high level of hormones being taken it can make some women feel sick. An IUD can only be used in this way if it is fitted within five days, but once it has been fitted it will function as a contraceptive for several years, if required.

Intra-uterine Devices

The IUD – the coil or loop – is a small object placed in the uterus to control conception. An IUD developed in the early 1900s had such a high infection rate that scientists quickly abandoned the device. In the 1950s, when plastics and powerful antibiotics were developed, research was reopened and the modern IUD was invented.

The first IUDs on the market were accepted with enthusiasm. Like the birth-control pill, the IUD offers excellent protection against pregnancy, and it is permanent until removed. A major advantage over the pill is that it allows the body to go through its natural changes every month, without alteration of the hormonal axis. After the birth-control pill, the modern IUD is the most effective method of reversible contraception.

IUDs come in many sizes and shapes, some impregnated with progesterone, others containing copper. No one knows exactly how the IUD works. Some scientists contend that the device prevents sperm from fertilizing the egg. Others say that the IUD causes changes in the lining of the uterus that make it impossible for the fertilized ovum to implant. Still others feel that the IUD causes the lining of the uterus and the fallopian tube to become so hyperactive that the egg cannot be fertilized, or if it is fertilized it falls out of the cervix and is discharged through the vagina.

Unfortunately, serious problems arose soon after the IUD came on the market. The IUD string, which hangs out of the cervix to track the presence of the device and to aid in removal, was originally made of braided Dacron. Bacteria could easily multiply and move between the strands of Dacron and into the uterine cavity, causing serious infection and in some cases death.

Today the strings are made of a single strand of plastic that retards bacterial movement. However, low-grade pelvic infections still occur and can result in tubal infections and obstructions. It is estimated that 10 per cent of IUD users develop some form of mild uterine infection that can potentially affect their fertility.

Sometimes an IUD can penetrate the wall of the uterus and pass into the abdomen. This poses no immediate physical danger, but it can have serious consequences for fertility. The omentum, a fatty curtain of tissue that hangs from the upper portion of the colon, engulfs the puncture in an effort to stop the spread of infection. Often the omentum does such a good job that the puncture goes by unnoticed. The only symptom shows up years later, when the woman is infertile because the omentum is stuck to the surface of the uterus and tubes.

The Right IUD

Infection with an IUD seems to occur more often in women who have never had a child because the uterus is smaller and more easily irritated by the device. The irritation creates an ideal surface for infection to take hold. Small copper-wire IUDs are recommended to protect women who have never had children. The copper leaches into uterine fluids and kills sperm. Women who have borne children and have a larger uterus can use larger IUDs, usually without copper, that rely more on size and configuration to induce continuous contractions of the uterus.

Risk of pelvic infection is also directly related to the number of sexual partners a woman has; the IUD, unlike barrier methods or the pill, offers no protection against such infections. Overall, therefore, in terms of protecting future fertility, the IUD is most suitable for older women who have already had children and who do not have multiple sexual partners.

A woman can become pregnant with the IUD in place (half the time the pregnancy will spontaneously abort) and can carry a child safely to term without removal of the device. However, most physicians recommend that the IUD be removed as soon as possible after a pregnancy is detected, to avoid life-threatening complications such as septicaemia, septic shock, and septic abortion.

Spermicides

When used alone, spermicides are an ineffective method of birth control; however, a spermicide combined with a condom or a diaphragm provides excellent protection against pregnancy.

Spermicides have some outstanding advantages. They can be bought over the counter without a doctor's prescription; they may offer some protection against the herpes virus and other venereal diseases; and they do not appear to affect future fertility. Spermicides contain a sperm-killing detergent, nonoxynol-9, which coats the sperm and chokes off their oxygen supply. They also contain a harmless, bulky substance that blocks the cervix and prevents any surviving sperm from entering the uterus.

Spermicides are marketed as foams, creams, jellies, foaming tablets, and suppositories. Whatever form is chosen, it must be inserted deep into the vagina and no more than thirty minutes before intercourse and must be reapplied before each new act of intercourse.

The foam, foaming tablets, and suppositories seem to offer the best protection when used alone. Even so, thirty women out of 100 become pregnant when using these forms of spermicides alone. The high failure rate is due in part to improper use. All spermicides are more effective when intercourse takes place in the missionary position. Spermicides tend to leak forward and run away from the cervix when other positions are used. Creams and jellies are less effective than foam because they usually contain less spermicide and fail to coat the cervix or vagina evenly. These agents are designed for use with a diaphragm.

Part of the problem with all the spermicides is that the sperm-killing agent, nonoxynol-9, is very effective in the test tube but less so in the vagina. Researchers have developed a new series of sperm-inhibiting enzymes that may prove more effective than present spermicides.

Side-effects

Occasionally men say they feel a slight burning from the spermicide. Women may experience mild vaginal irritations. These symptoms are rare and can usually be alleviated by changing brands.

The spermicide does not seem to change the cervical mucus or the pH of fluids within the vagina. However, spermicides do carry some long-term effects. A higher than usual number of late miscarriages and severe birth defects are reported in women who conceive while using a spermicide, theoretically because the spermicide damages the DNA of the sperm. Spermicides, however, do not seem to affect future fertility. Fertility is restored as soon as the woman stops using the contraceptive.

The Sponge

The polyurethane sponge was approved for use in the United States in April 1983; it is available in the United Kingdom under the trade names C-Film, Genexol and Ortho-forms. The sponge acts by blocking the cervix, absorbing sperm, and coating them with nonoxynol-9. Each sponge contains enough spermicide to provide twenty-four-hour protection, so that sexual relations do not have to be interrupted to reapply contraceptive. Sponges are available over the counter without prescription, and one size fits everyone.

The failure rate is about 16 per cent in a clinical setting. Although results in the general population are too early to evaluate, failure rates are expected to be somewhat higher. The side-effects of the sponge are similar to those associated with all spermicides, and the same precautions apply. Couples using these new contraceptives should be alert for further studies regarding side-effects.

Barrier Devices

Before the birth-control pill became available, condoms and diaphragms were the most widely used contraceptives in the world. They are safe and effective, protecting against both pregnancy and spread of venereal disease.

A diaphragm is a soft latex cup that a woman fills with spermicidal jelly or cream and inserts over the cervix. It acts as a barrier against the sperm and also holds the spermicide tightly against the cervix. It is awkward and sometimes inconvenient to use, especially for women who are not accustomed to intercourse. The condom is a thin, nearly transparent latex sheath that a man unrolls over his penis like a glove. Even though condoms fit like skin, most men feel that they interfere with sexual pleasure.

When the birth-control pill and IUDs came on to the marketplace, the older forms of contraception quickly went out of fashion. Now, more than two decades later, barrier contraceptives are coming back into style, largely to counteract the spread of venereal infection and to avoid the side-effects associated with newer contraceptives. Used correctly, barrier methods are effective and do not affect future fertility. However, proper use of these methods generally takes practice, motivation, and time. Therefore, barrier contraceptives usually work best for older women who have one sexual partner.

The Diaphragm

A diaphragm must be fitted by a physician or nurse; the fit should be checked every six months, after a pregnancy, or after significant weight loss. The diaphragm stays in place until at least six hours after intercourse. A spermicidal cream or jelly should be reapplied into the vagina with each act of intercourse. When a woman removes the cup and washes it out, she should check for any small holes or tears in the latex. Failure rates range from 6 to 29 per cent. Improper use and failure to check for pin-size holes contribute to the high variation in failure rates. The age and motivation of the woman using the diaphragm also have a great deal to do with success or failure. Younger women seem to have a higher failure rate, as do women who have some conflict about using a contraceptive. They have a diaphragm, but also an unconscious desire to get pregnant. It's easy to 'get caught' in a sexual situation without the diaphragm. The diaphragm is of no contraceptive use when it's sitting at home in the medicine cabinet. Even when it is used correctly, intercourse or normal vaginal swelling during intercourse may cause the diaphragm to slip out of place.

Side-effects are the same as those related to spermicides. Women who are allergic to spermicides or to latex will not be able to use the diaphragm. Future fertility is not affected.

The Cervical Cap

The cervical cap works in a manner similar to the diaphragm, but is not as popular. It has all the advantages of the diaphragm and, in addition, it can be left in place for several days.

The cap is held in place by the muscles around the cervix and is secured by suction. The cap comes in a hard and a soft version. The hard rubber cap, which does not require a spermicide, is somewhat difficult to fit. The soft cap, which is used with a spermicidal jelly, appears to be somewhat more effective. The failure rate of the cervical cap is similar to that of the diaphragm. The close-fitting caps do not appear to erode the cervix; the soft cap, which is used with a spermicide, carries the same hazards as all spermicides.

A new, permanent cervical cap made of thin moulded plastic is now under investigation. This cap has a one-way valve that allows cervical secretions and menstrual fluid to pass out of the vagina but prevents sperm from entering. Theoretically, the cap can stay in place for months at a time. The biggest problem with the permanent cap is that it must be custom-made for each woman who uses it. However, the cap may ultimately meet the needs of couples who want the safety of the diaphragm plus the convenience of an IUD or birth-control pill.

The Condom

The condom is one of the oldest forms of birth control. Early condoms were made of animal guts or bladders and originally were designed to prevent the spread of venereal disease. Modern condoms, made of synthetic rubber, are the most effective barrier method of contraception and disease prevention known today and are the world's most widely used contraceptive devices.

Condoms come in a wide variety of colours and textures. Some have a rippled surface to add friction during intercourse. The rubber of most condoms is impregnated with a spermicide. New manufacturing methods have virtually eliminated leakage. When a man uses a condom and his partner uses a spermicide, the combination is a highly effective contraceptive. The failure rate, which ranges from 5 to 25 per cent, is related to improper use.

The condom itself has no side-effects. The small number of men and women who are allergic to latex can substitute a special condom made of lamb intestine.

Coitus Interruptus

As a long-term approach to birth control, coitus interruptus is the least effective of all contraceptive methods. For the system to work, a man must be certain to withdraw completely before he has ejaculated even a single drop of semen. The first portion of the ejaculate is the most potent. Further, sperm deposited on the outer lips of the vagina can make their way up the vaginal canal and through the cervix. A woman's hymen does not have to be broken for conception to occur.

The chances of accomplishing complete, early withdrawal on a regular basis are virtually nil, making the failure rate extremely high, especially among young men, who have less muscular control than older men at the moment of ejaculation. Therefore, the greatest risk that accompanies coitus interruptus is pregnancy. Also, most men and women feel less sexual gratification with this method. However, there are no side-effects and no risks to future fertility.

The Rhythm Method (Periodic Abstinence)

Periodic abstinence is the only contraceptive method, other than complete abstinence, approved by the Catholic Church. The idea is to abstain from sexual intercourse on the days a woman is ovulating. The tricky part of this method is predicting ovulation. It's estimated that 25 per cent of all women using periodic abstinence as a contraceptive method become pregnant within one year. Women who have very regular menstrual cycles have a lower failure rate.

How It Works

There are four ways to use periodic abstinence: the calendar method, the temperature chart, mucus evaluation, and natural family planning.

To use the calendar method, a woman must first follow her menstrual cycle for several months. For a regular 28-day cycle, the period of abstinence would be ten days, between day 9 and day 19 of her cycle. Since many women have longer cycles, the period of abstinence may be as high as two weeks.

The temperature chart, which is somewhat more successful than the calendar method, involves temperature readings every morning. Temperature shifts upward midway through the cycle, just after a woman ovulates. It is safest to refrain from intercourse until three days *after* the temperature rises, when the ovum has presumably passed by the fertilization site in the fallopian tube. A temperature chart is an 'after-the-fact' dating system. Since a woman cannot tell beforehand on what day her temperature will rise, results are best when a couple abstains from intercourse for the first half of the woman's cycle. The failure rate using this method is only between 3·0 and 6·6 per cent.

If a woman has a very regular cycle and knows from past charts exactly when to anticipate a rise, she can risk intercourse early in the cycle, and stop five or six days before the rise. The failure rate, however, is much higher when a couple tries this approach – between 7 and 20 per cent. Also, illness can interfere with temperature readings, making the method somewhat unreliable.

The mucus method is based on observing changes in cervical mucus that take place when a woman is ovulating. Just before and during ovulation, the mucus typically becomes wet and abundant because of the high levels of oestrogen in the bloodstream. The mucus change generally lasts from one to three days and signals the time of maximum fertility. Intercourse is avoided on these days, and is resumed four days after the mucus returns to its thickened texture.

Natural family planning involves all three methods – calendar, temperature chart, and observation of cervical mucus. This approach can be somewhat more successful, but the couple must be strongly motivated. All abstinence methods require vigilance, and it's easy to make a mistake.

Rhythm methods work best for young, married women with regular menstrual cycles. As a woman grows older and her ovulation pattern becomes more erratic, it is difficult to tell exactly when the egg is being released from an ovary. The rhythm method carries no physical side-effects, but there is a certain amount of stress involved. The constant vigilance, as well as the uncertainty, is a strain for most people. The best candidates for this form of birth control are stable married couples who are determined to avoid other forms of contraceptives.

Abortion

In a voluntary abortion the fetus is removed from the womb mechanically by suction or D&C, or chemicals are introduced into the uterus to bring on contractions.

Before 1967 many women who had badly performed, illegal abortions came to emergency rooms in advanced stages of haemorrhage, infection, or septic shock. Many of these women died, and others became sterile. David Steel's 1967 Abortion Act has made abortion legal in certain circumstances, but 50 per cent of women seeking abortions are still forced to go outside the NHS. Professional care virtually eliminates the complications connected with the procedure.

Timing

Pregnancies are divided into three-month periods, called trimesters. The quickest, safest abortion is performed early in the first trimester of pregnancy, using a mild suction device. The procedure is usually performed under local anaesthesia in an outpatient clinic. The same technique is used to perform abortion later in the first trimester, except that the cervix must be more widely dilated. For this reason, most women have the procedure performed in a hospital under a general anaesthesia.

After the twelfth week of pregnancy, the fetus is usually too large for the suction method to work safely. Early in the second trimester, prostaglandins can be used to relax the cervix before the uterine contents are suctioned out. If the cervix is damaged, future pregnancies are at risk. This method, combined with a D&E (dilatation and evacuation), should be performed in a hospital under general anaesthesia.

Later in the second trimester, when the amniotic sac is larger, chemicals can be used to bring on contractions of the uterus. Contractions usually begin eighteen to twenty hours after the injection, and the fetus is then expelled. This kind of abortion carries a higher risk than the suction method and is extremely stressful for a woman.

Overall, the earlier an abortion is performed, the less the risk and the less the emotional trauma. Abortions are seldom performed after the twenty-fourth week of pregnancy. On those rare occasions when an abortion must be performed in the third trimester because the mother's life is at risk, a major incision is made through the abdomen and uterus to remove the pregnancy; this procedure requires a long period of recovery and carries the greatest risk of complication. Should the woman carry a subsequent pregnancy to term, she may have to have the baby delivered via Caesarean section.

The Rh Factor

When a woman has any kind of abortion she should have her blood type checked. A few women have Rh-negative blood. The term *Rh* is derived from the Rhesus monkey, in which researchers first discovered two categories of red blood cells. The first category contained a protein, called an antigen, and was labelled Rh positive. The second category, into which very few animals fell, did not have this protein. This category was called Rh negative. Red blood cells in humans fall into similar categories.

If the red blood cells from an Rh-positive person get into the bloodstream of an Rh-negative person, they will set off an immediate allergic reaction. The immune system of the Rh-negative person builds killer antibodies that will seek out and destroy the Rh-positive cells. This immune reaction is dose-dependent. A little challenge starts up the antibody killer system. A second dose usually results in a violent reaction in which the antibodies seek out and destroy all Rh-positive cells in their path.

When an Rh-negative woman becomes pregnant with an Rh-positive fetus, some of the fetal cells may leak into the mother's system, causing the initial antibody reaction. Because the infant is already fully developed, it is usually not affected by the killer antibodies. However, a second Rh-positive pregnancy will meet a fully developed antibody system; during early development the killer antibodies will enter the fetal blood system and destroy its red blood cells. This phenomenon is referred to as Rh disease. Depending on the force and length of the attack, the fetus may be severely anaemic at birth or may die in the uterus.

Fortunately, scientists have developed a drug which blocks the mother's immune system and prevents the Rh killer antibodies from developing. The drug is usually administered within seventy-two hours after an Rh-negative woman gives birth to an Rh-positive child. In certain rare instances the drug may be administered before the child is born. To guarantee the safety of future pregnancies, an Rh-negative mother should receive the drug after the birth of each Rh-positive child. If she gives birth to an Rh-negative infant, she will not need the drug.

During an abortion or miscarriage, fetal blood cells usually enter the mother's circulatory system. Since most fetuses are Rh positive, every Rh-negative woman should receive this drug following abortion or miscarriage.

Side-effects

A properly performed, early abortion usually has no side-effects and carries no risk to future fertility. Complications that occasionally arise from an abortion are usually caused by unskilled technique or by performing the abortion during the more advanced stages of pregnancy. The earlier the abortion is performed, the less risk of complications.

Some early research from Japan and England suggested that women who had abortions had a three to nine times greater chance of miscarriage in later pregnancies. These studies were done in the early days of legal abortions in these countries. More recent studies have shown that there is no correlation between induced abortion and miscarriage.

Permanent Sterilization

Vasectomy, in which the sperm-carrying vasa deferentia are tied off near their exit point from the testicles, was first performed in the late 1800s in the hope that it would relieve tumours of the prostate. It was not until a hundred years later that vasectomy became a common method of contraception.

Tubal ligation, the female version of vasectomy, was used as early as 1830, and has been common practice since the 1960s. Depending on the skill of the surgeon, the failure rate of vasectomy and tubal sterilization ranges from 0·15 to 0·20 per cent.

Vasectomy

Sterility does not occur immediately with vasectomy. Sperm stored in the upper portions of the vasa may take several weeks to pass through the sperm ducts. Two negative sperm counts at three-week intervals are required to confirm sterility.

The vasectomy technique is simple and effective, with little risk of complication. Some studies have suggested a correlation between vasectomy and stroke or heart attack later in life. Theoretically, sperm antibodies that cause arteriosclerosis may arise in men who have had vasectomies. These are highly speculative findings, however; at this time follow-up studies of men up to fifteen years after vasectomy show no significant correlation between vasectomy and heart disease or stroke.

The major drawback to vasectomy, of course, is that it is permanent. A handful of skilled surgeons can reconnect the severed ends of the vasa using microsurgical techniques, but this is an extremely expensive procedure. One alternative is for a man to have his sperm frozen before having the vasectomy. If he changes his mind later, he might then be able to impregnate his wife by artificial insemination.

Tubal Ligation (Sterilization)

Tubal ligation involves tying or blocking off the fallopian tubes to prevent sperm from reaching the egg. Today, several surgical techniques may be used; the surgeon may elect to burn the tubes by electrocautery, block them with a spring-loaded clip that snaps over the tubes, or entrap the tubes in a rubber band.

The tubes are reached through various kinds of incisions. The most common is a laparoscopy, a small incision made through the navel. Sometimes the surgeon reaches the tubes through a small incision made directly over the uterus. A less frequently used incision is a colpotomy, a small cut in the back of the vagina, through which the surgeon can grasp the tubes.

Effectiveness. All forms of tubal ligation are highly effective. Only one to two women out of every 1,000 get pregnant after a tubal ligation. In these cases, the sperm finds its way through a small opening in the tube, jumps the blockage, and finds the egg in the outer segment of the tube. This usually leads to an ectopic pregnancy, because the fertilized egg cannot get back to the uterus to implant. There are miraculous events in which the *egg* jumps the gap and passes into the uterus to be fertilized, resulting in a normal pregnancy.

Side-effects. With any surgical procedure involving anaesthesia, there is always a risk of side-effects. However, the chances of severe surgical complications from this procedure are low. Once performed, tubal ligation can be reversed only with major surgical reconstruction. Thus, only women who feel certain that they will never wish to have children or women who for medical reasons should not have children should select this contraceptive technique.

Reversals. Whether or not a tubal ligation can be reversed depends on three factors: the point at which the tube is tied off, how much of the tube was destroyed to effect sterilization, and the skill of the surgeon performing the reversal. The success rate is low. The best chance for reversal exists if the tube has been interrupted in the first portion, near the uterus.

A new technique to block fallopian tubes temporarily with removable silicone implants is being tested by the Food and Drug Administration (FDA) in America. The foaming silicone is inserted through the cervix into the uterus with a hysteroscope. Once the tubes are located, the silicone is pushed in and allowed to harden inside the tubes, forming a small plug. Later, when the plugs are removed, fertility should be intact.

The silicone technique requires skilled surgery. So far, there have been problems sealing both tubes, and reversibility has not been proved. The current failure rate is about 16 per cent. If the technique is perfected, however, it will revolutionize contraception. The implants have no side-effects, create no chemical changes within the body, and do not have to be manipulated by either partner.

The Future

The Biphasic Pill

Oral contraceptives involve taking one combination of hormones in the first phase of the menstrual cycle and another in the second phase. Triphasic pills are also available. The purpose of these modifications is to approximate more closely the natural menstrual cycle.

The Once-a-month Pill

According to Dr Gerald I. Zatuchni, director of the Program for Applied Research and Fertility Regulation, long-acting steroid contraceptives will soon be clinically tested in China. One pill, taken on day 1, 2, or 3 of the menstrual cycle, has been shown to suppress ovulation in monkeys. Major research programmes are also in the process of testing 90-day and 180-day systems, which are expected to be on the market in the next few years.

Male Birth-control Pills and Injectibles

Women will welcome the days when men can share the burden of contraception more equally. Researchers are investigating a combination injectible comprised of progestin and testosterone that will inhibit sperm production for ninety days. Danazol, a powerful new drug used to treat endometriosis, is being tried out as a male contraceptive. However, the drug, which inhibits the production of LH and FSH from the pituitary gland, has shown uneven decreases in sperm counts, and some men have complained that their sex drive is lessened on the drug. This combination requires further research, particularly in the area of side-effects, but it shows that there is hope for a reversible male contraceptive.

Anti-pregnancy Vaccines

The idea of vaccine against pregnancy has been in the research stage for over twenty years. It is based on the notion that some women naturally produce antibodies against sperm, particularly women who have been exposed to sperm from many different men. (Prostitutes, for example, are often infertile.) If such sperm-immobilizing antibodies can be developed in the laboratory, a woman could be vaccinated against pregnancy. Researchers estimate that it will be at least ten years before a contraceptive vaccine is available.

Long-lasting Injectibles

Several long-lasting injectibles are being tested around the world. The best known is Depo-Provera, an analogue of progesterone, which is injected once every three months. The drug has a failure rate of only 1 per cent, but animal studies show an increased incidence of breast tumours. Also, it may take two years for a woman to start ovulating after discontinuing the drug. Depo-Provera is used in over eighty countries but is not approved for sale as a contraceptive in the United States. In the United Kingdom it is available as a long-term contraceptive for women who cannot use any other method.

Noresthisterone is another injectible with a low failure rate, but it too appears to have many side-effects, including irregular bleeding and weight gain. It is only available as a short-term method. Several other injectibles being tested for fewer side-effects are at least five years away from general release.

Progesterone-T

A T-shaped IUD that delivers progesterone for one year is already on the market in America, but not yet in the United Kingdom. A new, long-lasting version, containing a different form of progesterone, is soon to be released in the United States. It can be left in place for up to seven years and is supposed to be more effective, cause less bleeding, and offer some protection against pelvic inflammatory disease.

LH-RH Nasal Sprays and Capsules

LH-RH is the releasing factor the brain uses to issue instructions to the pituitary gland. The hormonal axis in both men and women can be traced back to this powerful brain chemical. When a person receives synthetic LH-RH, the hypothalamus is blocked; as a result, the pituitary does not send the proper timed signals to the ovaries or testicles. In women, ovulation may become irregular and cease completely. In men, sperm usually fail to mature.

In the United States, LH-RH is available as a nasal spray which women can use each month before ovulation. Men can have a long-acting capsule that slowly releases the synthetic chemical implanted in fatty tissue anywhere in the body. LH-RH as a contraceptive is still under clinical investigation, and is not yet available in Britain.

Alternatives

32
Miracle Babies

Despite advances in medical and surgical treatment for infertility, there are still many couples who cannot achieve a full-term pregnancy. For women whose fallopian tubes are irreparably damaged or blocked by scar tissue, *in vitro* fertilization is a possible and exciting alternative. For women whose ovaries cannot produce healthy eggs, embryo transfer is a possible solution. If the husband is infertile, pregnancy can be achieved by means of AID (see p. 285 ff).

To skirt the emotional minefields that can accompany new reproductive technology, couples should first resolve their feelings about infertility. Not every person is able to accept the idea of having a child conceived in a test tube or having a child that inherits the genetic imprint of a stranger.

One especially difficult emotional aspect of all fertility enhancement techniques is their experimental status. Couples must be psychologically prepared for the likelihood that the procedure will fail. For some couples adoption or remaining childless may be preferable to having their hopes dashed yet again.

Before trying any of these procedures, husbands and wives need to discuss their feelings freely – both about the technique and about the possible outcomes. They should try to envisage how they will feel if the process doesn't work and decide how long they will keep trying if the technique fails the first time. These highly charged issues should be dealt with before any couple agrees to a new technique, because once a couple enters one of these miracle programmes, stress abounds. The best chance for success comes if both partners are stable, relaxed, and optimistic.

In Vitro Fertilization

There is perhaps no more controversial method of enhancing fertility than *in vitro* fertilization. It rings of futuristic genetic manipulation. It conjures images of robot-like generations, conceived in test tubes and manipulated by mad scientists. But *in vitro* programmes hold promise for thousands of couples who have no other means of achieving pregnancy. Louise Brown, the first test-tube baby, was born on 24 July 1978, the result of a decade of *in vitro* research by Drs

Robert Edwards and Patrick Steptoe in Oldham. Six years later these scientists had created 118 *in vitro* babies, and many more pregnancies were in progress. Howard Jones pioneered the technique in America at East Virginia Medical School. In Australia, Drs Carl Wood and Alan Trounson at Monash University revolutionized the *in vitro* method when they transferred a frozen embryo.

The breakthroughs performed by these scientists triggered a rush to *in vitro* research around the world. Other scientists, however, did not always find it easy to duplicate the technique. The basic steps of the procedure sound simple: remove an ovum from a woman, mix it together with some sperm in a test tube until one sperm penetrates the egg, then reimplant the fertilized egg into the woman's uterus. The embryo grows into a fetus and, *voilà*, nine months later a baby is born.

The process is anything but simple. Retrieving the egg at precisely the right moment of its maturity, gently nurturing the delicate conception process, and carefully balancing vital hormones make *in vitro* fertilization the most complex of all fertility enhancement techniques.

Programme Requirements

In the early days of research rigid criteria were established to define the ideal candidate for *in vitro* fertilization. These criteria held that a woman had to be under thirty-six years of age and ovulating normally. It was vital that the early experiments be free of any confusing elements that might cast doubt on whether the technique worked; therefore, the woman's tubes had to be irreparably damaged so there could be no possibility of natural pregnancy. The husband had to be completely fertile, with healthy, active sperm.

Today, as more and more clinics have opened, these restrictions have been relaxed, and couples with a wide variety of fertility problems may be accepted for *in vitro* programmes. Many clinics now accept women up to forty years of age, and a few even accept women up to forty-four, although their chances of success are slim. Some clinics accept couples who have prolonged and unexplained infertility (five years or longer) or women who have persistent endometriosis. Clinics sometimes accept infertile women even when the endometriosis is controlled or healed. A few programmes accept couples if the man has a low sperm count. Usually in these cases, artificial insemination should be tried first, since it is far less expensive and less traumatic than *in vitro* fertilization.

However, the main reason couples are accepted into *in vitro* programmes is to create a fertilization site outside the body for women who have badly damaged fallopian tubes.

In every case, at least one ovary must be normal and accessible. Scar tissue, cysts, or infections can keep one or both ovaries from producing healthy eggs. Sometimes microsurgery or laser surgery can be performed to free a scarred ovary and prepare it for *in vitro* fertilization. If a woman has difficulty ovulating, fertility drugs can be used to normalize her hormonal system. Above all, both the male and female partner must be free of infection of any kind. Researchers consider *in vitro* fertilization too complex and expensive a procedure to risk failure from elusive pathogens that infect sperm or the inside of the female pelvic cavity.

To achieve *in vitro* pregnancy, couples must be prepared to invest a great deal of time, and clinic directors caution that the chances of ultimate success are low.

In vitro fertilization is still an experimental process, and there is no single, precise way to perform the technique. Different clinics use slightly different methods; however, all involve similar essential steps.

Before a couple is accepted into a programme, a full check-up will be required. If a woman's ovaries are inaccessible or covered with scar tissue, she usually will have to undergo surgery to free the ovaries.

Once a couple has been accepted into an *in vitro* programme, the next step is usually a screening laparoscopy to make sure that the ovaries are fully accessible. The screening laparoscopy is not always done, and depends somewhat on the woman's previous medical records. The husband also will be evaluated, usually by semen analysis.

Growth and Retrieval of the Egg

After preliminary screening is completed, timing is all important. The treatment cycle begins on the first day of a woman's menstrual cycle and ends with the transfer of the fertilized egg into the uterus, usually on day 15. The first sequence for *in vitro* fertilization is the same as that for natural conception: the growth and release of a mature egg. Even when a woman's ovaries are functioning normally, *in vitro* specialists help the process along by using fertility drugs to make the ovaries produce several mature ova in a single month. The philosophy is that if more than one egg is fertilized and implanted in each cycle, there is a better chance of success. Multiple implants have been shown to increase the odds of successful pregnancy in a single cycle.

Between day 2 and day 5 of the cycle, a woman begins to take clomiphene or Pergonal, or combinations of the two to encourage egg growth. Most clinics seem to favour clomiphene, but the choice of fertility drug depends largely on the patient as well as on the experience of the clinic.

Ultrasound and Blood Tests. As the egg begins to grow, the woman visits the clinic daily for a series of ultrasound tests, which provide sonic images of the eggs developing inside the ovaries. Daily blood tests are usually taken to measure the rise of oestrogen and LH in the blood.

These tests help physicians gauge the growth of the eggs and discover the precise point at which they are ready to be released from an ovary. The eggs need to be nearly mature, but not so mature that they leave the ovaries spontaneously. If that happens, the physicians will not be able to retrieve them, and the woman will have to go home to try again the following month. Combined ultrasound and hormone testing can accurately predict the time of ovulation over 90 per cent of the time.

A woman stops taking the fertility drugs after five days. As the eggs near maturity, human chorionic gonadotrophin (HCG) is usually given to prepare for egg release. (HCG is a hormone manufactured during pregnancy that closely resembles LH.) The extra hormone helps along the body's natural surge of LH to eject the eggs from the ovaries.

Retrieving the Eggs. Just before the eggs burst out of the follicle, usually on day 13, the woman is taken to the operating room, where she is given a general anaesthetic. A member of the *in vitro* team inserts a laparoscope through her navel and carefully removes the eggs from the ovaries. Since the eggs may be ready at any hour of the day or night, the team must have several members who are equally capable of carrying out the procedure. And an operating room must always be available on short notice.

During the laparoscopy the physician removes all the mature eggs from the ovary by gentle suction. The aspiration procedure has been so well refined that if the eggs mature properly, retrieval is successful 90 per cent of the time. Sometimes the eggs fail to mature, and another attempt must be made in a subsequent cycle. The woman usually recovers easily from the laparoscopy; most often she remains in the hospital, waiting for the eggs to be fertilized and the embryo to be implanted in her uterus. If all goes well, the transfer should take place within forty hours, perhaps sooner.

Once removed, the eggs are placed in an organ culture dish and rushed to a highly specialized laboratory where a specialist in tissue culture examines them. Within a few moments, the specialist sends a report back to the surgical team, noting whether the eggs seem healthy and giving details about the condition of the granulosa cells that surround each one.

Each egg is placed in its own dish and bathed in a special culture medium; every clinic has its own formula for making the culture. The eggs are kept warm and allowed to mature fully while the sperm are processed. The first phase of the *in vitro* procedure is complete.

Fertilization

As the woman undergoes laparoscopy to retrieve burgeoning ova, the husband collects his semen by masturbation. While the eggs incubate, the semen liquefies and the sperm are then washed, or capacitated. Capacitation, which normally takes place in the woman's body, strips away the outer covering of the sperm and bares the acrosome warhead for egg penetration. It was once thought that only some mysterious substance inside the fallopian tube could strip off the membrane. Discovering how to wash sperm was a crucial factor behind the first successful *in vitro* birth. Today, sperm are separated from semen by centrifugal force and re-suspended in a fresh medium. If a man has a low sperm count, the sperm can be concentrated.

Each egg is combined with a quantity of capacitated sperm in a glass dish and placed in an incubator. As the technique has improved, fewer sperm are needed to fertilize a single egg; today usually 100,000 or 200,000 sperm are used. Fertilization, like egg retrieval, is a highly successful step of the procedure. After twelve hours, the technician places each dish under the microscope to discover if fertilization has taken place. This is a heart-stopping moment. In some ways, fertilization in a glass dish is even more magical than the secret union of sperm and egg within a woman's reproductive tract. Technicians and lay people alike stand in awe of nature's miracle.

When fertilization occurs, the fused cell is usually given a fresh bath and returned to the incubator, where it will begin to divide. After the cell divides several times, an indication that the embryo is developing normally, the technician notifies the other members of the team that the time has come to transfer the embryo.

Up to this point, the *in vitro* procedure is nearly flawless. Success in all timed phases of the technique ranges from 75 to 90 per cent, a figure that takes into account women who drop out before completing the preliminary work, the occasional failure of eggs to mature, and problems retrieving the egg from the ovary. The truly hazardous portion of the *in vitro* journey begins when the new embryo is ready for transfer into the nurturing environment of the uterus.

Embryo Transfer

The embryo is generally transferred to the uterus when it has grown to either four or eight cells. Researchers are still experimenting with the optimum time for transfer. Because implantation is the most difficult, and least successful, part of the *in vitro* process, the technique and skill of the team are important factors in the success rate.

Overall, embryo transfer seems to succeed only about 20 per cent of the time in any given cycle. To combat the low transfer rate, most *in vitro* specialists implant more than one fertilized egg at a time, doubling or tripling the chances for a successful pregnancy.

While the eggs are incubating in their special medium, the woman usually receives injections of progesterone to help prepare the uterus to receive the fertilized ova. When they are ready for implantation, the embryos are transported from the laboratory to the woman's bedside. The husband is usually present. The woman may receive a mild sedative before the transfer. As she lies on the bed with her feet in heel supports, the physician uses a speculum to open the vagina and expose the cervix. The transfer catheter is a long, curved sterile tube. With some air drawn into the tube to provide cushioning, the embryos are brought up into the catheter, along with a little neutral culture medium. The physician gently pushes the tip of the catheter through the cervix and ejects the fluid column.

Why does this simple technique so often fail? Researchers suggest two possibilities: eggs may be defective or immature when they are fertilized, or multiple implants may give off too much oestrogen, which counteracts the needed progesterone content of the endometrium. To succeed, the development of the embryos must be precisely synchronized with that of the endometrial lining of the uterus. If the endometrium lacks progesterone, the embryos will fail to implant, and the entire procedure will have been to no avail.

Following the transfer, most *in vitro* practitioners require their patients to lie in bed for several hours before leaving the clinic. The transfer is followed by two days of bed rest, either at the hospital or at home. Many physicians are now ordering blood tests over the week following transfer to ensure that enough progesterone is being supplied to the endometrium to support the pregnancy.

Chances for Pregnancy

Once a transfer is complete, the concepti must seek a nest within the uterus. Within the first twelve weeks 33 per cent of the transferred embryos spontaneously abort, and another 10–15 per cent are lost to late abortion. These are difficult and stressful months for the couple. Ultimately, a woman has only about a 10 per cent chance that an embryo will successfully cling to the inside of the uterus and result in a living baby.

The critical questions are how many cycles are needed, on the average, to achieve pregnancy, and at what point a couple should stop trying. Each cycle is a new ball game, and the odds of pregnancy (not birth) are about 20 per cent each time. If the pregnancy takes and aborts several months later, the couple has to decide all over whether they want to try the *in vitro* procedure again.

Obviously, these are emotionally loaded questions, and the decision about when to give up depends largely on the feelings of the couple.

In vitro fertilization can be extremely expensive, since most couples have to take time away from work, travel long distances, and pay for hotel accommodation for two weeks or longer in each attempted cycle.

Finding a Clinic

In Britain, there are two private IVF clinics at present, both very expensive. There are a few NHS clinics, but they usually accept women from their own area only. Although several more hospitals would like to start IVF programmes, they are prevented from doing so by lack of funds. IVF clinics require a GP's letter giving full details before they will make an appointment to see you.

Risks of In Vitro Fertilization

Even though *in vitro* fertilization takes place outside the body, there are several risks a woman should know about. They include intake of daily hormones, anaesthesia during egg retrieval, stress, and the risk of possible spontaneous abortion.

The greatest risk, of course, is to the embryo itself. Those embryos that do not cling will abort spontaneously. Once a baby comes to full term, however, it doesn't seem to be at any greater risk for birth defects than a child conceived in a natural manner. Edwards and Steptoe in England report that they have seen no serious defect in more than a hundred children; Trounson and Wood in Australia describe only one congenital abnormality occurring in sixty-five babies.

Controversy over Experimentation

All researchers have remarked on the improvement in the rate of pregnancy when more than one embryo is implanted. There is wide disagreement, however, on just how many embryos to transfer at one time. Several instances of twins, and even a few triplets, have been reported. Carl Wood has reported a total of ten sets of twins from a hundred *in vitro* pregnancies. In January of 1984 Dr Andrew Speirs, from the Royal Woman's Hospital of Melbourne, delivered the world's first quadruplets by *in vitro* fertilization.

NHS clinics limit the number of embryos replaced to three, but private clinics in Britain tend to replace all fertilized embryos in order to increase the chances of achieving a pregnancy quickly, so as to keep costs down.

The problem with multiple implants is the stress and risk they put on the mother. Often, women undergoing *in vitro* fertilization have had previous microsurgery and drug therapy. The added burden of multiple pregnancy can overstress the uterus and ultimately abort all the fetuses growing in the womb. There is also new evidence that when several follicles are induced to develop, they secrete too much oestrogen, which may adversely affect the endometrium. Further, having more than one child may be a tremendous emotional overload on a husband and wife already severely stressed by the fertility quest.

Investigators are now trying to decide exactly what number of transfers improves the chances of pregnancy without drastically increasing chances of multiple births. Trounson and Wood suggest that transfer should be limited to two in each cycle. Dr Jaroslave Hulka, professor of obstetrics and gynaecology at the University of North Carolina Medical College at Chapel Hill, says that the consensus of opinion expressed at a recent worldwide seminar in Helsinki was that three to four eggs give the optimum chance for pregnancy. Dr Luther Talbert, director of the Chapel Hill *in vitro* programme, is achieving a 12–15 per cent delivery rate by transferring three or four fertilized ova.

Freezing Embryos

The ultimate answer to this problem may be embryo freezing. Trounson and Wood began to study the possibility of freezing embryos in 1980. In 1984 the first baby born from a frozen embryo was delivered at Queen Victoria Medical Centre in Melbourne, Australia.

The tremendous advantage offered by embryo freezing is that several eggs can be retrieved at one time and fertilized. The embryos that are not implanted immediately can be frozen and stored for use in subsequent cycles. If the woman fails to get pregnant after the first transfer, or if she loses the baby, the frozen embryos can be thawed and transferred in a later menstrual cycle. Using frozen embryos spares the expense and physical strain of repeated hormonal stimulation and surgical removal of the eggs. The use of frozen embryos is far from routine, and there is much controversy about the morality of manipulating potential life in this manner.

In the future, the lengthy and complex *in vitro* process may be considerably streamlined, leading to a much shorter and less expensive process. Recently, surgeons in England eliminated the surgical laparoscopy to retrieve eggs. Instead, using ultrasound to locate mature eggs burgeoning on the ovarian surface, the surgeons inserted a long needle through the abdomen and aspirated the eggs off the ovary. The *in vitro* team then washed the eggs and sperm, mixed them together, and returned the cells to the uterus within four hours. Fertilization took place *inside* the mother's womb. This highly simplified technique led to three pregnancies out of thirty-eight egg retrievals, which compares favourably with the success rates reported by most clinics. This technique takes place in the gynaecology outpatient department under local anaesthetic; it thus eliminates the complex laboratory procedure of egg watching and fertilization and the surgical retrieval of eggs, and has aroused the interest of specialists around the world.

Embryo Transfer

In January of 1984 at the Harbor University of California at Los Angeles Medical Center, a woman gave birth to a baby that had been conceived in the body of another woman. The exact date of birth of the world's first embryo transfer baby is unknown, because the parents wish to remain anonymous. The medical team responsible for the birth of the baby was headed by Dr John E. Buster. This technique has not yet been tried in Britain.

Embryo transfer is the miracle needed for couples who are infertile because the woman's ovaries cannot produce healthy eggs. As long as she has a healthy uterus, she can nurture a fetus. The baby conceived by this method does not, of course, have the heredity characteristics of the infertile woman, since it has the genes of the husband and the donor woman.

Here's how embryo transfer works. A female donor volunteers to be inseminated with the husband's sperm. If she conceives, the doctors flush the embryo from her uterus five to six days later and implant it into the uterus of the wife. If all goes well, the wife will carry the baby to term and deliver it normally.

The Candidates

Candidates for embryo transfer are usually women whose infertility stems from irreparable damage to the fallopian tubes or women whose ovaries do not function. Even some women capable of conceiving and bearing children could be eligible for ovum transfer. A fertile woman who is genetically diseased, or in whom genetic analysis indicates a likelihood of passing a serious malady on to her offspring, might choose to gestate the fertilized ovum of a healthy donor rather than her own. Embryo transfer represents new hope as well for women who have tried *in vitro* fertilization or artificial insemination, but without success. By gestating a donor egg the woman gains the psychological benefit of intra-uterine bonding. The legal ramifications would probably be similar to artificial insemination by donor sperm.

Embryo transfer is fraught with emotional issues similar to those faced by couples who use artificial insemination by donor.

The Technique

Embryo transfer is not a surgical technique; therefore, it carries small physical risk to the donor or the recipient. The key to the transfer process is the matching up of the menstrual cycles of the donor and the infertile woman. This means that a large number of donors must be on call if an egg is to be produced at the precise time it is needed.

Assuming that the cycles are matched, on the day the donor ovulates, the husband is summoned to provide his sperm. The donor is artificially inseminated; five days later, the donor's uterus is washed out. In the lavage technique, a catheter is inserted through the cervix and about two ounces of a special nutrient fluid is gradually pumped in, gently showering the walls of the uterus.

Because the embryo rests on the mucus-covered inner walls of the uterine cavity and is not yet attached to its host, it can be swept into the lavage fluid, then into the exit port of the catheter, and on into a waiting laboratory vessel. A technician pours the lavage fluid into a clear plastic dish, which is placed on the heated stage of a microscope. The scope's special lenses help to spot the colourless sphere of cells nesting in the mucus and tissue debris of the pink fluid.

Once the ovum is identified, it is placed into a small amount of transfer medium and sucked up into a small catheter. At this point, the catheter is inserted into the cervix of the waiting recipient, and the embryo is delivered into the uterus. With luck, the recipient's uterus will be ready to support the embryo's growth. It takes about twelve days for a pregnancy test to reveal whether conception has ensued.

Success Rate

In the first embryo transfer project, twelve ova were recovered from twenty-nine lavage sequences. All the ova were transferred to recipient mothers, but only two were well-formed blastocysts capable of development. Both of the embryos – two out of twelve transfers – went on to become normal, healthy babies, yielding a success rate of 16.7 per cent.

Because so few embryo transfers have been attempted in humans, it's difficult to predict the potential success rate after the technique is perfected. However, the technique is known to be extremely successful in animal breeding.

Recently a Kentucky quarter horse gave birth by embryo transfer to a full-blooded male zebra at the Louisville Zoo. Successful embryo transfers have been accomplished in other animals as well: donkeys have given birth to horses as a result of such experiments, and individual breeds of cattle have given birth to other breeds. Such experiments are important because a similar procedure could be used to increase the populations of vanishing and endangered species.

The success of such animal transfers has made researchers optimistic over the potential success of human embryo transfer. Dr Buster believes that a woman should have a 33 per cent chance of pregnancy each time she receives a donor ovum. Such an optimistic result, however, depends largely on the availability of a fertilized ovum and the expertise of the team performing the transfer.

The Future

Researchers foresee a time when egg banks will be as popular as sperm banks. The first such egg bank opened in New York in 1985. With egg banks, donor eggs can be fertilized *in vitro* and the embryos frozen. In that manner embryos can be transferred to the womb of an infertile woman at the appropriate time.

The same principle of embryo transfer can be used in reverse: a woman who has no uterus or a defective uterus can have her egg fertilized with her husband's sperm *in vitro* and then implanted in another woman. This combination of *in vitro* fertilization and surrogate carrier could also be used by women who cannot carry a child because of a medical condition unrelated to fertility, such as high blood pressure. It is now medically possible for a child to have five parents: an egg donor, a sperm donor, a woman who provides a uterus to gestate the child, and the couple who raised the child. Any combination of parenting could be used to meet an infertile couple's desire for a child.

Although scientists and infertile couples around the world are enthusiastic about these medical advances, there are those who view the new conceptions with alarm. The future of fertility enhancement is closely tied to the emotional responses and viewpoints of many different kinds of people – scholars and philosophers, religious leaders and politicians, lawyers and doctors, and infertile couples. In the future, the ability of an infertile couple to have children may be limited not by medical technology but by decisions made by judges in the courtrooms of the world.

33
Brave New World

Robert and Marcia Davis tried for years to have a child. The verdict was that, because of a defective uterine cavity and weak cervix, Marcia could not carry for the full term. She had become pregnant three times and each time miscarried before the third month.

Adoption seemed to be the only course. The waiting-list for an infant was long, but the Davises were resigned. A friend told them about the possibility of a surrogate mother who could carry a child that would bear at least half of the couple's genetic imprint. Robert's sperm would be used to impregnate the woman, who would carry the child to term.

The three of them were nervous at first, but after a few meetings the Davises and Eleanor Greenwald began to feel comfortable. Eleanor had a child, a quiet six-year-old towhead. She had been married twice and the child was from her first marriage. Recently, she and her second husband had separated and Eleanor was having a difficult time working in a local supermarket and caring for her young son. After a few meetings they reached an agreement. The Davises would pay Eleanor $10,000 for becoming pregnant and carrying the baby to term. Eleanor would give up the baby immediately after it was born, for adoption by the Davises, and she would agree to abstain from sexual relations for a month after she became pregnant through the AID procedure. The Davises agreed to pay all medical bills.

The baby was born severely retarded, and in the attending physician's opinion the biological father of the child was not Robert Davis. Eleanor admitted that a few days before the AID procedure she had had sex with her estranged husband. But, she claimed, she had carefully douched after the encounter. Eleanor's estranged husband had a history of family genetic defects.

The Davises refused to accept the child. They had paid Eleanor half the $10,000 when the agreement was signed, but they would pay no more, and they would not pay any new medical bills.

Eleanor Greenwald sued the Davises for $5,000, plus medical expenses and the continuing cost of extraordinary care for the retarded child. She would never have carried a child to term, she claimed, if she had not been assured that the child would be taken and cared for by the Davises. The Davises filed a countersuit for breach of contract, asking for the $5,000 they had advanced Eleanor, plus their out-of-pocket medical expenses.

Robert and Marcia do not exist. Neither does Eleanor Greenwald. But the facts follow closely the issues in two cases heard in US courtrooms. (However, new techniques mean that we will be able to determine a child's parents with absolute certainty in the future, from blood samples.)

These are not simple issues. There are no white hats and black hats, no good guys versus bad guys. Each party has some right on its side and each needs some justice. But for complex, far-reaching questions, there are no simple answers.

Moral Dilemmas

Looking at the legal and moral questions raised by dealing with life and birth and death in new ways has become the thorniest problem of our age. According to philosopher Lisa H. Newton of Fairfield University in Connecticut: 'In pursuing techniques to provide children for the childless, we may, simply and commendably, be carrying on the task bequeathed to us from Aesculapius and Hippocrates, to use our God-given intelligence to improve the human condition. Or on the contrary, we may, in these attempts to impose human whims and wants on the most basic of life processes, be committing an intolerable trespass on domains best left to the working of God and nature; we may stand condemned with Prometheus for making off with the property of the deity.'

Expanding Technology

Expanding technology is probably the single most influential factor in our lives. Dreams are reality. We have, incredibly, been able to leave our planet and return. And in medicine we have extended the span of life, much reduced infant mortality and abolished smallpox from the entire world. But these great advances have posed new and difficult problems. Who has the right to make the decisions – the sort of decisions that only a short time ago were left to God?

If a couple is infertile but has an opportunity through advanced technology to have longed-for children, should the decision to use that technology to create new life be left to the couple?

Religious Guidelines

Some would say no. Some religious sects believe that most medical treatment intrudes on the province of the Almighty. Approaches to medical technology vary from one religion and sect to another, but all religious leaders express some discomfort over manipulation of the birth process.

The Roman Catholic hierarchy, which firmly opposes human intervention to *prevent* conception, also looks askance on conception enhancement techniques. There is no official church stand at the moment on such procedures as *in vitro* fertilization, but Father Kevin O'Rourke of St Louis University's Center for Health Care Ethics raised the enormity of the issue in *US News and World Report*: 'As genetic manipulation becomes possible – as we become capable of determining the very form of a human being – the ethical dilemmas are awesome.'

Jewish clergymen say that in general couples can use any form of fertility enhancement because it is their responsibility to procreate. In all cases, however, a child conceived through fertility enhancement must know the identity of its biological parents. There are a variety of restrictions that accompany this blanket permission, depending on which form of Judaism the couple practises. For example, masturbation is usually prohibited, which means that Jewish couples are unable to use any technique that involves masturbated semen. However, if the sperm cannot be retrieved by any other means, permission may be given, with the proviso that all sperm are used and none are wasted. The use of donor sperm is also prohibited by some groups because it is considered adultery for a woman to be impregnated with another man's sperm.

Legal and Ethical Issues

Should the decision about enhancement of fertility be left to medical science? Doctors today have much to say about matters of life and death. But as technology expands to give medical science greater power against disease, doctors have to perform under greater scrutiny and are regulated more carefully in the use of their power.

Issues such as abortion and *in vitro* fertilization mean that we have to consider when exactly life may be said to begin. If an ovum fertilized in a test tube is capable of sustaining life when transferred into a uterus, when does it have human rights under the law?

An American couple went to Australia in 1981 for a fertility enhancement procedure. Physicians removed and fertilized three eggs from the wife. All developed into embryos, and one was implanted in the woman's womb. The other embryos were frozen and stored. After ten days, the implanted embryo was aborted, and the man and woman left Australia, saying they would return at a future time.

In 1983, the American couple was killed in a plane crash. In addition to the moral questions surrounding the fate of the stored embryos, a further question was posed: Do the stored embryos have any future rights to the multi-million dollar estate left by the couple? The events have forced Australia to take a hard look at the laws that govern fertility enhancement, and the legislature will examine the question over the next year or so.

Artificial Insemination

There is little controversy surrounding artificial insemination using the husband's sperm. In the eyes of the law and most religious organizations, AIH is no different from natural means of conception. Artificial insemination using donor sperm, however, is a different matter.

The Roman Catholic Church opposes AID. The act of insemination with a donor's sperm is considered adulterous, and the child of an AID procedure is illegitimate. Orthodox sects of Judaism likewise oppose AID, although even Orthodox rabbis have, on occasion, sanctioned the procedure. The Anglican and Lutheran churches are in opposition to AID, although most other Protestant sects view the procedure with leniency.

In Britain, the husband must sign a consent form and he is the legal father of the child. In a divorce court, the husband may be awarded custody of the child.

But there is the possibility that a *child* conceived by an AID procedure may want to find its biological father. When interviewed on the network television programme *Good Morning, America*, a twenty-six-year-old woman said that her donor parent knew that a child would be born from his sperm. That he should remain anonymous to that child – who could not have been a party to the contract – she felt was wrong. Although she did not want financial support from her biological father, she did not rule out her right to such support. What this young woman wanted was to meet her biological father, to learn of her genetic history, and to discover if she has any half-brothers or -sisters on the father's side.

Surrogate Mothering

The other side of the AID coin is surrogate mothering, in cases where the husband is fertile, but the wife is not. It would seem logical that what applies to AID would apply here as well. That is far from the truth.

Surrogate parenting dates back at least to biblical days, when Abraham's infertile wife Sarah asked him to have intercourse with her servant Hagar so that they would have a child, but despite its biblical sanction, surrogate parenting is very controversial. Leaders of major religious groups have consistently withheld their approval of surrogate mothering and have, in many instances, actively condemned the practice. The Roman Catholic Church looks upon surrogate mothering as an adulterous act and, further, as baby selling. In fact, a major objection of almost all those who oppose surrogate mothering is the payment of money to the surrogate.

Surrogate mothering exists in almost a total legal vacuum. No laws specifically forbid the practice, but no laws sanction it either. In 1984, the Warnock Committee recommended that the practice be made illegal in Britain.

There are two major questions that cloud the legal status of surrogate parentage:

1. Is it lawful to pay a woman to bear a child for another person?
2. Who are the legal parents of children born out of the practice of surrogate motherhood (which includes the technique of artificial insemination)?

In America, several surrogate agencies are operating. The surrogate agreement, or contract, spells out all the rights and responsibilities of the consenting parties. But, according to Arthur Miller, these contracts are not enforceable, and in some areas are against public policy. Generally, there is no trouble and no legal intervention if the parties to the agreement fulfil their obligations. Most couples hold that the decision is between themselves and the surrogate, and that the choice is made without the coercion of any of the parties involved. But again, if the surrogate mother were to decide that she wanted to keep the child after it was born, most courts would probably permit her to do so.

In Vitro Fertilization

In vitro fertilization has an aura of 2001 about it, a glimpse into the future. Will all babies some day be conceived under a microscope and nurtured in a petri dish? Is the brave new world envisioned by Aldous Huxley upon us? Certainly the possibilities for genetic manipulation exist in the not-so-far-off future, but will we explore them? In some experimental cases, we probably will.

The greatest controversy surrounding in vitro fertilization today concerns the fate of fertilized embryos that are not transferred back into the mother's womb. Are these embryos life forms? If so, at what stage of life is the embryo considered an individual under the law? The present law holds that not until after twenty-eight weeks of pregnancy is the conceptus an individual protected by law. This cut-off date was established because after twenty-eight weeks a fetus is usually mature enough to live outside its mother's body.

New technology, however, has outstripped the law. Even though an embryo cannot survive on its own, it has the potential to be a human being. The questions are complex: for example, if legal status is given to a frozen embryo, does it have a legal right to come to term? If the embryo is damaged, does the life form have a lawsuit? If it is destroyed, is it murder?

In 1985, Enoch Powell introduced his Unborn Child Protection Bill, which aimed at making all experiments on human embryos illegal and even making *in vitro* fertilization very difficult. This Bill was eventually defeated but only after considerable delaying tactics by its opponents.

In 1984, a committee chaired by Dame Mary (now Lady) Warnock recommended that experiments on human embryos should be permitted up to fourteen days after fertilization.

Embryo Transfer

Philosophically, embryo transfer closely resembles artificial insemination, except that the child is conceived with a donor ovum instead of a donor sperm. Because of the similarity between the two techniques, many scientists believe that the same body of law that deals with artificial insemination should apply to embryo transfer. The technique has not yet been carried out in the United Kingdom.

The ethical and legal issues surrounding fertility enhancement techniques are so complex that they will provide many years of grist for the mills of judges, lawyers, and scientists, as well as for those ordinary citizens who seek fertility enhancement and those who wish to stop them. American philosopher Lisa H. Newton has written: 'It is time to de-mythologize reproductive research. Let us admit that all medical technology "tinkers with human life itself", that technology in general has been around much too long for us to continue viewing it with Victorian alarm, that dark mutterings about "provinces of the gods" are no longer the privilege of a nation that sends its rocketships about the universe. The poetic imagery meant to arouse our terror and disgust must be taken as empty unless backed up with specific ethical arguments . . . Human beings must answer to God (and to each other) for the use of these techniques.'

As scientists working with men and women who seek to fulfil their fertility potential, we believe that it is 'natural' to use our brains to do the best we can.

Appendices

Adoption

If you are unable to have a child of your own, you may want to consider adoption. It is important that the decision to pursue this course is taken by both partners, that husband and wife are equally sure that they have come to terms with their childlessness and see adoption as an acceptable way to create the family they long for. If you have any doubts about your ability to love an adopted child as if he or she were your own, or have any feeling that such a child would only be 'second best', then adoption is not right for you. To help you reach your decision, *Yours by Choice: A Guide for Adoptive Parents* by Jane Rowe (Routledge & Kegan Paul, 1982) is invaluable and is recommended reading for all prospective adopters. The British Agencies for Fostering and Adoption (BAAF) publish a very helpful handbook called *Adopting a Child*, which is available by post from 11 Southwark Street, London SE1 1RQ (the 1984/85 edition cost £1.50).

Adopting a Baby

There are very few babies available for adoption these days, partly because contraception is more effective and abortion more easily available, and partly because there is no longer any stigma attached to having an illegitimate child; this means that single mothers who decide to have their babies usually want to keep them. The adoption societies have very strict criteria for prospective parents: most agencies expect couples to be in their twenties or early thirties (thirty-five is usually the upper limit, although some accept that the husband can be older), to have been married for at least three years and to be in good health; they will usually only consider couples who are infertile and who have had time to come to terms with their infertility; you are unlikely to be considered if you are undergoing investigation or treatment and therefore still hoping to conceive. Even if you meet all the agency's requirements and are accepted for their waiting list, you may have to wait several years for your baby.

Adopting an Older Child

On the other hand, there are many older children in local authority care who are waiting for families to adopt them, and in these cases agencies are less strict in their requirements regarding age limits, infertility and so on. These children do have special needs – some belong to ethnic minorities, some are handicapped, some are siblings who should not be separated – and many will have been in care for some time, perhaps years, and may be emotionally difficult and insecure.

How to Set about Adoption

If you want to adopt a baby, the first step is to contact the adoption agencies in your area. Most local authority agencies will only consider people who live within their boundaries, although a few like to have one or two couples on their list from outside the immediate area, so it is worth contacting adjacent authorities just in case. Most independent non-denominational agencies are based in London, but some will consider couples from a wider geographical area. Large childcare organizations providing adoption services, such as Dr Barnardo's, the National Children's Home and the Church of England Children's Society have regional offices although they do not cover every county. Many Roman Catholic dioceses have their own adoption societies. The BAAF's handbook, *Adopting a Child* (see above) will help you find out which agencies you are eligible to apply to: it lists all the adoption agencies in the British Isles, tells you what geographical areas they cover, whether applicants have to be of a particular faith or denomination, and whether they have babies for adoption or only older children or those with special needs. It will also tell you which agencies' lists were open at the time of going to press, but as lists are opened when the need for new adopters arises, it is worth inquiring if the situation has changed since publication.

If you are a coloured family or are prepared to adopt a child with special needs, you will find that few, if any, restrictions apply, as there are many more such children in need of homes than there are couples willing to adopt them. The BAAF runs the Adoption Exchange Service for 'special needs' children, which is nationwide.

Once you have established which agencies to apply to, write them a letter giving personal details such as your ages, how long you have been married, why you want to adopt and what sort of child you are looking for. Be honest with yourselves, do not say you will take an older or handicapped child because it will get you on the waiting list more quickly if you know that you could not cope with the reality of adopting such a child, however desperate you are for a family. Tell the agency if you belong to an ethnic minority or a religious group, as, where possible, agencies like to place children in families of similar background. If the adoption agency is accepting applications, you will probably be invited to an information meeting where you will be told about the work of the agency and given an idea of their procedures, of how many babies they have for adoption each year (depressingly, it will probably be in single figures) and of how long their waiting list is. If you decide to proceed with your application, you will have to fill in a detailed form, have a thorough medical examination (including chest X-rays) and allow the agency to make inquiries about you with Scotland Yard and your local social services department. If all is well, you will be allocated a social worker who will see you a number of times over a period of several months, both individually and as a couple, at the agency and in your own home. They will want to know all there is to know about you, your lifestyle and your family background, as this will enable them not only to decide whether you would make good adoptive parents, but also give them an idea of the type of child to place with you. You may also be encouraged to talk to couples who have adopted children, so that you are aware of what is involved. Finally, the social worker's report is put to the agency's adoption panel who decide if you are to be accepted on to the waiting list as prospective adopters.

If you want to adopt a baby, you will probably have to wait years rather than months, whereas the notice you will get of your child's arrival will probably be days rather than weeks. When you take your baby home, he or she does not become yours immediately. For the first six weeks of the baby's life, the natural mother can change her mind at any time and ask for her baby back. At six weeks she signs an 'agreement to adoption' and at this stage the adopting parents can apply to the local county or magistrate's court for an adoption order. A couple adopting an older child must also apply for an adoption order to make the child legally theirs. In the case of a child with special needs, you may want to wait a little before applying, to give yourselves time to adjust.

Three months must elapse from the lodging of the application with the court to the date of the hearing, allowing time for the new parents and child to settle down together, for medical and character reports to be submitted to the court on behalf of the adopting parents by the agency, and for the natural mother to be interviewed by a court official to ensure she has not been coerced into giving up her child. If the natural mother changes her mind during this three-month period, she has to go to court to contest the adoption order; happily this very seldom happens. Once the adoption order is made, the child becomes legally yours, taking your name and nationality and becoming your heir just as if he or she were your natural child.

Costs

The main cost is, of course, the continuing cost of bringing up the child. Adoption agencies are not allowed to charge fees, although voluntary agencies may ask for a contribution to their costs, as they are charities. You and the child will have to have medical examinations, and you will be asked to pay for these; you will also have to pay for the adoption order, which costs very little unless the order is contested by the natural parents. In this case the legal fees will be higher, but it is usual to take out an insurance policy to cover this possibility; the agency will probably organize this for you for a small premium. Alternatively, legal aid may be available, depending on your income.

If you have adopted a child with special needs an adoption allowance may be available, and there are also allowances to help with the extra costs of caring for handicapped children.

List of Addresses

General

National Association for the Childless
Birmingham Settlement
318 Summer Lane
Birmingham B19 3RL
021-359 4887/2113

A self-help organization.
Advises people with fertility problems.

Child
Farthings
Gaunts Road
Pawlett
Nr Bridgwater
Somerset

A self-help group based in Somerset.

British Pregnancy Advisory Service
Austy Manor
Wootton Wawen
Solihull
West Midlands B95 6BX
05642 3225

AID Clinics, NHS and Private

(Clinics marked with an asterisk will take referrals from GPs)

Aberdeen (Scotland Health Region)

Professor Arnold I. Klopper
Department of Obstetrics and Gynaecology
Phase II
Royal Infirmary
Foresterhill
Aberdeen AB9 2ZB
0224 681818, ext. 3323

Barnstaple (South Western HR)

Mr J. M. McGarry
North Devon District Hospital
Raleigh Park
Barnstaple
North Devon
EX31 4JB
0271 72577, ext. 586

Belfast (N Ireland HR)

Professor W. Thompson/Dr D. D. Boyle
Department of Midwifery and
  Gynaecology
The Queen's University Institute of
  Clinical Science
Grosvenor Road
Belfast BT12 6BJ
0232 240503, ext. 3491

Bournemouth (Wessex HR)

*Ms Jean Stewartson
British Pregnancy Advisory Service
Dean Park Nursing Home
23–25 Ophir Road
Bournemouth BH8 8LS
0202 26174

Birmingham (W Midlands HR)

*Professor J. R. Newton
Department of Obstetrics and Gynaecology
Queen Elizabeth Medical Centre
Birmingham B15 2TG
021-472 1377

*Ms Cynthia Feasey
British Pregnancy Advisory Service
1st Floor
Guildhall Buildings
Navigation Street
Birmingham B2 4BT
021-643 1461

Brighton (SE Thames HR)

*Ms Pam Vaughn Jones
British Pregnancy Advisory Service
Wistons Nursing Home
138 Dyke Road
Brighton BN1 5PA
0273 506263

Bristol (S Western HR)

Mr M. G. R. Hull
Department of Obstetrics and Gynaecology
Bristol Maternity Hospital
Southwell Street
Bristol BS2 8EG
0272 215411

*Mr D. N. Joyce
Southmead General Hospital
Westbury-on-Trym
Bristol BS10 5NB
0272 505050

Cardiff (Wales HR)

*Miss Joan Andrews/Miss Shiela Walker
Antenatal Clinic (Infertility Clinic)
University Hospital of Wales
Heath Park
Cardiff CF4 4XN
0222 755944

*Mr R. W. M. Rees
59 Cathedral Road
Cardiff CF1 9HE
0222 397495

Clwyd (Wales HR)

Mr E. Parry
Haford
Ruthin Road
Denbigh
Clwyd
074571 3131

Doncaster (Yorkshire HR)

*Ms Frances Dunkley
British Pregnancy Advisory Centre
Danum Lodge Nursing Home
123 Thorne Road
Doncaster
South Yorks. DN2 5BQ
0302 25508

Edinburgh (Scotland HR)

Dr M. M. Lees
Infertility Clinic
Royal Infirmary of Edinburgh
Lauriston Place
Edinburgh EH3 9YW
031-229 2477

Exeter (S Western HR)

Dr B. Pepper/Mr D. W. Sykes
AID Clinic
Royal Devon and Exeter Hospital
  (Wonford)
Barrack Road
Exeter EX2 5DW
0392 77833, ext. 2480

Glasgow (Scotland HR)

Professor M. C. Macnaughton
Department of Gynaecology
Royal Infirmary
Glasgow G4 0SF
041-552 3400

*Mrs Margaret Gedeon
British Pregnancy Advisory Service
2nd Floor
245 North Street
Glasgow G3 7DL
041-204 1832

Hull (Yorkshire HR)

Mr A. G. Gordon
Gavin Brown Clinic
Princess Royal Infirmary
Salthouse Road
Hull HU8 9HE
0482 701151

Leamington Spa (W Midlands HR)

Ms Sandra Munroe
British Pregnancy Advisory Service

Blackdown Nursing Home
Old Milverton Lane
Blackdown
Nr Leamington Spa
Warwickshire
0926 34664

Leicester (Trent HR)

Mr C. R. Stewart
Leicester General Hospital
Gwendolen Road
Leicester LE5 4PW
0533 730222, ext. 636

Liverpool (Mersey HR)

Dr P. Walker
The Cranbrook Clinic
39 Rodney Street
Liverpool L1 9AA
051-709 2203

*Ms Susie Wilkinson-Jones
British Pregnancy Advisory Service
Merseyside Nursing Home
32 Parkfield Road
Liverpool L17 8UJ
051-727 1851

London (NW Thames HR)

Dr G. Barry Carruthers
55 Wimpole Street
London W1M 7DP
01-486 4646

Dr J. Glatt
144 Harley Street
London W1N 1AH
01-486 0090

Mr A. V. Hirsh
112 Harley Street
London W1
01-935 6588

Dr L. Hughes
99 Harley Street
London W1
01-935 9004

*Dr Maurice Katz
128 Harley Street
London W1N 1AH
01-486 9018/9019

Dr B. A. Mason
25 Weymouth Street
London W1N 3FJ
01-631 1583

Dr R. Curson
Gynaecology, Endocrinology Unit
5th Floor (NWB)
King's College Hospital
Denmark Hill
London SE5
01-274 7711, ext. 2516

London (NE Thames HR)

Professor R. W. Shaw
Department of Obstetrics and Gynaecology
Royal Free Hospital
Pond Street
London NW3 2QG
01-794 0500

Mr S. J. Steele
Academic Department of Obstetrics and
    Gynaecology
4th Floor
Thorn Institute
Middlesex Hospital
Mortimer Street
London W1N 8AA
01-636 8333

Guys Hospital
St Thomas's Street
London SE1 9KT
01-407 7600

London (SW Thames HR)

Mrs T. R. Varma
St George's Hospital
Lanesborough Wing
London SW17
01-672 1255, ext. 4177

*Mrs Jill Butler
British Pregnancy Advisory Service
2nd Floor
58 Petty France
London SW1H 9EU
01-222 0985

Maidstone (SE Thames HR)

*Dr Alan Pentecost
Maidstone Hospital
Maidstone
Kent
0622 29000

Manchester (N Western HR)

*Dr R. W. Burslem
24a St John Street
Manchester M3 4DU
061-834 4945

Professor V. R. Tindall/Dr E. H. Pease
Department of Obstetrics and Gynaecology
St Mary's Hospital
Hathersage Road
Whitworth Park
Manchester 13
061-224 9633, ext. 494

Palatine Family Planning Association
Manchester

Newcastle (W Midlands HR)

Mr A. W. Clubb
Grove House
11 King Street
Newcastle ST5 1EH
Staffs.
0782 614174

Nottingham (Trent HR)

Professor E. M. Symonds
Fertility Clinic
University Hospital
Queen's Medical Centre
Hucknall Road
Nottingham NG7 2UH
0602 700111

Oxford (Oxford HR)

*Professor A. C. Turnbull/Mr P. D.
  Bromwich
Maternity Department
Nuffield Department of Obstetrics and
  Gynaecology
John Radcliffe Hospital
Headington
Oxford OX3 9DU
0865 64711, ext. 7571

Salford (N Western HR)

Dr Pathak/Dr Anderson
Hope Hospital
Salford
Lancs

Sheffield (Trent HR)

*Dr G. W. Pennington
Consultant Chemical Pathologist
Jessop Hospital for Women
Leavygreave Road
Sheffield S3 7RE
0742 29291

Professor I. D. Cooke
Department of Obstetrics and Gynaecology
University of Sheffield
Jessop Hospital for Women
Leavygreave Road
Sheffield S3 7RE
0742 29291

Southampton (Wessex HR)

Mr G. M. Masson
Princess Anne Hospital
Coxford Road
Southampton SO2 4HA
0703 777222

Swansea (Wales HR)

*Mr P. Bowen-Simpkins
69 Walter Road
Swansea
West Glamorgan SA1 4QA
0792 55600

Taunton (S Western HR)

Mr E. Wallace
Department of Obstetrics and
  Gynaecology
Musgrove Park Branch
Taunton
Somerset TA1 5DA
0823 73444

Watford (NW Thames HR)

*Dr B. E. Bean
Subfertility Clinic
Peace Memorial Hospital
Rickmansworth Road
Watford
Herts. WD1 7HH
92 25611, ext. 131

Windsor (Oxford HR)

*Dr C. B. Butcher
Clarence House
Clarence Crescent
Windsor
Berks. SL4 1BU
95 69999

In Vitro Fertilization Clinics

Based on information collected by the National Association for the Childless
(A letter of referral from a GP is required.)

Private

Mr Patrick Steptoe
Bourn Hall Clinic
Bourn Hall
Bourn
Cambs. CB3 7TR
0223 315955

Mr Ian Craft
Humana Hospital Wellington
Wellington Place
St John's Wood
London NW8
01-586 8861

Dr Bridgett Mason
Hallam Medical Centre
77 Hallam Street
London WIN 5LR
01-631 1583

Dr Jack Glatt
144 Harley Street
London WI
01-486 3860

Professor Robert Shaw
Academic Department of Obstetrics and
  Gynaecology
The Royal Free Hospital
Pond Street
London NW3 2QG
01-794 0500, ext. 3736

Dr D. K. Edmunds
Chelsea Hospital for Women
Dovehouse Street
London SW3 6LT
01-352 6446

Dr Brian Lieberman
Manchester Fertility Services
BUPA Hospital
Russell Road
Whalley Range
Manchester
061-226 0112

Dr Webster
The Park Hospital
Sherwood Lodge Drive
Arnold
Nottingham NG5 8RX
0602 208111

Professor Ian Cooke
Department of Obstetrics and Gynaecology
Jessop Hospital for Women
Sheffield S3 7RE
0742 29291

Mr R. Low
Consultant Gynaecologist
Nuffield McAlpin Clinic
25 Beaconsfield Road
Glasgow 12

National Health Service

Mr Robert Sawers
Birmingham Maternity Hospital
Queen Elizabeth Medical Centre
Edgbaston
Birmingham B15 2TG
021-472 1377

Mr D. N. Joyce
Department of Infertility

Southmead General Hospital
Westbury-on-Trym
Bristol
Avon BS10 5NB
0272 505050

Head of Department of Obstetrics and
  Gynaecology
Addenbrooke Hospital
Hills Road
Cambs.
0223 245151

Dr D. K. Edmunds
Chelsea Hospital for Women
Dovehouse Street
London SW3 6LT
01-352 6446

Dr Brian Lieberman
Regional IVF Unit
St Mary's Hospital
Hathersage Road
Manchester M13 0JH

Dr Martin Lees
The Royal Infirmary of Edinburgh
Lauriston Place
Edinburgh EH3 9YW
031-229 2477

Dr W. P. Black
Consultant Gynaecologist
Glasgow University Department of
  Obstetrics and Gynaecology
Ward 31
3rd Floor
Surgical Block
Castle Street
Glasgow G4 0SF

Assistant Professor Robert Harrison
1 St James Street
Dublin 8
01 537941

Independently Funded
Voluntary contributions may be requested

Mr Marcus Setchell
Department of Obstetrics and Gynaecology
The Royal Hospital of St Bartholemew
London EC1A 7BE
01-600 9000, ext. 3212

Stuart Campbell, Professor and Head of
  Department
John Parsons, IVF Team Leader
Academic Department of Obstetrics and
  Gynaecology
King's College Hospital
Denmark Hill
London SE5 8RX
01-274 6222

Professor Robert Shaw
Academic Department of Obstetrics and
  Gynaecology
The Royal Free Hospital
Pond Street
London NW3 2QG
01-794 0500, ext. 3736

Mr Robert Winston
Department of Obstetrics and Gynaecology
Hammersmith Hospital
Du Cane Road
London W12
01-743 2030

Adoption

British Agencies for Adoption and
  Fostering
11 Southwark Street
London SE1 1RQ
01-407 8800

Publishes information on adoption and will give advice on adopting children with special needs. Their booklet *Adopting a Child* contains a list of addresses of all the adoption agencies in England and Scotland.

Parent to Parent Information on Adoption
  Services
Lower Boddington

Daventry
Northants. NN11 6YB
0327 60295

A self-help group for adoptive parents and prospective adoptive parents.

Harmony
22 St Mary's Road
Meare
Glastonbury
Somerset

Information for inter-racial families.

Glossary

ABDOMEN. Roughly, the 'belly'; scientifically, that part of the body lying between the chest and the pelvis. It contains the stomach, lower portion of the oesophagus, small and large intestines, liver, pancreas, spleen, gall bladder and urinary bladder and in women the uterus, tubes, and ovaries.

ABDOMINAL PREGNANCY. A pregnancy growing in the abdominal cavity. Rare cases have been known to survive after CAESAREAN SECTION.

ABORTION. The premature expulsion of an embryo from the uterus. When an abortion is deliberate, it is known as an induced abortion, voluntary abortion, therapeutic abortion, or termination of pregnancy. When it occurs naturally, it is known as a spontaneous abortion or a miscarriage.

ABSCESS. An accumulation of pus.

ACROSOME. The cap on the head of a sperm.

ACUTE. Sudden in onset and short in duration, said of an illness; cf. CHRONIC. Neither term necessarily implies severity.

ADENOHYPOPHYSIS. The front portion of the pituitary gland.

ADENOMYOSIS. A condition in which the ENDOMETRIUM invades the uterine muscles.

ADHESION. A band of scar tissue that binds organs together; adhesions tend to form after infection or operation.

ADRENAL GLANDS. Two small glands, one atop each kidney, that secrete several hormones, including some sex hormones.

ADRENAL HYPERPLASIA. An enlarged adrenal gland producing excess hormones; associated with CUSHING'S DISEASE.

AGGLUTIN. A substance that causes clumping; when sperm clump together (agglutinization), a man's fertility may be reduced.

AID. Artificial insemination by donor's sperm.

AIH. Artificial insemination by husband's sperm.

ALLERGEN. Any agent (drugs, foods, pollen, sun, heat) that causes an allergic response in the body.

AMENORRHOEA. Absence of menstrual periods.

AMNIOCENTESIS. Removal of a small sample of AMNIOTIC FLUID from the uterus between the fourteenth and sixteenth week of pregnancy for chromosome analysis. Used primarily in women over thirty-five.

AMNIOTIC FLUID. The liquid that surrounds the developing fetus in the womb.

AMPULLA. A pocket at the upper end of the VAS DEFERENS in which some sperm are stored.

ANDROLOGIST. A specialist in diseases related to men.

ANOREXIA NERVOSA. Loss of appetite, leading to dangerous weight loss. Believed to be psychological or emotional in origin. Sufferers are usually women. When body weight falls sharply, ovulation and periods cease.

ANOVULATION. Failure of ovulation to occur.

ANTEVERSION. The normal, forward position of the uterus in the pelvic cavity.

ANTIBODY. A substance produced in the body that attacks foreign bacteria or viruses. Some men and women produce antibodies against sperm that can cause infertility.

ANTIGEN. Any foreign substance that causes the body to produce antibodies against it.

APOCRINE GLANDS. Scent-producing glands.

ARRHENOBLASTOMA. A rare tumour of the ovaries that may produce excess male hormone and stop ovulation.

ARTIFICIAL INSEMINATION. Injection of semen by syringe into a woman's cervix. If a husband's semen is used, it is called AIH ; if a donor's semen is used, it is AID.

ATROPHIC VAGINITIS. An irritation of the vagina resulting from lack of oestrogen (dry vagina).

AUTONOMIC NERVOUS SYSTEM. Regulates blood vessels, heart rate and other bodily functions that occur automatically.

AZOOSPERMIA. Complete absence of sperm in semen.

BARR BODY. Raw genetic material found in all cells of normal females but not in males ; a condensed X chromosome that appears in the periphery of the nucleus of a cell that contains more than one X chromosome. The number of Barr bodies is X – 1. If the cell is XXX, then two Barr bodies will be seen. Thus, a male with XY has no X-condensed chromosome.

BARTHOLIN'S GLANDS. Two pea-sized glands just inside the vagina that secrete lubricating mucus. The glands can swell shut if inflamed and are subject to ABSCESS.

BASAL BODY TEMPERATURE. The temperature of the body at rest.

BENIGN. A tumour that grows slowly but does not invade surrounding tissue. Benign tumours are not dangerous. Cf. MALIGNANT.

BICORNUATE UTERUS. A uterus with two branches, or 'horns'. The malformation is a result of incomplete development before birth.

BIOPSY. Surgical removal of tissue for analysis.

BIPHASIC. The normal pattern of BASAL BODY TEMPERATURE, showing an upward shift in the middle of the menstrual cycle ; temperature remains elevated until the next period starts.

BLASTOCYST. A fertilized ovum that after a few days' development attaches to the inside wall of the uterus.

BLIGHTED OVUM. A fertilized ovum that fails to develop after implanting in the uterus and aborts spontaneously.

CAECUM. The section of the large intestine between the colon and the small intestine.

CAESAREAN SECTION. Delivery of a child through an incision in the abdominal wall rather than through the vagina.

CANCER. A malignant growth.

CANCROID. Soft cancer caused by a micro-organism that is highly infectious.

CANDIDA. A yeast-like fungus, often the cause of vaginal itching. See MONILIASIS.

CANNULA. A small, hollow instrument used to introduce material into the body or remove material from the body.

CAPACITATION. The washing away of a sperm's protective coating.

CASTRATION. Commonly, the removal of testicles; also refers to the removal of ovaries or their destruction by radiation.

CAUTERIZE. To coagulate or destroy by applying heat.

CERVICAL MUCUS. The secretions surrounding the cervical canal. The amount and texture change during ovulation to allow sperm penetration.

CERVICAL OS. The opening of the cervix.

CERVICAL SMEAR. *See* PAP TEST.

CERVICITIS. Inflammation of the cervix by bacterial or fungal infection. May temporarily affect fertility.

CERVIX. The neck of the uterus, opening into the vagina.

CHLAMYDIA. A micro-organism found in the GENITO-URINARY TRACT; may be transmitted by sexual contact.

CHROMOSOME. A cell that carries the material determining hereditary characteristics; a sex chromosome determines sex. *See also* GENE.

CHRONIC. Of prolonged development and duration, said of a condition or infection. Cf. ACUTE.

CILIA. Tiny hairlike projections that grow out of some cells.

CIRCUMCISION. Generally, removal of foreskin from the penis. Can also describe removal of extra skin from the clitoris.

CLIMACTERIC. The period in women's lives when menstruation gradually stops. 'Male climacteric' is sometimes used to mean ageing in man.

CLITORIDITIS. Inflammation of the clitoris.

CLITORIS. The external erectile tissue located above the urethra in women; the most sensitive point of female genitalia.

CLOMID. Brand name for the non-steroid OESTROGEN clomiphene citrate, a fertility drug used to stimulate ovaries.

COITUS. Sexual intercourse between male and female.

COITUS INTERRUPTUS. Withdrawal of the penis from the vagina before ejaculation.

COLON. The portion of the large intestine from the CAECUM to the rectum.

COLPOSCOPE. A small, low-powered microscope used to examine tissue in the vagina.

COLPOSCOPY. Examination using a COLPOSCOPE.

COMBINED-FACTOR INFERTILITY. Failure to conceive due to the relative infertility of both partners.

CONCEPTION. Fertilization of an ovum by a sperm.

CONCEPTUS. A fertilized ovum or, later, the embryo, fetus, placenta and other membranes.

CONDOM. A sheath usually made of latex placed over the penis to prevent conception or spread of infection.

CONDYLOMA ACCUMINATA. A kind of wart caused by a virus.

CONDYLOMA LATUM. A flat, wet wart of secondary syphilis, usually found near the anus or on the penis.

CONGENITAL. Developmental; present from birth.

CONIZATION. Excision of abnormal parts of the cervix.

CONTRACEPTION. Prevention of pregnancy; birth control.

CONTRACEPTIVE CREAM. A creamy substance containing a sperm-killing agent inserted into the vagina for birth control.

CONTRACEPTIVE FOAM. A foaming substance containing a sperm-killing agent inserted into the vagina for birth control.

COOMBS TEST. A laboratory procedure used to detect the presence of proteins, usually antibodies.

CORNUA. The 'horns' of the uterus – the point at which the fallopian tubes enter the uterus.

CORPUS CAVERNOSA. Two of the three cylinders that make up the penis. The third is the CORPUS SPONGIOSUM.

CORPUS LUTEUM. The 'yellow body' that develops in the ovarian follicle after it has released an egg. It secretes PROGESTERONE.

CORPUS SPONGIOSUM. One of the three cylinders that make up the penis. *See also* CORPUS CAVERNOSA.

COWPER'S GLANDS. Tiny outgrowths of the urethra that secrete fluid to neutralize urine and help the passage of sperm through the urethra.

CRYOCAUTERY. Destruction of tissue by freezing.

CRYOPRESERVATION. Preservation of tissue by freezing.

CRYPTORCHISM. Undescended testicles.

CULDOCENTESES. Withdrawal of undesirable fluids from the pelvic cavity through the back wall of the vagina.

CULDOSCOPE. A telescopic instrument inserted into the pelvis through the vagina.

CULDOSCOPY. Examination of the pelvic organs with a CULDOSCOPE.

CULDOTOMY. Cutting into the pelvic cavity through the back vaginal wall.

CULTURE. A laboratory procedure in which organisms such as bacteria are allowed to develop for easier identification.

CURETTAGE. Scraping of the uterine lining with an instrument known as a curette.

CUSHING'S DISEASE. A rare condition in which a pituitary tumour causes the adrenal glands to produce excess hormones. Named after Harvey Cushing, an American neurosurgeon. Cushing's disease can prevent ovulation.

CYST. An abnormal, encapsulated accumulation of fluid, fat, or semi-solid material.

CYSTITIS. Inflammation of the bladder.

CYSTOCELE. A condition in which the bladder and front wall of the vagina sag so that the bladder bulges through the vaginal opening.

CYSTOSCOPE. An instrument used to examine the inside of the bladder via the urethra.

CYSTOSCOPY. Examination of bladder using a CYSTOSCOPE.

CYTOLOGIST. A physician who specializes in the study of cells.

D&C. *See* DILATATION AND CURETTAGE.

D&E. Dilatation of cervix and evacuation of uterine contents by suction.

DANAZOL. A drug used to treat ENDOMETRIOSIS, marketed under the brand name Danol.

DECAPACITATION FACTOR. A factor contained in the MALE PILL used to prevent conception.

DES. *See* DIETHYLSTILBOESTROL.

DETUMESCENCE. Shrinking of the penis or clitoris following erection.

DEXAMETHASONE. A cortisone-like compound that is used to reduce adrenal gland secretions.

DIABETES MELLITUS. A disturbance in METABOLISM that causes the blood sugar level to become very high.

DIAPHRAGM. A dome-shaped device inserted in the vagina, against the cervix, for birth control.

DIATHERMY. A method of applying heat to parts of the body. Often used in female sterilization to destroy part of the fallopian tube.

DIENOESTROL. A synthetic OESTROGEN.

DIETHYLSTILBOESTROL (DES). A synthetic OESTROGEN that may cause serious lesions in unborn children if given to a pregnant woman.

DILATATION AND CURETTAGE (D&C). A minor surgical procedure in which the cervix is dilated to permit scraping of the uterine wall with an instrument called a curette.

DILATOR. Any device used to widen a body opening.

DNA. Deoxyribonucleic acid; the part of the cell that contains and transmits the genetic code.

DOUCHING. Rinsing of a body cavity for hygiene.

DOWN'S SYNDROME. A birth defect characterized by an extra chromosome in pair No. 21. The abnormality results in moderate to severe mental retardation. Also called mongolism or trisomy 21.

DUCTUS DEFERENS. See VAS DEFERENS.

DYSMENORRHOEA. Painful menstruation.

DYSPAREUNIA. Painful sexual intercourse, usually during penetration of the vagina by the penis.

DYSPLASIA. An abnormality of some cells of the cervix, vagina, or vulva in which some, but not all, layers are abnormal.

ECTOPIC PREGNANCY. A dangerous condition in which a fertilized ovum attaches itself outside the uterus (usually in a Fallopian tube) and begins to grow.

EGG. Female sex cell, female gamete, ovum.

EJACULATE. Seminal fluid expelled during ejaculation.

EJACULATION. The act of expelling semen from the penis at orgasm.

EMBRYO. An early stage of prenatal development, to the eighth week of pregnancy. Thereafter, the term FETUS is applied.

ENDOCRINE GLANDS. Glands that make and secrete hormones, including the adrenals, pancreas, pituitary, ovaries, testicles and parathyroid glands.

ENDOCRINOLOGIST. A specialist in the study of hormones.

ENDOMETRIAL BIOPSY. Removal of a small part of the endometrium for examination under the microscope.

ENDOMETRIAL CYTOLOGY. PAP TEST taken from inside the uterus.

ENDOMETRIOSIS. A condition characterized by abnormal growth of endometrial cells in areas of the pelvis outside of the uterus.

ENDOMETRIUM. The mucus membrane that lines the uterus.

ENTEROCELE. A bulging at the top back wall of the vagina.

ENZYME. A substance that regulates biochemical reactions within the body.

EPIDIDYMIS. The coiled structure outside the testicles in which sperm are stored.

EPINEPHRINE. A chemical that controls or affects fright reaction and body functions related to the lungs, heart and uterus. Also called adrenalin.

EPISIOTOMY. An incision made between the vagina and rectum to ease the delivery of a baby.

ERECTION. Engorgement of erectile tissues with blood (in the penis or clitoris) during sexual intercourse.

ERPC. Evacuation of retained products of conception; DILATATION AND CURETTAGE performed after a miscarriage.

ESCUTCHEON. The triangle of short, curly pubic hair covering the MONS VENERIS in the female.

ETHINYLOESTRADIOL. A synthetic OESTROGEN.

EXCISE. To cut away or remove surgically.

EXTRACORPOREAL FERTILIZATION. *See* IN VITRO FERTILIZATION.

FALLOPIAN TUBE. The long, narrow tube between an ovary and the uterus. After release of the egg from the ovary, the tube transports the egg to the uterus.

FEBRILE. Having a high fever.

FERTILITY. The ability to produce offspring; a woman's ability to conceive and carry a child or a man's ability to impregnate a women.

FERTILITY DRUGS. Drugs that stimulate an ovary to release an ovum.

FERTILIZATION. Penetration of ovum by sperm.

FETUS. An unborn CONCEPTUS after eight weeks in the uterus.

FIBROADENOMA. A non-malignant tumour made up of glandular and fibrous tissues.

FIBROID. A benign tumour that, when it occurs in the uterus, may distort the uterine shape so that it cannot support pregnancy.

FIMBRIA (pl. FIMBRIAE). The finger-like end of the fallopian tube that catches the released ovum.

FOLLICLE. A small sac in the ovary in which the ovum develops.

FOLLICLE-STIMULATING HORMONE (FSH). A hormone produced by the pituitary gland. In women it is secreted cyclically and is responsible for ripening the egg. In men it is essential for sperm growth.

FORESKIN. The skin covering the head of the penis or clitoris.

FRACTYL. A synthetically produced LH-RH.

FRENULUM. The fold where the labia and clitoris merge.

FRIGIDITY. The inability of a woman to reach orgasm.

FRUCTOSE. A type of sugar present in semen.

FSH. *See* FOLLICLE-STIMULATING HORMONE.

FUNDUS. The upper portion of the uterus, farthest away from the cervix.

GAMETE. Sperm or ovum; the male or female sex cell.

GARDNERELLA. A bacteria causing common vaginal infection.

GAS GANGRENE. An infection caused by the bacterium *Clostridium*, which may lead to tissue death. May occur after miscarriage or incomplete abortion.

GENE. A unit of heredity located in a fixed position on a given chromosome.

GENERAL ANAESTHESIA. A type of sedation that causes unconsciousness, as opposed to LOCAL ANAESTHESIA, which sedates a specific area of the body.

GENERIC. The chemical, rather than the brand name of a drug.

GENITO-URINARY TRACT. The excretory and reproductive systems in men and women.

GLUCOSE TOLERANCE TEST. A laboratory test used to detect DIABETES MELLITUS, adrenal abnormalities, and HYPOGLYCAEMIA.

GOITRE. Enlargement of the thyroid gland, usually caused by deficient iodine in the diet.

GONADOTROPHINS. Pituitary hormones that stimulate the reproduction system.

GONADS. The primary sex glands; the ovaries in a woman and the testicles in a man.

GONORRHOEA. An infection spread by sexual contact, caused by the bacteria GONOCOCCUS NEISSERIA.

GRAAFIAN FOLLICLE. The lead follicle that matures in one ovary each month and eventually ovulates.

GROWTH. An abnormal collection of tissue, such as a polyp or tumour; may be malignant or benign.

GYNAECOLOGIST. A specialist in the care of the female reproductive system.

HABITUAL ABORTION. Recurrent, spontaneous premature loss of a fetus.

HAEMATOMA. Local swelling due to abnormal collection of blood.

HAEMORRHAGE. Uncontrolled bleeding.

HCG. *See* HUMAN CHORIONIC GONADATROPHIN.

HEMOPHILUS A family of bacteria some of which are responsible for vaginal infection. *See* GARDNERELLA.

HEPARIN. A chemical used to prevent blood from clotting.

HERNIA. Rupture or projection of an organ through an abnormal opening.

HERPES SIMPLEX. A cold sore or fever blister caused by a virus; found on the mouth or genitals.

HERPES VIRUS. A group of viruses causing genital oral, and skin infections and meningitis.

HERPES ZOSTER. Shingles; manifests itself often as a skin eruption, especially around the waist. Caused by a HERPES VIRUS.

HIRSUTISM. Excessive hairiness.

HMG. *See* HUMAN MENOPAUSAL GONADATROPHIN.

HORMONE. A chemical secreted by the endocrine glands that circulates in the blood to regulate many body functions. Hormones are also made synthetically.

HOSTILE MUCUS. Mucus that immobilizes or destroys sperm.

HOT FLUSH. Sudden flushing of the skin, often associated with the CLIMACTERIC.

HPG. *See* HUMAN PITUITARY GONADATROPHIN.

HSG. *See* HYSTEROSALPINGOGRAM.

HUHNER TEST. *See* POSTCOITAL TEST.

HUMAN CHORIONIC GONADOTROPHIN (HCG). A hormone secreted by the placenta during pregnancy. Its presence in the blood indicates a positive pregnancy test. May be used with other hormones in treating infertility.

HUMAN MENOPAUSAL GONADOTROPHIN (HMG) FOLLICLE-STIMULATING HORMONE. Extracted from the urine of post-menopausal women; used in the treatment of fertility problems. *See also* PERGONAL.

HUMAN PITUITARY GONADOTROPHIN (HPG) FOLLICLE-STIMULATING HORMONE. Obtained from the pituitary glands of cadavers; used in treating some fertility problems.

HYDROCELE. Swelling of the scrotal sac due to accumulation of fluid.

HYDROSALPINGES. Blockage and resultant swelling of the fallopian tubes.

HYDROTUBATION. Flushing of the fallopian tubes to test for obstruction, to treat some types of tubal blockage, or to wash the tubes after surgery.

HYMEN. Maidenhead; the membrane that partially blocks the entrance of the vagina in virgins. May or may not be present depending on past trauma or individual physiology.

HYMENECTOMY. Surgical removal of the HYMEN.

HYMENOTOMY. Surgical incision in the HYMEN.

HYPERMENORRHOEA. Excessive menstrual bleeding.

HYPERPLASIA. Abnormal enlargement of an organ or tissue of the body.

HYPERTENSION. High blood pressure.

HYPERTROPHY. Excessive enlargement of an organ of the body.

HYPOGLYCAEMIA. A low level of sugar in the blood.

HYPOMENORRHOEA. Scanty menstrual bleeding.

HYPOSPADIUS. A CONGENITAL abnormality in which the urethra is found on the underside of the penis rather than at the end.

HYPOTENSION. Low blood pressure.

HYPOTHALAMUS. The portion of the brain directly above the pituitary. Controls many body functions, including regulation of pituitary hormones.

HYPOTHYROIDISM. A low level of activity of the thyroid gland.

HYSTERECTOMY. Surgical removal of the uterus.

HYSTEROSALPINGOGRAM (HSG). X-ray study done by injecting dye into the uterus to examine the interior of the uterus and fallopian tubes. Also called tubogram or uterogram.

HYSTEROTOMY. Surgical opening and closing of the uterus for removal of a tumour or for repair.

HYSTEROGRAM. X-ray of the uterus.

IMMUNE SYSTEM. The body's defensive response to disease or infection; white blood cells are the most important component of the system.

IMMUNOLOGIC RESPONSE. The presence of antibodies in the male or female that immobilize or kill sperm.

IMMUNOSUPPRESSIVE DRUG. A drug used to stop the IMMUNE SYSTEM from attacking a foreign presence in the body.

IMPLANTATION. The precess by which the fertilized ovum attaches itself to the ENDOMETRIUM.

IMPOTENCE. Inability of the male to produce or maintain an erection.

INCISION. A surgical cut.

INCOMPETENT CERVIX. A cervix that dilates prematurely during pregnancy. May cause loss of the fetus.

INFECTION. Contamination with harmful organisms.

INFERTILITY. Inability to produce offspring. May be permanent or may refer to a prolonged, temporary status.

INFLAMMATION. Pain in tissue as a result of injury, irritation, or infection.

INSUFFLATION OF THE TUBES. See RUBIN'S TEST.

INSULIN. A hormone secreted by the pancreas that regulates levels of sugar in the blood.

INTERNAL PELVIC EXAMINATION. A physical examination in which the physician feels the shape of the internal reproductive organs of the female by inserting two fingers into the vagina while pressing down on the abdomen with the other hand. Also called bimanual examination.

INTERSTITIAL CELLS. Testicular cells that produce the male hormone TESTOSTERONE. Also called Leydig's cells.

INTRAUTERINE. Within the uterus.

INTRAUTERINE DEVICE (IUD). A device inserted into the uterus to prevent pregnancy.

IN VITRO FERTILIZATION. Fertilization that takes place outside the body. Also called extracorporeal fertilization.

ISTHMUS. The narrow area of fallopian tube closest to the uterus.

IUD. See INTRAUTERINE DEVICE.

KETO STEROIDS, KETOGENIC STEROIDS. Waste products of the adrenal system found in urine. Analysis of 24-hour urine specimen for these products can indicate how the adrenal system is functioning.

KAROTYPE. A photograph of the arrangement of chromosomes in the nucleus of a cell.

KELOID. Overgrowth of scar tissue.

KLEINEREGEN. The presence of pink, brown, or red stain in cervical mucus at the time of ovulation.

KLINEFELTER'S SYNDROME. A developmental abnormality in the male characterized by an extra X chromosome in the sex gene. Usually results in sterility.

KRAUROSIS. The dry, itchy condition of outer genitalia in women, usually occurring after menopause.

KRIEGS AMENORRHOEA. Upset of the normal menstrual cycle during wartime. The change in menstrual function is probably related to the hormonal changes associated with stress and anxiety.

LABIA MAJORA. The large lips of the vagina; the fold of skin across the vaginal orifice; part of the vulva.

LABIA MINORA. The inner lips of the vagina; part of the vulva.

LACTATION. Production of milk in the breast.

LAPARASCOPE. A telescopic instrument inserted through a small incision in the navel to directly examine the pelvic cavity.

LAPAROSCOPY. Examination with a LAPAROSCOPE.

LAPAROTOMY. A major surgical procedure in which the abdomen is opened through incision in the abdominal wall.

LESION. Any break in tissue; sore, ulcer, tumour.

LEUKOPLAKIA. White patches on mucus membranes.

LEUKORRHOEA. A white, vaginal discharge.

LH. See LUTEINIZING HORMONE.

LH-RH. Releasing hormone from the hypothalamus which activates FSH and LH in men and women.

LIBIDO. The sex urge.

LICHEN SCLEROSIS ET ATROPHICUS. A skin condition of the outer genitalia similar to KRAUROSIS.

LIGATE. To tie or bind.

LINING OF THE WOMB. See ENDOMETRIUM.

LIPOMA. A fatty tumour.

LOCAL ANAESTHESIA. The use of a drug to numb a small area of the body. Cf. GENERAL ANAESTHESIA.

LUMEN. The inside of a tube in the body.

LUTEAL PHASE. The phase of the menstrual cycle after ovulation when the CORPUS LUTEUM is secreting PROGESTERONE.

LUTEINIZING HORMONE (LH). A hormone secreted by the pituitary gland. In women it is produced cyclically to stimulate the CORPUS LUTEUM to manufacture PROGESTERONE. In men, it stimulates testicular cells to produce TESTOSTERONE.

LYMPH NODES. Structures that produce blood cells to filter certain foreign elements out of the bloodstream.

LYMPHATIC SYSTEM. A 'secondary' circulation system consisting of glands, ducts, fluids and nodes. The communications network for the IMMUNE SYSTEM.

LYMPHOPATHIA VENEREUM. Sexually transmitted disease that affects the LYMPHATIC SYSTEM.

LYSIS OF ADHESIONS. Surgical removal of scar tissue.

MALE PILL. The popular name for any experimental substance taken by men to prevent conception.

MALIGNANT. Capable of causing death, usually used in reference to cancer. Cf. BENIGN.

MAMMOGRAPHY. An X-ray procedure for examination of the breast.

MARSUPIALIZATION. A surgical procedure in which the ends of a CYST are sewn to form a sort of pouch.

MASTECTOMY. Surgical removal of the breast.

MASTODYNIA. Painful breasts.

MELANOMA. A malignant, pigmented mole that invades the LYMPHATIC SYSTEM and bloodstream very quickly. Usually appears as a flat, black mole on the skin and is diagnosed only through wide excisional BIOPSY. The tumour has been known to go across the placenta and transfer to the infant in the woman's uterus.

MENARCHE. The first menstrual period for a female.

MENINGITIS. An inflammation of the lining of the brain.

MENOPAUSE. The time of life when menstruation ceases due to ageing of the ovaries.

MENORRHAGIA. Excessive menstrual bleeding.

MENSTRUAL CYCLE. A cycle of approximately one month in the female during which the ovum is released from an ovary, the ENDOMETRIUM is prepared to receive the fertilized egg, and blood and endometrial tissue are lost via the vagina if pregnancy does not occur.

MENSTRUATION. Loss of blood at the end of the menstrual cycle.

MESTEROLONE. A male sex hormone used to improve sperm production.

MESTRANOL. The chemical name for an oestrogenic component used in oral contraceptives.

METABOLISM. The daily chemical reacions of the body (conversion of sugar to energy, food to protein, protein to hormones and so on).

METASTASIS. Movement and growth of cancer cells from one area in the body to another.

METORRHAGIA. Bleeding between periods.

MICROSURGERY. Surgery performed on minute body structures with the use of microscopes.

MISCARRIAGE. Spontaneous loss of the fetus or embryo from the womb.

MITTELSCHMERTZ. Pain felt at ovulation.

MOLAR PREGNANCY. Change of a pregnancy into a fleshy, mole-like tumour.

MONGOLISM. See DOWN'S SYNDROME.

MONILIASIS. Infection of the skin or mucus membrane by a yeast-like fungus.

MONS VENERIS. Mount of Venus; the fatty area between the navel and vagina. Also called mons pubis.

MORNING-AFTER PILL. A contraceptive pill (usually DIETHYLSTILBOESTROL) taken after coitus rather than before.

MORPHOLOGY. Structure or form.

MORULA. A fertilized ovum after a few day's growth, when it becomes a ball of cells.

MOTILITY. Ability to move.

MUCORRHOEA. Abundant production of mucus at the time of ovulation.

MUCUS. A clear secretion from any mucus membrane that keeps the membrane moist.

MYOMA. A benign tumour of uterine muscle tissue.

MYOMECTOMY. Surgical removal of a MYOMA from the uterine wall.

NABOTHIAN CYST. A CYST of the cervix.

NEEDLE BIOPSY. Removal of a small amount of tissue for microscopic examination.

NEOPLASM. New growth of any tissue.

NIDATION. Attachment of the fertilized ovum to the ENDOMETRIUM.

OBSTETRICIAN. A specialist in the care of pregnant women.

OESTROGEN. A major female sex hormone, secreted mainly by the ovaries in women and in smaller amounts by the adrenals in men and women.

OLIGOMENORRHOEA. Scanty menstrual flow.

OLIGOSPERMIA. Low sperm count.

ONANISM. Another term for COITUS INTERRUPTUS. Named for the biblical Onan, son of Judah, who spilled his seed on the ground.

OOCYTE. A primitive cell that becomes an ovum.

OOGENESIS. The development of ova from primitive to mature eggs.

OOPHORECTOMY. Surgical removal of an ovary.

OPHTHALMOSCOPE. An instrument used to examine inside the eye.

ORAL CONTRACEPTIVE. A substance (such as the birth control pill) taken by mouth to prevent pregnancy.

ORCHIDITIS. Inflammation of the testicles.

ORCHIDOPEXY. A surgical procedure to bring undescended testicles into the scrotum.

ORCHIDECTOMY. Surgical removal of the testicles.

ORGASM. The climax of the sexual act, marked in the male by ejaculation of semen and in the female by vaginal contractions.

PAGET'S DISEASE. A type of inflammation around the nipple of the breast; rarely, inflammation of the vulva. Also a non-malignant bone disease.

PANCREAS. The organ behind the stomach that produces INSULIN as well as performing other functions.

PAP TEST. Popular name for the Papanicolaou test, in which cervical cells are examined under a microscope for abnormalities. Also called cervical smear test.

PAPILLOMA. Small skin tumours (warts, polyps, skin tags)

PARASYMPATHETIC NERVOUS SYSTEM. A division of the autonomic nervous system that assists in controlling respiration, heart rate and digestion; also contols erection of the penis.

PARATHYROID GLANDS. Four small glands in the thyroid that control serum calcium and phosphorus levels.

PATENCY. Openness, as of the fallopian tubes.

PATHOLOGIST. A physician who examines tissue specimens.

PELVIC INFLAMMATORY DISEASE (PID). Generalized infection of the reproductive organs of the female.

PELVIS. A structure encased by the iliac bones and sacrum, supported by muscle and pelvic ligaments. It contains the reproductive organs and bladder and supports all the abdominal organs and intestines.

PENIS. The male organ through which urine and semen are emitted.

PERGONAL. Brand name for a mixture of 50 per cent LUTEINIZING HORMONE and

50 per cent FOLLICLE-STIMULATING HORMONE, extracted from postmenopausal female urine. A potent ovulation induction drug, it has been known to produce multiple pregnancies.

PERINEUM. The membrane between the vagina and the anus.

PERITONEUM. The tissue covering the inside of the abdominal wall.

PERITONITIS. Inflammation of the PERITONEUM.

PESSARY. A device placed in the vagina, usually to support a misplaced uterus.

PHIMOSIS. Difficulty pulling back the foreskin of the penis or clitoris.

PINEAL GLAND. A small gland in the cranium whose function is not well understood.

PITUITARY GLAND. A gland located at the base of the brain that is responsible for many hormone secretions in the body, including FOLLICLE-STIMULATING HORMONE and LUTEINIZING HORMONE.

PLACEBO. An innocuous substance given surreptitiously in place of drugs; sometimes cures illness by suggestion.

PLACENTA. A spongy substance in the uterus that serves as a conductor between mother and fetus.

PNEUMOPERITONEUM. Introduction of gas into the peritoneal cavity.

POLYCYSTIC OVARIES (PCO). A condition in which many ovarian cysts prevent fertility. Also called Stein-Leventhal disease.

POLYP. A small growth on tissue.

POSTCOITAL. After intercourse.

POSTCOITAL TEST. Examination of the cervical mucus shortly after intercourse to determine how well sperm are surviving inside the female body.

PRECANCEROUS. A condition that may become malignant in the future.

PREDNISONE. A cortisone-like compound about three times stronger than cortisone.

PREGNANCY. The condition of being with child, from the moment of conception until delivery.

PREMARIN. Brand name of a hormonal component of 'conjugated oestrogens' derived from horse OESTROGEN.

PREMATURE EJACULATION. Early expulsion of semen by the male during intercourse, causing loss of erection.

PREMATURE MENOPAUSE. Menopause occurring when a woman is in her thirties or earlier. The cause is not known.

PREPUCE. Foreskin; the skin covering the head of the penis or clitoris.

PROCTOCELE. *See* RECTOCELE.

PROGESTERONE. The major female hormone secreted by the CORPUS LUTEUM and other organs during pregnancy.

PROGESTIN. A classification of drugs that produces progesterone-like effects on the body. Acts primarily on the lining of the uterus.

PROCTOSCOPY. Examination of the lower colon with a telescopic instrument via the anus.

PROLACTIN. A pituitary hormone that stimulates milk glands in the female.

PROLAPSE. The dropping of an organ.

PROLIFERATIVE PHASE. The period of the menstrual cycle between menstruation and ovulation when OESTROGEN is the dominant hormone.

PROSTAGLANDINS. Hormones in the blood that have an effect on METABOLISM and blood vessels and that cause the mouth muscle to either contract or relax. Prostatic fluid is very rich in prostaglandin substances.

PROSTATE GLAND. A large, walnut-shaped gland surrounding the male uerthra; contributes a large portion of fluid to semen.

PROSTATECTOMY. Surgical removal of part or all of the prostate gland.

PROSTHESIS. Any artificial device used to replace part of the body.

PSEUDOCYESIS. False pregnancy; a condition in which a woman believes she is pregnant when she is not.

PSYCHIATRIST. A physician who studies and treats mental and emotional disorders of all kinds. Treatment may involve drugs and shock therapy.

PSYCHOSEXUAL COUNSELLING. Help by trained experts in sexual problems that are psychological in origin.

PSYCHOTHERAPIST. A person who treats emotional problems by focusing on mental rather than physical responses.

PUBERTY. The time of life in males and females when sexual organs mature.

PUBIC. Relating to the frontal area above the male and female genitalia.

PUBOCOCCYGEUS MUSCLE. The muscle that partially surrounds the vagina.

RADIOGRAPHER. A technician who takes X-rays and similar tests.

RADIOISOTOPE. A radioactive element used to look for or treat tumours.

RADIOLOGIST. A physician who interprets X-rays or other films of the body. May also be skilled in using X-rays for the treatment of tumours.

RADIOPAQUE. A substance that allows the inside of hollow organs to be seen in X-rays.

RADIOTHERAPY. The use of X-rays to treat tumours and cancers.

RECANALIZE. To rejoin, usually tuberous structures.

RECTOCELE. Dropping of the wall of the rectum.

RECTUM. The lowest part of the large intestine.

RETARDATE EJACULATION. Ejaculation after withdrawal of the penis from the vagina.

RETINA. The layer in the back of the eye where colour and dark and light receptors are located.

RETROGRADE EJACULATION. Semen that backs up into the bladder instead of out of the penis on ejaculation. Sometimes a side-effect of DIABETES MELLITUS.

RETROGRADE MENSTRUATION THEORY. A theory for the origin of ENDOMETRIOSIS holding that endometrial cells, which are normally shed through the vagina during menstruation, back up into the fallopian tubes and then find their way to other parts of the body.

RETROVERSION. The condition in which the uterus is angled backwards rather than forwards in the pelvis. Occurs in one out of every five women. Also called retroflexed uterus and tipped uterus.

RH FACTOR. The presence of absence of Rh antibody on red blood cells; 85 per cent of the population have the Rh antigen (Rh positive), 15 per cent do not have it and are said to be Rh negative.

RH INCOMPATIBILITY. Mismatching of an Rh-positive father with an Rh-negative mother in which the child may carry the RH FACTOR. The mother's IMMUNE SYSTEM may try to destroy the RH-positive child, resulting in newborn jaundice or even death in the womb.

RHYTHM METHOD. A method of contraception in which intercourse does not take place in the middle two weeks of a woman's menstrual cycle, when she is presumed to be ovulating.

ROUND LIGAMENTS. Bands of tissue that help hold the uterus in position.

RUBIN'S TEST. A test for infertility, seldom used today, in which carbon dioxide is blown into the uterus and escapes through the fallopian tubes if they are open. Also called tubal insufflation.

SALPINGITIS. Inflammation of the fallopian tubes, usually due to infection.

SALPINGOLYSIS. Surgical removal of an ADHESION around the fallopian tubes.

SALPINGOGRAM. X-ray of the fallopian tubes.

SALPINGO-OOPHORECTOMY. Surgical removal of a fallopian tube and ovary.

SALPINGOPLASTY. Surgical repair of fallopian tube.

SALPINGOSTOMY. A surgical procedure to open the fallopian tubes at the fimbrial end. *See also* FIMBRIA.

SCMCT. *See* SPERM-CERVICAL MUCUS CONTACT TEST.

SCROTUM. The skin and muscle that hold the testicles.

SEBUM. An oily substance secreted from pores.

SECONDARY INFERTILITY. Infertility in a couple who have already had one or more successful pregnancies. Sometimes called one-child sterility.

SECRETORY PHASE. The second half of the menstrual cycle after about day 14 when the ENDOMETRIUM is preparing to receive the fertilized egg.

SEDIMENTATION RATE. A blood test for determining the presence of an infectious process in the body.

SEMEN. The milky fluid of the ejaculate comprised of sperm and secretions from the PROSTATE GLAND, SEMINAL VESICLES and COWPER'S GLANDS.

SEMEN ANALYSIS. Laboratory study of semen under the microscope to examine the number, size, shape and motility of sperm.

SEMINAL FLUID. *See* SEMEN.

SEMINAL VESICLES. Two small glands behind the bladder in males through which the VASA DEFERENTIA pass. These glands produce a highly acidic fluid that comprises more than half of the semen.

SEMI-IMPOTENCE. Inability of the male to maintain an erection long enough for intercourse.

SEMINIFEROUS. Seed-carrying.

SEMINIFEROUS TUBULES. Long, thin tubes in the testicles in which sperm are formed.

SENILE VAGINITIS. *See* ATROPHIC VAGINITIS.

SEPTICAEMIA. Blood poisoning.

SERUM PROGESTERONE TEST. A blood test to measure the amount of PROGESTERONE in the blood. Used to determine if a woman has ovulated.

SEXUAL DYSFUNCTION. The inability to perform sexually.

SHIRODKAR PROCEDURE. A stitch or insertion of a kind of plastic around the cervix at about the thirteenth or fourteenth week of pregnancy to prevent spontaneous abortion.

SPERM. Short for SPERMATOZOON.

SPERM COUNT. A laboratory examination to count the number and characteristics of sperm in the ejaculate. Cf. SEMEN ANALYSIS.

SPERMATOGENESIS. Development of sperm into maturity.

SPERMATOZOON (pl. SPERMATOZOA). The fully developed male reproductive cell.

SPERM-CERVICAL MUCUS CONTACT TEST (SCMCT). A test in which the female's cervical mucus is mixed with her partner's seminal fluid and examined under a microscope to see if the mucus is hostile to the sperm.

SPERMICIDE. Any substance that kills sperm.

SPINNBARKEIT. The thready consistency of cervical mucus.

SPIROCHETTE. An organism that carries SYPHILIS.

SPLIT EJACULATE. A method that seeks to inseminate the woman with the first part of the ejaculate, which contains more sperm. The first part is collected in one container and the second part in another container.

STEIN-LEVENTHAL SYNDROME. *See* POLYCYSTIC OVARIES.

STERILE. Permanently infertile.

STERILIZATION. A procedure that terminates fertility by interrupting the male or female reproductive system.

STEROID. A chemical that acts to modify or mediate body functions, such as induction of ovulation, allergic reaction, healing, sex drive and metabolism of water.

STILBOESTROL BABY. A child born of a mother treated with DIETHYLSTILBOESTROL (DES) during pregnancy.

STRICTURE. The narrowing of any canal or tubal structure of the body.

SUBFERTILITY. A delay in producing offspring due to some problem in conception.

SUTURE. A surgical stitch.

SWIM. Sperm-washing insemination method; a laboratory procedure for removing antibodies from sperm.

SYMPATHETIC NERVOUS SYSTEM. *See* PARASYMPATHETIC NERVOUS SYSTEM.

SYPHILIS. A contagious venereal disease caused by bacterium.

SYSTEMIC. Pertaining to the whole body, rather than a localized area.

TAMOXIFEN. A fertility drug.

TEMPERATURE CHART. The chart kept by a woman of her daily body temperature to determine when or if she ovulates.

TERATOMA. A type of tumour made up of tissue that is out of its normal place in the body.

TESTES. Testicles, male gonads in which sperm are produced.

TESTICULAR BIOPSY. Removal of small section of testes for microscopic examination.

TESTOSTERONE. The major male sex hormone secreted by the testes.

TEST-TUBE BABY. Popular term for a child produced by fertilization outside the body.

THERMOGRAPHY. A diagnostic technique that measures the amount of heat given off from an area of the body.

THERMOLYSIS. Surgical use of a heat-producing device to remove an ADHESION.

THYROID GLAND. An endocrine gland situated in the neck in front of the windpipe that controls many body functions.

TIPPED UTERUS. *See* RETROVERSION.

TISSUE. A group of similar cells.

TISSUE TYPING. The process of matching recipient and donor before organ transplant.

T-MYCOPLASMA. A micro-organism that may be responsible for some miscarriages. *T* stands for *tiny*.

TOXIN. Poison made by micro-organisms.

TOXOPLASMA. A protozoa that may infect women during pregnancy, causing abortion or brain damage in the fetus.

TRICHOMONAS. A parasitic organism that may be transferred during sexual intercourse. May cause vaginal burning and itching in the female.

TRIGONITIS. Inflammation of an area of the bladder.

TUBAL INSUFFLATION. *See* RUBIN'S TEST.

TUBERCULOSIS (TB). An infectious disease that may affect many areas of the body, most commonly the lungs.

TURNER'S SYNDROME. A condition in women in which a sex chromosome is missing, causing infertility.

ULCER. An inflamed break in tissue.

ULTRASOUND. A diagnostic technique that uses sound waves, rather than X-rays, to visualize internal body structures.

UMBILICUS. The navel; belly button.

UNDESCENDED TESTIS. A testicle that has not descended into the scrotum.

UNICORNATE UTERUS. A CONGENITAL abnormality of the uterus; literally, having one horn.

URETER. A tube that carries urine from the kidney to the bladder.

URETHRA. A tube that carries urine from the bladder out of the body.

URETHRITIS. Inflammation of the urethra.

URETHROCELE. Falling of the urethral wall.

URETHROSCOPY. Examination of the urethra with a lighted instrument.

UROLOGIST. A specialist in urinary systems in men and women, and genital and urinary systems in men.

UTERINE. Pertaining to the uterus.

UTERUS. The womb; a hollow, muscular organ in the woman in which the fetus develops.

VAGINA. The birth canal; the passage between cervix and vulva.

VAGINISMUS. A spasm of muscles around the opening of the vagina that makes intercourse painful and difficult.

VAGINITIS. Inflammation of the vagina.

VARICOCELE. A varicose condition of scrotal veins; may cause infertility.

VARICOCELECTOMY. Removal of varicose veins of the testicle.

VARICOSITY. Swelling of a vein.

VAS DEFERENS (pl. VASA DEFERENTIA). The tube that connects the EPIDIDYMIS to the prostate gland.

VASECTOMY. Surgical interruption of the VAS DEFERENS for permanent sterilization.

VASOEPIDIDYMOSTOMY. Surgical operation to open a blocked passage between the VAS DEFERENS and the EPIDIDYMIS.

VASOGRAPHY. X-ray of blood vessels.

VASOVASOSTOMY. Rejoining of the severed ends of the vas deferens to restore fertility after a VASCETOMY.

VENEREAL DISEASE. Any disease transmitted by sexual intercourse.

VESTIBULE. The entrance to the vulva.

VIRILIZATION. The 'mannish' appearance of a woman, often caused by taking male hormones or by tumours producing male hormones.

VIRUS. A microscopic infective agent that may overcome a host. Viruses are considered to be the smallest living molecules.

VULVA. The female genitals outside the vagina.

VULVOVAGINITIS. Inflammation of the vulva and vagina.

WHITES. *See* LEUKORRHOEA.

ZYGOTE. A fertilized ovum.

Index

Semen analysis (*contd.*)
  shape of sperm, 186–7, *188*
  sperm count, 185–6
  spontaneous abortion and, 301
  after varicocele surgery, 257
  viscosity, 183
  volume, 184
  when to collect a sample for, 183
Seminal vesicles
  absence of, 275
  anatomy of, 54–5
  infections in, 274
Seminiferous tubules, 52
Septum, uterine, 241–2, 294
Serono, P. Donini, 210
Serono Pharmaceuticals Company, 210
Serophene, *see* Clomiphene
Sertoli's cell-only syndrome, 265
Sertoli's cells, 62, 63, 68, 193–4, 196
Sex chromosomes, 8. *See also* Chromosomes
Sex-determination techniques, 289
Sexual abuse, 38, 125–6
Sexual arousal
  clitoris and, 12, 13
  labia minora and, 11
  vaginal secretions during, 18
Sexual development, *see* Puberty
Sexual dysfunction, *see* Sexual problems
Sexual history, 121–3. *See also* Psychosexual
    history
Sexual intercourse (sexual activity). *See also*
    Orgasm; Sexual arousal; Sexual problems
  deposit problems and, 77–8, 277–80
  diabetic men and, 279
  frequency of, 277
  history of, 121–3
  laboratory tests after, 145, 148–52
  lubricants for, 175, 278
  nipple discharge and, 132
  number of partners, 122
  paid during, 19, 122, 227–30
  pelvic inflammatory disease (PID) and, 218–19
  pleasure in, 126–7
  puberty and, 23–4
  technique for, 277–8
  timing of, 122, 174
  types of, 122
  urethra and, 16
Sexual problems, 93, 175. *See also* Impotence
  history of, 126
  of men, 77–8, 278–9
Sheehan's syndrome, 124

Silicone technique, for blocking the fallopian
    tubes, 325–6
Sims, J. Marion, 10, 148, 283
Sims-Huhner test, 148
Skene's glands, 14, 16–17, 18
Skin, 130, 180
Smegma, 11, 59
Smoking
  by men, 172, 176
  spontaneous abortion caused by, 297
Spallanzani, Lazzaro, 2–3, 283
Specialists, *see* Fertility specialists
Speculum, 134
Speirs, Andrew, 337
Sperm, 62. *See also* Ejaculation; Semen analysis
  abnormal shapes of, 150
  accumulation of, 276
  agglutination of, 189, 274–5
  antibody reaction to, 45, 122, 151, 189–92, 239–40
  capacitation of, 65, 67, 335
  deposit problems and, 277–8, 280
  discovery of, 2
  drugs and quality of, 172
  in epididymis, 52, 54, 65
  freezing of, 276, 287
  motility (swimming ability) of, 52, 185, 287
  normal fertilization and, 3–5
  pelvic inflammatory disease (PID) and, 218
  postcoital test of, 149–51
  production of, *see* Sperm production
  protective membrane of, 6
  shape of, 186–7
  spontaneous abortion and, 301
  washing, 274, 276, 335
Spermatic cords, 52, 265
Spermatids, 63
Spermatocytes, 63
Spermatogonia (mother cells), 62, 63, 65, 195, 261, 262, 264
  absence of, in Sertoli's cell-only syndrome, 265
  chemicals and, 268–9
  chemotherapy for cancer and, 270
  radiation and, 268, 270
  testicular biopsy and, 195–7
Sperm banks, 286–7
Sperm count, 67–8, 72–3, 185–7
  decline in, 79–80
  normal, 186
  previous, 176
  procedures for, 185–7
  too high, 186